A STUDY OF U.S. ARMY TACTICS

HORSEMANSHIP

AT LITTLE BIG HORN

A HORSEMAN LOOKS AT THE CUSTER BATTLE

By Robert E. Doran

Copyright © 2007 by Robert E. Doran

All rights reserved. No part of this book shall be reproduced or transmitted in any form or by any means, electronic, mechanical, magnetic, photographic including photocopying, recording or by any information storage and retrieval system, without prior written permission of the publisher. No patent liability is assumed with respect to the use of the information contained herein. Although every precaution has been taken in the preparation of this book, the publisher and author assume no responsibility for errors or omissions. Neither is any liability assumed for damages resulting from the use of the information contained herein.

This book is non-fiction and is about real people and events.

ISBN 0-7414-4056-3

Illustrations and maps are by the author unless otherwise noted.

Published by:

INFINITY
PUBLISHING.COM
1094 New Dehaven Street, Suite 100
West Conshohocken, PA 19428-2713
Info@buybooksontheweb.com
www.buybooksontheweb.com
Toll-free (877) BUY BOOK
Local Phone (610) 941-9999
Fax (610) 941-9959

Printed in the United States of America
Printed on Recycled Paper
Published June 2007

IN MEMORY

"CHARLEY" (Leo Tuff)
1969-2002

He was the best friend that a horseman could ever have. Charley has gone on to Fiddler's Green, where he was put on permanent Pasture Duty. I know that I will see him again. He taught me how to ride like a Cavalryman!

DEDICATED:

Walter M. Camp, 1867-1925. Walter Camp as a historian hobbyist, interviewed many of the officers, enlisted men, civilians, and allied and hostile Indian participants of the Battle of the Little Big Horn. In doing so he solved many of the mysteries of the Custer Fight. His proposed book on the Indian Wars went unwritten and his research material scattered for decades. Camp's monumental effort has given us new insight into this Icon of the taming of the American West. **(See SOLVING THE CUSTER MYTHS, pg. 15 pp)**

Mel Andersen, For teaching me how to understand and love horses and the many horse packing trips into the High Unita Wilderness Area.

William D. Wolverton, Colonel, USA, 1834-1910. William D. Wolverton graduated from Princeton University as a Doctor in 1861. He entered the U. S. Army as an Assistant Surgeon in August 1861. He would serve his country for another thirty-seven years. On June 26, 1876 he was promoted to Major and assigned to the Seventh Cavalry Regiment for the next seven years. As a family ancestor and a "Custer" ghost from my past, he may have given me the spiritual guidance for my lifetime fascination about the Custer Mystery.

National Archives, Military Record of William D. Wolverton:
Civil War: August 1861 to April 1864.
Entered U.S. Army, August 5, 1861. Commissioned Lieutenant, Assistant Surgeon.
Seminary Hospital, Georgetown, D.C.
Fort Pickens, Florida (Post Surgeon)
Department of Gulf
Department of the South
10th Army Corps

Post Civil War Service: August 1864 to March 1869.
Promoted Captain July 28, 1866.
General Hospital, Fort Monroe, Richmond, Virginia
Baton Rouge, Louisiana
New Orleans, Louisiana
Greenville, Mississippi

Frontier Service: March 1869 to 1876
Fort Snelling, Minnesota: March 1864-1876
Fort Abercrombie, Dakota Territory
Nashville, Tennessee

(The "Custer" Years) Seventh Regiment: August 1876 to 1883
Promoted Major **June 26, 1876**
Fort Abercrombie, Dakota Territory (August 1876)
Standing Rock, Agency, Dakota Territory
Fort Abraham Lincoln, Dakota Territory

Washington Barracks, D.C., December 1883 (Post Surgeon)
Fort D. A. Russell, Wyoming
Fort Douglass, Utah Territory
Fort Schuyler, New York
Fort Omaha, Nebraska
Promoted Lieutenant Colonel May 6, 1893 (Deputy Surgeon General)
Watervliet Arsenal, New York August 1893:
Department of the Columbia, Oregon/Washington (Chief Surgeon)

Retirement from Active Duty: December 15, 1898.
Promoted Colonel, U.S.A. April 23, 1904

TABLE OF CONTENTS

PREFACE: 9

FORWARD: 13

SOLVING THE CUSTER MYTHS: 15
Modern cavalry buffs that reenact how the U.S. Army rode and deployed their men and horses have created new insight into the Frontier Army of the Custer Era. Two very important early researchers, Walter M. Camp and John Stands In Timber, have given us many clues as why the army was defeated. Combined with their personal interviews with many of the participants, and their knowledge of the terrain now makes it possible to understand the Battle of the Little Big Horn. This extensive research combined with the horsemanship experience of today's cavalry reenactors now makes reconstructing the battle far more complete. With the new knowledge of the Old Army's horsemanship training of their men and horses now sheds additional light on what happened at the Custer Fight.

THE U.S. ARMY HORSEMANSHIP PROGRAM: 29
The regulated training and deployment of the various units of the Seventh Regiment expose the myths and deception created by the human participants. The methods of how the U.S. Army trained their men and horses will be reconstructed. Today, their methods can be considered to be very modern and an effective means of teaching young men from industrial urban settings how to ride properly astride a horse. Many of the "Old Army" cavalry reenactors of today have reinvented these methods. Understanding the importance of the army's regulated gait will solve the time/distance mystery of and why the terrain features controlled the Custer Battle. The drill tactics employed during the Custer Era explain how and why the individual regimental units were deployed. The evidence left us by the army's horses' eclipses the faulty testimony of the human participants as to the time, distances and events.

PROLOGUE: Decision in Medicine Tail 47
Bugler John Martin is sent back to Captain Fredrick Benteen with a written message. Other messengers are revealed in Walter Camp's interviews with Battle participants. John Martin could not have carried the "Come on, Bring Packs" message!

CHAPTER ONE: The Divide to Medicine Tail 51
The "Custer Trail" is revealed using the regulated gait of the army horses rather the guesswork of the human military participants. Walter Camp's detailed civil description of the early 1900s trails and the U.S. Government mandated Blake/Marshall surveys of the late 1880s now can be used to establish the exact routes used by the army. The army followed established "roads" knowing that they would lead to a good crossing of the Little Big Horn River. The only fear that the regimental officers had was that the expected villages would escape! The actual route can now be traced to Medicine Tail Coulee.

CHAPTER TWO: The Reno Valley Fight 75

The actual location of the Reno Valley Fight will be revealed for the first time! Tactical errors by Major Marcus Reno in the deployment of his men and horses caused him to establish his skirmish line prematurely. Reno's lack of leadership and the rumor of the poorly located led horses being threatened by the warriors caused a breakdown in military order. His decision not to hold the "Woods" position becomes a major factor in the swarming of warriors against Custer's advanced front.

CHAPTER THREE: The Bad Blood Between Benteen and Custer 101

Revealed for the first time is the role that Captain Fredrick Benteen played concerning the movement of the Pack Train and his failure to supply reinforcements. It was an act of indifference and insubordination that could have led to his conviction by a Court-Martial board. The bad blood between Custer and Benteen may have contributed to the tragic destruction of all five companies on the Custer Field. Benteen's relationship with Custer is traced to his pronounced vindictiveness when it came to obeying a number of standing orders, written and verbal, concerning his expected role as a reserve battalion commander.

CHAPTER FOUR: The Left Scout to Reno Hill and Beyond 105

Other messengers sent to Benteen are revealed in Walter Camp's interviews with Battle participants. Custer may have irritated Benteen by controlling his actions. Benteen's Left Scout may have been designed to reconnoiter the South Fork of Ash Creek. Was Benteen ordered to halt and wait for the Packs? Sergeant-Major William Sharrow is seen at the Morass with additional orders. A pivotal mystery messenger is revealed. Benteen has trouble with Captain Thomas Weir. Benteen snubs Sergeant Daniel Kanipe's short-cut order, and unsaddles his horses after reaching Reno Hill. Benteen orders Hare to expedite ammo mules. Benteen's refuses Weir's request to go forward to the sounds of Custer's fighting. Second Lieutenant Luther Hare is sent by Benteen to recall Weir's advance. Benteen finally goes forward after another messenger arrives from Custer He is requested by other officers to take over after the obvious failure of Reno to be able to command. Benteen becomes the "Hero of Reno Hill" and wins future support from his fellow officers to cover up his true role as a reserve battalion.

CHAPTER FIVE: Martin's True Order 123

The Custer Battalions are halted again in Medicine Tail Coulee. John Martin could not have carried the famous "bring packs" order as it is written! Benteen's cover up in the Reno Court of Inquiry, and its forced perjury by wittiness was designed to deceive the Court of his role on the first day of fighting. The actual content of Martin's message may have been altered by Benteen to cover up his disobedience of several direct orders to advance without the Pack Train. Benteen was made to look as if he did all he could do to render aid to Custer's advance front. He may have altered Martin's original order to cover up his failure to carry out previous orders.

CHAPTER SIX: Medicine Tail to Finley Hill and Beyond 151

The deployment of the First and Second Battalion as separate units to different ford crossings can now be revealed. Upon seeing additional villages downstream Custer halts and divides his forces in Medicine Tail Coulee. A lengthy halt occurs in Medicine Tail for the First Battalion. The Second Battalion is sent northward to find a downstream crossing as part of an enveloping attack on the lower villages. Their subsequent early encounter with John Stand In Timber's "Young Warriors" is revealed. Captain George Yates deploys Company E too early near Medicine Tail. The secrets of the Gray Horse Company can now be exposed and their relationship to the skirmishing on the Luce and Nye-Cartwright Ridge areas. The aborted crossing at the Minneconjou Ford, and the retreat of the First Battalion to Finley Hill is reconstructed. Custer chooses the yet to be "Calhoun Hill" area as his "high-ground" defensive area for the First Battalion. The inability of both battalions to affect simultaneous crossings now causes separate defensive stands.

CHAPTER SEVEN: The Custer Fight 163

A detailed study of the actual fighting by the individual companies on the Custer Field can now be reconstructed. The Second Battalion is forced to retreat from the lower fords and establishes a temporary skirmish line north of the Battlefield. The two battalions are now separated by one-mile distance, and Custer attempts to reunite them. This action turns into disaster when the archaic bow and arrow was used to stampede Company C from Finley Hill. Additional strategic errors by Captain Yates may have defeated Colonel Custer's planned withdraw to the relative safety of the timber in the valley. The segmented fighting of the First and Second Battalion is based on the actual company assignments of June 25. Other researchers have consistently misplaced Company L in the wrong battalion to explain their final position on Calhoun Hill. The author's twenty-year research into the U.S. Army horsemanship-training program can now explain the actual tactical deployment and the skirmishing on the Custer Field. However, the poor training of the enlisted men and a serious understaffing of both enlisted men and officers served to defeat the Seventh Regiment. Additional tactical errors committed by Captain Yates may have caused an escalating destruction of the Second Battalion. The mystery of the Gray Horse Company and the establishment of the South Skirmish Line can now be fully explored. The defeat of the South Skirmish Line by teenage pre-society "Suicide Boys" caused the final defensive "Last Stand" on Monument Hill. The "Last Seven" men run for the timber, and the last man to die is suggested.

SUMMARY: 191

APPENDIX:
The Luce Artifact Finds Grid Map 195
NPS Master Artifact Finds Arial Photo Survey 197
Green's Fold-Out Map 198
Company Formation 199
Squadron Formation 200
Skirmishers as Flankers 201

Custer Fight - Phase 1 202
Custer Fight - Phase 2 203
Custer Fight - Phase 3 204
Custer Fight - Phase 4 205
Custer Fight - Phase 5 206
Seventh Regiment Roster-Enlisted Men 207
Enlisted Men and Officers Killed Off Field 208
U.S. Government Horses 209
Packs 210
Pack Train Assignments 210
Summary of Orders sent to Benteen 211
Trooper Bob Doran 212
Notes on Documentation-Bibliography and End Notes 213-228

PREFACE

Ever since I was nine years old I have had an interest in the Battle of the Little Big Horn. better known as "Custer's Last Stand". It would soon turn into what has been described as an obsession. Is it possible that a life time "obsession" may be the result of a family ghost in your past who is trying to get your attention?

My father's family name was Wolverton. By age ten he was adopted and his surname changed. When I was yet pre-school age my father and mother took me to visit his family relatives in Delaware County, Pennsylvania. There an elderly woman and her sister talked about their father who had been an U.S. Army officer during the Civil War. They thought that he had been a General and they still had had his sword. It was the sword incident that haunted me and later I was able to identify it as an officer's ceremonial cavalry saber, but still not knowing who my illustrious Civil War family member was.

Many years later, while researching my family ancestry, I discovered that a Colonel Charles D. Wolverton **(See Dedication: pg. 3)** was the only Wolverton to have served in the U.S. Army as a commissioned officer during the Civil War. In August 1876, he became a battle replacement for Lieutenant George Edwin Lord, assistant surgeon for the Seventh Regiment of Cavalry who had been killed at the Battle of the Little Big Horn. Major Wolverton would serve in the Seventh Regiment for the next seven years. He knew all of the surviving Custer Battle officers. I now feel that my obsession with the Custer Fight has come from that family ancestral connection.

Sometime in 1947, when I was nine, my nineteen-year-old brother and some of his "adult" friends went to see the movie; *They Died With Their Boots On*, starring Errol Flynn as General Custer. I was not invited for obvious reasons. Afterwards, around the breakfast table, he and one of his buddies were discussing "Custer's Last Stand" in glowing terms They described how hordes of Indians surrounded and rode wildly around Custer and his men, and then decimated them to the last man. There stood the heroic Custer and all of his remaining men, standing like sheaves of wheat, until he fires the last shot. Suddenly, I interrupted their "adult" conversation and with a great shout I proclaimed, "No, that's not how it happened!" All I got were silent stares, and without any further conversation, breakfast was soon over. It seems that little brothers are to be seen, not heard. I still have no idea why I just blurted out this historical correction to Hollywood's 1939 version of the Custer Battle.

After all, I had no interest in the subject and I did not have a clue how the real "Custer Fight" had been fought. In 1960 when I made my first trip to then the Custer Battlefield National Monument, I just knew that Hollywood was wrong. Now some sixty years after this early episode with Errol Flynn, my interest has now turned into a passion that Patty Kluver, a Southeastern Montana ranch-woman would describe as being my "Magnificent Obsession" Now after some forty trips to Montana, and a lifetime of trying to solve the "Custer Mystery," I think that I now have the answer. It is all about that magnificent creature the Great Spirit gave to us, what biologists call *Equus Caballus*, the horse.

Having grown up in the Northern Appalachian Mountains of Pennsylvania, I had no interest in horses in this poor faming country, some sixty miles from Camptown, the home of Walter

Mason Camp. It would be in his footsteps that I would follow some fifty years later along his "Custer Trail" up the Rosebud River to the Custer Battlefield. On my first trip west, I had to stop and identify the familiar aroma of western sage brush that does not grow in Pennsylvania. On my first trip to the Custer Battlefield it seemed to be a familiar place. They call it Dejavu, but it seemed as if I had been there before.

Soon after moving to Northern Utah I attempted to learn how to ride a horse for the first time. I had the same experience when I begun to ride horses for the first time in my life. The smell of their sweat, and the rhythmic rocking motion all seemed strangely familiar to me. Some other horsemen said that it seemed that I was a natural born horseman considering that I was almost forty years old and had never been on a horse before!

After many visits to the local "rent-a-horse" stables proved to be a disaster, I was invited by a co-worker to come up and ride his ranch-trained horses. I was blessed with the acquaintance a "Horse Whisperer." But, in the Old West ranching environment of Northern Utah, they are just called "Old Time" livestock men that have that rare quality of "horse sense". That horse whisperer was Mel Andersen of Kaysville, Utah. He trained me in the old Cowboy-Way of horsemanship. He became a lifetime friend and taught me how to understand and love horses. It was this understanding of horses that helped to resolve my fifty year quest for answers about what happened along the banks of the Little Bighorn.

Fortunately, in 1977 the same year that I began my horse training, I had began to research the Walter M. Camp Collection housed at Brigham Young University (BYU) in Provo, Utah, fifty miles from where I lived. BYU Press had just published Kenneth Hammer's book, *Custer In '76*, the year before. In this massive collection of Walter Camp's interviews with Custer Battle participants there are a lot of statements about the army's horses. With my newfound horse sense, this valuable collection led me to reconstruct the possible role that the U.S. Army's horsemanship might have played in the Custer Fight.

Soon I would learn that many of the early High Plains ranchers had deep roots in the "Custer" era! A number of former enlisted men of the Seventh Regiment became the early ranchers in Southeastern Montana, becoming part the first generation of the livestock industry in that region. Much of the tradition of what we call today the "Cowboy Way" is of the residual "Old Army" culture. Especially in how they trained and handled their horses.

This book is to some extent about horses, how the U.S. Army trained and utilized them. I hope that all good horsemen and non-horsemen alike can enjoy this study. And, perhaps come to the understanding that the army horses may have determined the final outcome of this military battle. If Custer and his men had been infantrymen at the Little Bighorn, most likely there would not have been such a defeat, and we would not have today the John Ford and John Wayne visual but false image of the real Frontier Cavalry. Certainly, not anything like the Errol Flynn version!

During the same time frame of my Camp Collection research my involvement in a mounted reenactment unit in Northern Utah made me become aware of the many centuries of military horse training protocol. What started out to be a simple parade cavalry unit resulted in my twenty-five years of research into the U.S. Army training program. This late Nineteenth Century program of U.S. Army horsemanship, which evolved over 150 years, became obsolete by the mid-Twentieth Century. When W.W. II converted the U.S. Mounted Service into mechanized units, the Old Army horsemanship training became a lost art. By the 1940s, without another new generation of military horsemen to orally pass down the traditions, this time honored program became lost to history!

I would like to share this lost experience with you, and let you discover yourself what may have happened at the Custer Fight. Perhaps many of the traditional die-hard "Custer Buffs" will continue to disagree with my conclusions, but this no nonsense "horse sense" approach tells another tale. One must keep in mind that everything the officers and men of the Seventh Regiment did on June 25, 1876 evolved around the use of their horses.

Please, come with back with me to the days when the U.S. Cavalry rode not in helicopters, but on horse back. It can be a very interesting trip. But beware that becoming interested in this historical event and horses in general, can be become very habit forming. As my old friend and fellow Custer researcher, Dee Brown titled his best selling book, *Bury My Heart at Wounded Knee*, I would like to paraphrase and say, *Bury My Heart in Montana.*

FORWARD

This is not a revisionist effort to correct the prevailing literature on the Battle of the Little Big Horn. But it is more of a deconstruction of the time line and physical locations of the true "Custer Trail". This is done by using today's restoration by cavalry reenactors who have recreated how the U.S. Army trained their men and horses. Above all in how the they were deployed and the protocol set by army regulations of the "Custer Era". For far too long this horsemanship aspect has been overlooked by other Custer writers who in the past have just speculated on where the events unfolded and the deployment of incorrect battalion assignments have contributed in perpetuating the "Custer Myths".

The following statement about John Martin's role came about secondary after the correct Custer Trail was resolved by much ground work and the use of the Blake-Marshall Survey published for the first time in this study. The inevitable conclusion came about when the author tried to recreate the text of Martin's true order sent from Medicine Tail Coulee.

John Martin could not have carried the historical "bring packs" message. His predecessor, Sergeant Daniel Kanipe had already delivered another order that countermands any future pack train order. Besides there is evidence of other messengers being sent earlier to Captain Fredrick Benteen to expedite the Pack Train. Perhaps as many as eight individual orders may have been sent to Benteen on June 25, which at least three concerned the movement of the Pack Train.

This concept *is not* the main thesis of this book. The author came to this conclusion long *after* reconstructing the horsemanship aspect based on his research as a Custer Era cavalry reenactor. The glamour of the John Ford and John Wayne Hollywood versions of the Frontier Army clouds one's perspective as to the true history of this historical event.

This deconstruction of the Custer Fight by using actual U.S. Army horsemanship protocol as a control factor has not been done before, at least not to the depth that this book will attempt. Other military trained sources have skirted around the subject. The Reno Court of Inquiry has many "hidden" clues as to gross violations to the tactical deployment of their horses. When the officers were not busy protecting Captain Frederick Benteen, their "Hero of Reno Hill", they left their guard down.

This book will reveal how Benteen may have altered and manipulated his famous "last message" which he claimed was carried by his bugler, John Martin. If the Custer Icon is authentic and in its original wording, then it had to been sent much earlier in the Battle timeline. That means there was a second and different written order, the one the John Martin carried. The most probable candidate for the "bring packs" order, if it existed at all, would have been Corporal Henry Eldon French, of Company C. He was assigned to the Headquarters Staff and carried the pivotal Pack Train order some forty minutes *earlier* then Martin's message! The final conclusion of the author is that there was but *one written message,* allows for Benteen's blatant alteration with his inclusion of the wording "bring packs, PS bring pacs."

There were other written messages written on June 25. Second Lieutenant Hare sent one to

Custer when he and Fred Gerard saw their "running" Indians at 2:00 PM. And, there was the Staff's written "memorandums," when the battalion assignments were made at 12:10 PM. Of course there was the "Herendeen" dispatch to General Terry, carried by Private Nathan Short of Company C, written at 3:10 PM. **(See author's article, *The Man Who Got to the Rosebud*, published by the Little Big Horn Association *Research Review*, Winter 2002)**

The publication of the Blake-Marshall survey maps for the first time in this work now allows for identifying the actual "Custer Trail." A more accurate blueprint of the topography, rate of march, and events can now be reconstructed. For the first time the true location of Major Marcus Reno's Valley Fight can now be located. It is now identified as being much further to the east then the traditional Garryowen Loop site. Also, the legend of the "Gray Horse" Company and its role in the early skirmishing will now be explained.

Also for the first time, three other unrecognized skirmish sites by Custer's battalions are identified. Their strategy rational can now be suggested and the actual fighting by the individual battalions on the Custer Battlefield is now understood. The fact that the First and Second Battalions of Captain Keogh and Yates were operating as separate battle units can now be told. This is in part due to the excellent research of the two finest "Custer" researchers ever to look into this seminal event. Walter Camp and John Stands In Timber had solved the "mysteries" long ago. But, their voluminous research material had not been fully understood nor examined from the view point of the 1876 U.S. Army horsemanship that was involved. That is where today's cavalry reenactors can come together with their research and resolve many of the "Custer Myths."

Strongly recommended is that the reader will study the next two sections, ***Solving the Custer Myths*** and ***The US Army Horsemanship Training Program***. The first will introduce the reader to new criteria that have not been considered in past reconstructions. The second will reveal the structured horse training protocol that shaped the outcome of the Custer Fight. Both will help the reader to understand how the author developed this new and nontraditional thesis for the Battle of the Little Big Horn.

 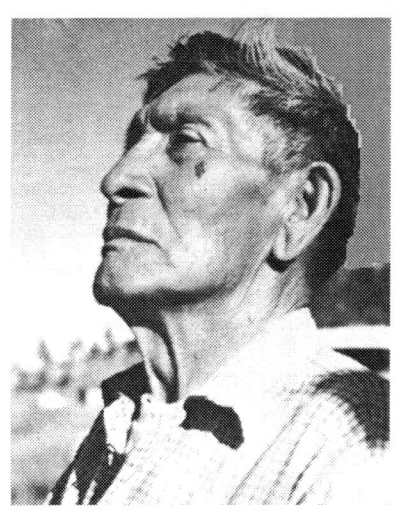

Walter Mason Camp
1867 - 1925

John Stands In Timber
1884 - 1969

Walter Camp was a railroad civil engineer who made a hobby of researching the mysteries of the Custer Battle. In the early 1900s Camp interviewed over sixty battle participants and made sixteen field trips to Montana. He was planning to publish his findings, a hope that failed with his untimely death at age fifty-five.

John Stands In Timber was born in Montana as a member of the Northern Cheyenne. He was educated in a private school and returned to become the self-appointed historian of the Northern Cheyenne at the Lamedeer reservation in Montana. In the early 1900s he interviewed many of the Cheyenne who had fought at the Little Bighorn. His mentor was Peter J. Powell, an ordained protestant minister assigned to Lamedeer. Stands In Timber's research was deposited in Powell's Indian School in Chicago and remains un-inventoried and unpublished.

SOLVING THE CUSTER MYTHS

This is not just another speculative "Custer" book about the Battle of the Little Bighorn. This study is about that wonderful creature, the horse. How the U.S. Army trained and deployed their horses may have shaped the "Custer Battle." This factor has never been fully explored before! Horses were the same a hundred years ago as they are today. Most horsemen understand the saying that a well trained horse is a "honest horse". The gentle nature and honesty of the horse tells the real story behind all of the human distortions that have become known as "Custer Myths."

After the disaster on the Little Bighorn, the two legged participants generated misconceptions and outright deception. This study will deal with some of them, but there are too many to expose for what they are, legend making. Nor is this book just about the Custer factions that helped to create the myths, it is about the reality of the simple role played by the horses.

The Battle of the Little Big Horn: The history books call it the Battle of the Little Big Horn. But, to the Sioux and Northern Cheyenne it was the place where the greasy grass grew, and a good place to hunt and graze their horses. It was here on their Greasy Grass Creek in Southeastern Montana they defeated the U. S. Army. The blue-coated invaders were intent on destroying their villages and altering their way of life remaining as free roaming large game hunters. The U.S. Government wanted them to become good Christian farmers who would stay on land not of their choosing.

The "People," as they called themselves, had not always been game hunters of the High Plains. They had been driven from the eastern woodlands of the Trans-Mississippi and Ohio River valleys by the Anglo-American hunger for land. But, on the High Plains they thrived on massive herds of Buffalo, Elk, Mule Deer and Antelope, once thought to be endless. The Great Spirit blessed them with the horse when they were driven out of their ancestral eastern woodland homes onto to the Great Plains. They became horsemen that would have no equal. It was the horse that offered them their free roaming way of life. Before that they were fixed-land farmers. Quickly they mastered the hunting of the sacred Buffalo and the art of becoming good horsemen! The Washington bureaucrats soon defined those who refused to live on fixed land called "reservations" as renegades. A better term for them would be the "Winter Roamers," or the ones that stayed away from their assigned reservations in Dakota Territory and toughed it out in the Powder River region of Montana Territory.

The pure Winter Roamers looked down on their "Summer Roamers" relatives who went onto the U.S. Government sanctioned reservations in Dakota Territory for the winter. Here they were guaranteed enough meat from the white man's cattle and were issued sugar and coffee. It was their addiction to this staple that earned them the nickname "coffee coolers" by the Montana Territory winter dwellers.

By the end of the Civil War, the radical right of the Johnson Administration caused a landmark decision from the U.S. Supreme Court in 1867. It was to set the scene for the Indian Wars that would follow. This new ruling abrogated all previous legal obligations made between the U.S. Government and Native American tribes. All previous treaties made by the Department of State were ruled to be invalid, as Indians were no longer considered as foreign nations. The Department of War would now be in charge of all Indian affairs. But, the men and officers of the army were now caught between the rock of the Grant Administration, and the hard place of the harsh Indian policy of Phillip Sheridan and William Sherman.

The most dramatic social change was in the creation of the new Indian Department by the Grant Administration. A coalition of national civil reformers and Christian religious leaders now ran the show. This quiescent governmental affair became the predecessor to the present Bureau of Indian Affairs (B.I.A.). The U.S. Army would no longer be involved with social interaction with Native American tribes. There is compelling evidence they fared better under the U.S. Army before this radical change in national policy. After this change corruption, greed and social reformers ran amok among the Western Tribes.

In the winter of 1868, Lieutenant Colonel Armstrong Custer's Seventh Regiment decimated the Southern Cheyenne village of Black Kettle on the Washita River in western Oklahoma Territory. The total destruction of the Indian's lodges, camp equipment, winter food supplies and over 600 head of horses would be a precursor for the things that could have happened on the Little Bighorn. The Grant Administration was sending a strong message of its new

"Indian" policy. In 1876, the U. S. Army became a pawn in the politically-charged "Indian Problem" in Washington and was ordered to destroy the Montana winter-roamer's way of life. These were the wild bands that refused to live on the reservations assigned to them by the Indian Department. The destruction of their villages would set them on foot without food or shelter. However, the worst devastation would be the decimation of their horse herds. This loss would crippled their ability to make a living as wild game hunters on the high plains of Southeastern Montana. Seemingly, one of the main objectives of this new policy was to kill as many of their men, women and children by direct warfare or starvation.

The policy makers of the Grant Administration thought that with the destruction of the winter roamer villages they would be forced to live on fixed reservations. General Sherman referred to this strategy as the solution to the "Indian Problem," a term reminiscent of Germany nearly seventy years later. The plan called for them to become farmers and good Christians overnight in the Bad Lands of South Dakota. But becoming either was not likely.

The true religion of the People, as expressed by the nineteenth century Ogallala-Sioux warrior Black Elk and the twentieth century Red Power advocate Vine Deloria was that the concept of individual land ownership was not what the Great Spirit had promised the Chosen People of the Great Plains. The White Man's Eucharist was not a good substitute for the Sundance renewal ceremony.

The last great fight of the Sioux and Northern Cheyenne to remain as free roamers occurred during the Great Sioux Campaign of 1876. Here, with their allied tribes they won an empty victory over a small segment of the U. S. Army. The unprecedented consolidation of their massive villages had never been seen before, or after this watershed conflict. Within the next few years most would be subjugated on their assigned reservations. In reality, these reservations would become nothing more then prisoner of war camps. Their horses and firearms were taken away from them. Now they could no longer hunt the scared buffalo, which were disappearing very fast from the High Plains.

The systematic destruction of the buffalo herds was part of the same political policy that sent the army against people now politically deemed as "Hostiles". They may have won their battle with Custer, but they lost the war that President Grant, and Sherman and Sheridan had instituted against them.

In 1876, when the U. S. Seventh Regiment of Cavalry went into combat on the Little Bighorn, they comprised of just over 600 officers and enlisted men. They were undermanned, poorly trained, and ill-equipped. Under the existing Federal Laws, they were to have almost 1000 officers and enlisted in the twelve companies. And, there was also the polarization of the military leadership of their executive officer, and acting regimental commander, Lieutenant Colonel Armstrong Custer. Heading the Pro-Custer faction was Captain Thomas Weir with Captain Fredrick Benteen best representing the Anti-Custer splinter group. This internal bad blood played a major part in the development of the Custer Fight. This struggle represents the worst of the human element and has caused many of the "Custer Myths" to develop a cult-like status. But, the resolution of these "myths" may be found in the study of their non-human counterparts, the horses!

This seminal event occurred over a three-day period from June 25, to June 28, 1876. The "hostiles" were able to defeat the "Elan" of the U.S. Army, leaving behind over fifty percent causalities among their officers, enlisted men, civilians, and allied Indian Scouts. This pitched battle was fought over half-dozen combat sites with but four identified today. The actual site of the Reno Valley Fight and some of the "Custer" Battalion's preliminary skirmishes will be revealed for the first time in this study.

The villagers left the battlefield in honor, but they went away in sorrow. They had to leave behind some one hundred of their warrior husbands, and family members. More then half of these causalities would later be described as the "Suicide Boys". They had self-pledged to throw away their lives in the next fight with the soldiers. They were the teenage sons, cousins, and nephews that were too young to be considered full-fledged society warriors. The full story of the deaths of these young "boy" warriors was too painful to be discussed, as the People thought they had digressed in their faith as the Chosen People. And, that the Great Spirit had abandoned them by their deaths in the Custer Fight. Their way of life and faith had been broken by this ill-omen of things to come.

The villagers left behind the defeated and entrenched soldiers to lick their wounds, and to be rescued by their expected reinforcements. This threat of more soldiers coming from the north prompted the villagers to leave. They had enough of the killing, and the more important camp logistics of grazing, sanitation and the feeding of thousands of people with fresh meat were critical reasons. Their unexpected victory left them overwhelmed, but they knew that the soldiers would return, and this time with a much larger force.

Another general misconception of this battle is that the entire Seventh Regiment fought and was killed on a single battlefield on the same day. Only one-third the Regiment was killed with the Custer Battalions, on or near the present Custer Battlefield. The balance of the Regiment held out for three days, on a separate defensive site, located four miles away. There, on their entrenched hilltop position, the remaining two-thirds of the regiment staged a desperate two day fight, fighting against "hordes of Indians."

Valid estimates of just how many Native Americans were at the Custer Fight indicate there was a minimum of 7000 Sioux and Northern Cheyenne, and their allied tribesmen, in the consolidated villages along the Little Bighorn. On June 22, Custer told his officers not to expect less then 1000 and perhaps as many as 1500 lodges out in the field. By the method that the army used this could represent as many as 7000 to over 10,000 men, women and children. And, no less then a warrior force of 1500. According to the seasonal migration of the buffalo, their villages were expected to be in the area of the Rottengrass and Lodgegrass tributaries of the upper Bighorn and Little Bighorn Rivers. The last thing the army expected was to find the villages gathered in one place. This unprecedented congregation was the major factor in the defeat of the Seventh Regiment. However, the army's own horsemanship training and deployment tactics may have proven to be their worst enemy.

Early Researchers: Walter M. Camp and John Stands In Timber were exceptional history researchers without peer. Dedicated to their avocations as hobbyist historians, they pursued their lifetime interest with a zeal that few academic scholars ever achieve. Neither became rich from their pursuit of the preservation of the story of the Little Bighorn Battle. In fact, they both expended a great deal of their time, effort and financial means to obtain their stories of this High Plains episode. This event not only changed the lives of those involved, but it also changed the lives of these two extraordinary men. Today's dedicated researchers are in debt for the efforts they made, and their legacy of many hundreds of research notes and material that have gone unnoticed for over a half-century. Only a part of Walter Camp's massive collection of field notes and interviews have only recently received due notice. However, John Stand In Timber's effort to preserve the history of the Northern Cheyenne has fallen through the financial cracks of an archival limbo.

Walter Mason Camp: Walter Camp was from a culturally rich Anglo/ American environment. He was born in a small Northeastern Pennsylvania town named after his family progenitors. His ancestors came from England in 1631, and founded Camptown in the late 1790s. Later, the songwriter, Stephen Foster immortalized this small rural community when he penned his famous ditty, *Camptown Races*. Walter Camp was born here in 1867. He became a lifetime railroad man. At age sixteen he was already a "Trackwalker" for the Lehigh Valley Railroad. It was there that he learned telegraphy, which was on the cutting edge of railroad technology. He graduated from Pennsylvania State College as a Civil Engineer in 1891. He soon went to work for railroads in California where he leaned "hands on" civil surveying, and structural drafting. **M40, pg 1 (See BIBLIOGRAPHY, pg. 220**

He found his niche later when he went to work for electrical railway systems in Oregon. With this new skill, Camp became an advocate for electric railroading for the rest of his life. He participated in the design of the New Orleans streetcar system in the 1890s. He served in many capacities of railroad construction from a civil surveyor to track foreman. To improve his knowledge, he obtained a Masters Degree from the University of Wisconsin, in Steam Engineering and the new field of Electrical Railroading. For a time he taught civil engineering to graduate students. But, it was in Chicago in 1896 that he took the position as technical editor for a prestigious trade journal, *Railway Review*.

Here he discovered his true calling as a writer, and would remain as their chief technical editor for the next twenty-six years. He became their "In House" expert on track building. Walter Camp literally wrote the book on the subject, He authored what is still considered to be a premier textbook on railroad track building. Just like their animated horse cousins, the "Iron Horse" technology has not changed very much!

However, due to economics and perhaps declining health, Camp would spend the last three years of his life on his dairy farm, in Northwestern Indiana. He became a free lance writer for this same trade journal, and was never to miss a deadline. Upon his death in 1925, his Chief Editor, Willard Smith, called him the most informed man that he had ever known. His last weekly column had arrived in the mail the week of his funeral, on time and ready for publication!

Walter Camp became intrigued with the Custer Battle as early as 1898. But, it was his first trip to Montana in 1903 that prompted his investigation into what was already a National Icon. He said the written "facts" about the Custer Battle did not agree with what he saw in Montana. The terrain simply did not match what he had read about the battle. As a civil surveyor, his trained eye told him that what was being written was already becoming a "Custer Myth."

Camp then began his own pursuit for the truth, which lasted for another twenty-two years. At first, he wanted to write a history of the Seventh Regiment. But, by 1920, at the annual conference for the Order of Indian Wars, he announced that he had collected enough material to expand his writing to cover the entire Indian Wars period from 1854 to 1890. Eventually, he wrote a preface and laid out many of the photos and chapters of his proposed history. But five years later, upon his death, his proposed book remained unwritten and would never be published. **M40, Camp/Hammer. pg. 10 (Address by Mr. W. M. Camp"** *Winners of the West,* **Vol. X, No. 11, October 30, 1933 (Reprint of address given in January 17, 1920)**

His extensive research notes and interviews soon became scattered or remained in storage. In the early 1930s his material was dispersed from Indiana to Colorado. But, in 1968 Brigham Young University (BYU) was able to purchase the single largest known portion of the "Camp Collection." But, it lay un-inventoried and un-indexed for the next six years. However, by 1974, with a grant from the Custer Battlefield Historic & Museum Association, Dr. Kenneth Hammer was able to inventory and typescript much of the "Custer" portion of the BYU collection. He had already type-scripted the Camp material housed at the Lilly Library of Indiana University (IU), the so-called "Lilly" collection.

Doctor Hammer, a noted economics historian and Custer scholar, began a meticulous effort to work with the fragmented pieces of Camp's hand written field notes, correspondence and personal interviews with over one hundred Custer Battle participants. At one point the BYU Camp Collection, including Dr. Hammer's some 1100 pages of typescripts, occupied over sixteen feet of library shelf space! In 1976, BYU Press published *Custer In '76*, Dr. Hammer's effort to record the Custer portion of the Camp material housed at Brigham Young University. But, even then he was not able to publish all of it.

As this author was to discover certain facets of the Custer portion still remain unpublished, and some may never have even been microfilmed. Custer scholar, Bruce Liddic has not yet been able to find some of the photocopies and notes that this author made on the three rolls of microfilm now available from BYU Because of the on and off microfilming process conducted during the 1980s at BYU there is doubt that they recorded all of the material.

With over 1100 pages of typescripts, from the BYU Custer material alone, Dr. Hammer and subsequent researchers have failed to understand the importance of this massive collection. And no one has yet published any of the other forty some U.S. Army and Indian battles and skirmishes that Camp also investigated. The author was able to view the original Camp material from 1977 to the early 1980s. Then, due to sporadic microfilming, portions of the original material would be put off-limits for viewing. Only as new microfilm became available, were a small number of researchers able to view the collection over the next twenty years. In general, and to the "Custer World" in particular, many history students remain uninformed about this very valuable and primary source material.

Eventually several non-interpretive "Camp Collection" books were published. But, in essence they remain "sterile," without the compassion and zeal that marked Walter Camp's original efforts. They were written by researchers that do not have the engineering training of Walter Camp, nor his humanistic approach in his interviewing skills. What these "Camp Books" are missing are the many horsemanship clues as to the role that the army's horses played in the Battle. Because of this deficit these authors continue to perpetuate many of the Custer Myths that Walter Camp tried to expose. In the BYU collection, there are many scraps of field notes, written in Camp's cramped and almost unreadable handwriting. They were reminders written to him to look up a particular participant or a single facet of his interviews and research. It was his engineering style of asking questions that led to the many good resolutions he suggested. It is oblivious that Camp had great more knowledge about the Custer Battle then was ever put on paper.

By obtaining the official U.S. Army Muster Rolls and military pension records from the General Services Administration (G.S.A.) Camp was able to identify those who may have been at the Little Bighorn Battle. And he verified their participation from other enlisted men whose presence he had already established as being there. In this manner he was able to interview some one hundred men known to have been at the Little Bighorn Battle. Eventually, he also interviewed over two hundred Sioux warrior participants and their relatives who had watched the Battle. He also contacted a number of the civilian participants. He used modern technology of the Twentieth Century such as the telephone, typewriter, and ammonia "spirit" copiers for his research. He also utilized an amazing number of library archives, both public and government. But, his preferred method was to locate his informants, travel to their homes, and conduct a one on one interview.

He once commented that he never wrote anything down in front of his informants as he thought that it would intimidate them and possibly make them reticent. As soon as possible after the interview, he would prepare a summary of the interview, in his own wording. Rarely did he ever use direct quotes, but knowing of his painstaking engineering methods, you can believe that his recorded interviews were accurate interpretations. Today, to be able view the BYU Camp material, one must be satisfied with the three massive rolls of microfilm. There are also the many hundreds of typescripts prepared by Dr. Hammer, not only from BYU, but the Lilly Library collection of the Robert Ellison portion and the so-called Colorado portion of the highly segmented Camp Collection. Also, the National Park Service at the Little Bighorn Battlefield National Monument obtained another unknown portion of Camp papers that were recovered from a barn in Eastern Colorado in the late 1980s.

John Stands In Timber: The Northern Cheyenne tribal historian, John Stands In Timber was born but eight years after the Custer Fight. While his family was being held as prisoners of war, Stands In Timber was able to attend the Haskell Institute in Kansas. Here he became well versed in the English language, and later he used this asset to write about his cultural heritage. He returned to his native Northern Cheyenne reservation in Montana and would spend a lifetime recording the history of his people. However, his efforts did not fare as well as Camp's better preserved effort.

In the 1950s, Stands In Timber's primary advocate became Peter Powell, an enlightened Episcopal priest who was assigned to the Northern Cheyenne Reservation in Lame Deer, Montana. This was where Stands In Timber lived and was also the headquarters for the Northern Cheyenne agency. For over ten years Father Powell maintained more then a passing interest in Stands In Timber's effort to preserve the "Old Way" of the Northern Cheyenne. Father Powell was able to publish several well accepted anthological works on the Northern Cheyenne due to his relationship with John Stands In Timber. **M76 (See Bibliography, pg 217)**

During the early 1900s, Stands In Timber had taken many of the old time warriors to their former battle sites. This included the fight on the Little Bighorn River, known today as the Little Bighorn Battlefield National Monument. There they reenacted their roles. Stands In Timber recorded their stories, and carefully marked their battle sites with small rock monuments that represented each individual warrior's story. Each of these cairn monuments represented the participation of an old warrior. But, human activity on the Custer Battlefield has destroyed most of Stands In Timbers' rock memorials. Those "little stone piles" have been scattered by the uninformed and uncaring relic hunters. When Stands In Timber died in 1967, he took most of his "Custer" knowledge with him. Book writers picked his brain for his anthropological knowledge, but very few ever took the opportunity to walk the Custer Field with him. By the late 1950s, when "Custer-mania" was at its height, Stands In Timber had developed cataracts, and he could not see well enough to find all of his old "warrior markers." At the age of eighty-five, John died in Lame Deer. His mentor, Father Powell interrupted his schedule to travel from Chicago to Montana to bury his old friend. **M53**

History was not so kind to their collaborated efforts. Stands In Timber's shed full of newspaper clippings, and his massive undertaking to record his People's history disappeared into the archives of the Saint Ignatius Indian program in Chicago. This effort, promoted by Father Powell and sponsored by his Episcopal Diocese was to help a stone age people into the Twentieth Century. In recent times this effort has failed to stay financially solvent. The Gods of War have not favored the winners of the Custer Fight.

The Time Puzzle. It took a railroad man to discover what official time the Seventh Regiment used. In their testimonies at the Reno Court of Inquiry, the officers referred to "regimental" time. Walter Camp obtained the Northern Pacific Railroad's timetables for May 1876. He discovered that Bismarck was then using St. Paul railroad time! The headquarters for the Northern Pacific was located in St. Paul, Minnesota, along with General Terry's military headquarters. The Regiment's garrison at Fort Abraham Lincoln, located across the Missouri River from Bismarck, was officially operating on St. Paul railroad time. **LILLY 616 (See Citations, pg. 221)**

The difference in longitude between St. Paul and the Little Bighorn Battlefield is fourteen degrees, seven minutes, and thirty some seconds. Since each fifteen degrees of longitude represents one-hour, this difference represents fifty-six and one half minutes in time. When the officers said that they crossed the Divide at Noon, St. Paul time, it was about 11:03 AM local time. According to the Hardin, Montana newspaper official sunrise and sunset for June 25, 1976, was at 5:22 AM and 9:04 PM Mountain Daylight Savings Time. This leaves fifteen hours and forty-two minutes of official daylight.

There is also about an additional half hour of twilight, before and after official sunrise and sunset times. When the Seventh Regiment marched up the Rosebud, reveille call was at 4:00 AM, St. Paul regimental time. That means that in Eastern Montana, reveille would be in the dark, about one and one half hour before sunrise. They would then march two hours later at 6:00 AM, some forty minutes after sunrise. Since the sun set about 8:00 PM in St. Paul, it would become too dark to see by the same time by 8:30 PM in Montana.

This is important because it can be used to determine the end of the fighting on the Custer Battlefield. Camp's informants agreed that the firing from the north seemed to stop as soon as they left their advanced position, known today as Weir Point. Some of them said that it was between two to three hours after they returned to Reno Hill that the warriors' firing on their position ceased when it became to dark to see. That places the end of the Custer Fight between 5:30 to 6:30 PM. However, Fredrick Gerard, who had stayed in the valley, said that he heard firing from Custer's northerly position that lasted until near darkness.

Walter Camp's Maps: Walter Camp carried a barometer with him on many of his trips to

Montana. He used this scientific instrument in the same manner as all surveyors. He would record the local barometric pressure, and by using standard mathematic calculations, he could obtain the local altitude. Then he could estimate the elevations of a given terrain feature by using a local datum point. Camp would also have had the use of a surveyor's "hand level." This small hand held device will give estimated angles of a sighting and using trigonometry tables; he could determine the terrain elevations by adding this information to his local datum point. In early 1910s, Camp had a large-scale map made of the Little Bighorn Valley. He had a draftsman prepare a "master" map of the Little Bighorn Valley, done in black "Indian" ink on linen. That is typical of an engineer, since his hand printing was almost unreadable, he would have a professional draftsman prepare the map. Then, he could run a number of "blueprint" copies from his master map, by using the old Osiliad ammonia process. This blueprint process was common before the era of computer drafting. Segments of surviving Camp blueprint copies are published in this study

Map Orientation: In the writings of most Custer authors, there is great confusion about compass direction and map orientation. The reader is advised that when interpreting topographical maps, as used in this book, that they are oriented to the earth's True (longitudinal) North. The United States Geological Survey (U.S.G.S.) topographical maps are used for civil property descriptions. This can be confusing to those who are "topographically challenged." A person's "built-in" sense of direction may not align with their visual conception, while on or near the Custer Battlefield or in its environs.

Most of the geographical directions in this study will be given as a general reference based on the U.S.G.S. True North orientation, and not magnetic compass heading. They will be given in *Italics*. For all magnetic compass readings, keep in mind that the U.S.G.S. "Topos" of the Custer Battlefield area should be used with a magnetic variation of sixteen degrees from their True North orientation. That is where the earth's magnetic field causes a compass deviation of sixteen degrees to the east of True North. Most Custer students become confused in the field when it comes to describing general directions as to what is north or south when compared to the U.S.G.S. surveys. In reality, the Little Bighorn Valley and Custer Battlefield lie on a true Southeast to Northwest magnetic direction.

Walter Camp was a trained civil surveyor. However, in his Custer research notes, he used an archaic notation system to express his magnetic compass readings. This author has converted Camp's recorded compass headings to a more conventional reading in azimuth degrees. For example, when Camp expressed his magnetic compass heading of "S., 22 Deg. W. or 22 Deg. W. of South," in this study it will be expressed in a true azimuth heading of 202 degrees. Azimuth magnetic compass readings are expressed as 360 degrees for north, 090 degrees for east, and 180 degrees for south and 270 degrees for west. This method will be used in this study for the convenience of the field researcher. **BYU 299 (See Citations, pg. 223)**

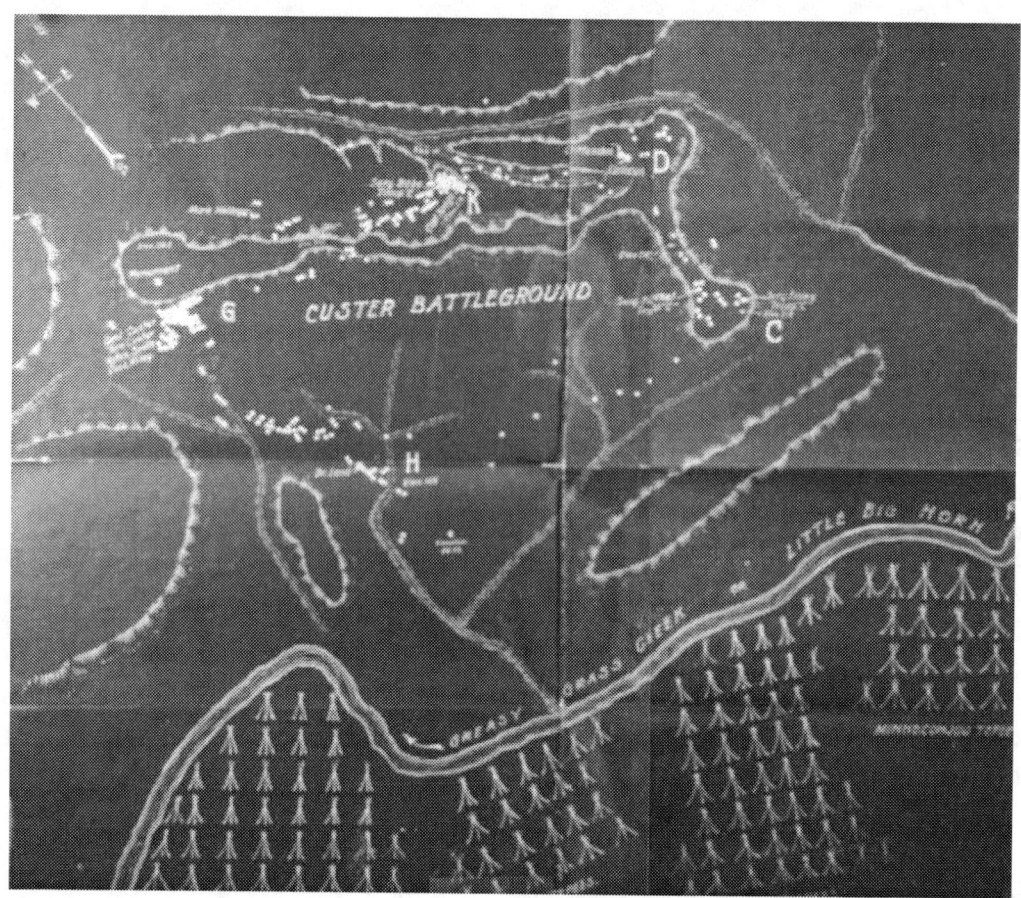

Permission from BYU Archives and Manuscripts Department

SEGMENT OF WALTER CAMP'S BLUEPRINT MAP

SCALE: -------------------- 1/4 MILE

Originally done in black Indian ink on white linen by a professional draftsman, Walter Camp was able to run off multiple copies of his "master" by the Osiliad ammonia process know today as a "Blueprint." Copied on heavy paper stock, Camp carried or mailed a number of these copies to his participants. They include Private James Rooney, of Company F (mailed) and Lieutenant Winfield Edgerly (in person). Only three of his blueprint maps are known to exist today and they are housed in the Special Collections Department at Brigham Young University in Provo, Utah. The above segment is that of his unannotated third copy. All of the Blueprint maps were about eighteen by thirty-six inches. Severe fold lines can be seen on all of those that survived.

For those who are less familiar with U.S.G.S. maps, the one square mile "Township" sections are identified by section numbers and are arranged in an East to West numerical order, up to thirty-six sections. This pattern repeats itself alternating along a base line. All U.S.G.S. "Quadrangles" titles are shown on an index for each State. The one showing the Custer Battlefield is called the Crow Agency S. E. Quadrangle.

Property Descriptions: First, the Range and Township designations are given along an established east-west base line, and then the Township Section number. This is further broken down to a 160 acre quarter Township section, and continues quartering down to the smallest 1/16th section, that of a forty-acre section. Therefore, a standard one square mile

Township Section contains four quarter sections of 160 acres, or a total of 640 acres. This Township Section system is used for all property descriptions in the United Sates, and was inherited from England after many centuries of property recording for taxation purposes.

Usage of U.S.G.S. Quadrangles is impractical in the field, unless you are very familiar with them and have a "witness" corner-section monument, a fence line, or some other physical orientation point. They can be very disorienting since they are based on True North longitudinal alignment, and not magnetic compass headings. However, all U.S.G.S. "Quads" show the regional magnetic variation at the bottom of each quadrangle sheet. The magnetic variation at the Custer Battlefield is sixteen degrees. The usage of U.S.G.S. topographical maps, as reproduced in the appendix, allow the reader to see the terrain features as represented as contour lines. They are shown at twenty foot intervals and their datum elevations are measured above mean sea level by barometric pressure. Only the current 1967 U.S.G.S. editions are used as background in this book as they show the accurate terrain contours.

They were created by a method known as the Photogrammetric process. That is where high altitude aircraft photographs are used to reproduce the latest versions of all U.S.G.S. Quadrangle surveys. The film is transferred onto a standard format that equals seven and one half minutes of longitude. This is called the so-called standard U.S.G.S. 7 1/2 (minute) Quadrangle and it represents seven and one half minutes of longitude and at the latitude of the Custer Battlefield represents an east to west distance of about six miles. On this format, at the latitude of the Custer Battlefield, one inch equals 2000 feet.

All U.S.G.S. topographical surveys published prior to 1967 were done by what is called an "Eyeball" ground survey. That is where on-the-ground surveyors actually plotted the more interesting features of a township section. On uninhabited and less interesting areas, they would add conjectured terrain features. For example, the terrain features around the so-called "Nye-Cartwright" area, where today known army skirmishing occurred, is not valid. They were drawn in by subjective guesswork, and physically do not intend to represent the actual terrain. They were not surveyed by men on the ground, but just "eyeballed" from a distance by experienced field surveyors. A good example of this major problem is found in Jerome Greene's *Evidence and the Custer Enigma*, first published in 1973. Greene was a seasonal NPS ranger at the Custer Battlefield in the late 1960s. Although the more accurate 1967 photogrammetric aerial survey of the Crow Agency Quadrangle was available, the author/publisher used the earlier and much older edition done as early as 1896. **M36**

This older non-aerial version is very inaccurate. Greene's foldout map of "Artifact Finds" is of the older 1896 version and is very misleading. Especially the terrain features around the Nye-Cartwright area do not represent the true terrain area at all. This error has led many Custer scholars to misplace terrain features such as the true "Luce Ridge." The terrain features on these older editions do not reflect the actual terrain. Except for the one square mile of the Custer Battlefield, the earlier U.S.G.S. special edition was created by "eyeball" guesswork.

However, within the same time period of Greens tenure, the National Park Service started to use United States Department of Agriculture (U.S.D.A.) aerial photographs for plotting their artifact finds. Several of these 24 X 24 square inch aerial maps were spliced together to form a large composite map, where most of the then known "Custer" artifacts found outside of the one-square mile Custer Battlefield, were plotted by an alphanumerical system. Segments of this National Park Service (N.P.S.) Master Artifact Find master artifact aerial-photo map are reproduced in the appendix from personal photographs taken by the author in the 1980s.

While Greene's foldout topographical map does show the correct artifact alphanumerical numbering taken from the NPS master U.S.D.A. aerial-photo, they were transposed onto the incorrect terrain features of the much earlier U..S.G.S. eyeball survey. Perhaps the logistics of copying the U.S.D.A. master Ariel-photo was overwhelming in 1973, but at least the more accurate 1967 edition of the U.S.G.S. quadrangle should have been used. This poor choice has led many Custer Buffs to be misinformed as to the actual locations of the artifact finds, especially on or near the Nye-Cartwright/Luce Ridge area. For a period of time, the original U.S.D.A. master artifact map hung on the wall of the then 1970s library in the basement of the visitor's center at the Little Bighorn Battlefield. However, very few researchers even know of its existence. **See Appendix: N.P.S. Aerial Survey and Greene's Map, pg. 194-195**

Most of the mileage distances in this book are conveniently rounded off to "tenths" of a mile. This decimal system is given for a field researcher who has permission to walk or drive a vehicle over the terrain in question. Then a pedometer or the vehicle's corrected odometer can be used. Those researchers lucky enough to be able to ride on horseback can use the built-in odometer that all horses have. It is called a natural gait, and can be expressed in miles per hour by experienced riders.

Camp's Field Trips: Between 1908 and 1920, Walter Camp made at least sixteen trips to the Custer Battlefield. Normally, he used his railroad pass to travel from Chicago to Rosebud, Montana. There he would rent a wagon and team, and make the two hundred mile round trip to the Custer Battlefield. He usually went during his summer vacations in July or August. He would mount an odometer on one of the wagon's spooked wheel. That way he was able to record the distance as he traveled along the "Custer Trail." By faithfully recording the odometer's readings, he could accurately calculate the distance in miles.

Camp's field notes contain many of these trail distance recordings. Many of these were typed scripted by Doctor Hammer, when he reviewed the Camp material housed at Indiana University (IU), referred to in this study as the Lilly (Library) Collection. What is important is Camp's written description of the "Custer Trail" that he made on one of his many trips. As early as 1911 he recorded his return trip up Reno Creek to the so-called "Divide. " His compass headings and "station" mileages allow researchers to be able to trace his "Custer Trail" today. **LILLY 6162, LILLY 558**

In 1917, Camp placed a bronze plaque, now known as the "Camp Marker" on the divide crossing between the Reno Creek and Davis Creek trail. He used a square metal "lard" can as a mold for the cement base for his plaque. He mixed the dry cement with water taken from the upper Davis Creek. Camp also placed similar markers on four other Indian Wars battle sites. In particular, the exact location of the 1876 battle site of Slim Buttes between the Sioux and General George Crook would not even be known today without the extraordinary efforts of Walter Camp to preserve this piece of history. This author has used Camp's meticulously recorded mileage distances, and found them to be highly accurate when compared to modern vehicle odometers. In some cases, Camp's more accurate measurements are used rather then the author's vehicle, or when traveling by horseback over the "Custer" trails.

Camp also prepared a civil survey of the "grave markers" on the Custer Battlefield! It was done on large "field" survey linen that has a waterproofing "waxy" surface. He recorded each individual Custer "tombstones" with a numbered triangle. Today, in the field, a serious researcher can verify Camp's painstaking accuracy. Very few scholars even know of the existence of these maps at BYU, because in 1977-1995, they were kept separate in the "Map Room," and not with the balance of the Camp material! Unfortunately, the Grave Marker "map" is almost un-reproducible, due to its size and the faintness of the original pencil drawn features. Obliviously, Camp had hoped to have his Chicago based draftsman copy it in more permanent Indian Ink.

Another important factor was Camp's 1909 field trip that he made with Daniel Kanipe and Peter Thompson. Both were former enlisted men from Company C, one of the so-called "Custer" companies. Also, both were at the Battle, one as messenger who was sent back to the Pack Train, the other as a drop-out from the Custer battalions. It was former Sergeant Kanipe that gave us the best clue for the exact number of burials on the Custer Battlefield. In his 1909 field trip with Walter Camp, he pointed out that wherever there were clusters of two or three grave markers, in 1876 there had been but one burial! By elimination of the some sixty surplus "phantom" markers, found within a three yard circle of each other, and set up in 1886 a more accurate picture of the actual fighting is obtained. Daniel Kanipe had helped to identify and bury his former line sergeants, August Finckle and Jeremiah Finley. He also found where his First Sergeant Edwin Bobo had died. Later he would marry his widow.

In 1920, Camp made his last trip west to the Battlefield. This time he would travel by automobile for the first and only time. That year he doubled his vacation time and took a month to visit Montana. Earlier he mentioned being interested in a "Reo" model vehicle, which he later purchased, that was part modern pickup and car combination. It had a short bed behind the enclosed two-seat cab. It would have been the ideal vehicle for all of his camping and surveying gear. Camp recorded that on this auto trip up Davis Creek, that with a little filling in of the washes, an automobile should be able to negotiate the original "Custer" trail. He does not say whether or not he made it all the way up with his new vehicle, but knowing of his tenacity, and his engineering skills, he most likely did!

Camp mentioned that officials from Custer County planned to establish a graded automobile road up Davis Creek from Busby to Crow Agency. It would be called the "Custer Memorial Highway," for the anticipated motorized tourist trade. The Custer tourist did come, now at a rate of some 400, 000 a year, but not by the Davis Creek "Memorial" highway. We know that it was never constructed, as many Custer Buffs have discovered when trying to drive it today without a four-wheel drive vehicle. It is a tribute to Camp's "magnificent obsession" that he was able to negotiate this mostly road-less area of the High Plains from Chicago to Crow Agency. But his travels paid off with his voluminous notes that he recorded.

The Blake/Marshall Survey: The Dawes act of 1887 established the township civil property system to the once "wild" land areas surrounding the Custer Battlefield. Enrolled members of the Crow Nation were to be allotted 160 acres of each quarter section for families then living on the Crow Reservation. This allotment system required that a civil survey be done to establish the exact boundaries for each Township Square.

In the Bureau of Land Management (B.L.M.) district office in Billings, Montana, are the original drawings of the 1890s land surveys of the Crow Reservation. This discovery was a major breakthrough in solving the mystery of the terrain that the Custer forces marched over to reach their final battlegrounds. The U.S. Congress had mandated that the Crow reservation to divide into Township Squares for enrolled Crow families. What is important to this study is that the existing trails/roads of the post Custer era are shown on these hand drawn land surveys.

Over a period of ten years civil surveyors laid out the standard one mile grid for the Little Bighorn Valley and its benchland environs. This established two different property ownerships, one for Trbal Lands and the other for individual enrolled Crow families. The interesting thing for this study is the defining of established "roads" that existed in the 1890s. A few of these roads were established by U.S. Government intrusion, such as the "Crow to Busby" Stage Road. In the 1880s, a telegraph line was established, which later was replaced by a telephone line. It is also recorded on these surveys that it originally ran up Reno Creek, or as the author prefers the traditional Crow name, Ash Creek.

The Blake/Marshall surveys also show the existing "roads" on the upper reaches of Reno Creek and Davis Creek. These are most likely the same "trails" that were used in 1876. These roads are the same today except where they have been altered for the use for motor vehicles. Automobiles can climb steeper than horses so most of these early roads now have more direct grades than the original trails created by four-legged game animals or travois trails.

What is of particular interest is where the lower Reno Creek "Route to Crow Agency" road is shown crossing at the latter Hartung and Echleman Fords, seen in Sections 11 and 12. The upper Reno Creek road (labeled as the "Sawmill Road") can be seen. With Walter Camp's detailed written descriptions and the Blake/Marshall surveys, one can trace today much of the original "Custer" route of 1876. For the most part, the present county graded school road follows the original trail, except where it ends in Section 20, two and one half miles west of the Camp Marker on the Divide. **See Blake-Marshall Survey, pg. 55-56**

THE PROPER MILITARY SEAT

Lt. Boniface's 1890s trooper exhibits the proper military seat for a mounted soldier. Except for the gauntlets, near side carbine scabbard, and canvas leggings this photo represents the Custer Era soldier's proper tack and arrangement of accouterments. Note that the infamous carbine sling is missing after the introduction of the Craig bolt-action carbine as the standard sidearm. **See Custer Era Horseman, pg. 196.** *(Source: H2, The Cavalry Horse and his Pack, by 1st Lt. Jno. J. Boniface, 4th Cavalry-1903)*

THE U.S. ARMY HORSEMANSHIP PROGRAM

The man who carelessly writes of history or without exhausting every possible source of information is bound to have some things incorrect, and the historical writer who is indifferent to facts does not know the harm he is doing.

Walter Mason Camp

Walter Camp wrote this preface for his proposed history of the Indian Wars, a book that he hoped to have published by the early 1920s, but was still unfinished at the time of his death in 1925. **LILLY 616**

As a horseman looking at the Battle of the Little Bighorn, this author has discovered a new perspective that may help to resolve many of the "mysteries" of this seminal event. By analyzing how the U.S. Army trained and deployed their men and horses, a new and startling viewpoint starts to emerge. The methods that the army used may have shaped the outcome of the Custer Battle?

The understanding of the deployment of the army's horses has been largely overlooked in the past. The cavalry tactics that were used in the 1870s was dictated by the army's horsemanship training program. Both officers and enlisted men were trained to respond in a given manner to a certain "horse" situation. The movement of mounted men over a given terrain was dependent on this training. Virtually everything the U.S. Army did in this military engagement evolved around the use of their horses.

Today we now have far more feasible military scenarios, thanks in part to modern military reenactors who have reconstructed how the army of the Custer Era trained, and tactically deployed their men and horses. Through trail and error they have rediscovered the lost art of the military protocol that was used some seventy years before the mechanization of the U.S. Army's "Mounted Service" of the 1930s. The military strategy and ethical protocol used during the Custer Era will also be examined. Again, thanks to today's "Civil War and Frontier Army" reenactors, we now have a more complete picture of how these findings can be applied. If we combine these unique findings of horsemen who have recreated the methods used by the U.S. Army, then perhaps many of the unanswered questions on what happened at the Custer Battle can now be resolved?

In the past, "Custer Books" have concentrated on the frailties and prejudices of the human participants. We need to look at the rider, and not the writer! This book focuses on the horsemanship, the distances and the actual terrain that the so-called "Custer Battalions" marched over to reach their final battlefield.

The Army's Horsemanship Training Program: The following reconstruction is primarily based on the 1883 U.S. Fourth Regiment of Cavalry official Drill Manual sent to the author by the present First Calvary Division's "Horse Platoon," an official U.S. Army mounted ceremonial unit at Fort Hood, Texas. The 1883-4 time frame in which it was written is close to the Custer Era drill tactics. Actually, drill manuals did not change very much from Phillip St. George Cooke's Civil War issue. But, the Frontier Army cavalry tactics were evolving as this rare manual proves. **O4**

The first thing an army recruiter did was to sort out who would go to the cavalry. This was simple, all of the new men over five foot six to five foot seven inches and weighing more then 150 pounds would be automatically be sent to the infantry. The army wanted cavalrymen to be small men and not weigh too much!

The procedure of training military riders and horses evolved over a long period of time. The European Armies had developed it over many hundreds of years. The U.S. Army borrowed and adapted these time-honored methods, especially those from the British Army. The "Custer" horsemanship can be traced back the era of General George Washington.

For Custer Era enlisted men there was no basic training as we understand today. Initial military training for the new recruit destined for frontier duty was conducted at the Jefferson Barracks, south of St. Louis, Missouri. Here the men were taught the basic military order and ethical protocol. From a month or longer the new enlisted men were held here for later assignment to a Mounted Regiment. The essentials of barracks life were taught, and an introduction to that necessary icon of the army, the army sergeant! **M47**

This was about the only training experience the new men would receive. As far as they would ever get to be a cavalryman was when they mucked out a stall in the stable for an officer's horse. It would not be until they were sent to their regiment that they would start their training with army horses. During the "Custer Era" the entire U.S. Army horsemanship program was done at a company level, at the enlisted man's new regimental assignment. The dream of General Phillip Sheridan for a centralized Mounted Service training center was not fulfilled until some forty years after his death. That was when U.S. Army School of Cavalry was established at Fort Riley, Kansas in the 1920s. The reader must be aware that in the late 1800s, not many young men were trained horseback riders. Horses were expensive to own, and if you lived in a rural area, you rode behind the horse in some sort of conveyance. If you came from a large urban area, you would not have a riding horse, unless you were from a wealthy family.

The overwhelming majority of the new recruits had most likely never ridden astride a horse in their life before. However, before the new recruit was trained to ride horses, the Dismounted School of the Soldier (Infantry) was taught as "instruction on foot" from the manual. They would be instructed in such fine points as how to from a rank, count off by fours, order of arms and movement in a dismounted unit. The prescribed marching steps, flank movements, how to oblique in quick step, double quick step, and the other movements used by an infantry man would be taught. Everything was done by the numbers and "by the "book," just like the military today, army life has not change that much.

The initial training for the Mounted School of the Soldier in his new company was expected to take at least two months. Here they would be assigned to older and well-disciplined horses. But, they would be required to change horses every day during the training period of at least one hour each day. They were expected to master the proper "military seat." No saddles were ever used in the initial training. They used an issued bed blanket with a "surcingle" chinch over the "saddle" blanket. They first learned to mount and ride bareback without the doubtful benefit of a saddle with stirrups.

At first new cavalrymen were taught to use the "snaffle-bit" bridle, using both hands on the reins. They most important thing that they were taught was the proper methods of safe handling of horses in the confinement of closed ranks. They practiced daily how to mount and dismount properly and learned how to lead a haltered horse and how to put on a bridle. All of this mandated practice was what the army called proper "ground training." Knowing how to handle your mount safely from the ground was very important. This was first step of learning how to ride the army way. **H6, O4**

When they had properly learned how to walk, trot, and canter the horse without a saddle, they were given a saddle without stirrups! Again, once they had mastered the walk, trot and canter without stirrups, they would graduate to a full saddle. Once they mastered riding at all gaits again, they were finally integrated into the ranks of the other experienced company riders. Again, the cycle of the walk, trot, and gallop, but now with the more aggressive curb bit, using just the left "bridle hand" was mastered.

Weather permitting; the Army performed what was called "close order" mounted drill every day, except on Sundays. This was done for up to four hours, and six days per week. This was where a squad, platoon, company or even a full battalion would march closed up, stirrup to stirrup around the parade ground. They would perform all of the required formation maneuvers. The actual purpose of this rigorous training was to keep the horses in condition in case they were called to go into the field for an extensive amount of time. It could take up to two years to produce a proficient rider by these time-honored methods. That a majority of the enlisted men in the Seventh Regiment were not sufficiently trained to be "good riders", is the key to understanding their role in the Battle of the Little Bighorn. Some 100 raw recruits had been sent to the Seventh Regiment just before the Custer Battle.

One of Walter Camp's informants was retired General Hugh Scott, who in 1876 was a Second Lieutenant battle replacement direct from his West Point graduation. Scott told

Walter Camp that of the more then one hundred raw "recruits" sent to Fort Abraham Lincoln before the Custer Fight most had little or no training in safe "ground" handling of their horses. This means that if they could not control their horses from the ground, they were considered to be poor riders when mounted. On the 1876 Sioux Campaign that resulted in the disaster on the Little Bighorn River, these recruits were forced to walk the three hundred miles from the Seventh Regiment's post at Fort Abraham Lincoln to the Powder River in Montana. Obviously, their company commanders did not consider them to be trained well enough to ride in the ranks. They had not yet been assigned to a company horse! Well over 100 of these men were left behind at the newly formed supply base at the mouth of the Power River. How could such mismanagement exist in the élan regiment of the US Army? **LILLY 108**

This sad state of affairs was but another legacy of the regiment's acting executive officer, Major Marcus Reno, and his lack of managerial skills in handling men and horses. In the prolonged absence of Lieutenant Colonel Custer, Reno would not permit the companies the time to train their new men to be capable riders. His official excuse was that the logistics of the pending campaign demanded that all of the men to be put to work in the government warehouse in Bismarck and in ferrying the supplies over the Missouri River to the army post. Proper training of the men was not the only thing wanting on Reno's watch. In the spring of 1876 the government issue of horse tack, and the men's accoutrements and clothing were sorely missing under the new Grant Administration economic policies.

The regiment was a makeshift outfit of Civil War surplus items, but with some newer authorized 1874 issued gear. Anything made from expensive leather ranging from saddles to boots was in short supply. A number of men did not have the necessary riding boots that are required by all horsemen. The high top boots prevent abrasions of the riders' lower leg caused by the jouncing gait of a horse against the exposed stirrup straps of the McClellan saddle. Enlisted men Henry Lange and Able Spencer of Company E said that they were forced to wear the low quarter garrison "brogan" shoes for their entire enlistment from 1872 to 1877. Either this was an example of poor management at the company level or of the Regimental Quartermaster, or just another sign of the cost cutting of the Grant Administration? **BYU 215 (Lange)**

The army purchased only gelded (neutered male) horses. They never placed stallions or mares in their company herds. U.S. Army mounts were selected carefully on their conformation and soundness. The purchasing officer was judged on his "Horse Sense." At least two officers in a regiment were assigned to this duty. The nominal age of all army horses was between six and seven years old at the time of purchase. This older age was considered the optimum for the horse's ability to learn quickly; any younger, with their shorter attention spans, were considerer to be a deficit. The new horse "recruit" was placed into a company herd, but not ridden for the first two years. This was done so the animal could adjust to the routine sights and sounds of an army post. Horses psychologically thrive on routine. By the age fifteen, the "older" cavalry mount was considered ready for retirement. By then, the animal had many miles on its built in odometer. In the 1876 Sioux Campaign alone, the average marching distance on the Seventh Regiment's horses was 2000 miles. **H6, H10**

The average weight of an army horses was in the 900 to 1100 pound range. Their height as measured at the withers (shoulder neck) was between 13 to 14 1/2 hands (four inches to a "hand"). Their breeding today could be considered to be that of a modern thoroughbred-quarter horse conformation. Army horses were purchased at an official U.S. Government remount stations, or from an accredited horse breeder under government contract. **H6**

Commissioned Officers were required by Congressional Law to purchase their own horses, usually bought from the same source as the company horses. The average purchase price could range from $150 to over $250 per horse. The average officer's annual income was but $1500. Now you can now see why a high value was placed on the horses. Lowly enlisted men could be had for only thirteen dollars per month. After nearly ten years of training and care, the investment in an army horse was much greater than that of an enlisted man.

Horses have three natural gaits, the walk, trot and the gallop. Anatomically, the fore feet control the direction and the rate of their forward movement. Their hind quarters supply the propulsion that makes them go forward or backwards. And, they all have a built in "odometer" that can be used to estimate accurately how far an army column traveled in an overland march.

The natural gait of horses has been studied for centuries. Not until motion pictures has their natural rhythm and mechanics have ever been fully understood. Before this many theories were developed to explain how the various gaits of a horse functioned. A schematic form of notation was developed to describe the timing and order of movement of the feet. Like musical notes, the actual placement of the individual feet became a scientific study decades before motion pictures of the film industry solved the mystery!

Gaits may be classified as being either natural or acquired. The acquired (artificial) gaits were never used by the military. The Army classified the natural gaits as the walk, trot and gallop. Gaits can be further classified as either being on the diagonal or on a lateral movement. This applies to which feet are in unison at any time. The term beat is the sound that the feet make when striking the ground, either one foot or two feet in unison. The term time is the interval between successive beats, or phrases of the stride. The stride is the distance between successive imprints of the same foot. Step is the distance between two successive imprints of the two forefeet or hind feet. It should be one half of the stride, except where pronounced lameness exists. An examination of these hoof prints can pin point lameness.

Gait can be said to be collected when the length of the stride is shortened and the center of gravity shifts to the rear quarters. The natural gait of a walk is defined as a slow four marched beat on a diagonal stride. In different animals, the walk may differ from as slow as two miles per hour, or as fast as up to six miles per hour, depending on its natural gait. You cannot have hundreds of horses moving forward at their own natural gait! It's the same with infantry; the men are marched at a regulated pace. The U. S. Army set the official walk at as being three and one half to four miles per hour. This was a natural gait that the horses were trained to consistently achieve in the ranks. Again, you cannot have some horses traveling faster or slower in the ranks.

The trot can be defined as a "leaped" or fast two beat diagonal gait. It can be a slow (short), ordinary, or the long racing variety. The slow trot is not collected. The ordinary trot is a perfect two-beat gait. The army set the ordinary trot at eight miles per hour. The long or racing trot of up to ten miles per hour was never used by the military.

The gallop may be defined as a fast "leaped" or three beat diagonal gait. This is the familiar "clarity-clop" sound that the motion picture sound editors like! A slow gallop was called a canter, or in Western riding terms a "lope." Faster "racing" galloping is also considered to be natural gaits. The speed at which a horse can gallop can vary between from six to over forty miles per hour. For the military, the "maneuvering" gallop of a formation was to be held between twelve to fourteen miles per hour! However, a faster full gallop could be achieved between sixteen to eighteen miles per hour, but only in smaller units and with perfect ground conditions. The army rarely used this faster gallop, no mater how hard the moviemakers try to make you believe! **H6**

When Major Reno "charged" down the Little Bighorn Valley, he ordered a collected "hand" gallop of about twelve miles per hour. This was a rare event, and Reno's horsemanship skills were to be put to the test, and he failed. That failure of his horsemanship will be discussed in the Chapter Two on the Reno Valley Fight. These regulated gaits and the constant drill training created a compact unit of experienced horses and men that could travel over most terrain in an orderly manner. The operative word "orderly" must be kept in mind when analyzing what happen at the Little Bighorn Battle.

When the so-called "Custer Battalions," traveled to the Little Bighorn down what is now called Reno Creek, they averaged a "fast walk" of five and a half miles per hour. Eventually, they were to never to travel any faster then an average of seven miles per hour. Researching the history of the Pony Express this author discovered this natural gait. Pony Express horses maintained a walk/trot gait for an average of fifteen miles between their remount stations. Overall, cross country their horses averaged seven miles per hour for the entire some 2000 mile route This little known logistic of the Pony Express is used as the natural rate of march of Custer's horses when the distance is known, but the actual time element is missing.

This "magic" gait of seven miles per hour can now be used in this study. This natural gait can be used to estimate the time of marching by the various Seventh Regiment units. Particularly where the distance is known between geographical locations in the battlefield environs. An accurate timetable of plus or minus five minutes can now be established by using this rate of march. It is the average speed of a fast walk and a slow canter. Cavalry officers of the Custer Era were proud of their ownership of a good watch! By keeping their timepieces wound and synchronized daily, they could estimate very accurate mileages of how far they had traveled by keeping track of the time that the horses had marched. On all cross-country marches, an officer kept an officially itinerary of the daily marches. .

The average rate of march can now be set for all four of the major components at the Battle of the Little Bighorn. They are the combined First and Second Battalions, or the so-called "Custer Battalions," Benteen's Third Battalion, Reno's Fourth Battalion, and the Pack Train with Company B acting as a rear guard. By using the above-established gaits, as defined by the army-training program, we can use these marching rates quite accurately. When horses are placed into a compact formation, they learn to coordinate their gait with each other.

Tactical Training: Every morning the men would count off by fours for each dismounted platoon. They would keep that numbered rank position throughout the day. Number "Four" would become the horse holder for the other three horses in his rank. Army regulations required all of the horse holders to stay mounted whenever the platoon or company was dismounted. This sound practice was based on the theory that a well trained rider mounted on a disciplined horse was far safer then being on the ground trying to manage 4000 pounds of excited horse flesh! Far more "horse accidents" occur when men are deployed on the ground. A trained mounted man is far safer mounted than working on the ground with the same horse. This is an established "given" that all "good" horsemen should learn quickly. **O4**

The First Platoon would always be designated to be the right of any formation. The Second Platoon would be on the left, no mater what direction they were facing. The men and horses were trained to perform all of the prescribed maneuvers at a walk, trot, and a gallop. On a march in an "open" column a number of the company's non-commissioned officers would act as "File Closers." They would ride close to the outside to the non-aligned file to insure the lateral alignment of that rank. By literally pushing inward they would forced the men to yield to pressure to keep the files closed up.

When dismounted, the men were trained to march in the British style of "quick and double time" movement when being moved on foot from one point to another. To visualize this think of those old British war movies where they use that high stepping animated walk, and then you will have a good idea how the "Custer" era soldiers looked when they were being moved from one place to another. Keep this image in mind, as many of the Indian accounts refer to the soldiers "running as if they were tired," during the Custer Fight. The historical link between the U.S. Army and their Anglo military heritage was but a short one!

The "Lance Corporal" was considered to be a non-commissioned officer, and he acted as a visible guide. There was always another "principle guide" in the first file of the First Platoon, another non-commissioned officer, but he never carried the Guidon. The Lance Corporal was always positioned at the head of the first file of the Second Platoon. By carrying a "Guidon" flag the men to his rear in that file would align on his position. The reason for this arrangement was for ceremonial parade formations where the Guidon flag was required to be in the center of a single rank when the when the men formed into a line. This is not what you see in the Hollywood movie versions, where the Guidon is always placed in the first rank at the front of the company! The proper placement of the Guidon (Lance Corporal) is outlined in all of the cavalry manuals. **O3, O4. See also Appendix, pg. 199**

The formation of an "open column" was conducted with the standard average of four inches of space between the men's knees, and a four-foot interval from the croup to the nose of the horses. This created a front some twelve-foot wide when they were in the standard formation of a column of fours. A full company of eighty men would then be some sixty-six yards in length. The buglers rode as pairs at the front and center of a marching column. They were always to be mounted on gray horses. In the first file of every second rank was to be a non-commissioned officer (N.C.O.). He could be a Corporal or above in rank. In addition, there were job "specialist" ranks such as Farrier, Blacksmith, and Saddler that were considered to be non-commissioned officers. The First Sergeant, who was the administrative non-commissioned officer, always rode at rear of the Second Platoon in the first file.

Platoon leaders, usually the First and Second Lieutenants, rode at left of the first rank in their platoon, assuming that the dress alignment was to the right. Company commanders were required to ride on the outside of the First Platoon leader, in the first rank. The platoon sergeants also rode on the left flank acting as file closers. They "pushed" the men on the outside file towards the alignment file, left or right. Alignment could be to the left, but the file numbers never changed. **O4**

The number one man was in the first file and always on the right flank of a column of fours.

The standard formation for all parade drill or an open route march was that of a column of fours. The 1883-drill manual of the Fourth Regiment of U.S. Cavalry calls the column of fours the standard formation. The walk was the habitual gait. However, this is not what you see in the Hollywood versions. **O4**

The movie makers always show a cavalry command in a column of twos. The main reason was that they never had enough trained men and horses to flesh out a full size company. If you had eighty untrained movie extras whose horses were not part of an integrated horse herd, all trying to ride closed up in a column of fours, than you ended up with disorder with horse fights. And, they did not go galloping madly all over the terrain, as no sensible horseman would endanger his mount or the other riders, especially in such close contact as the army rode. Now you know why they created all of those "regulations" and trained their men to ride safely. Or else they were transferred to the infantry. There are "riders" who sit on a horse, and then there are good horsemen who ride a horse! They understand both the inside and the outside of a horse. A wise man once said, "There is nothing as good for the inside of a man, as the outside of a horse." That was the level of "horse sense" that the Mounted Service wanted their men to achieve.

Not all would achieve this expectation. Prior to 1876 it was mandated that a company was to have a minimum of eighty enlisted men in the ranks. In full muster before leaving Fort Lincoln in 1876, the Seventh Regiment averaged but sixty-two men. By the time they reached the Little Bighorn, due to assignments to the packs and elsewhere this average dropped to about thirty-eight, with the smaller companies having only twenty-two men to be put on a dismounted skirmish line. **See Appendix: Enlisted Men Roster, pg. 207**

After the Little Bighorn disaster the U.S. Congress increased the army's minimum company strength from eighty to one hundred enlisted men. Does not this sound like the military appropriations of some recent National Administrations when it comes to military spending? The fiscal year after the Custer Fight, the entire U.S. Army went for a full year without pay because Congress failed to pass a military appropriation bill. Only after the leading political cartoonist, Thomas Nast (hence the name "Nasty Cartoon") published a scathing cartoon scenario showing a skeleton wearing a army uniform was Congress shamed into passing the belated Army appropriation bill. It is a tribute to the U.S. Army's professionalism that they did not mutiny over the hardship of serving for a year without pay!

The more familiar modern eight-man "squad" was not officially recognized during the Custer era. The smallest unit then was the forty-man platoon. The term "trooper" was not yet commonly used, although many of the younger officers had started using that term. Apparently, First Lieutenants wanted to be distinguished from the lowly Second Lieutenants by having them to be being addressed as "Mister," just as the U.S. Navy still address their Ensigns. By the turn of the century this holdover from the British Army fell out of favor.

The accepted ethical protocol was that there would be no fraternization between enlisted ranks and commissioned officers. All of the enlisted ranks were prohibited from speaking directly to a commissioned officer, without first having permission from his First Sergeant. And, then it should be a matter of life or death. This etiquette was ingrained into the U.S. Military Academy graduates, and it caused serious problems between the two cultures, that of the lowly enlisted men and his superior officer. As a farm boy from Ohio, Custer was a rare exception of this rule.

Captain Thomas French was to learn this military ethic the hard way. In 1879, French was unceremoniously kicked out of the army when he was accused of getting high on opiates stolen for his company Farrier, and than he got drunk off duty with some enlisted men. This may have been a case where a good combat officer sunk to the level of the lowly enlisted man. His behavior was not acceptable and he was summarily convicted and dismissed from the army with the added insult of the recommendation from President Hayes that it should be a permanent separation

The U.S. Army in the Nineteenth Century was still very much patterned after the British Army caste system of distinction between wealthy upper-class and the more "common" man. The enlisted men were taught to salute their officers with the British style of "telegraphing" a sideways snapping of the arm, with the palm of the hand outward and thumb down. However, the officers were required to use the more refined form of saluting, one that all of the U.S. Military use today. The enlisted men were also taught the smart style of a British "About Face", with a high lifting right knee, and the foot stomping and quick pivoting of the upper body. Just like you see in all of those old British war movies!

In the late 1850s, members of an official U.S. Army inspection tour of the European armies, supervised by General George McClellan, were impressed with the stylish uniforms of the Prussian Army. To the chagrin of all good leather workers, who love the natural russet color of leather, the leather accouterments of the Civil War and the Frontier army were to be dyed black! Soon, any manufactured leather equipment would become an economic issue under the Grant Administration. However, the Seventh Cavalry did still have some older Civil War issued rawhide-covered saddletrees, as several authentic "Custer Battle" saddles have surfaced, still in their original tan rawhide leather.

All of the newly issued Custer era saddles had the standard Civil War hooded stirrups covers removed along with the leather "sweat" skirts that covered the stirrup straps. These life saving and comfort features were just another cost reduction of the post Civil War economy. In case of a fall from a horse, the hooded stirrup kept a man's foot from becoming lodged in the stirrup and being dragged to their death. The skirt prevented the uncomfortable rubbing of the rider's legs on the bulging metal stirrup buckles and hard leather cinch straps.

Another questionable army regulation was the very dangerous usage of a shoulder sling to carry the carbine while the rider was dismounted. This ill-logical system demanded that the rider would never be able to leave his side arm on his horse after he dismounted. The theory was that if the horse stampeded with the weapon it deprives the man of his sidearm! The shoulder sling required the enlisted man to be linked by a snap to the carbine ring on the left side of the breech. This floating snap was permanently attached to the shoulder sling. This system prevented the rider from dismounting without having the weapon come along with him. In photographs of the time period, you can see where the men have unsnapped the link and would leave the carbine lying around anywhere on the ground. Try walking any distance with a forty inch long carbine hanging down between your legs. Then you will know why the men immediately unattached the weapon from the sling when they were dismounted. With this obtrusive weapon system, the men had to hoist the carbine up to shoulder level just to be able to mount their horses.

At the Custer Fight, some of the companies of the Seventh Regiment experimented with the system that the civilian scouts were using. They carried their long arm weapon diagonally across the pommel (front) of their saddle. Company C was one of those known to be doing this. They used the issued leather "carbine socket" lashed sideways through the coat strap slots in the McClellan saddle. But they still had to keep the shoulder sling linked to the carbine. After all, it was still a required army regulation!

The standard carbine "socket" was normally strapped to the off (right) side of the saddle rigging was still a death trap for any man who fell off his horse to the right side! The weight of his body hanging against the mandated carbine sling would just jamb the carbine barrel deeper into the socket. Most likely he would be severely injured or killed while being dragged upside down between his horses' legs. After the 1880s this very dangerous devise was slowly replaced by new socket that had a split metal ring covered with leather. Now you know why some of the companies were now starting to carry the carbine across the saddle. Not until the 1890's when the Craig bolt action carbine was issued was this archaic and dangerous system done away. It was replaced with the full length "western style" carbine scabbard mounted on the "near" (left) side of the horse. **See Boniface photo, pg. 29**

Men who were dismounted on a skirmish line were deployed on an interval of a prescribed six yards. This is important to note as archaeologists from the National Park Service have discovered a possible skirmish line of expended shell casings at six yards (eighteen feet) intervals near the Calhoun Hill loop road entrance. **See pg. 196**

No matter what you have heard, the famous McClellan was an excellent equestrian saddle. Adopted from the European armies, this lightweight but rugged saddle was easy on ones rear end. That is if you learned to sit the proper military "seat" for which it was designed. Its free hanging stirrups allowed for great leg cues. However, the exposed stirrup straps without "fenders" (skirts) can allow for discomfort on an extended march, as they will cut into your inner knees. Custer's personal McClellan had well worn "sweat" fenders, but Commissioned Officers were required to purchase their own tack along with their personal mounts. By regulation, officers were prohibited from using issued gear, especially the U.S. Government horses, but that was quite often ignored on the frontier posts.

On an open route march, the men rode mounted for about the first fifty minutes of each hour of marching. For ten minutes or more, they would dismount and led their horses. After the first hour of march there would be a highly supervised "shake down" halt of a greater duration. This allowed the men to care of bodily functions and the tightening up loose saddles and gear. During the day's march on every hour they would repeat the ride/walk routine. This was to prevent saddle sores, allow the horses to cool down and the fact that horses thrive on routine. When the trail was steep enough, either ascending or descending, they would be required to dismount and dismount and lead their horses. Today, you will not see Western style "Cowboy" riders doing this, but they were not supervised like the army men!

In any given open terrain march there are what the army defined as "obstacles" to be negotiated. This could be a ditch, fence line or just a horse accident-waiting-to-happen on tricky terrain. In the early Twentieth Century, officers and enlisted men were expected to learn to ride the "hunt" seat. **O4**

That is where the men and horses were able to jump difficult obstacles without changing gait. The eastern seaboard Confederate Cavalry was born to the hunt seat, and was able to ride circles around the "heavy" plodding Yankee cavalry riders. And so could the Sioux and Cheyenne warriors who were trained to ride as soon as they could walk. The Northern Cheyenne warrior, Wooden Leg tells of how they would "roughhouse" with each other as part of their natural horse training. They would strive to throw another rider off their horse, especially into a cactus bed.**NA5, H10**

On upper Ash Creek (Reno Creek) there were a number of side drainages that created "slow-down" obstacles for the thirty foot wide Squadron formation of the First and Second Battalions. The heavily used game and travois trail had deep "troughs" going in and out of these drainages. Any natural barrier such as at a ford crossing, ditch, fence or wall was considered to be an obstacle. The method that the Mounted Service used to train their men and horses to over come these barriers were logically based on good horsemanship.

The men had to learn to ride with the natural balance of the horse, without fear of falling and not freezing up. The rider and the horse had to learn to trust each other. A good rider is one that never shows nervousness, as a horse can sense sudden tenseness in his rider, and the confidence bond comes unraveled. For the most part, the Custer Battle was a challenge between two cultures of horsemanship, but it was when the army was forced into a defensive posture they where defeated.

The standard military technique to negotiate an obstacle was by having the outside files of twos, or even a single file if necessary, to break from the formation, and pass over or around the obstacle. With the default alignment being to the right, the first and second set of files would increase their gait, while the other files held their gait. Then by an oblique movement of thirty degrees to the right, they would negotiate the obstacle. The other files would then fall in behind them and reform on the other side of the obstacle. After the files had passed the barrier, they would oblique back to the left and reform the former formation, nearly always that of a column of fours! By this "leap frog" technique the cavalry could just about accomplish passage through or over any obstruction. The key to remember was that after the first set of files passed the obstacle they would allow the other files to catch up by maintaining their former gait or even slowing down! **O4**

The style of jumping taught by the U.S. Army was called the "Hunt Seat." The modern "Jumper/Hunter Class," as seen in English style horse shows is one of the finest forms of horsemanship! But, to this author, the number one form of horsemanship is the "Reining Horse" class, as seen in Western riding and indicates the author's bias for the working ranch horse. Here, all of the advanced elements of equine training come into play. The rider and the horse become as one. The competition Reining Horse rider is shown the pattern just before entering the arena. He can not use any visible cues, physically or verbally. A very integrated course where a change of leads spins and controlled backing is closely scrutinized and scored. This is when a talented horse can out score the rider's performance.

Another form of advanced horsemanship is found in the European High School form of Dressage. By the 1920s, the newly founded School of Cavalry at Fort Riley trained cavalry officers to compete at international levels of Dressage. But, even as early as the "Custer Era," the army trained their men to perform simple Dressage movements such as the "passage," or side pass. This elegant form of a lateral side stepping motion allows for a diagonal realignment in the ranks. But, when a larger change in direction is required, the left or right "Oblique," by rank and file was done at a prescribed thirty-degree angle. This was but a few of the "basic" maneuvering formations taught in the daily mounted drills on the parade ground. Like a "ripple" a well-trained platoon or company could accomplish this technique even at the faster gallop. **O4, H10**

The primary reason for this no-nonsense training was for the protection of the horse. Paramount was the prevention of injuries to U.S. Government horses. Preventing "horse-accidents" was the motivation for the highly regulated drill maneuvers. This system evolved over many centuries of accepted "good horsemanship." It was based on the number and severity of "horse-accidents" known to occur. Prevention of these accidents was the key word in the army's horsemanship training. The initial high cost and the many years of training made the cavalry horse a valuable commodity. All Company and Regimental officers were held responsible for an out of service injury and or loss of the Government horses placed in their charge. Especially during the "Custer" era, any officer found responsible for the injury or death of too many government horses, due to poor training, would have a very short career.

During the Civil War, General Custer developed an excellent reputation for being a good manager of men and horses. This was one reason for his dramatic rise to a divisional commander, with the rank of Major General (Brevet), the highest rank in the U.S. Army that could be held by a field commander. He supervised some 6,000 men. During his days at West Point, Custer excelled in all of the horsemanship training and he set equestrian records that remained for a long period of time. As a youth he developed the understanding of horses at his father's blacksmith shop in Ohio. Then, blacksmiths were the local horseshoer and veterinarian for the local community. Some have said that Armstrong Custer was a born horseman.

In the U.S. Army the term "Blacksmith" meant the same thing, one that shoed horses. However, the term "Farrier" meant one who was a veterinarian's assistant. There was at least one Blacksmith and Farrier assigned to each company. The rank and file men were not allowed to clean even their own horse's feet! Some enlisted men were known to injure the horse's feet with the misuse of a hoof pick. Once a day the company Blacksmith and Farrier would check the horse's condition and take the proper corrective procedures. By regulation there was to be a Veterinarians assigned to cavalry regiments, but the army had to hire civilian horse doctors, as there were yet no army trained Veterinarians. But, on the frontier it was not always possible to find a Veterinarian. However, there was a Veterinarian assigned to the Seventh Regiment in 1876, but he did not go on the summer campaign that ended in the loss of nearly over four hundred of the regiment's government horses.

Another major fallacy that pervades throughout this study is the misconception that the cavalry always fired their weapons from horseback! Except for the exceptional use of the revolver for close-in action, the men were always deployed as skirmishers on foot to use their side arms, especially the Springfield carbine which was the authorized weapon in 1876. Most "Custer Buffs" are convinced that the Indian Wars Army went into action firing from horseback, just like you see in all of those John Ford and John Wayne Hollywood movies. As today's military reenactors have discovered nothing could be further from the truth. From the way the Custer Fight evolved, nearly all of the fighting was done dismounted. They had lost the offensive, and for defensive measures they would have been dismounted. For the most part, the action on the Custer Field was a dismounted infantry action, for both the army and the warriors. **LILLY 24 (Camp)**

Any defensive action with the carbine would be done as dismounted skirmishers. Try rapidly shooting and reloading a powerful weapon like the .45 caliber Springfield carbine from horseback with any accuracy, and you will soon realize why the army dismounted to do so. Besides, with men mounted in a marching column just the left file could fire, and than just to the left front. Even when formed into a single rank of skirmishers, they could just shoot at a very limited angle to the left forward of the line. The men were trained to dismount, link up and advance on foot at the double time as skirmishers. The front rank would knell, while the second rank fired from a standing position over the front rank, the same tactics as used by Infantry. **O4**

General George B. Thomas, during the Civil War, pioneered the method of using horses to take men from Point A to Point B and then to dismount and fight on foot. He has been credited with developing this method of using cavalrymen trained to fight as infantrymen. There simply was not enough time to properly train the men to be good horsemen, so they were more heavily trained in infantry tactics.

Firearms: Many of the late Civil War horsemen were armed with an excellent weapon, the Spencer .50 caliber carbine. This was a lever-operated repeater with a tube magazine for metallic cartridges. In 1876, the Government warehouses were filled with thousands of surplus Spencer carbines. There were also many Sharp single shot rifles and carbines stored as what we now think of as war surplus. A few of these "surplus" weapons found their way to the Little Bighorn, and were used by Sioux and Cheyenne warriors against the U.S. Army soldiers.

A recently discovered memo, originally sent in 1874 by a cavalry commander to the U.S. Arsenal at Harper's Ferry, requested to have his regiment issued Civil War surplus weapons, specifically the .50 caliber Spencer carbines. His request was rejected by a higher command in Washington. That request was submitted by the executive officer of the Seventh Regiment, Lieutenant Colonel G. A. Custer!

The U.S. Army weapons review board in the early 1870s mandated that a single shot breechloader was to be the official side arm issued to all U.S. soldiers. The Springfield Armory originally designed a .50 caliber weapon, but it was downsized to .45 caliber because of high muzzle blast. Often referred as the "trapdoor" model, because of the later designed storage compartment in the butt plate, this post-Custer era modification was a direct result of the Little Bighorn. Due to the sometime failure of cartridge ejections, a segmented cleaning rod was issued and it was stored in the trap-door compartment. The real culprit causing spent cartridges to jam in the breech was the soft copper casings. The Custer era weapon had no cleaning rod "trap door" and the copper cartridge casings were an economic consideration as the original design that called for brass casings. By 1874, the downsized .45 caliber model became the standard issued firearm and was used in the Custer Fight. An irony of history was the fact that one of the review board members was Major Marcus A. Reno! This official review board refused to accept any repeating action weapons, as they were considered "wasteful" for a well-trained marksman! The foolishness of this theory was that there was no regular marksmanship training program in the army until nearly the turn of the twentieth century. Officially, regiments were allowed a very small number of cartridges per year for the training of their men. There is no doubt that many of the new recruits that went to the Little Bighorn had never even fired their weapons before June 25.

As most enlisted men, who have ever served in the Armed Forces, knows there is vast difference of the world of commissioned officers and the world of the enlisted men. One persistent "Custer Myth" is that the men each carried fifty rounds of carbine ammunition on their person. Virtually all of the Seventh regiment officers made this claim. But, thanks to modern military history reenactors who have painstakingly reconstructed the uniforms and authentic issued gear, and have also researched the actual tactics of the Custer Era, we known this blanket claim not to be true.

The men at the mouth of the Rosebud had been issued 100 rounds of carbine ammunition. Just as today, cartridges were packaged in twenty round cardboard cartons. This is equal to five cartons of twenty rounds each. At least one of Camp's enlisted informants said they had been issued but eighty rounds, or four cartons. The question that needs to be asked is just how the men managed to carry "fifty" rounds on their person. That is the equivalent of two and one half cartons.

The Seventh Regiment, in part a tribute to the forward thinking of its acting commander, was experimenting with what will become known as the "prairie" cartridge belt. By adding a looped cartridge sleeve made of canvas over a regulation leather belt the men would have a better means of carrying carbine ammunition on their person. They were made by the regimental saddlers who were responsible for maintaining all of the leather tack and saddles. Peter Thompson said that not all of his Company C's prairie belts were completed in time and he did not have one on the Sioux Campaign of 1876. There just is not enough room on a thirty some inch waist belt to accommodate fifty loops. Besides, of all of the authentic so-called Custer Era cavalry "prairie" style cartridge belts now in museum collections, there is not one that has fifty loops. The largest number is forty; the exact number to contain two cartoons of issued ammunition. You will still have to subtract space for the revolver holster and its required so-called "cap box." And then there is the problem of the men that were issued the modified Civil War cartridge boxes. They only held a maximum of twenty rounds. What did they do with the other thirty rounds? And, still there is the mystery of how the men were able to get the other four cartons into the tiny Civil War half moon shaped saddle bags? The later 1874 issued rectangular bags were larger, but could barely hold the individual man's reserve ammunition. These were the tactics that Custer and all of his battalion and company officers were faced with in the Battle of the Little Bighorn. True history cannot be changed just to appease a non-horseman fallacy. With these startling criteria in mind, we can now put those Custer Myths to rest.

The Role of the Pack Train: The U.S. Army also included mules in their livestock inventory. In the late 1870s, the inclusion of mules was a new experiment. They were to replace the more costly draft horse for heavy freight hauling. Brigadier General George Crook, who earned the enlisted men's nick name of "Rosebud George" from his 1876 Sioux Campaign, was to gain fame later in his Arizona campaigns as a pioneer of army mule pack trains. By the 1890s, this economic measure became an integral part of most cavalry regiments. Rather than having freight hauling non-cavalry horses, the six-hitch mule team rapidly replaced them. But, it would be their role as pack animals that made them acceptable. **H2**

During the 1876 Montana campaign, the Seventh Regiment was among the very first to incorporate this feature. Custer was on the cutting edge of military technology. But, his officers were very skeptical, and rightfully so. They did not have the experience or the training to create an efficient pack train with wagon mules. But that would all change within the next decade with better training and breeding of pack mules. The eventual elimination of the heavy army freight wagon and the necessary wagon teams was a breakthrough especially for the difficult terrain encountered during the Southwest Apache wars.

The stocky army mule was a product of the breeding of a selected female (dam) horse with a known male (sire) donkey. Eventually, this breeding program would develop into the large mule of today called the "Mammoth Jack" riding mule popular with Western riders. What we call "mulishness" is in reality an undesirable trait from the horse! Of course, the southern plantation farmer had used mules for hauling and riding for many decades before the military discovered them. The Seventh Regiment's first time usage of a mule pack train in 1876 would become a controlling factor for what happened at the Little Bighorn Battle.

The use of a Pack Train was a new experience for the Seventh Regiment. The Pack Train crossed the Divide twenty minutes after the other eleven companies. At the average interval of ten feet between ranks, the Pack Train's normal length would be about a quarter mile in length or 440 yards. All of the men and officers involved with the Pack Train agreed that at no time was it longer then 500 yards long going down Ash Creek. In all of Walter Camp's interviews, they all agreed that going down Ash Creek; the Packs had very little difficulty. This differs from the impression that some of the officers tried to leave at the Reno Court of Inquiry. It seems that Benteen and certain others were striving to create a different picture.

Lieutenant Edward Mathey reported that at the Powder River 160 mules were assigned to the Pack Train to carry the regiment's rations, ammunition and camp equipment. Private Dennis Lynch said that just the leaders and swing mules were taken for the new Pack Train. He was emphatic that the "wheelers" were left at the Powder River. This is contrary to the concept of Lieutenant Edward Godfrey who maintained that only the larger "wheel" mules were used. This is one of many "Custer Myths" that the good Lieutenant would create in his writings soon after and for many years after the event! An unknown additional number of mules were used for the officers, scouts and civilians. **M33, M40, pg. 138, & BYU 388**

The Pack Train may have had a total of some 200 mules. Crossing the Divide on June 25, the packs were kept in a column of twos. One enlisted man was assigned to each set of two mules. A lead rope held in his right hand, guided the first mule, while the second one was led in tandem. Another lead rope was tied from the crupper (rear rigging) of the first mule to the halter of the second mule. Each company had at least two "outriders," and possibly one civilian packer available to repack or tighten up a slipping load. **See Appendix: Packs diagram, pg. 210**

Again, it was Godfrey who gave the incorrect impression that seven men were assigned from each company. He was speaking for his company alone, as his Company K was the smallest unit in the regiment. In fact the overall average number was nine men from each company! When the regiment started up the Rosebud, the Quartermaster officer would have estimated the number of pounds of rations needed per company, based on its exact number of enlisted men assigned to that company. From this calculation it was determined that 160 mules would then be needed. That is the exact number given by reporter Mark Kellogg from his source, Lieutenant Mathey. **H2 & BYU 168 (Kellogg's Notes)**

Based on the ratio of one enlisted man for each two mules, then eighty leaders would be needed. Add to this a minimum of one non-commissioned supervisor plus two "outriders" from each company would be required to flesh out the pack train. For example, Dennis Lynch, who was with his company's packs, told Walter Camp that his Company F had fourteen mules and ten men assigned to the company packs. When Company F went up the Rosebud they had fifty enlisted men. This means that only seven men had to lead the mules while the three others acted as supervisor and outriders. This ratio of men to mules is used to estimate the correct number involved in the regiment. The exact number of men assigned to the packs depended on the actual number of men in the company. Each mule could carry an average of 250 pounds. **See APPENDIX: Pack Train Assignments, pg. 210.**

The number of pack mules assigned to the five "Custer" companies alone was seventy. Fifty men would have been required to control them. There were an additional number of personal "strikers," and other assignments to the packs. Along with McDougall's Company B, there could have been up to 180 men with the entire Pack Train and rear guard on June 25. And, there may have been at least one civilian packer assigned to each company. Walter Camp obtained the names of at least twelve civilian "packers" known to have gone to the Little Bighorn and not the far lesser number of five or six as implied during the Reno Court of Inquiry.

In this time frame, officers referred to the entire pack train as being the "packs", and not as the individual mules. Lieutenant Jonathan Boniface makes this quite clear in his would be primer for younger cavalry officers, *The Cavalry Horse and His Pack*. This established army terminology must be kept in mind when Lieutenant W.W. Cooke used the term "packs" in his written message to Benteen! That is if those words were ever in the original written message at all. **H2**

Each mule could carry between 300 to 400 pounds, including the weight of the packsaddle. The estimated total weight of the men's ration, camp equipment, and the reserve ammunition for the entire regiment could have exceeded well over 30,000 pounds, or fifteen tons! This would make the 160 mules have an average pack weight of less then 200 pounds. From the loading charts in Lieutenant Boniface's pack manual makes it quite clear that Custer's pack mules were not over loaded. **H2**

Two styles of packsaddles were used. The most superior was the traditional "Aparejo" pack saddle derived from thousands of years of development in the Middle East. It consisted of a large pad that was filled with natural soft material such as straw, and bundles of small diameter sticks for support. Its natural contour fitted on the mule's back and was kept in place by a simple chinch strap. Unfortunely, there was a very limited number of Aparejo pack saddles in the regiment when they separated from the wagon train at the Powder River.

The other packsaddle used was the forerunner of the now traditional "sawbuck" saddle, still popular with Western riders. Consisting of a dual cross design of wooden supports lashed to the pack animals back, this type requires a special rope rigging called the "diamond hitch." It was this system that caused all of the problems of loose and fallen packs going up the Rosebud. Major Reno discovered this on his earlier Powder River scout, and he had but six companies of packs to contend with. **H2**

Each company was issued 2000 rounds of reserve carbine ammunition. This was packed in two wooden boxes containing 1000 rounds each. Within each box the 1000 rounds were distributed in fifty cardboard cartons of twenty rounds each. Each ammunition box weighed a total of 110 pounds. The proven Aparejo pack saddles could handle both ammunition boxes on one mule, as side packs. This was because of the unique design and reliability of the ancient Aparejo packsaddle. But, the less flexible sawbuck saddle pack could carry but one ammunition box per mule. It was placed on the top, between the valley created by the side packs. These had to be limited to fifty pounds each, which was weight of one box of bacon or hard-bread. All of the individual side packs had to be equal in weight in order to balance the load. **H2**

The average rate of march of the Pack Train from the Divide to the 2:00 PM/ Hartung Morass was close to three and seven tenth miles per hour. The ten and one half miles was covered in two hours and fifty minutes! The pack mules could be trotted for short periods of time. When Lieutenant Luther Hare requested rapidity to get the packs from Mathey's Knoll to Reno Hill, the entire train was "whipped" into a "blazing" seven miles per hour gait, covering the one and a quarter mile distance just in ten minutes! The entire distance of fourteen miles from the Divide to Reno Hill was covered by the Pack Train in four hours. This includes an approximate fifteen minute halt on the "Big Flat." The head of the packs arrived at the Reno retreat position by 4:20 PM, just as Godfrey recorded in his field notebook. This amount of time translates an overall average rate of a regulated walk of three and three quarter miles per hour. And, certainly not the much slower gait that Fredrick Benteen tried to make the Reno Court believe.

Some writers think that when Custer sent Benteen the so-called "P.S., bring packs" message that he wanted the individual ammo mules to be cutout for "his" five companies. The logistical nightmare of this theory makes this argument impractical from a horseman's view. There were almost fifty "packers" from the five companies alone, and with a possible ten ammunition mules. One Camp's informants made it clear that the "ammo" mules were scattered throughout each company.

The problems of sorting out those men and mules would be overwhelming. Also consider the fact that when Lieutenant Hare arrived with his urgent request for ammunition, only two ammo mules were ever sent forward to Reno's men! This fact should be enough proof of the fallacy that that Custer wanted the reserve ammunition. The smaller expedited ammo mule train would then be exposed to flanking attacks on its way forward. And, Custer would not have wanted the entire Pack Train exposed to flanking attacks as they proceeded to a safer position on the bluffs. As his experience at the Washita Fight proved, the Pack Train was Custer's Achilles Heel, and protecting it was greatest in his mind!

PROLOGUE

THE DECISION IN MEDICINE TAIL

About halfway down to Little Bighorn we came into full view of the village and here he halted command and Cooke wrote out the message to Benteen
John Martin, paraphrased by Walter Camp

As Lieutenant Colonel Armstrong Custer marched towards his future battleground, at some point he halted his command and had his Adjutant Lieutenant William Cooke write out a dispatch. Bugler John Martin was now handed this message to take to his company commander, Captain Frederick Benteen. According to today's accepted historical version it read:

> Benteen
> Come on, Big
> Villages, be quick
> bring pack.
>   W.W. Cooke
> PS Bing pacs

According to Benteen this was the content of Martin's message. But in this version its expressed military logic is that of a Pack Train expediting order. If this version is in its original text and has not been altered, than its military value would be more correct if sent much earlier in the Custer Battle timeline, some forty minutes earlier.

At the time, U.S. Army officers referred to their pack trains as the "packs." Apparently, the emphasis was for Captain Benteen's reserve Third Battalion to advance the regiment's entire pack train to Custer's forward position, and as fast as possible. The hurried inclusion of the words, "bring pack, PS bring pacs" makes that assumption quite clear.

The Medicine Tail Halt: But, John Martin could not have carried this historical version of the "bring packs" message. In an interview with Walter Camp, Sergeant Daniel Kanipe revealed how he had already been ordered to have Benteen to take a shortcut to the bluffs, and travel to Custer's new front, and as quickly as possible! And, there is no mention of "packs" in this pre-Martin order. Another fragmentary note from the Camp Collection hints at yet an even earlier messenger, who may have delivered a similar order to Benteen, soon after he reached his "Morass." Was this messenger someone other then John Martin? An order sent much earlier in the Battle time line?

Benteen, with a lot of help from his fellow officers, successfully convinced the Reno Court of Inquiry, that he received but one written order, and that it was delivered by an enlisted man from his own company. John Martin was selected to serve on Custer's Headquarters Staff by a time honored U.S. Army method. As much as other Custer "Buffs" try to malign John Martin's foreign origin as an Italian immigrant, how he ended up on Staff duty with his regimental commander is important to understand.

Some Custer researchers seem to think that Benteen was playing a joke on his nemesis by sending a raw untrained and ignorant Italian who could not speak English very well! Not so, if we apply the process of how enlisted men were assigned to Daily Duties (D.D.) such as fatigue and guard duties, and other detached duties. The Officer of the Day (O.D.) would request the daily assignments on the evening before. Only those enlisted men who were considered to be the sharpest, as far as military decorum and uniform appearance were selected by their platoon line sergeants. The First Sergeant, who was the administration Non-Commissioned Officer (N.C.O.) of the company, would make the final cut. So it appears that Martin was considered to fit all of those requirements. The company commander would never be involved in such daily routines.

John Martin had served in his home country of Italy's military for a decade starting at the early age of fourteen. Immigrating to the United States in 1873, he enlisted in the Seventh Regiment less then two years before the Custer Battle. As a former military musician he was able to master the intricate cavalry bugle calls of the U.S. Army. Apparently, he had enough intelligence to become proficient in an endeavor that can not be faked. One area of interest in the Reno Court of Inquiry was that every time Martin referred to distances, the record gives his responses in the English measuring system such as miles, yards, and feet! It makes one wonder how accurate the verbatim record is since Martin grew up with the metric system in Europe. Perhaps it was the civilian stenographer, who changed Martin's replies, as it does not seem possible that Martin, in two years would have adapted that quickly? **M41 & M71**

THE HISTORICAL VERSION

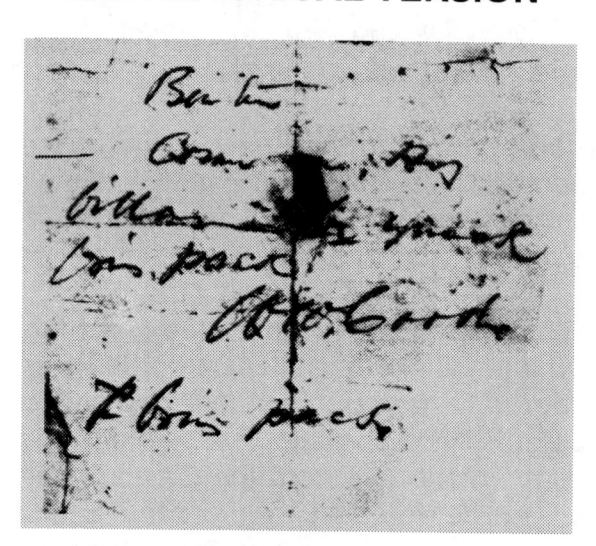

FACSIMILE A

1. Benteen
2. Come on, Big
3. Villages, Be quick
4. ***bring pack***
5. W. W. Cooke
6. ***PS bring pacs***

(Bold Italics by author)

Note: Neither the first usage of the word "bring" or the letter "p" in Line 4 does not match the same word or letter in Line 6. Is this evidence of a possible alteration of the original message? It should be noted there seems to be thin pencil lines inside the letters "W. W." that may be tracing lines. **(For author's version, see FACSIMILE B, Chapter 5, pg. 141)**

It was written in pencil on four by six inch yellow lined note paper common to all field officers. Today it can be seen in the Library at the U.S. Military Academy at West Point, New York. Colonel Charles F. Bates, with the earlier help of Retired U.S. Army General William D. Brown, the last Chief of Staff of the U.S. Army Mounted Service, had Benteen's Custer Battle "memento" donated to the Academy by 1942. He was the same General Brown that purchased the bulk of Walter Camp's Custer research for Robert Ellison in the early 1930s.

Benteen's Perfidy, The Bogus. and Only "Last Message": As this narrative will show, that at least one other messenger, Daniel Kanipe, and possibly two other couriers had already delivered countermanding orders to Benteen, long before he received "Martin's" order.

Benteen never carried out the expressed intent of any of them! The U.S. Army calls this an act of insubordination. The probable role of Benteen and his relationship with the Pack Train will be explored. Benteen may have withheld other important "secrets" about his role with the "Packs" from the Reno Court of Inquiry. Also, the part that he played in the mysterious "bring pack" order will now be revealed. **See Chapter Five, pg. 123 (See also Summary of Orders to Benteen on June 25, 1876, pg. 211)**

Courtesy of Dr. Jeffery B. Johnson, 54 mm pewter miniature diorama

FIRST AND SECOND BATTALION "SQUADRON" FORMATION

Sergeant Daniel Kanipe described this wide front marching formation as used by Custer from the Divide Halt to where he was sent back. After Martin's 'Big Hill" halt into "Fours," the command was now sixty feet wide. (Shown)

CHAPTER ONE

THE DIVIDE TO MEDICINE TAIL

The Seventh Cavalry was like a pack of bloodhounds following a scent.
Walter Camp

The Battalion Assignments and Military Protocol: Without the exact known battalion assignments in effect on June 25, incorrect assumptions will always be made as to their deployment on, or near the Custer Battlefield. At the beginning of the 1876 Sioux Campaign, the Seventh Regiment was formed into two wings of two battalions each. Upon arrival at the Powder River, on June 10, the Right Wing, consisting of Companies B, C, F, E, I and L, were assigned to reconnoiter up the Powder River, June 11-19.

Captain Thomas B. McDougall stated that his Company B was assigned to the First Battalion, under Captain Myles Keogh. Later, Sergeant Daniel Kanipe said that his "Company C was also in Keogh's Squadron." Sergeant James E. Wilson, in his report to the Chief of Engineers, included a portion of the diary of First Sergeant James Hill, Company B, who was on the Powder River scout. On June 13, Sergeant Hill recorded in his diary that "Companies C and B scouted the creek (Mizpah Creek) in a northerly direction," indicating that the two companies were in the same battalion.**BYU239-42, & BYU127**

Civilian correspondent Mark Kellogg also recorded the battalion commanders, but he did not list the individual company assignments. Base on the above sources, it is apparent that the Wing/Battalion assignments from mid-May to June 20, 1876 where as follows: **BYU127**

The Right Wing:

Commanding: Major Marcus A. Reno

First Battalion:
Commanding: Captain Myles W. Keogh.
Company I: First Lieutenant James E. Porter.
Company C: Captain Thomas W. Custer.
Company B: Captain Thomas M. McDougall.

Second Battalion:
Commanding: George W. Yates.

Company F: Second Lieutenant William Van W. Reily.
Company E: First Lieutenant Algernon E. Smith.
Company L: First Lieutenant James Calhoun.

The Left Wing:

Commanding: Captain Frederick W. Benteen

Third Battalion:
Commanding: Captain Thomas B. Weir

Company H: First Lieutenant Francis M. Gibson.
Company D: Second Lieutenant Winfield S. Edgerly.
Company K: First Lieutenant Edward S. Godfrey.

Fourth Battalion:
Commanding: Captain Thomas H. French.

Company A: Captain Myles Moylan.
Company G: First Lieutenant Donald McIntosh.
Company M: First Lieutenant Edward G. Mathey

On June 22, when the Seventh Regiment began its march up the Rosebud River, the wing and battalion formations were suspended. During that evening's officer's call, acting Regimental Commander, Lieutenant Colonel G. A. Custer, in an unusual frame of mind, stressed his dependence on the regiment's officers and their judgment. He challenged them to be individually responsible for their companies. His demeanor was very unlike the usual bombastic Custer, and perhaps a precursor of things to come?

After the regiment crossed the divide on June 25, the exact same battalion assignments that existed under the wing formation were re-established. There were new assignments given to former battalion commanders who were now reassigned within the battalions. There was no switching of companies from one battalion to another due to nepotism as suggested by non-military minded researchers. The exact formations on June 25 can now be reconstructed as being:

First Battalion:
Commanding: Captain Keogh

Company I: Lieutenant Porter
Company C: Second Lieutenant Harrington.
Company B: Captain McDougall.

Second Battalion:
Commanding: Captain Yates.

Company E: Lieutenant Smith
Company F: Lieutenant Reily.
Company L: Lieutenant Calhoun

Third Battalion:
Commanding: Captain Benteen

Company H: Lieutenant Gibson.
Company D: Captain Weir.
Company K: Lieutenant Godfrey.

Fourth Battalion:
Commanding: Major Reno.

Company A: Lieutenant Moylan.
Company G: Lieutenant McIntosh.
Company M: Captain French.

* **Author's opinion that on June 25, Thomas Custer was acting as Aide de Camp on his brothers staff.**

** **French replaced Mathey due to his assignment to the Pack Train.**

Since Custer's Headquarters Staff traveled with the First and Second Battalions to the Custer Battlefield, the non-military researchers have concluded that the two battalions fought as a single unit under Custer's personal command. This is a major misconception and always leads to incorrect assumptions about the deployment of the individual battalions. Military tradition defines a Headquarters Staff as a "floating" independent command unit, free to move from one theater of a battle to another. This lack of understanding the important roles that the battalion commanders played in the Battle has clouded the perception of the passage of the "Custer Companies" from Medicine Tail Coulee to the Custer Battlefield.

Mission: The Army knew that a game/travois trail would soon lead to good crossing of a river. These "roads" always took the path of least resistance and would be the best way for a compact formation of horsemen to be able to move quickly over unknown terrain. This concept is called a "Reconnaissance-In-Force."

The Battle of the Little Big Horn and the Vietnam War's search and destroy missions had something in common. In 1876, the army's primary goal was to locate a small village, capture it, and destroy its lodges, along with the food stores and household goods. The captured pony herds were to be decimated, putting the villagers on foot. These were the same successful tactics used by Custer nine years earlier against the Southern Cheyenne village of Black Kettle on the Washita River. This was to set an example for the other expected scattered villages. This valid theory was that without shelter, food, clothing and horses, the "hostiles" would not be able to survive the harsh winters on the High Plains. They would be forced to go to the reservations already established for them in the Dakota Territory. The capture of women, children and old men, as prisoners of war, was never a consideration, nor an option. The only fear that any of the Seventh Regimental officers had, was that the villages would escape from them!

The Custer Trail: The actual "roads" that were used by the army controlled the time element essential in being able to deconstruct the Custer Battle. Many of these roads would later become the early stage, wagon and rancher roads. Part of today's county graded roads overlay the original trails. Only with the coming of the automobile have the routes of these early "roads" have changed to any degree. The regimental officers followed these "roads" to go to the Little Bighorn Valley, as they knew that wherever they crossed the river, there would be a good ford crossing **See Blake-Marshall Survey, East Section, pg. 55-56**

Prelude, The Crows Nest Incident: At sunrise on the morning of June 25, 1876, a detail of Allied Scouts and one U.S. Army officer made observations from a high point to become known as the "Crows Nest." What they observed would shape of the Battle of the Little Bighorn. The Scouts had been observing signs of an encampment since sunrise. The Crows said they could see "campfire" smoke and "worms" that they thought were pony herds. On the same hand, the Arikara Scouts describe seeing not only the smoke, but also some of the lodges along with visible pony herds.

When dealing with translations of the native tongues of the Scouts, especially those of the Crow Nation, one must be careful. As Thomas La Forge pointed out, the difficulties of the understanding the Crow language was great. The Ree Scouts described their village sighting as being near the White Rocks area of the Middle Ash (Reno) Creek. It was implied that the Crows' sightings were in the far more distant Little Bighorn Valley. Perhaps both sightings were one and the same, and at a much closer location than the Crows sightings? **NA2**

When Colonel Custer first arrived on the Crows Nest, he was directed by Second Lieutenant (Mister) Charles Varnum to observe a small village on the Middle Fork of Ash Creek. As he stated in a letter to Walter Camp in 1909, Varnum said that with his naked eye he was able to see at least two lodges standing on Ash Creek. The Crows tried to have him verify their more long distant sighting, but the Crows had made their sighting with "a cheap spy glass." However, even with his more powerful army binoculars, Varnum could see nothing in the far distant Little Bighorn Valley. He pointed out his Ash Creek sightings to Custer when he arrived much later in the morning. These Ash Creek lodges could still be seen by the time of Custer's late arrival at 11:00 AM. **M40, Pg. 59**

Custer at first failed to verify Varnum's sighting upon his first visit. He blamed this on the "fogging" of his old Civil War binoculars. Perhaps he thought this was due to the decomposition of the rubber seals. He then threw them down on the ground, only to be rescued by one of the Crows. It was Curly who would put Custer's old glasses to good use later in the day when he would observe the fighting on Calhoun Hill after he left the battlefield. Custer left the Crows Nest skeptical that any villages had been sighted. Perhaps, with cataracts and advanced deterioration of his eyesight, due to long term ultraviolet exposure and approaching middle age, Custer may have had just poor eyesight.

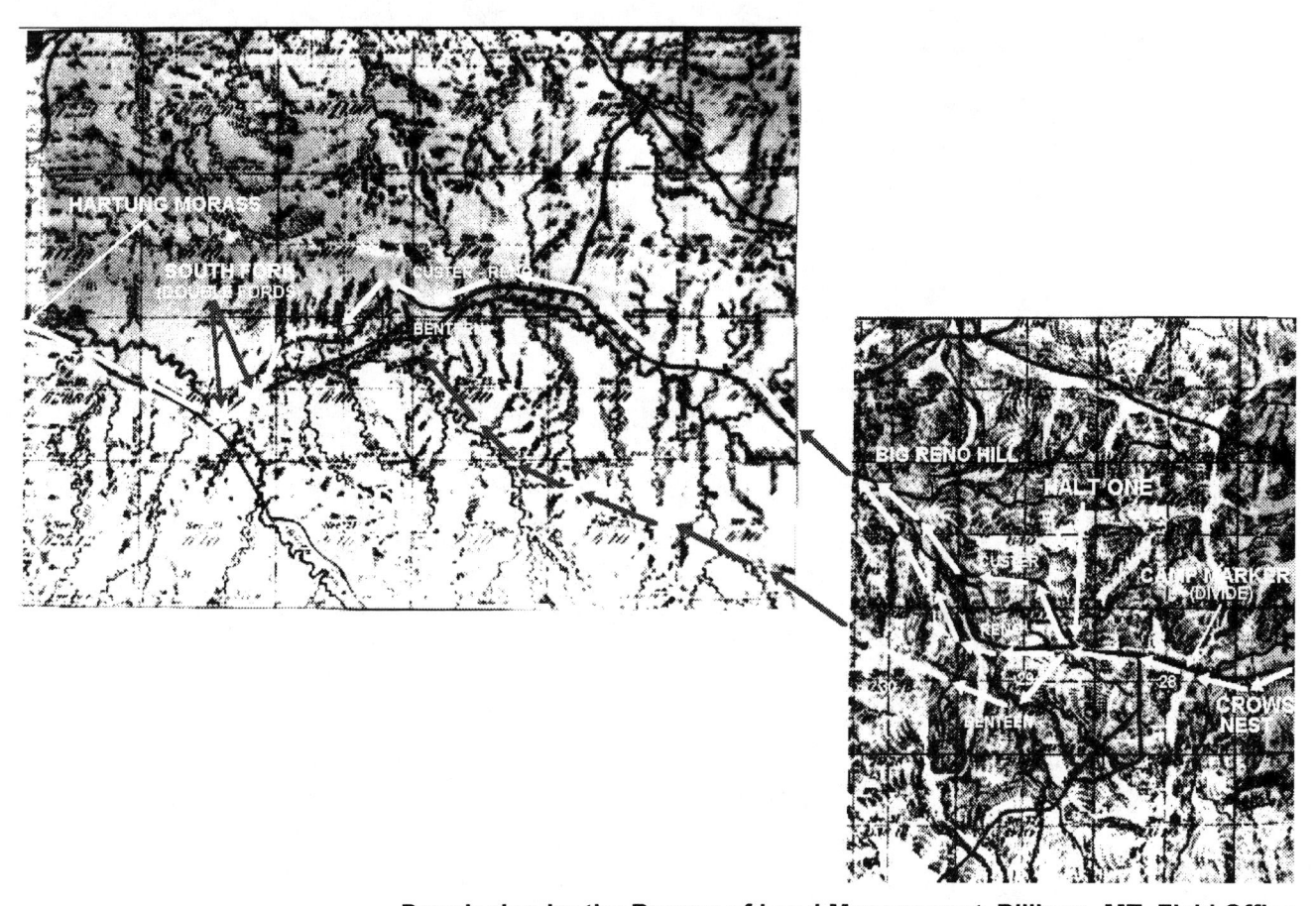

Permission by the Bureau of Land Management, Billings, MT. Field Office

BLAKE - MARSHALL SURVEY - EAST SECTION
Annotations in white by author.

SCALE: -------------- **1 MILE**

The Blake-Marshall Survey was mandated by the U.S. Congress to establish a Township Square system on the newly established Crow Reservation in Eastern Montana. Each enrolled Crow family living on the reservation would be allocate 160 acres. The balance of non-farmable land was designated as tribal land. The above artwork was developed from photographs taken by the author of the original surveys housed in the Bureau of Land Management field office in Billings, Montana. Some six sheets of hand drawn plats on velum and Indian Ink were done between 1883 and 1903. The importance of these surveys is that early reservation roads are shown. Most of these were the original travois/game trails used by the army in 1876. Walter Camp surveyed the Reno Creek road with a wagon odometer. He called it the "Custer" Trail. It starts at his divide marker in Section 28 and runs westward down Upper Ash Creek. There a number of "slow downs" of side drainages that forced the thirty foot wide Squadron formation of the First and Second Battalions to loose perhaps five minutes. Called a Reconnaissance in Force movement, this Civil War tactic allows for a large body of horsemen to travel fast, but with a shortened column. The army was following established original trails created by annual migration of large game animals and Native American tribes. The officers knew that such travois trails would lead to good crossings of the Little Bighorn River. The total distance by this trail is an approximate eight miles from the Camp Marker to the junction of the South Fork of Ash Creek. The author prefers the traditional Native American name of Ash Creek to the present name of Reno Creek.

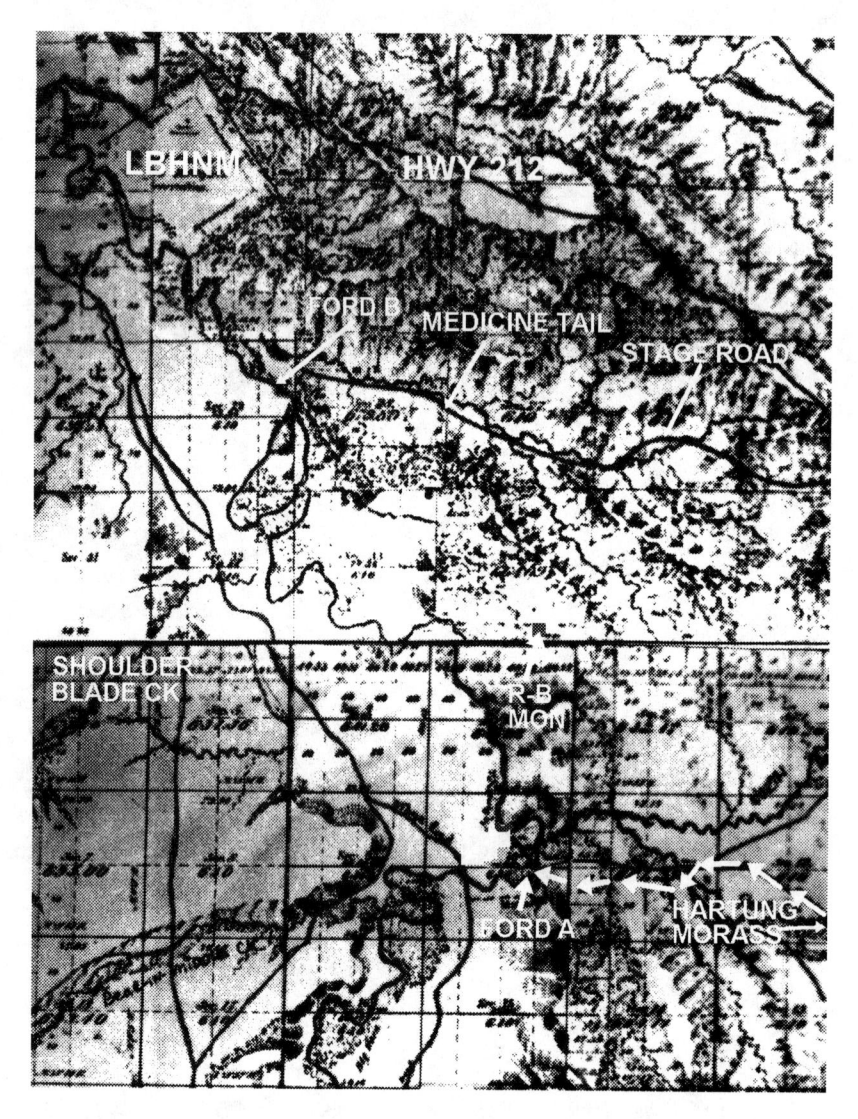

BLAKE - MARSHALL SURVEY WEST

Annotations in white by author.

SCALE: --------------- 1 MILE

The major trails in the valley are shown in the upper left section. Conducted between 1883 and 1903, the Blake-Marshall Survey shows features that existed in that time frame. However, many of the major roads were trails that existed at the time of the Custer Fight. To be noted is the later Busby-Crow Agency stage road in Medicine Tail Coulee as it directly leads to Ford B area. The existing railroad is not shown, or is the later "Reno Canal" irrigation project of the early 1900s.

The Crows Nest Again: On his second visit to the Crows Nest, with Lieutenant DeRudio's new European field glasses, Custer now conceded that the Ree Scouts had indeed seen an encampment on Ash Creek. The Crows were later quoted as saying they were able to detect their sightings in the Little Bighorn Valley at sunrise. There was but one Crow interpreter there, and that was Mitch Bouyer. The army officers were not convinced. Even the Arikara Scouts seemed skeptical. Considering the straight-line distance of fifteen miles, and with the high blocking terrain of the east bluffs, it is very doubtful that the Crows ever saw anything definitive of the massive encampments that would soon be proven to exist in the Little Bighorn Valley.**M40 & NA2**

Modern day experiments, such as those carried out by Owen B. Williams and this author has failed to prove the Crow's more distance sightings. By the use of 200 mm photo lens, which is about the same power of the army's eight power binoculars, at sunrise on June 25, 1976, this author was not able to verify the Crows' version of what happen in 1876. The higher terrain of the east bluffs prevents any view downstream from the Denny farm building. Since this location is at least two miles farther upstream from the Shoulder Blade Creek encampment of the Hunkpapa village, it is very doubtful that the Crows were able to see anything definitive of the massive encampments in the Valley!

In the late afternoon on the day before the Battle, the Crow Scouts were sent to a known Crow "War" observation point still called today the "Custer Last Lookout." This prominent high place location is eight miles from the valley. It is located six and one half miles east of the Custer Battlefield entrance, and one mile north of present Highway 212. It dominates the divide and is a pyramid shape in appearance. The Crows returned to the Busby area after dark and reported to Custer that due to the setting sun, they could not tell if there were villages in the Little Bighorn Valley! From their "Lookout" it was but eight miles to the downstream camps on Onion Creek, the same ones that would be discovered by the "Custer" Battalions on June 25. For the location of Onion and Shoulder Blade Creeks, **See VILLAGES pg. 69**

Perhaps Custer's trust in the Crows report of seeing nothing from their "war observation" point was very misplaced? But the next morning, from the Crows Nest, the collective eyesight of the Crows became greatly improved! But, their sightings of horses and campfire smoke may not have been in the Little Bighorn Valley at all. They may have been speaking of the same small village camped near the forks of Ash Creek. If so, then this village was only a straight line of six miles from the Crows Nest, and not the more distant fifteen miles to the Little Bighorn Valley. No matter where the sightings were, the army had found its quarry. To understand how this misplaced village, and its effect on the outcome of the Battle, one must start at the beginning, when the regiment crossed the watershed divide between the Rosebud and Little Bighorn Rivers.

The Divide Crossing: Approximately at Noon, St. Paul Regimental time, eleven companies of the Seventh Regiment crossed this divide. As Walter Camp expressed it, the Seventh Cavalry was like a "pack of bloodhounds following a scent!" Since then Custer scholars have debated the route that his battalions used to arrive at their final Battlefield. Comprised of the First and Second Battalions, this advanced unit followed a well established lodge pole/game trail down Ash Creek for nearly all of its thirteen miles. In the environs of the Little Bighorn drainage there are today a myriad of trails, salt roads and present day graded roads. Is it possible to establish exactly which trails were used? The answer is yes, if aspects of the U.S.

Army's Horsemanship are applied. The use of horses has never been fully explored before, and this paper will concentrate on their usage, rather than the conflicting human "eyewitness" testimony as to the times and distances of its human participants.

The First Halt, the Battalion Assignments: The Seventh Regiment followed a well-defined travois trail across the Rosebud/Little Bighorn divide. Nine tenths of a mile west of the "Camp Marker," a short halt was made to allow the companies to be formed into four battalions. Since Captain McDougall's Company B had already been assigned to the Pack Train, this left the First Battalion with just Companies C and I. This formation halt occurred in the northeast 1/4 section of Township Section 29, as seen in the Blake/Marshall Survey. **See pg. 55 (Halt One)**

For the next ten minutes the companies would be halted. Several overlooked clues that concern the standard U.S. Army procedures are found in the Reno Court of Inquiry, and in Benteen's own writings. Captain Myles Moylan said that his company assignment came in the form of a "Memorandum." That is military lingo for a written order. Benteen said that when the command halted near the divide that both Custer and Cooke were "figuring on paper" what soon turned out to be the new battalion assignments! Most likely it was Adjutant Cooke that rode down the column to the selected battalion commanders. This means that Captains Yates, Keogh, Benteen and Major Reno all had received a memorandum. This is important to note, as the last two never mention this fact after the Battle, or in the Inquiry. Perhaps because it was such a routine matter, that they "forgot" to mention it? The other two commanders were dead, so we do not know what they had to say about this very ordinary procedure. **M71, pg. 219**

Surviving battalion officers stressed the point at the 1879 Inquiry, that there was but one written message ever sent from Custer on the day of the Battle. Did John Martin carry the only written message, according to the orchestrated testimony of those officers most concerned with receiving any orders from the Regimental Staff? Now we know of other written messages, the multiple battalion assignment "memorandums." The reader is encouraged to keep in mind other possible written orders that seemed to have slipped through the cracks of the Reno Inquiry!

The First and Second Battalions marched together in a Reconnaissance In Force movement. Sergeant Kanipe told Walter Camp that all five companies marched a column of twos, ten files wide. That is where each company's front is on a line with each other. This formation of more then one platoon or company marching together had become popular during the Civil War. It allows for a more compact unit and the length of the command is shortened. This formation was maintained from the divide halt to the point where Sergeant Daniel Kanipe was sent back to Captain McDougall. **M40, pg. 92 & LILLY32 (Kanipe's sketch)**

According to Kanipe, the five companies were arranged from left to right as Companies E, F, and L for the Second Battalion, and Company I, and C for the First Battalion, and in that order. This is what some of the officers that Camp interviewed referred to as marching in platoons, or as in a "squadron" of companies. When Lieutenant Edward McGuire created his first version of his Reno Court of Inquiry map, he labeled Custer's companies as being "Squadrons." And, he diagramed a typical squadron formation, just as Sergeant Kanipe described. Acting as "Foragers," a five man detail from Company F was sent in advance of the First and Second Battalions. This was a standard army procedure and they would stay within communication distance just ahead of the main command. Their responsibility was to scout the condition of the trail ahead of the advancing Squadrons. By hand signals, and perhaps by bugle, they would signal the Headquarters Staff, or a battalion of impending obstacles and a necessary change of gait or direction. **See APPENDIX: Squadron Formation, pg. 200**

The Custer Trail: From the Battalion Formation Halt, the First and Second Battalions would continue to follow what Walter Camp's called his "Custer Trail" route as seen in the Blake/Marshall survey. They went to the right, over a rise in the terrain in the southeast 1/4 section of Township Section 29. For a short distance Reno's Fourth Battalion continued straight ahead, but would soon be forced to cross over to the right bank of upper Ash Creek. Benteen's Third Battalion turned thirty degrees to the left to gain access to the ridges that would become his "Left Scout." Soon, both Custer and Reno would reach the first major crossing on Upper Ash Creek. Referred today by local ranchers as the "Big Reno Hill," an intersecting road runs down North Davis Creek. Here it joins the original telegraph and later telephone line from Crow Agency to the Northern Cheyenne village of Busby, Montana.

At this point Reno's Fourth Battalion was forced to drop in behind the advanced battalions traveling with Custer's Headquarters Staff. The reason is that no defined trail ever existed on the left bank of Upper Ash Creek. There is a prevalent "Custer Myth" that Reno paralleled Custer from this point on down Ash Creek. This major horsemanship misconception is dispelled by the fact that no military unit the size of a battalion would have been sent where there was not an established trail that could not be reconnoitered in advance by foragers. The army was not blazing a trail, not at this critical point in time. They all felt that the villagers were getting away from them.

The Blake/Marshall survey solves this misinterpretation of the roads that existed in 1876. From this point, Reno would follow behind the other battalions until he was sent into the advance near the mouth of Ash Creek. The main trail now runs along the right bank until it reaches the South Fork area. The First and Second Battalions, traveled the Upper Ash Creek from the Divide to the South Fork at a fast walk/slow trot. They covered the eight miles in ninety minutes for an average rate of just less than five and one half miles per hour.

The Double Fords at South Fork: Less then three tenths mile East of the junction of the South Fork of Ash Creek, the main trail now crosses over to the left bank of Upper Ash Creek. However, within a short distance, it crosses over the South Fork, creating a second ford, about 100 yards upstream (*south*) of the present county bridge on the county gravel school road that goes up Ash Creek. The main trail will now stay on the left bank until it reaches the Little Bighorn River.

The White Rocks Area: It was in the vicinity of the South Fork that the first signs of a recently abandoned village were first encountered. When the First and Second Battalion reached the South Fork of Ash Creek, near the White Rocks area, they encountered abandoned lodge poles and cooking fires that were still burning, along with other camp equipage. It was very obvious that a village had just been camped there!

The Fleeing Village: Soon after the Custer Battle, Captain J. S. Polland reported that he had interviewed returning hostiles (Summer Roamers) at Standing Rock Reservation. His report strongly suggests the possibility of a small band of reservation Indians having been camped on Ash Creek by the mid-afternoon of the day of the Custer Battle; they would have almost been run over by the army soldiers. It now appears that this may have been the same encampment seen from the Crows Nest on the morning of June 25. This is supported by Frederick Gerard's usage of the word "town" to describe a small band of Indians that he saw "running" down Ash Creek, from a knoll near a "Lone Tepee." This may have been one of Captain Polland's villages on its way to join the Winter Roamers. When these Summer Roamers became aware of the advancing battalions of the Seventh Regiment, the women and children quickly stripped off the valuable lodge covers and hurriedly packed their household goods. In wild disorder they fled down Ash Creek. As they approached the Little Bighorn River, they would realize that they did not have enough time to cross. The river was now at its full spring-swollen snow melt from the Bighorn Mountains, located fifty miles upstream in Northern Wyoming. **LILLY 806-7, M71, pg. 84 & 181.**

At a point near the Ford A crossing, they diverted northward to another crossing on Lower Ash Creek, very near its mouth. Here they remained hidden in the river bottom timber. The army would pass by them on both sides. Was this Gerard's "Town" that had fled in haste from the abandoned South Fork campsite?

The Arikara's Lone Tepee: About one and three tenths mile west of the South Fork, the army came upon the first of several abandoned lodges. This first lodge now becomes Lone Tepee Number One **(LT1).** It stood off the trail to the right. The Arikara Scouts were the first to arrive, and riding around it they counted coup on the lodge cover. Some of the Arikara Scouts said that they entered the lodge and ate some of the food stores found there, as they were very hungry. Perhaps, this explains the sudden disappearance of Mister Varnum's Ree Scouts? Most likely, this lodge may have been a family lodge, and was part of the same village seen earlier from the Crows Nest, but was now abandoned. **NA2, MIDDLE ASH CREEK, pg. 61**

When Custer's Squadrons passed this singular standing lodge, they soon diverted from the main trail. One-half mile east of the Fellows Ranch landing strip, they began to follow a more prominent and fresher lodge pole trail; one created by the villages had fought General Crook on June 17, over on the Rosebud. This new lodge pole trail now diverted to the right (northwest) fifty yards past the Ree's Lone Tepee. Within the next two and half miles from the South Fork crossings, this well-defined travois trail would cross again to the right bank of Ash Creek. Here the villager's "Crook" trail went through a pronounced wet area that some would later call a morass. This "morass" is located on the old Robert Hartung property in the southeast 1/4 section of Township Section 12, on lower Ash Creek. Bob Hartung was a former chief of maintenance with the National Park Service. He was a brother-in-law to Hank Weibert, a well known local "Custer" buff. **MIDDLE ASH CREEK, pg. 61**

The 2:00 PM Crossing and the Hartung Morass. Soon after passing the site of the Ree's Lone Tepee, Custer diverted from the main trail and he began to follow the larger and fresher of these two trails. Near 2:00 PM, and another one and three tenth mile, they would come to a natural depression where artesian water had created a large morass. This will later become known later as "Benteen's Morass," but the Custer Squadrons were the first to arrive.

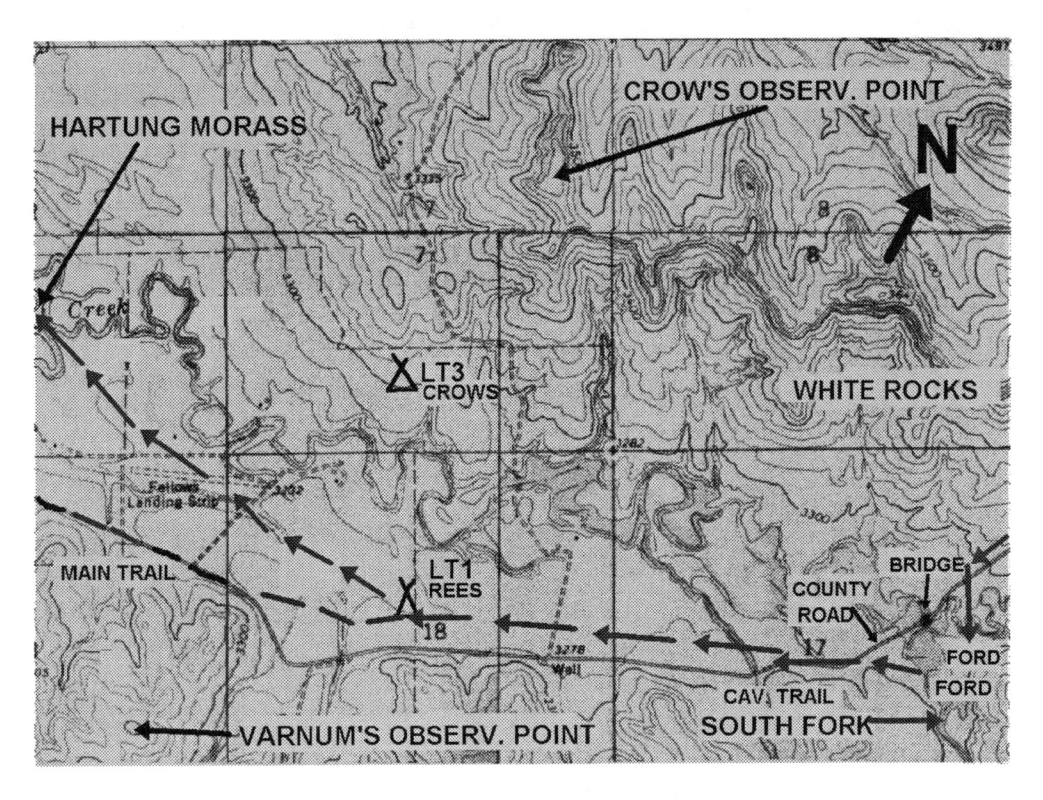

ASH CREEK-MIDDLE

SCALE: ---------- 1/4 MILE

The advanced battalions discovered a hastily abandoned village site west of the South Fork of Ash Creek. This was the same village as seen earlier from the Crows Nest by Varnum and the Ree Scouts. Even though this small encampment fled directly to the Ford A area on the left bank, Custer would veer off fifty years past the Ree's "Lone Tepee" **(LT1)***. This direction took the army over the Hartung Morass crossing and onto the "Big Flat" where they discovered Lt. Lee's "Lone Tepee"* **(LT2). See pg. 64**

The Crow's "Lone Tepee" **(LT3)** *is seen in Section 7 and is correctly identified in Ray Meketa and Thomas Bookwalter's book, "Search for the Lone Tepee" published in 1983. However, there has never been a known trail on the right bank of* **Middle Ash Creek***. Besides, Camp's civil research and the Blake-Marshall Survey do not indicate that there was ever a major trail in this area. Custer's advanced battalions were traveling in a wide* **Recognizance In Force** *movement called "Squadron" marching that does not allow for the army to create their own trail. The First and Second Battalion were following an already established trail.*

The trail passed from the southeast to northwest through the southern end of a fifteen-acre sunken marshy area that today still holds artesian water when the rest of Ash Creek has dried up from summer heat. There is a pronounced exit trough on the west side of this area. Reno's Battalion was now signaled to follow the advancing Custer Squadrons already on the right bank. Some forty minutes later, the Benteen Battalion would arrive at this same point, later to become named after him. What occurred at **"Benteen's Morass"** *would soon become the focal point in the developing Battle.*

Gerard's First Knoll: At the time that Custer was crossing the Hartung Morass, Frederick

Gerard and Second Lieutenant ("Mister") Luther Hare rode up onto a small double knoll ridge located three tenth mile west of the Hartung Morass. From here they were able to see the fleeing village, which by now were approaching the Ford A area. Gerard would yell at Custer, "Here are your Indians, running like Hell (devils)." Mister Hare, knowing that Custer had not heard Gerard, now sent a written note to Custer that Indians were now in his front. What was not made apparent was that this was a fleeing village with pony drags, and not a warrior force. Hare does not seem to have distinguished the difference. Is it possible that what Hare and Gerard were seeing were the same small village that had just fled from near the White Rocks area? This was the same area earlier in the morning where Mister Varnum and the Ree Scouts said they had seen at least two lodges and pony herds. **M71, pg. 112.**

The Second "Lone Tepee," The Burning Lodge: About eight tenth mile southwest of the 2:00 PM/Hartung crossing, a second standing lodge was seen by many of the Reno and Benteen contingents. Some reported that a singular corpse was ceremoniously laid out inside this abandoned lodge. This one now becomes the so-called "Lone Tepee" of the later Reno Court of Inquiry, in 1879. This was Lieutenant Jessie M. Lee's focal point of his time/distance reconstruction of the Little Bighorn Battle. It would forever create confusion by the Court Prosecutor's misguided effort to create a starting point for the witnesses testifying at the Inquiry.

It was located on the left bank of the North Fork of Ash Creek. It stood partly obscured in a small side drainage ravine to the northwest of the "Big Flat," where the villages had camped the day before the Crook Fight on the Rosebud. Piles of brush had been placed around its base to discourage predators from getting at the corpse inside. It was near this burial lodge site that the Rees were threatened by Custer to be dismounted for failure to press the attack on Gerard's fleeing village, which by now was but one half of a mile ahead on the left bank.

It would be at this same point that Reno's Battalion was now ordered forward, but not to go into the valley, but to bring the fleeing village to bay. This is an important factor that has been overlooked in the reconstruction of this stage of the Little Bighorn Battle. At this point, Custer was quoted as promising Reno full support with his "battalions." When this order was given, Reno had not yet been ordered over the river. It was also at this time that Lone Tepee Number Two was set on fire by the advanced detail of foragers from Company F. This burial lodge now becomes the "Burning Lodge," as noted by members of Benteen's later arriving battalion.

Mister Varnum's Observation: About fifteen minutes before the Custer Squadrons crossed the 2:00 PM Hartung Morass, Mister Varnum went to a high point southeast of Middle Ash Creek, across from the 2:00 PM crossing. From here he could see a massive encampment of lodges in the Little Bighorn valley, some four miles away. It was Sitting Bull's Hunkpapa village, camped at the mouth of Shoulder Blade Creek. Varnum could see them to the west of the intervening east bluffs of the Little Bighorn Valley. He then proceeded to play catch up with the Headquarters Staff, and about twenty-five minutes later, he reported the second sighting of their quarry to Custer. Lieutenant Hare's written note concerning Gerard's Fleeing Village had just arrived moments earlier. **See ASH CREEK-MIDDLE, pg. 61**

The Third "Lone" Tepee: About the same time that the advanced Custer Battalions were crossing the South Fork, Mitch Bouyer and four of the six Crow Scouts diverted to higher ground to the north, known to the Crows as the "White Rocks" area. They proceeded to climb the ridge adjacent to this area that terminated in high ground overlooking the Big Flat and the North Fork of Ash Creek. After observing lower Ash Creek for a period of time, they descended to the right bank again, and it was at this point that they discovered another burial lodge. It was located on the right bank of Ash Creek, almost opposite of the Ree's Lone Tepee Number One! This becomes the "Crow's" Lone Tepee Number Three. This "Lone Tepee" site has been identified by Custer researchers, Ray Mekita and Thomas Bookwalter in their 1983 booklet, *The Search for the Lone Tepee.* **See ASH CREEK-MIDDLE, pg. 61**

North Fork Trail Separation: It was at the location of the "Burning" Burial Lodge (Lone Tepee Number Two) where the Reno Battalion was sent forward, that another division in the trail occurred. An old unused trail went straight ahead and crossed the North Fork of Ash Creek about a half mile ahead of the Burning Lodge. This trail would soon become the Pack Train's "shortcut." It led directly to what will become known as "Mathey's Knoll."

The Echleman Fords: The major travois trail now left the "Big Flat, "and crossed over again to the left bank. There are even today three shallow troughs to be seen here. The reason for this diversion was that on June 18, the day after the Crook Fight on the Rosebud, the consolidated villages would travel south to the Lodge Grass, Montana area of the Little Bighorn Valley. Soon after crossing at the Echleman Fords, this new trail would continue southward over the bluffs to new campsites on the Little Bighorn, some twelve miles to the south. These triple fords are on the old Echleman property in the east 1/4 mid-sections of Township Section 11. They are approximately one and a quarter mile from the Hartung Morass. They are named for another of Hank Weibert's brothers-in-law, all early German immigrant families that settled on the Crow Reservation in the early 1900s.

Ford A and Gerard's Second Knoll: Less then a quarter mile *south* of the Echleman Fords this very pronounced trail continued due *south* after crossing over the main Lower Ash Creek trail. A five man detail and the Ree Scout Stabbed were sent to check out on this divergent trail. This is proof that Custer was no longer following the heavy trail left by the villages that had gone against General Crook on the Rosebud. This broad trail continued to by-pass Lower Ash Creek and takes a direct path over the *east* bluffs to the Lodge Grass, Montana area some ten miles upstream (*south*) of the Custer Battlefield. But it was here that another major trail was picked up at this intersection of several trails. The question that needs to be asked is why did Reno and Custer both ignore the very pronounced, but older trail that was created on June 18, the day after the fight on the Rosebud. **NA2 pg. 116, M40, pg. 188**

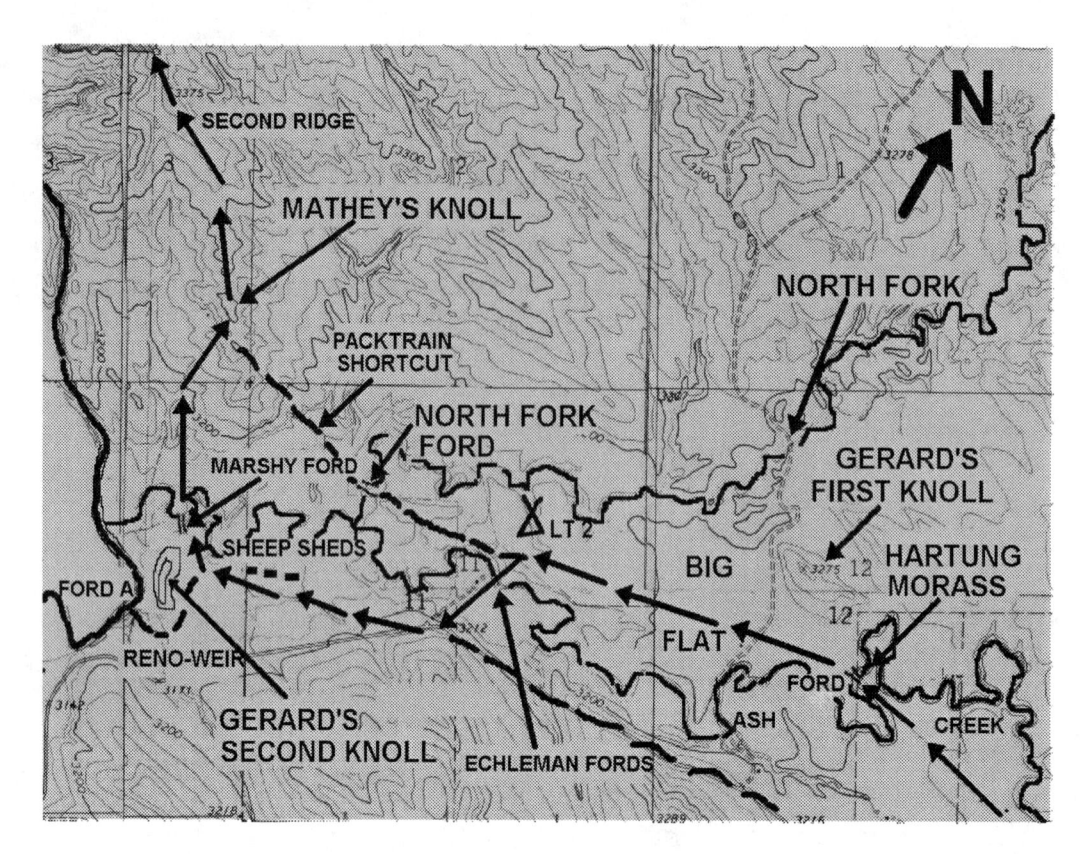

ASH CREEK-LOWER

SCALE: ----------- 1/4 MILE

*From Gerard's First Knoll in Section 12 he saw a fleeing village with travois packs that he described as a "Town." They were on the opposite side of Ash Creek and when Custer received Lt. Hare's note he ordered Reno's battalion to bring them to bay. The foragers from Company F was ordered to set fire to the "Lone Tepee" that was a burial lodge **(LT2)**. This burning burial lodge becomes the focus of Lt. Lee's orientation at the later Reno Court of inquiry.*

Custer's advanced battalions will now follow Reno's battalion over the Echleman Fords and came within a quarter of a mile of crossing over Ford A. However, near Gerard's Second Knoll in Section 10 the First and Second battalions would now head north. Was Custer now committed to a military pincer movement on a massive village seen in the valley thirty minutes earlier by Mister Varnum? If so, the die was cast for the defeat of his two battalions.

The army would leave the Ash Creek Valley by a trail later used by automobiles to reach Reno Hill from the south. The original trail went over the Second Ridge to Reno Hill.

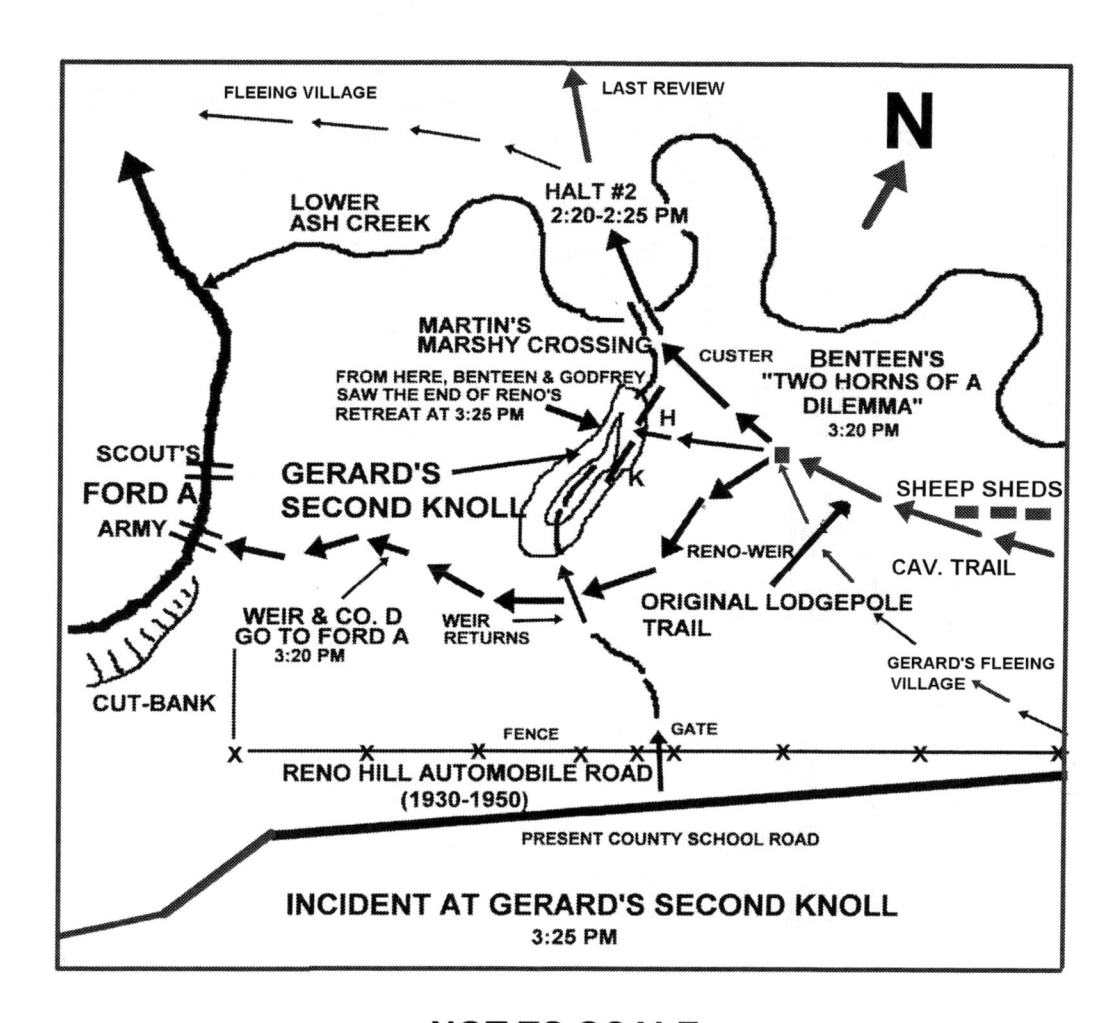

[Map: Incident at Gerard's Second Knoll, 3:25 PM — labels include: FLEEING VILLAGE, LAST REVIEW, LOWER ASH CREEK, HALT #2 2:20-2:25 PM, N, MARTIN'S MARSHY CROSSING, FROM HERE, BENTEEN & GODFREY SAW THE END OF RENO'S RETREAT AT 3:25 PM, CUSTER, BENTEEN'S "TWO HORNS OF A DILEMMA" 3:20 PM, SCOUT'S FORD A, ARMY, GERARD'S SECOND KNOLL, H, SHEEP SHEDS, RENO-WEIR, CAV. TRAIL, WEIR & CO. D GO TO FORD A 3:20 PM, WEIR RETURNS, ORIGINAL LODGEPOLE TRAIL, GERARD'S FLEEING VILLAGE, CUT-BANK, FENCE, GATE, RENO HILL AUTOMOBILE ROAD (1930-1950), PRESENT COUNTY SCHOOL ROAD]

NOT TO SCALE

The Speer Ranch sheep sheds location and Benteen's "Two Horns of a Dilemma" separation point on the Custer/Reno cavalry trails is noted. Gerard's Second Knoll, is where Benteen and Godfrey would later observe Reno's retreat from the valley is also noted. The Gerard and Lt. Hare "Fleeing Village" escaped into the timber bottom as seen in the upper left corner. Just north of Halt #2 Custer's staff paid homage to the passing First and Second battalions, his last military review of his beloved Seventh regiment.

Varnum's Report: Within moments after the Reno Battalion had left, Varnum reported to Custer that some twenty minutes earlier, he was able to observe the tops of a large stationary village downstream in the Little Bighorn Valley. Perhaps, with his Intelligence Officer's latest report, Custer now decided to abandon his promise to support Reno's advance with one or more of the "his" battalions. Gerard's "Fleeing Village" had just fled over the original Ash Creek main trail, leaving very fresh signs of their pony drags. Even though a north bound fresh lodge pole was evident on this left bank trail, Reno now choose to follow another older trail that went northwestward, passing by where the Speer Ranch sheep sheds would later be erected. **M37, pg. 17**

The Headquarters Staff, with the First and Second Battalions continued to follow Reno's advancing battalion. This is important to remember, as Benteen would latter come to a separation in the cavalry trails, which he referred to as being his "Two Horns of a Dilemma."

Here, the trails divided with one leading to another crossing on Lower Ash Creek, and the other to the river crossing now known as Ford A. Evidently, Custer was more intrigued by Varnum's newest report of fixed villages being seen downstream in the Valley. High ground was now needed for an observation point. Reno and Custer continued to follow the Speer Ranch sheep shed trail. The Crows later pointed out where the "*Spear* Camp" was located, as recorded by Hugh Scott in 1921. It was where they and Reno passed by on their way to the river crossing. **M37, pg. 17.**

Daniel Kanipe told Walter Camp that he thought Custer may have diverted to the north after he reported seeing a large group of Indians on what will become known as Benteen Hill. He reported his sighting to First Sergeant Bobo, who told Second Lieutenant Henry Harrington, who in turn passed it on to Captain Tom Custer who was serving on his brother's Headquarters Staff. His "Indians" were of course a gathering of tribal police who had just signaled the villages in the valley of the approaching soldiers.

By now, Gerard's fleeing village had disappeared! It was now for the first time, that Reno was ordered to cross the Little Bighorn River with his battalion and enter the Valley. Most likely it was Lieutenant Cooke that delivered this new order, as he had traveled to the Ford A area with Captain Keogh. Custer may have incorrectly guessed that the fleeing village may have already crossed the river, and was getting away.

Gerard's Second Knoll: About one mile west of the Echleman Fords, there is a pronounced knoll located near the mouth of Ash Creek. Gerard referred to this location as from where he saw warriors racing up the Little Bighorn valley to mobilize against Reno's advance. This is not the same knoll where earlier he saw his fleeing "town," but a different and a second knoll that he described in his testimony at the Reno Court of Inquiry. This now becomes known as Gerard's "Second Knoll." Just before reaching this point, Gerard described seeing a fresh travois trail, crossing over the Reno/Custer trail from the South. This was of course his Fleeing Village, now seeking refuge in the timber bottom, *north* of Lower Ash Creek. It was at this junction of Gerard's northbound travois trail that now becomes the separation point for the "Custer's' Squadrons, the First and Second Battalion, and the Reno Battalion.

Obviously, Custer was now planning to make a long end run over the bluffs, and attack Varnum's villages from the downstream side. His direct promise of support to Major Reno had come earlier when Reno was ordered to pursue Gerard's fleeing village, some ten minutes earlier. Now, without any further orders that we know of, Custer turned sharply to the north. When he left the Ash Creek Valley, he cast the die for the ultimate defeat of the five companies. Is it possible that Custer had abandoned Reno to his own fate?

Or as suggested with the reported appearance of both Adjutant Cooke and Captain Keogh at the Ford A area, perhaps Reno may have been issued an additional orders, ones that have never been revealed. However, Custer was still unaware that downstream (*northward*) of Varnum's Hunkpapa village, there were more massive encampments extending well down the valley. This unprecedented historical factor of these nearby consolidated villages would suddenly require a new strategy. It was this remarkable aspect that would soon become the primary cause for the defeat of Custer's two battalions. Also the apparent lack of effective reconnaissance on Custer's part was another factor. He was still traveling in a Recognizance In Force mode. And, it would prove fatal in the next two and one half hours!

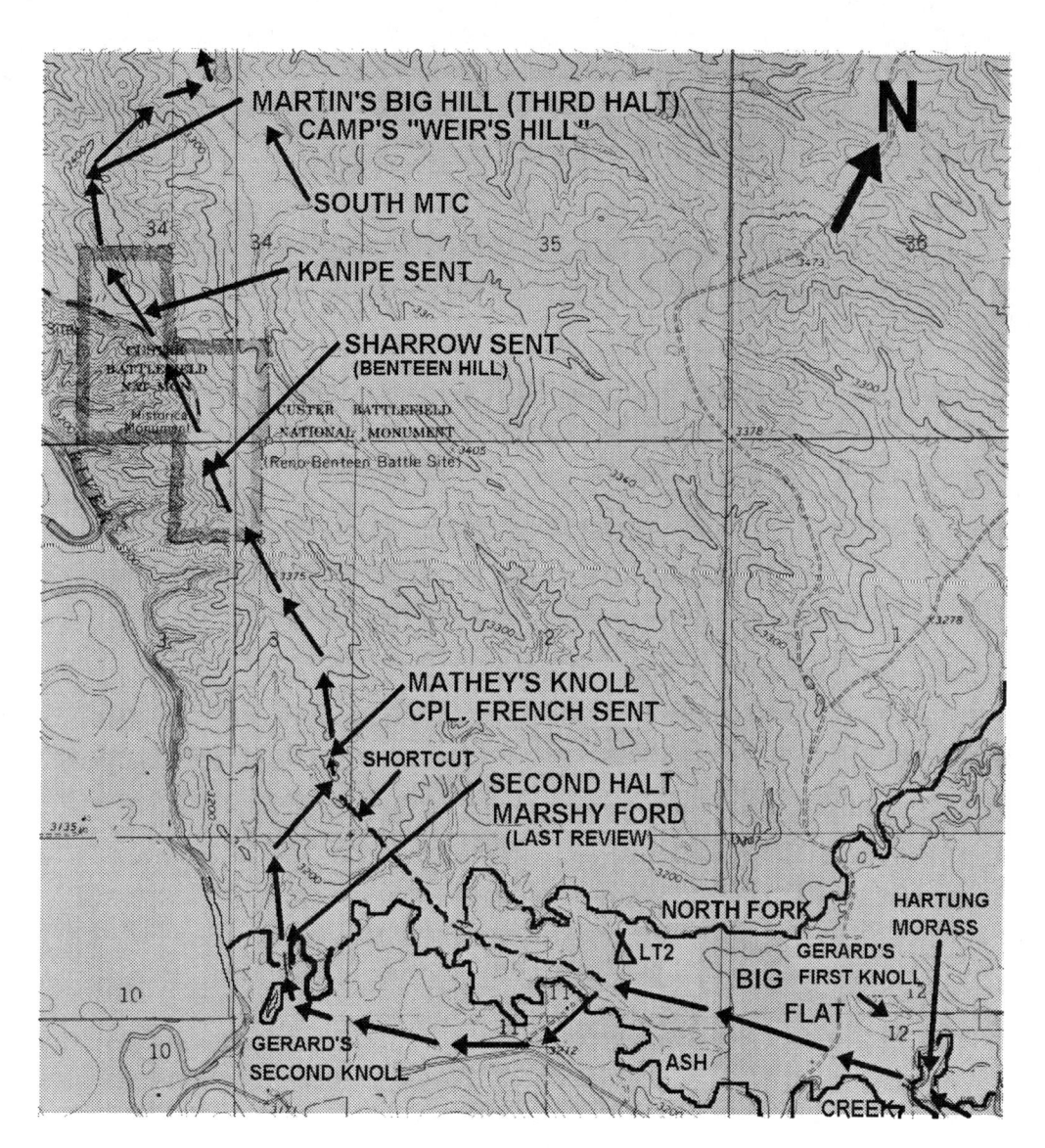

CUSTER TRAIL 1

SCALE: ----------- 1/4 MILE

*Gerard's First Knoll is seen in Section 12. Lt. Lee's "Lone Tepee" is shown as **LT2** in section 11. This burial lodge becomes the "Burning Lodge" after the foragers from Company F were ordered to set it on fire. **Gerard's Second Knoll** is in Section 10 and is located in the mouth of Ash (Reno) Creek. **Martin's "Big Hill"** is seen in Section 34. **South MTC** is Godfrey's "eastern" route of the two battalions.*

*Benteen's "shortcut" mandated by Custer, a verbal order delivered by Kanipe, was an old trail that ran from the crossing on the **North Fork** to **Mathey's Knoll**. It would be used later by the Pack Train to reach Reno Hill.*

*The term the "**Big Flat**" was coined by Hugh Scott when he visited the area in 1910. It was a traditional site for holding the Sundance ceremonies. Originally some of the Natives American referred to Reno Creek as Sundance Creek.*

The Reno Hill Auto Road Crossing: The trail now divided with one going northward to the east bluffs, to become known later as the Reno Hill automobile road. John Martin referred to the next Lower Ash Creek crossing as being at a "Marshy Place." In the 1930s, early day tourist would use this original crossing on Lower Ash Creek as an automobile road to gain access to the Reno Hill area. Here Custer would turn north and crossed once more to the right bank of Ash Creek. By turning north he was effectively putting into effect a "pincer" movement on the villages, yet unseen by him, but verified by his trusted Intelligence Officer, Second Lieutenant Varnum. **See Incident at Gerard's Second Knoll, pg. 65**

The Second Halt of the "Custer" Battalions: The two battalions were now halted for the second time since the battalion assignment halt near the Divide. Inside an oxbow meadow north of Martin's "Marshy Place" the men of the First and Second Battalions were briefly halted. Actually it was only the right flank files of Company C that stayed halted for the duration of this reforming halt. The trailing companies had to close up due to the delay of crossing this narrow crossing by a column twos or perhaps by a single file. It could have taken a minimum of five to ten minutes to effect this difficult crossing.

Custer's Last Review: About 100 yards *north* of this crossing, Custer's Headquarters Staff gave their final review of his soldiers. Peter Thompson described how the Staff pulled off to the right, and paid homage to the First and Second Battalion as they passed forward. **R4**

Mathey's Knoll: Within the one half mile, the advanced column reached the summit of Mathey's Knoll. It was here that new crucial battle plans were put into effect. From here, Custer could now see Varnum's village in the Valley, but not likely the other large encampments located further downstream. Due to the higher elevation of the East Bluffs blocking the view *northward*, the Onion Creek camps could not be seen.

This apparent lack of additional reconnaissance would soon come back to haunt Custer when he would reach Medicine Tail Coulee. From Mathey's Knoll, Custer could also now see Benteen and the Pack Train on his back trail. Benteen was only ten minutes from entering the 2:00 PM /Hartung Morass. The head of the packs was just crossing the South Fork Fords, only a mile and a half mile behind Benteen. Is it possible that Custer now sent an order to Benteen and the Pack Train at this time? It seems quite logical that he may have done so. The location of this first observation point is in the extreme southeast corner of the southwest 1/4 section of Township Section 3. By the trail from the 2:00 PM/Hartung Morass it is two and one half miles. It is named for Lieutenant Edward Mathey, as it was here that he later met Mister Hare on his ammunition expediting ride.

The First Ridge Approach: The Squadron continued northward on a well-defined game trail. It ran along over the second ridge that ran parallel to the East Bluffs. Later, automobiles would use this same trail before the present National Park Service paved road from the North was constructed. By this route it is one and three tenths mile from Mathey's Knoll to Reno's future retreat position on the bluffs. There is still today a distinctive trail that runs along this ridge. It now terminates at the southeastern corner of the Reno/Benteen defensive site.

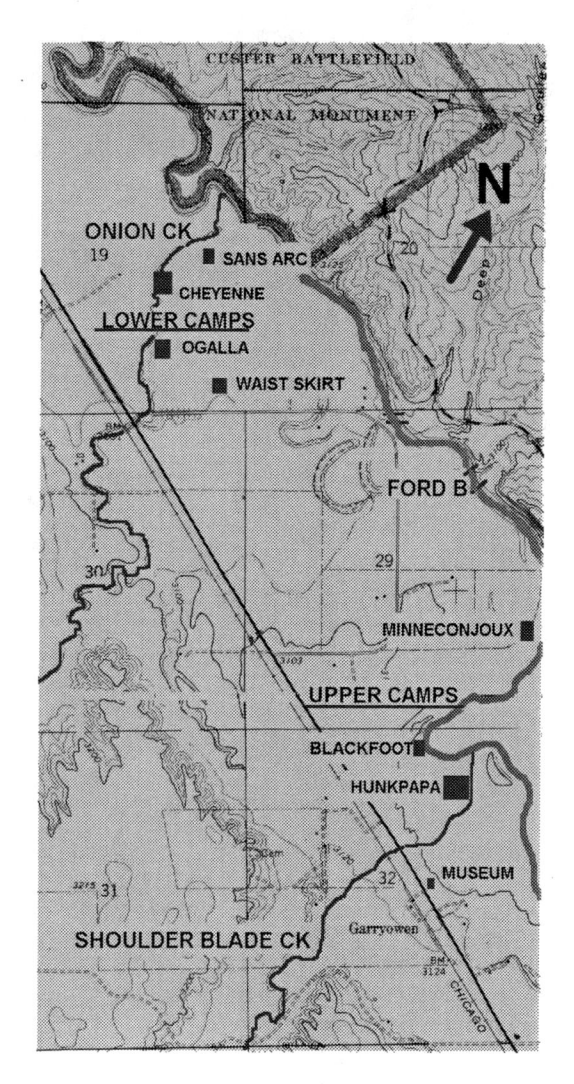

VILLAGES

SCALE: -------- 1/4 MILE

Some 1000 to 1500 lodges were located between Shoulder Blade Creek to the south and Onion Creek to the north. A gap of one and a half mile separated the Upper Camps (south) from the Lower camps of the Northern Cheyenne. The army could see only the Hunkpapa Village and Blackfoot Sioux encampments from Mathey's Knoll.

The combined strength of the villages June 25 represented some 7,000 people. Custer's pre-battle army intelligence report of 1000 to 1500 lodges was correct. But the military did not expect them to find a consolidated encampment such as this one. This unprecedented historical gathering was a primary factor in the defeat of the Seventh Regiment.

NOTE: *The later Reno Canal irrigation projects of the early 1900s would cut-off and change the flow of Onion and Shoulder Blade Creeks. This route of this canal has been deleted from the author's maps but can be seen on current versions of U.S.G.S. quadrangles.*

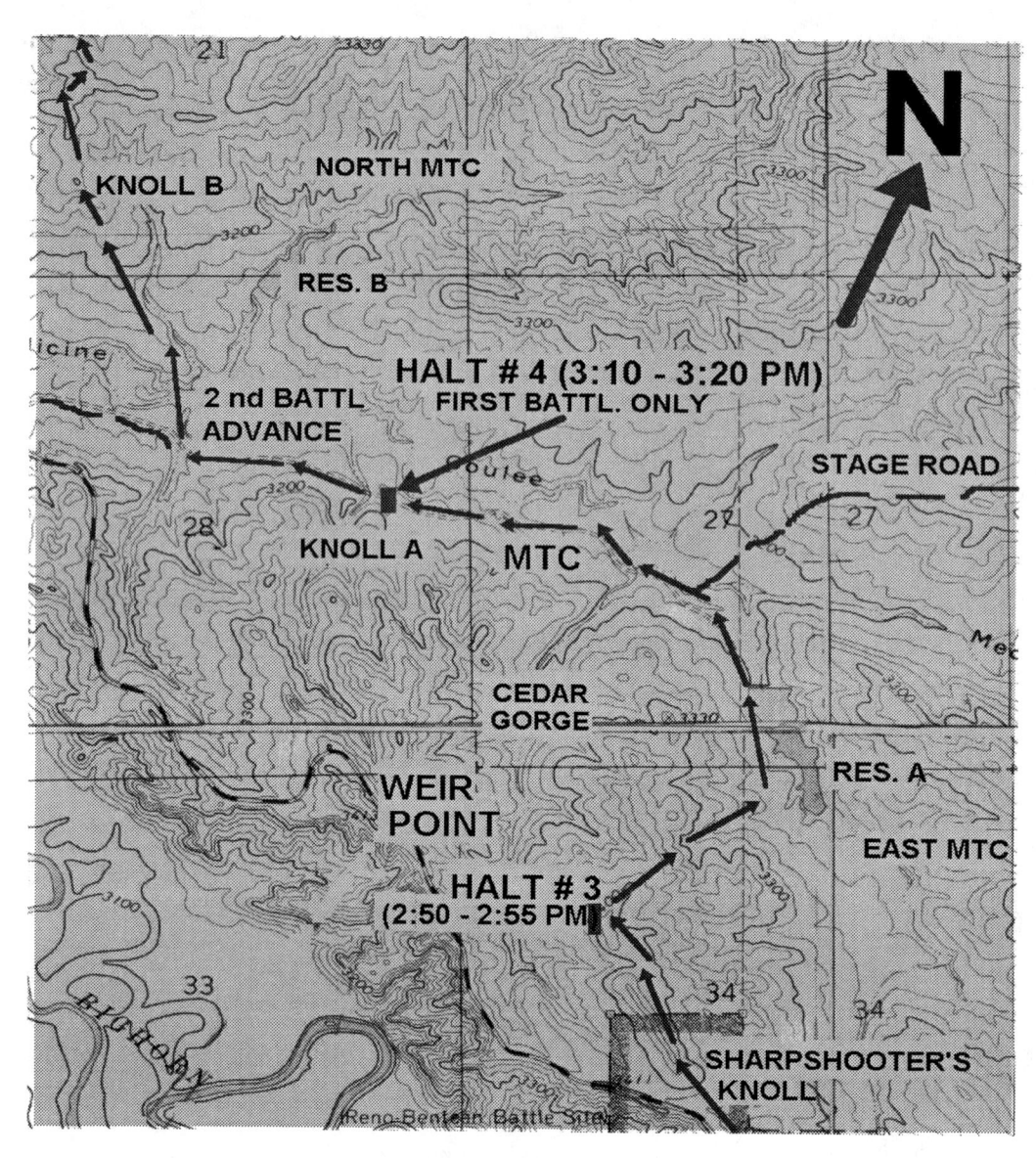

CUSTER TRAIL 2

SCALE: ------------ 1/4 MILE

*John Martin was sent from Medicine Tail Coulee **(MTC)** at **Halt #4** with his written order. The First Battalion halted here while the Second Battalion was sent north to flank the Onion Creek camps. When the "Young Warriors attacked the rear of the advancing second battalion at 3:20 PM it marked the beginning of the Custer Fight.* **See Young Warriors Route, pg. 169-170**

Kanipe Sent Back to McDougall: At a point about three tenths of a mile north of the present monument on Reno Hill, and just below the southern end of "Sharpshooter's Ridge," Sergeant Daniel Kanipe, of Company C, was sent back to Captain Thomas McDougall. According to Kanipe, the wording of his verbal order to McDougall was to "hurry up," and "come across country" (shortcut) to the bluffs. Is it possible that this "shortcut" order also pertained to Benteen? It is now 2:45 PM **M40, pg. 91-95. See also text pg. 130.**

We know that Kanipe intercepted Benteen by 3:25 PM **(See Chapter Five, pg. 130)**. This time interval of forty minutes makes his rate of travel of almost four miles per hour (4.2 mph) that of a regulated walk. Apparently, Kanipe's horse was very tired, as Company C had been on Reno's Powder River excursion and, thanks to Reno's unabashed disobedience, all of the horses of the First and Second Battalion had been ridden an extra two hundred miles!

This "come across country" shortcut was of course the North Fork trail that intersected with Mathey's Knoll from the Big Flat campgrounds. This intersection on the Big Flat was one mile west of the Custer/Reno 2:00 PM Hartung crossing. When Custer was on Mathey's Knoll, he could not failed to have noted the more direct route to the bluffs, rather then the roundabout trail that passed the future Speer's sheep sheds and crossed at Martin's difficult "Marshy" crossing. It now becomes apparent that Custer wanted both Benteen and the entire Pack Train to be brought forward to an advance position somewhere north of Mathey's Knoll. They both were directed to take the shortcut by the more direct North Fork trail. We will soon see evidence of this order.

The Third Halt, The "Into Fours" Formation: Soon after ascending the high ridge now known as Sharpshooter's Ridge, the third halt of the battalions was made. It was two and six tenths miles from the second halt on Lower Ash Creek. They were still following the defined trail that goes over this hill/ridge complex. It was here, on what John Martin described as being on a "Big Hill" that the Custer Squadrons were again ordered to halt, this time to form into fours, the standard formation for pending combat. **M40. Also Custer Trail 2, pg. 70.**

According to Sergeant Kanipe, up to now they had been traveling in a column of twos. But, when he left he had not yet been ordered to load his carbine. It was also most likely at this Third Halt that the men were ordered to load their carbines. A number of live rounds of .45 caliber carbine ammunition have been found in this vicinity. Under pressure, some of the mounted men may have dropped a few cartridges as they fumbled to load their carbines at this brief halt. Army regulations prohibited the men from having the Springfield carbine loaded with a live round in the chamber while riding in the ranks. That was due to a fault in the original design. The 1874 model had just a two click hammer mechanism, full cocked and half cocked. When set on half cock, the breech had a tendency to come open on a jouncing horse. This allowed dirt to enter the chamber. But, to place the hammer full down on a loaded round in the chamber caused frequent accidental discharges in the mounted ranks. Not until the later post-Custer Battle model, when a safety stop was incorporated into the hammer, were the men allowed to keep a loaded weapon while mounted. Until then, the men had to be told when to load the carbine.

Martin on Military Horsemanship: In John Martin's 1908 interview with Walter Camp, he delineated the exact commands that he was now ordered to blow on his bugle at this halt. They were:

    1.   Attention
    2.   Fours Right
    3.   Column Right
    4.   March

The first bugle command shows that the command was at a halt, as only a halted command can be called to attention. The second is a preparatory command, and it supports Kanipe's statement that they had been in column of twos. The third signals the direction and the final command puts them into motion. These standard commands are outlined in all of the Mounted Service tactical manuals. After thirty-two years, John Martin had not forgotten his bugle training. Benteen's "poor dumb" Italian immigrant that was supposed to have been "thick headed and dull witted," and "not cut out to be a cavalryman", seems to have won the battle as who was the better soldier. **M40, pg. 140.**

It was most likely at this time that Mister Varnum's valley sighting of the Gray Horse company along the bluffs took place Doug McChristian, former N.P.S. historian at Little Bighorn Battlefield National Monument, did a compelling analysis of this sighting as happening at this time and most likely on John Martin's Big Hill, also known to Walter Camp as Weir's Hill". **M59**

After performing the Into Fours maneuver, the command left Martin's Big Hill ridge, and turned to the right. This would lead them down into the South Fork of Medicine Tail Coulee. They were now blazing a new trail of their own. The primary reason for this diversion was that the front of the new column of fours had now doubled in width to some sixty feet. This wide formation could not continue to march over the Martin's Big Hill/Sharpshooter's Ridge complex that now became too narrow for the new wide front. The advance team of foragers would have signaled a need for a change in direction. Good horsemanship requires that horses not be ridden in parallel along on a steep slope, as it puts to much stress on their lower legs. **H5, H8, H9, H6 &**

According to John Martin, upon reaching the drainage of the "South Fork" of Medicine Tail, there they made another ninety degree turn this time to the left. This now sent the so-called "Custer" companies into history. There was no turning back from the fatal decision made on lower Ash Creek. Custer's planned pincer movement on the village that Mister Varnum had located would soon turn into disaster.

Just as the Custer battalions left Martin's "Big Hill" Halt, Reno's men in the valley below now opened fire for the first time after being deployed on foot. It was now 2:55 PM based on the time/distance reconstruction calculated using the horses' gait, and not the varying human estimations.

The Crow Scouts Revisited: After having made their observations from the high ground north of the White Rocks area, Mitch Bouyer and his four remaining Crows Scouts caught up with the advancing battalions on the Big Flat near the now burning burial lodge, the one that the prosecutor of the Reno Court of Inquiry, Lieutenant Jessie Lee would refer to as the "Lone Tepee." Before Bouyer and the four Crow Scouts could arrive, Custer had ordered the other two oldest remaining Crow Scouts to go to the bluffs and observe the Valley. This may have occurred immediately after Varnum's report of lodges in the Valley. However, White Swan and Half Yellow Face may have misunderstood, or they decided not to expose themselves this close to their traditional enemy, the Sioux. Instead, they followed Reno's advance across the Little Bighorn River. They would soon participate honorably in the later Reno Valley and Hilltop Fights. Apparently their noncompliance was noticed by Custer, as he now ordered Mitch Bouyer and his three remaining Crow Scouts to take the place of the other recalcitrant Crows. They were to go forward and observe the warrior movements in the

Valley. Although they would use Custer's soon to be proposed "shortcut" trail they soon fell behind the Custer battalion's faster moving horses which continued to follow Reno's Battalion across the Echleman Fords. **M39**

Or was it, as Lieutenant Bradley experienced earlier in June, that whenever his Crow Scouts got near the Sioux/Cheyenne camps on the Rosebud River they would start to become very hesitant to go forward. Bouyer and now with but three of his Crows fell in behind the First and Second Battalions which by now had reached what will become known as "Mathey's Knoll." It was Curly that was now missing.

Curly's Disappearance: When Custer would later halt on Martin's "Big Hill," (Halt #3) Bouyer by now had only three of his Crows. It was Curly that was missing, starting a controversy that would haunt him the rest of his life. However, as retired NPS historian Mardell Hogan points out in her Little Bighorn Associates Research Review article, Curly may have fallen behind when he tried to find White Swan, his warrior mentor. But, White Swan had already crossed the river with Reno's forces. Arriving too late at Ford A, Curly may have then decided to rejoin Custer's faster moving battalions, which he later caught up with in Medicine Tail Coulee. **M75**

Custer now ordered Bouyer and the three remaining Crows to go forward to high ground now known as Weir Point. They were to observe the villages, and to report back their findings to Custer. A five man detail may have accompanied them. However, they continued past Weir Point, and apparently without reporting anything back to Custer, they continued further *northward* along the bluffs.

Arriving on a high knoll, now known as "Crow Hill," they fired a few rifle rounds into the Minneconjou village directly below them. Arriving here five minutes after the opening shots from Reno's skirmish line; they would remain here for at least another five minutes. Here, the three Crows were ordered by Bouyer to go back, as their job was done. They had found their quarry, the Sioux and Cheyenne. As they were leaving, the three Crows observed Custer's Battalions now entering the upper end of Medicine Tail Coulee. The time was now 3:05 PM. **See Custer Trail 2, pg. 70**

The Busby to Crow Stage Road Trail: After traveling about one mile from Martin's Big Hill halt, the "Custer Squadrons" reached another well-established travois trail. This major trail ran from the Rosebud Valley to the present Crow Agency. It followed the North Fork of Davis Creek, and went down Medicine Tail Coulee to the Minneconjou (Ford B) crossing. Later, this well traveled trail would become the primary stage road between Crow Agency, Busby and the Northern Cheyenne Agency at Lame Deer, Montana. On the night march of the June 25 early morning hours, up Davis Creek, Custer warned the advanced companies not to take the "right" fork in the trail. This was the later stage road trail that ran up North Davis Creek. Custer had been ill advised by the Crows not to take this easier passage over the Wolf Mountain range. It follows much of present Highway 212 from Busby. Instead of the Ash Creek route, this northerly trail would have placed the Regiment hours earlier and only a half-mile upstream from the Onion Creek encampments. This strategic location would have placed the regiment halfway between the upper (Hunkpapa), and the lower (Ogallala) villages. **See VILLAGES, pg. 69**

The Crows later claimed that Custer, on the late evening of June 24, had asked them about a place where he could "hide the regiment" near the Divide. He was going to wait until the morning of June 26, and then attack the villages in the Little Bighorn Valley. Why would Custer think that any villages would still be there? After all, it was at the Busby campsite on June 24 that the Crows recommended the more difficult "left" hand trail up Davis Creek proper. There were more hiding places for the regiment. The easier and more direct route went up the North Fork of Davis Creek. But, it was an open route with few or no places to hide that many horses and mules. This whole Crow story smacks of contrivance, as if you could silence some 200 "Rocky Mountain Canaries" (mules) from whistling their tunes!

The problem with their little "story" was that the Crows had just returned from a late afternoon reconnaissance of the Little Bighorn Valley. They had traveled the some forty-five miles round trip to the traditional Crow "Custer Last Lookout," only to return after dark to tell Custer that they could not see any villages due to the setting sun! Or did they even go much beyond the Busby bend? As Lieutenant James Bradley, Colonel Gibbons Chief of Scouts tells of his problems with the Crow Scouts that whenever they came in near contact with the Sioux, they would become very lethargic, and start to balk in going forward. The other problem is that no one had yet seen any villages in the Valley that is until the next morning. Perhaps Custer's trust in the Crows was very misplaced?

The Fourth Halt in Medicine Tail: Bouyer was now seeing for the first time the massive encampments at the mouth of Onion Creek, now alone he would leave Crow Hill by 3:05 PM. and traveled up Medicine Tail to met Custer's advancing companies. He met them about one and three tenths mile east of the Ford B area. It was here that Custer would halt his two battalions, and for the First Battalion, a much longer period of time. This now becomes Halt Number Four. According to Walter Camp's odometer measurement, it occurred in the east mid-section of Township Section 28. He had measured 6185 feet (1.3 miles) from the Minneconjou Ford to where he thought the halt occurred. Traveling the one and eight tenth miles from the Third Halt on Martin's Big Hill in fifteen minutes, Custer again halted the two battalions in Medicine Tail Coulee!

Was it because of the new information that Bouyer had just bought to him? From this halt, Custer could just see the very upstream end of the Ogallala village, but not the other encampments on Onion Creek, those of the Northern Cheyenne, Sans Arc and other smaller villages. Most likely it was this sighting that caused this new halt. According to John Martin, it was also at this time Custer and Cooke hurriedly discussed something, and then he was sent back with a written message to Captain Benteen. **LILLY 131**

This extended halt would remain unknown until Walter Camp suggested that such a delay did occur in Medicine Tail Coulee. He thought that this halt might have been as long as thirty to forty-five minutes, a time far too long for consideration. What was the reason for this lengthy halt and the sequence of decisions made at this crucial time? **See Chapter Six, pg. 151**

Courtesy of R. N. Wathen Jr. - 1976

ARIEL VIEW OF RENO VALLEY FIGHT

SCALE: -------------------- 1/4 MILE

CHAPTER TWO

THE RENO VALLEY FIGHT

On the retreat it was every man for himself and the Sioux took the hindmost.
Private Daniel Newell, Company M.

Reno was whipped out of the valley, and his command fled in great disorder!
Walter Camp

The Reno Valley Fight: In his proposed book, Camp wanted to use the above statements for the conclusion on the Reno Valley Fight. This disastrous episode of the Custer Fight was but one of many contributing factors that resulted in the defeat of the regiment. But, it may have been the primary one for the total destruction of Custer's five companies on a battlefield four miles downstream. Walter Camp identified the true location of the Reno Fight with his compass headings that he observed from the present Weir Point. His recorded 202 degrees azimuth intersects just west of the driveway of the turn of the century "Man Paints His Body" homestead **(Old Pitsch farm)**. Reno responded incorrectly by dismounting when the Otter Creek drainage blocked his forward movement. He was still a mile from the first village located on Shoulder Blade Creek. Reno had deployed into a very wide mounted line of three companies too early. His dismounted line stretched some 150 yards out into the valley floor.

Reno's First Skirmish Line was advanced on foot for 100 yards and with a Right Wheel movement ended up on a new "second line" in reversed order. The result was that his led horses, which had been taken down into the lower bench of the "woods" area, were now in reverse order. During the retreat, men from Company G were trying to mount Company M's horses. Reno had violated army regulations concerning the proper deployment of the led horses and the wrong tactical deployment. Reno's military errors and the fact that he skirted too close to the timber which allowed his command to become boxed in by the Otter Creek was a major factor in his Valley Fight. At the time this small cross-drainage was too deep to be negotiated by a rapidly moving mounted command.

Reno's major failure was that he did not maintain a mounted offensive. And, within minutes of halting and withdrawing into an adjacent wooded area, there were no defensive actions taken. However, the turning point in the Battle of the Little Big Horn was the retreat of the Fourth Battalion from the upper valley. This action allowed for the release of almost the entire warrior force, and they would soon swarm Custer's two battalions. The military breakdown of Reno's battalion was a direct result of his failure to properly manage his men and horses.

When Reno halted and dismounted his men they were still nearly a mile from the closest village. And, there was a rather small opposition in his immediate front. His short lived valley fight occurred within four miles was within walking distance by horse of the soon to be Custer Battlefield. Reno's actions in the valley fight remain controversial. Even its actual site remained a mystery until Water Camp turned his trained civil engineering eye on its true location. Over a fifteen-year period of interviews and on his many trips to Montana, Camp was able to locate the actual site. His civil engineering experience gave him insight on how to match the known events with the terrain. From his massive first hand information and sixteen field trips he was able to pin point the Valley and "Woods" battle sites. They are not located in the now accepted "Garryowen Loop" area, but further upstream than has ever been suggested before. **LILLY 45**

As an experienced surveyor, Camp used a typical engineering method to record his location of Reno's battle-site. He simply went a high terrain feature above the valley and made a visual observation from a high place now designated by the National Park System (NPS) as "Weir Point." When he first visited the Custer Battlefield in 1903, no one knew where either site was located. The U.S. Army was then responsible for the management of the Custer Battlefield. Then there were no interpretive services as today. From the highest point on the present Weir Point, Camp recorded 202 magnetic azimuth degrees that intersected with his location of the Reno Valley Fight.

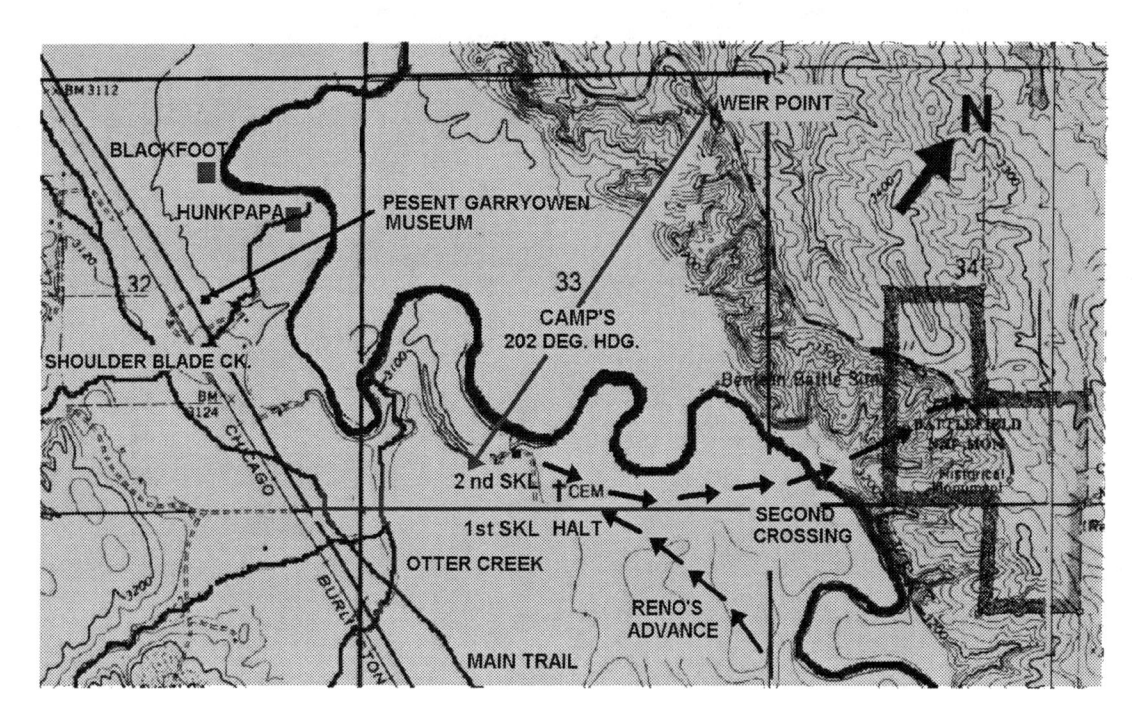

RENO VALLEY FIGHT

SCALE: ----------- 1/4 MILE

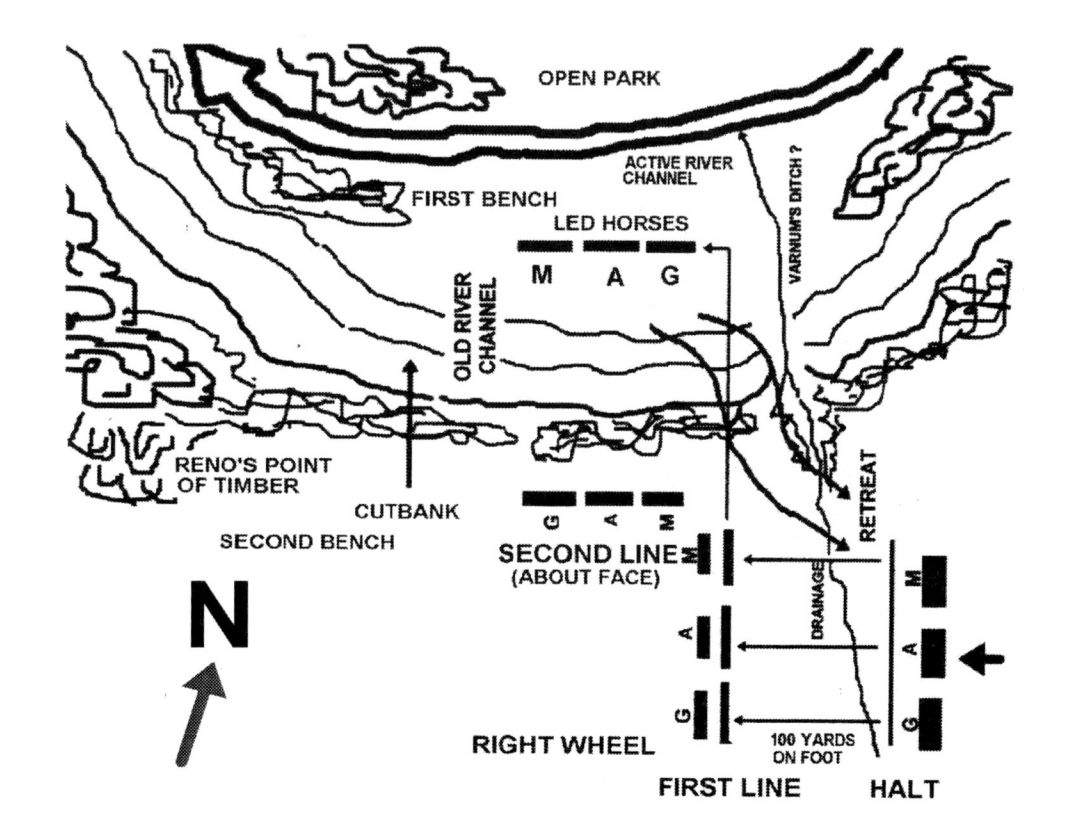

VALLEY FIGHT SCHEMATIC

NOT TO SCALE

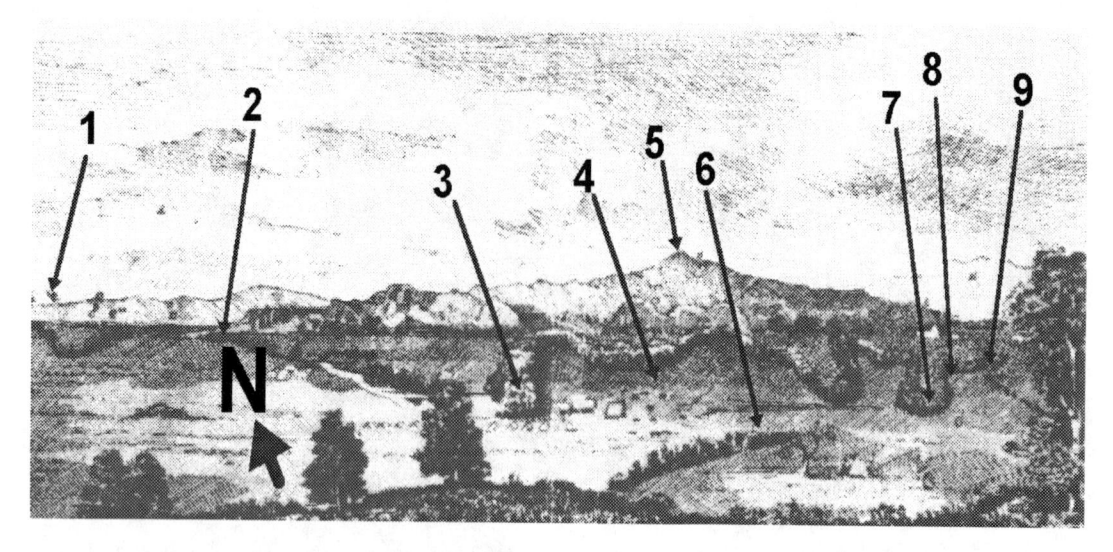

NEW YORK GRAPHIC'S DRAWING - JULY 1877

KEY:

1. Custer Battlefield.
2. Ford B.
3. Blackfoot Sioux bend.
4. Future Garryowen Loop.
5. Weir Point.
6. Shoulder Blade Creek.
7. Reno's "Point of Timber" (Gibbon).
8. Gibbon's Ford (See Reno Court of Inquiry).
9. Otter Creek

From a field sketch made by a newspaper artist from the *New York Graphics*, published in July of 1877, one can easily today line up the terrain features with Camp's Valley Fight location. Colonel Gibbon described the location of Reno's "Point of Timber" as being at the third river bend downstream from Reno's second crossing. This places his skirmish line less then a mile from his second crossing. The most prominent river feature seen in the 1877 newspaper sketch is easily identifiable today as the "Blackfoot-Sioux" encampment bend. The Blake/Marshall survey, published for the first time in this study, shows where this river bend changes direction to the east, and is the first major loop downstream of the so-called "Garryowen" location of the first post office in the valley.

The Blackfoot-Sioux's upstream neighbor, the Hunkpapa village, was located at the mouth of Shoulder Blade Creek, *north* of the present "Garryowen" store/museum complex. This was the largest encampment on the Little Bighorn and it covered at least five acres in size. This large encampment of Sitting Bull's people was the closest village to Reno's dismounted skirmish line. And it was still a mile distance away! Somewhere between these two points, his second crossing and the Hunkpapa village, Reno halted his command. But, exactly where was his "Point of Timber" located?

This physical analysis of the known terrain features now suggests that Reno's battalion was first halted and dismounted in the southwest 1/4 section of Township Section 33. This location is but three quarter mile due west in a straight line from Reno's second crossing. It lies just beyond the driveway of the Old Pitch family farm house, located at the burial pit discovered in the 1930s. A small iron fenced enclosure now marks the site were a number of Reno dead were uncovered by Crow Agency workers. Hank Weibert's father was one the workers. **See pg. 75, RENO VALLEY FIGHT, MASS GRAVE**

The presently accepted Reno battle site at the "Garryowen Loop," one that hardly existed in 1876, is in neighboring Township Section 32. It is another three quarter mile further downstream from the actual site as suggested by Camp/Gibbon and the 1877 newspaper sketch. Some of the men from Company G said that after they halted, they could see a *large village* from the far left of their first skirmish line. Here they were seeing either the somewhat smaller Blackfoot-Sioux village, or the much larger Hunkpapa encampment located near the next river bend downstream from the present Garryowen Loop. The U.S. Government's Indian Department had issued army "duck" canvas to the reservation summer roamers as replacement for the now scarce buffalo skin lodge covers. The white appearance of this substitute material stood out in contrast to the camouflage like color of the animal skin lodges. The Hunkpapa village was most likely masked by the tree line in the later formed Garryowen Loop, which then cut into the second bench much further to the north.

Some of Reno's officers claimed that the "lodges" they saw were only *a few hundred yards* away from their line! This gross exaggeration was part of the "smoke screen" orchestrated by Reno's attorney. It was designed to cover up the fact that when Reno halted, he was still a considerable distance from any of the villages. What they did not want known was the real reason of Reno halting in the first place. And, it was not because there were too many Indians!

The testimony of the civilian doctor, H. R. Porter, exposes this distortion. Early in his testimony, he said that it was not until he entered the timber that he saw the "main village" at least a mile away. He saw about 1000 lodges through an opening in the woods. At the same time, he also noticed a singular standing "tepee," only one quarter mile away. Here the deception of the smoke and mirror act of Reno's fellow officers fell apart. **M71, pg. 194.**

Does Doctor Porter's singular tepee sighting now become their large "village," the one that Reno had been ordered to charge. This misconception went unchallenged by the Court. However, one lodge does not make a village. But, Doctor Porter's tepee stood very close to Reno's subsequent "woods" position. Lieutenant Lee changed his line of questioning of Doctor Porter, whose testimony now differed from Reno's officer's estimate of just how close Reno had gotten to the villages. Was it one quarter of a mile, or Doctor Porter's more distant one mile?

Indian accounts strongly suggest that Doctor Porter's singular tepee sighting was part of a sun dance ceremony site, located a mile upstream from the upper villages. It was near the place were the soldiers were hiding on their horses in the wooded area. **M71, pg. 194-196**

Camp interviewed retired army officer Jessie M. Lee in 1912. He was the prosecutor for the U.S. Army at the 1879 Reno Court of Inquiry. Lee told him that the "Court" (Colonel Wesley Merritt) had "dammed him (Reno) with faint praise." Camp quotes another unidentified army officer who was in a position to know the "feeling" among the sitting Board of Inquiry. He said they were lenient with Reno for but one reason. And that was because Reno's "hesitancy" and "conservatism" probably saved the balance of the regiment from the same fate of Custer's other five companies and that was of their total annihilation. However, Camp's anonymous officer went on to say that he believed that if Reno had held the timber, he would have been able to hold his ground without losing as many men as he did when he retreated. This unidentified officer may have been none other then Colonel Wesley Merritt, the ranking officer on the Inquiry Board. Although Camp never interviewed Merritt, Jessie Lee told Camp, in a guarded Victorian age politically correct manner, that it was Colonel Merritt that coined the phrase "faint phrase."

Camp's own opinion was that if Benteen had reinforced Reno in the valley, together they could have held many Indians away from Custer. Camp's conclusion was by the army, fighting on two points in the valley and at the same time, might have stampeded the Indians. But we know that Benteen did not enter the valley, as he was working on a separate agenda of his own. He went on to say that Reno's action resulted not from cowardliness, but from an error in judgment, and nothing more.

Reno Sent Forward: To fully understand Reno's action, we need to start at the point where his battalion was sent forward to "pursue fleeing Indians, who were on the jump just ahead of them," a statement attributed to Frederick Gerard. From a knoll just northwest of the present Hartung Morass, Frederick Gerard saw a small Indian "town" of pony drags (travois) fleeing on the opposite side of Ash Creek. Most Custer researchers have misinterpreted Gerard's usage of the word "town," as recorded in the Reno Court verbatim testimony. **M71, Pg. 84**

It has been misunderstood that Gerard made this sighting from the bluffs overlooking the valley. And, that his reference to a "town" was that of a fixed village in the Little Bighorn Valley. This misconception is dispelled if one reads Gerard's testimony carefully. He speaks of his separate observations as being from two different knolls. Especially, if you consider his usage of the word "town" as referred to a moving village, one with travois ponies and men, women and children on the move. Was it possible that Gerard's town was the fleeing village from the South Fork area?

As the soldiers approached their encampment this errant small village made a hurried exit and fled downstream to the Ford A area. They were Summer Roamers out on a lark from the confinement of the Dakota reservations. But, now at 2:00 PM, they were still one mile east of that point, when Gerard and Hare reported their sighting to Custer. It was at this time, near Lieutenant Lee's "Lone Tepee," after reading Hare's written communication that Reno's Fourth Battalion was now ordered into the advance. Most likely Gerard's and Mister Hare's "running Indians" (Gerard's "town") were the same Indians that had been earlier camped in a village near the South Fork area. When Custer's advanced Squadrons almost ran over their camp, they packed up and fled toward the valley. This may have also been the same "village" that the Crow Scouts thought they had seen in the valley of the Little Bighorn. But, the Ree's more moderate judgment was that the "village" was in the White Rocks area near the South Fork of Ash Creek, and far closer to their lookout than the more distant Little Bighorn!

However, it was Varnum's new verbal report made soon after Reno was ordered to pursue the fleeing Indians that caused Custer to change his plans. Only some twenty-five minutes earlier Varnum had seen the Shoulder Blade Creek encampments from his high observation point located on the left bank of Ash Creek, some two miles east of the Ford A. area. Approximately one mile west of the Hartung Morass at 2:10 PM, Reno was sent forward to pursue Gerard's "Fleeing Village." Both Adjutant Cooke and Custer had issued this verbal order.

Their words were that Reno would be fully supported by either the First or Second Battalion, or both! But, it is important to note that Reno was not yet ordered to cross the Little Bighorn River, at least not from the "Lone Tepee" area. Unable to catch the faster traveling villagers, that had pony drags, women and children, the Fourth Battalion would soon arrive at what will become known as Gerard's "Second Knoll." It was here that the Scouts halted and were observing the activities of the hostile warriors seemingly advancing upstream in the valley. Gerard joined them and they wisely waited for the army before they crossed over the river into the valley.

From here, Gerard turned back to warn Custer, and when he met Adjutant Cooke he told him that the warriors were now advancing toward their position. He was positive that Custer's battalions were in the immediate vicinity when he met Lieutenant Cooke, who was very close to his second knoll. Walter Camp noted this prominent terrain feature in his field notes. He said that it stood right in the mouth of Ash Creek a quarter of a mile east of Reno's crossing at Ford A. Gerard's Second Knoll now becomes the focal point for the further deployment of Reno's Battalion.

Just east of this knoll the travois trail divides with the right hand branch headed *north* to what John Martin said was Custer's next crossing on Lower Ash Creek. **(MARSHY PLACE)**. The other branch swings to the left around Gerard's Second Knoll to Ford A. Some of Reno's officers observed Lieutenant Cooke and Captain Keogh traveling together just behind Reno's advancing battalion. Perhaps, finding no "running Indians" east of the knoll was the reason that Reno was now ordered to cross the Little Bighorn.

Gerard's Second Knoll is located 400 yards north (magnetic) of the Ford A area. The trail from the Echleman Fords that Reno, Custer, and then later Benteen would use passed by sheep sheds that would be later erected by the Speer Ranch in the 1890s. The Crow Scouts pointed out the trail used by Reno to General Hugh Scott during his 1919 visit. Just east of his Second Knoll, Gerard noticed a distinct and fresh lodgepole trail that crossed northward over their trail. He mentioned seeing this travois trail in his testimony, but the Recorder Lee ignored this very important clue. This places the arrival of the Fourth Battalion a few minutes before 2:20 PM. Today, at the Ford A area, there are two pronounced "troughs." The army used the one to the left (upstream), while the scouts crossed at the downstream trough. **NA4**

There is a continuing "myth" that Reno "watered" his horses at Ford A. This concept is unacceptable, as the procedure for "officially" watering the horses was a highly regulated army protocol. Some of the men's horses may have balked to take a sip of the better tasting spring water run off from the Big Horn Mountains. Horses have a highly developed sense of taste and smell. Up to now the water had been brackish and alkaline in taste. Mister Hare said that Reno had allowed the men "plenty of time to water" their horses, taking as much as ten minutes to cross. At the same time one of Reno's platoon sergeants complained that they had a hard time with the men for not allowing the horses to stop mid-stream to sip a little water. He also complained how the men could not keep their intervals as it had become very ragged. Just another example of how poorly the men were trained in good horsemanship. Was the enlisted men's tail wagging the dog? Perhaps, the officers just did not have that much control over their men **M40, pg. 65 (Hare)**

It was very near Gerard's Second Knoll that Reno was first ordered to cross over the Little Bighorn River and enter the valley. The Court and the sworn testimony of the officers in Chicago in 1879 overlooked this second order and its messenger, Lieutenant Cooke. But, too many other witnesses saw Cooke, along with Keogh, near the Ford A area at this time. Adjutant Cooke was upset by the too fast pace that Reno's men were now using when they reached the river crossing. According to Private James Wilber of Company M, Cooke had yelled at them, "For God's sake men don't run those horses like that; you will need them in a few minutes." Meantime, Gerard's Fleeing Village had disappeared. **M40, pg. 148 (Wilber)**

They can be discounted as being players any longer in the new scenario now being played out by Custer. By turning *north* he had other plans on his mind. Lieutenant Lee seemed to be informed about the possible presence of Gerard's "running Indians" in the area just east of Ford A. In an unexpected direct line of questioning of Mister Varnum, he was asked that after passing Custer's "Command" on his way to Reno's crossing, did he see any Indians to his immediate right front. Varnum seemed to be flustered as he tried to avoid answering this simple question. Perhaps, the good Lieutenant had not attended the daily pre-testimony briefings, held by Reno and his attorney at their hotel? Varnum's evasive answers does raise questions as to how much preliminary information Fred Gerard may have given to the Court in closed door hearings?

After all, Gerard had described seeing a fresh lodgepole trail that crossed over the trail that Reno was following. And, it was located near his Second Knoll, and also very near the Ford A area. The other and more important question which remained unasked by the Court was: why Reno did not continue to follow this "quite of a large" lodgepole trail if he was sent to bring the fleeing Indians to bay? It is interesting to note that after Gerard's testimony, Second Lieutenant Varnum was the very next witness called by the Court. **M71, pg. 90**

Apparently, the answer may be in that Reno was now ordered to cross the river and attack the Hunkpapa village, as just reported to Custer by Mister Varnum. In his testimony, Varnum describes how he seen fixed tepees in the valley, "an hour or more" early from a high bluff south of Ash Creek. We know from our reconstruction of the advance of the three battalions down Ash Creek, that Varnum's sighting took place by 1:45 PM. He was on a high knoll located three quarter mile southeast of the Hartung Morass. In his testimony, Varnum fails to mention that he had reported this sighting to Custer. He had caught up with his Commander just as Reno's battalion was pulling out to chase Gerard's "running Indians."

Lyman Gilbert, Reno's private civilian attorney tried to discredit Gerard's testimony. He pointed out that not only was Gerard a civilian, but also he was "living in sin," because he had an Indian wife. Also, Gilbert made sure that the Court knew of Gerard's dismissal as an official army interpreter, a position that paid well. He had been fired by Reno. Of course Gilbert was inferring that Gerard was one of those vindictive dirty stinking squaw men. Reno's high priced attorney must have been the original "Philadelphia Lawyer". **M71, pg. 126**

But this ploy to discredit Gerard's revealing testimony worked. The additional insult by Lieutenant Lee was when he questioned Gerard's veracity about seeing a fresh lodgepole trail so near the river, one that Reno had ignored. Asked if he would recognize such a trail, Gerard sarcastically replied that he had been in Indian country for thirty-one years, and he thought that he would know one when he saw one. After this unwarranted attack on his credibility, Gerard became a very unwilling witness. Lieutenant George Wallace, who was the regiment's Engineering Officer and the official itinerarist for the Rosebud march, testified that by his watch they had reached the Little Bighorn River by 2:20 PM, St. Paul regimental time. Allowing ten minutes for the battalion to cross would not be unreasonable at this point. And, perhaps add another ten minutes for reforming on the left bank. This area was described as having a lot of downed timber. Afterwards, Reno ordered his command into an orderly and progressively faster pace downstream by 2:40 PM. His orders were to attack and seize the village sighted by Mister Varnum. It was yet some three miles downstream in a straight line.

After crossing the river, Reno had to reform his "scattered" men, more evidence of how poor horsemen they were. Reno then did something very unorthodox according to Lieutenant Wallace. He did not agree with Reno's tactical choice of deployment. Reno now ordered all three companies "Into Line" as mounted skirmishers. Then he ordered a regulated gait of a hand gallop between twelve to fourteen miles per hour. Company M was on the right flank, with Company G being held in reserve in the rear. This was the formation allowed by army regulations, but usually used when in the immediate presence of the enemy.

At this time, the warriors were over two and one half miles away, and content to mask their activities by riding back and forth stirring up a huge dust cloud. Gerard's ominous warning about warriors racing up the valley was incorrect. Reno's "combat ready" deployment came far too early and would soon prove to be the first of many tactical errors. So far, except for this early single rank formation, Reno was performing in the regulated manner of a good cavalry officer. But, that would soon change!

As soon as the command reached the hand gallop rate of march, Reno ordered his reserve company, Company G "Left, Into Line." The other companies had to slow their gait to the trot in order for Company G to be able to join them in their single rank line. Now all three companies were now riding abreast of each other at one of the fastest gait allowed. Good horsemen understand that when horses are allowed to gallop that you can not always expect them to rapidly slow down without problems. Perhaps Major Reno was not a good horseman?

The battalion's movement now became ragged and it signaled horse troubles to come. Also, Lieutenant Wallace testified that at the time of Company G's slow down that the warriors surged forward towards their newly formed line. This was at the point when things began to become unraveled. Wallace later testified that Reno's "Into Line" formation was not the proper type of an attack on a stationary Indian encampment. He thought that the standard column of fours would get the job done rather then the much wider front of an extended line. Especially after Reno ordered his reserve company into the line.

The line was now extended across the valley floor to some one hundred fifty yards in width. Compare this exceptionally wide formation with the column of fours width of twenty-five yards for the Custer Squadrons, a ratio of six times greater. And three companies were charging down the valley floor at a blistering pace for which most of the men and their horses had not been trained to accomplish. In his testimony, Reno referred to a ravine located 200 to 300 yards downstream from where he would halt. Many hundreds of Indians were now "*disgorging*" from this "ravine". His vague description implies that his ravine was perhaps Shoulder Blade Creek, and that "*straggling parties*" of Indians that were now flanking his command causing him to be thrown on the defense and the need to halt. He estimated that there were 500 to 600 Indians now going around to the rear of his command. However, from the "point of timber" where he halted, it was still one and quarter mile (2200 yards) further downstream to the mouth of Shoulder Blade Creek. The problem with Reno's testimony was that it was neither his "straggling" Indians nor his "ravine" which was "disgorging" them that caused him to halt and dismount his men! It was a much smaller "ravine" now called "Otter Creek." **M71, pg. 590 (Reno's "Ditch")**

Unfortunely, Reno was at the same time making a fatal mistake by skirting too far to his right along the river channel. If he had just traveled further out to the left in the valley, by as little as a half mile, he would have been able to follow the established main trail that runs up the valley. The villagers had just used this trail to go to their present location from their upstream location near Lodgegrass, Montana on June 22. The crossing at Ford A was not a major trail and had not been used by the now consolidated encampments after the June 17 Crook Fight on the upper Rosebud.

This lack of horsemanship judgment would cost Reno any possible victory of seizing any of the scattered villages. It was not hundreds of straggling Indians now getting in the rear of his command that caused Reno to halt and dismount his men, but a serious "horse obstacle" now looming very large in front of his charging line of men and horses. The charge of Indians around the rear came after his halt.

In the Little Bighorn Valley, there are several cross drainages that cut deep into the valley floor. One of them is called the Otter Creek drainage. Its origins are in the benchland adjacent to the "Denny" farm buildings. It crosses Township Section 5 and enters the Little Bighorn River in the southwestern corner of Township Section 33. It was here that Reno's tactical error of skirting too close to the river now created a horseman's nightmare of monumental proportions. He failed to consider that such a deep cutting channel would soon "box" him in and created a disaster. **See Reno Valley Fight, pg. 77**

We know from the Camp research that a ten man detail of foragers from Company M was riding in front of the battalion. It is a standard army practices to do so. They would have signaled that an impassable obstacle was in their immediate front! But, as Sergeant John Ryan of Company M told Camp, he and his foragers had gotten too far ahead of the mounted line. The soon to be impassable "obstacle" would become the mouth of Otter Creek where it empties into the Little Bighorn River.

It was far too deep and wide to be negotiated by Reno's wildly charging and straggling mounted line. Today this natural drainage is now used for irrigation and has been altered to be straight and far shallower. Camp noted this in his 1910 field notes that this natural drainage was now being used for irrigation, and that its mouth had been cut deep into by the river channel. Several of the valley fight participants said that there was a deep "coulee" 900 to 1200 yards ahead of their line. From this "ravine" as Reno would later refer to it, many

Indians were pouring out before he halted. Was Reno referring to Otter Creek as his "ravine," which he estimated to be a half mile ahead of his command? **M71, pg. 562**

Reno now committed his second tactical error, one of many to come. He had the battalion slowed to a halt while he tried to asses this sudden tactical problem! A number of men were not able to control their horses. Some of the better horsemen were able to "turn" their excited horses and return again to the battalion. But several were swallowed up by the "hordes" of Indians and were never seen alive again. Later, one of several heads was found in the village, and one had red hair. The grisly discovery was later identified as Private John Armstrong, of Company A.

Reno then made his single biggest mistake. He decided to halt the men and deploy them as dismounted skirmishers. His military options before he halted were to slow his gait and order a change of direction by a "Left Oblique," so the command could pass around this obstacle. But this was not practical from a formation already in a very wide single rank. Normally this was done from a column of fours. He could have ordered the line back into a column of fours, but there was neither enough time nor distance. And, most likely the horsemanship training necessary to do this was just not there. This was when Reno's earlier decision to form a mounted skirmish line in his mad dash down the valley would now come back to haunt him. When he halted and dismounted, his battalion was still over three-quarters of a mile away from the nearest encampment.

What did he expect the men to do, march on foot at the double time for the rest of the distance? But, if the ravine that Reno referred was indeed Otter Creek, it was still at least 800 yards in his front. Reno's military indecisiveness by halting now lost him the momentum of any continued offensive action. In fact, it now turned the battalion into the role of a defensive measure. The warriors now moved into a much closer position and started to flank the troops. Before Reno's dismounting of his men, the relatively small number of about two hundred warriors had keep their distance, satisfied to create a dust screen by riding back and forth in the valley. This was to allow time for the pony herds to be driven into the upper camps located near Shoulder Blade Creek. A small number of Arikara Scouts had gone onto the west benchlands to capture those pony herds. The roles were changed by Reno's deployment of his men on foot. The Sioux now became the hunters, and they were now after the army's horses.

Any offensive momentum was now lost. Cavalry is at its weakest when thrown into the defensive posture of being dismounted. Approximately four tenths of a mile upstream of the mouth of Otter Creek, Reno halted and formed an ill-conceived dismounted skirmish line. This was a decision that would create nothing but confusion and a disaster in the making. A mounted line would have intervals of about one yard, but a dismounted line could be deployed at an extended standard six yard interval. However, Sergeant Culbertson in his testimony said that the line was only 250 yards meaning that they were deployed at a closer three yard interval. **M71, pg. 367**

Another possible reason for an early halt in this area was the presence of another but much smaller cross drainage "ditch," as mentioned by Mister Varnum. He discovered it on his way out of the woods on the retreat. His knew that his horse was not a jumper and he had become the brunt of other officer's jokes for having purchased a mount that would not jump. On their wild flight from the woods position, he knew that his horse would not jump the up coming drainage ditch. He was positive that he would be over taken and killed by the pursuing warriors. He said that not only did this horse jump it at this time; but that it was the first and last time that his horse ever jumped anything. Varnum thought that the reason was that his horse was more frightened then he was. Varnum's drainage would later become the low wet area where today a small iron fence enclosure marks the grave for several of Reno's retreating dead. The Custer "Unknown Soldier" buried at the present Garryowen museum complex came from the discovery of this mass grave in the 1930s by a reservation work party, and Hank Weibert's father was one of the workers.

At the time of the initial halt, Company M had been on the right of the line. At first the men were advanced on foot at the prescribed animated double time. The dismounted line was advanced for about 100 yards using this fatiguing high stepping walk, before being halted to form the first stationary skirmish line. It was just upstream of what would be later referred to as Reno's Point of Timber. This would soon become the so-called "Wood's" position. Later, some of Reno's officers talked about the command being ridden toward a heavily wooded area where the river made an abrupt bend to the north. This was the direct result of Reno having chosen to have ridden too close to the river channel. Simply, he had gotten the battalion boxed in!

The first line was established at right angles adjacent to an old "dry" river channel. Company M's right flank was located next to this channel. Walter Camp discovered that the three companies had halted near the present driveway to the old Crow homestead originally owned by "Paints His Body." More recently, this old homestead has been called the "Old Pitsch" house. This original Blake/Marshall forty acre allotment is located in the southwest 1/4 section of Township Section 33. The first skirmish line was on a northeast/southwest magnetic alignment with the general direction of the valley. But, the line would soon be swung around; one enlisted man described it as like a swinging barn door. This is the classic description of a right wheel maneuver right out of the army drill manual.

This second line was now ninety degrees to the first, and it was now located right on the embankment of the Reno's Pont of Timber overlooking the old river channel. After an About Face command, Company M would now be on the left of the line. How this new movement occurred would soon become smothered in the deception and the plausible denial of the 1879 investigation into Reno's role in his Valley Fight. There is a mystery of exactly just how Company M, which was on the right of the advancing line going down the valley, ended up being on the left of this "second" line? This flip-flop can be answered by examining the drill tactics of the army's mounted service, and what the warriors were doing at the time when the soldiers halted and dismounted.

Essentially, when Reno first halted it was because of the obstacle called Otter Creek. At first the relatively small number of warriors was content to zigzag creating a dust cloud that masked their intentions. However, when the soldiers got off their horses, the warriors now circled around the left of the first dismounted line, which extended over one eight mile out into the valley. The problem was that this flanking ride by did not leave any targets to shoot at in their immediate front. Reno's straggling Indian parties were now ninety degrees to his line. But soon there were new warriors who seemed now to disgorge out of his ravine, which of course was the mouth of Otter Creek. Reno now swung his first line in a clockwise direction, what the army calls a Right Wheel maneuver. **03 & 04**

We know that Reno had to have ordered a Right Wheel, because it inverted the companies' original positions on the line. Company M, which had been on the right flank, was now on the left of this new line. Because the line was facing the wooded area they had to be ordered to perform an About Face. This now places them facing their flanking targets, Reno's "straggling" Indians who were bent on getting in the rear of his now dismounted command. However, it was at this time that Reno committed his worst error in horsemanship. U.S. Army drill regulation requires that at all times the led horses be maintained at a prescribed six yard distance behind the dismounted skirmishers. But, for some inexplicable reason, someone now ordered that all of the battalion's led horses to be taken down into the dry river channel. This old channel was some fifteen feet below the valley floor.

The Board tried without success to find whom it was that ordered this unorthodox maneuver. Captain Moylan said that it was done for better security for the horses. But none of Reno officers would say who it was that ordered this inane procedure that led to disaster when Company G tried to mount the wrong horses some thirty minutes later. But, the bottom line is that the blame must fall on Major Reno's shoulders. The tragedy was that when the led horses were taken by file a right flank movement down into the abandoned river channel, they were then forced to turn left to maintain the advance of the marching to the first skirmish line. But, when they were halted behind the new second line, the sequence of the company horses was now reversed! The horses' alignment remained the same, but now Company G's horses were on the left of the led horses' final halt.

While the men from Company G were now on the right of the new skirmish line, their horses were now being held behind the position of Company M, which was now on the left of the line. This action occurred while the skirmish line was being wheeled to the right, after it had marched downstream for at least 100 yards. This "horse" blunder seemed to have gone unnoticed, that is until Reno and Moylan with his Company A decided to flee the wooded area. Company A had been in the middle of the defunct skirmish line, so their horses were not effected by the inverted led horse arrangement. It was Company G and M that would discoverer that they were trying to mount each other's horses. The men just took what ever set of linked up horse they found and rode out pell-mell, to join the rest of the other fleeing men.

That is when all pandemonium broke out, and the deteriorating breakdown in military order just increased. Company G paid the penalty for Reno's mismanagement of his men and their horses. They ended up with the highest percentage of causalities in Reno's rout from the valley. Captain Benteen, who was not there, blamed the tragedy of Company G on its commander, Lieutenant Donald McIntosh. Benteen said it was McIntosh's "slow poking ways" that got him into all that trouble. Of course, Benteen's reference was a racial one, as McIntosh was part Native American from Canada. Benteen was never publicly known of saying anything derogatory against Reno. I guess that drinking buddies hang together?

Soon after Company G had been posted on the new second line, Lieutenant Wallace said that he and his company commander, Lieutenant McIntosh, each took a portion of Company G and went into the woods to check on the rumor that Indians were "getting at their horses." Exactly who ordered this movement has never been determined. Apparently, it was not Reno, who along with Moylan had gone into the timber very early. Did McIntosh take it onto himself to reconnoiter the timber that lay some twelve feet below his position? If so, he would pay the highest price along with many of his men. With Reno's quick departure from the "Woods" area, McIntosh could not find his personal horse, as it had already been taken along by Company M along with many of the others. He jumped on one of the company horses and rode it up onto the valley floor. The last that anyone saw of Lieutenant McIntosh was out on the valley floor when his horse began to buck with the picket rope and pin dangling behind the horse's rear legs. This allowed the perusing warriors to circle around him like hungry wolves attacking their prey. The enlisted man, whose horse McIntosh had taken survived by being forced to remain behind in the woods, but his company commander did not survive. Officers were not accustomed to having cavalry gear on their horses, as their orderlies always took care of their privately owned horses. **M40, pg. 119 (Rutten)**

Although Wallace said that he only took a "squad," inferring eight men, the entire company was not on the line soon after they had faced about on the second line placement. The rear of this second skirmish line was now perched on the edge of a high cut-bank that formed the west side of the dry river channel. The led horses were now positioned down on the lower bench north of an old abandoned river channel in the area between the dry channel and the active river channel.

Along the right bank of the active river channel, there was about a five acre open park where a Sundance camp had been located. Wallace said that he soon retuned with his men only to find Captain Moylan ready to "charge" with his Company A men. Moylan had just ordered his men in from the line. Wallace had lost contact with McIntosh and the remainder of Company G. When Reno and Moylan fled the woods, many of the men with Company G, along with others, could not find their assigned horses when they entered the woods area. Of course, they were trying to mount the wrong horses, with the transposing order of the led horses. This was another tactical mistake made by Reno that the Court was not interested in perusing. After all, they were charged with only investigating Reno's alleged "drunkenness and cowardliness." Legally, they could not dig deeper into his incompetence and mismanagement of his men and horses, all of which were highly prescribed by army regulations.

This incompetence was a charge for which Reno would have been convicted in a trail. But, the army and the new administration of President Rutherford B. Hayes did not seem to be interested in placing real blame on its living officers. It was easier to let the "Dead Lion" Custer to take the full blame.

The men stayed on the second skirmish line for about ten minutes, or less. That was about the length of time most of the men had to wildly fire their small amount (twenty to thirty rounds) of ammunition they carried on their person. Private Stanislas Roy of Company A said that he had fired all twenty of his cartridges. However, others said that they fired only four or five. **M40, pg. 112 (Roy)**

Company A, located now on the right flank, after the mysterious disappearance of Company G, decided to have their alternate files, numbers one and three of each rank, sent into the timber to retrieve their reserve ammo from their saddle bags. One or more of their line sergeants made this decision. This act now reduced the number of men on the line by one third. The Court was never able to discover whom it was that ordered this move. However, Varnum testified that it was Moylan that ordered the alternate files into the woods to retrieve the reserve ammunition from the saddle bags And exactly where was the good Captain at this time? Why, he was hiding in the woods, mounted on his horse next to Major Reno. That was where Lieutenant Varnum testified to finding his company commander when he went into the "woods" early. This was when the entire line collapsed on its own! When the men of Company M saw Company A's men running at double time into the woods, they also got up, and without orders they joined in with them and simply abandoned the line! They would be soon joined with the small balance of Company A. After that, the valley skirmish line just did not exist any more.

That is how Private Thomas O'Neill described it to Walter Camp. He said that there was a cry that "the Indians were getting their horses!" Of course, what may have increased the breakdown of military order was the "rumor" that the Indians were now killing their led horses in the woods! This may have been more then just a rumor; although nobody at the Inquiry ever mentions that any of the horses had been killed before the retreat. However, Colonel John Gibbon would testify that when he went into what was pointed out to him as being Reno's "Point of Timber," that he saw a "number" of dead government horses in the "woods" position. Perhaps the rumor indeed had substance in fact. Horses usually scream very loudly when injured, perhaps the men on the valley floor could have heard them? **M71, pg. 555 (Gibbon)**

It was at this point in time that military order started to break down and the men began to panic. O'Neill said that once the men had started to leave the line there was no stopping them. It did not help that their superior officers had not demonstrated much confidence by hiding in the wooded area. **M40, pg. 107**

According to some of Camp's enlisted men, Captain Thomas French was the only officer that was still on the line, as he was the only commissioned officer assigned to Company A. First Sergeant William Heyn, of Company A, said that there were no officers on his line for the duration of their deployment. French said that by now all of the other officers were hiding behind the trees. Sergeant Ryan of Company M, said that earlier he saw Second Lieutenant Benjamin Hodgson walking up and down the "line" encouraging the men to fire low.

Second Lieutenant Varnum had been assigned to the Arikara Scouts, but his regular company assignment was with Company A. He said that as soon as the line was established, he had gone into the woods to find Captain Moylan. And there he was with Reno, both mounted, and Moylan was yelling at the top of his lungs that they had to charge. Varnum said that he wondered in what direction his bellowing Captain intended to charge.

This same break down in military order would soon occur on the Custer Battlefield. The men were poorly disciplined and unsupervised by a lack of commissioned and non-commissioned officers alike. Sergeant Ferdinand Culbertson testified that the inexperienced men could not keep their intervals very well in the deployment of the line. Also, they fired too rapidly once the second line started firing. Is not this more evidence that the new recruits had not been properly trained during Reno's tenure as acting regimental commander at Fort Abraham Lincoln?

Sending the horses into a thickly wooded and brush filled area, such as described by Colonel Gibbon and some of the other officers, defies all good horse sense. Gibbon described the area as being a tangle of brush mixed with sizable trees and much fallen timber. This was where Reno's "Point of Timber" had been pointed out to him, the same place where he also found a number of dead U.S. Government horses. He described the "cut-bank" behind the line as being from twelve to fourteen feet above the first bench of the riverbed. Plus there was a dry river channel at least twenty feet in width that separated the led horses from the line. That makes the placement of the led horses some fifty feet or more from the line. And that was more then three times the regulated distance.

To make matters worse, at some point early in the dismounted deployment, Company G was removed from the line. This incident was not pursued by the Court, which amounts to total indifference in pursuing justice, as ninety percent of Company G would soon be abandoned, and killed by this movement. Lieutenant Wallace said that twenty men of his men from Company G had never been on a horse before their arrival at Fort Lincoln. He also stated that when he entered the woods, Reno and Moylan were already mounted. And this was very early in the fighting. Civil War tradition was that line officers would remain mounted during an action to insure confidence in their men. Cavalry Regulations required that officers, trumpeters and the horse holders stay mounted whenever the men were put on foot. But it is doubtful that Reno and Moylan remained mounted just to insure confidence in the men, they where ready to get the hell out of there!

After the Little Bighorn Fight, Moylan was accused of showing the "white feather," along with Reno. After all, they both lead the "charge" to the rear, and both arrived well ahead of everyone else on the bluffs, some three hundred feet above the valley.

Several of the officers testified that when they entered the wooded area, they had to bend down on their horses to avoid tree limbs and they had to follow very narrow game trails. The cover of heavy brush and the sizable cottonwood trees allowed perfect cover for the warriors to infiltrate the area and go after the led horses. And that is just what happened. Within ten minutes of the skirmish line being deployed, the rumor spread like wildfire along the skirmish line that the Indians were killing ("getting") their horses in the woods. And if the dead horses later found by Gibbon's men reflects an incident that occurred before Reno's stampede from the woods, then the "rumor" might have some substance.

During the Inquiry, all of the officers gave Reno credit for having issued all of the orders up to the halting and deployment of the line. But no one would say who gave the orders after the line was created. It seems to have hit a nerve when Prosecutor Lee asked who had issued the order for the withdrawal of the line from the valley floor. Suddenly no one knew who had ordered the abandonment of the valley floor position. For once, the witnesses were telling the truth; it appears that no one ordered the men from the line. Based on what was told to Walter Camp, and with a careful reading the verbatim record of the Inquiry, it is now apparent that the line collapsed on its own. It was the men that abandoned their position; military order had broken down. There are two reasons that the officers did not want to talk about it. One was that the Court would not have believed them; the second is that all of them, except Captain French, were now hiding in the woods. The next obvious question they wanted to avoid was why they were not on the line with their respective companies? The rumor that the Indians were getting at their horses and the exodus of Company A's alternate men into the woods to retrieve their reserve ammunition, were the reasons everyone just went into the woods. The officers were powerless to stop them, since most were not on the line anyway.

Captain French was not invited to appear at the Reno Court of Inquiry in Chicago! An irony of history was that on the very first day of the Inquiry convening on January 13, 1879, Captain French was also on trail in another military jurisdiction. He had been charged and convicted of "fraternizing" and drinking off duty with enlisted men. His sentence was to be dismissed by the U.S. Army. Apparently, the military courts were more interested in an officer's off-duty morals then in their competency under fire in combat. It makes one wonder if French's bogus conviction had any thing to do with his willingness to present very damaging testimony against Marcus. Reno?

After all, he was a good combat officer, as his role in the Valley Fight proves. And, his misbehavior with alcohol and fraternizing with the lowly ranks of the enlisted did not start overnight. After all, it was Captain French who said that he thought about shooting Reno at his Second Crossing. A common thought for a man who rose up through the ranks as an enlisted man during the Civil War. His proposal for putting a "stray" bullet into Reno was because for Reno's disastrous rout from the timber and losing half of his command!

The Rout from the Valley: By the time the Fourth Battalion fled the woods position they had very few causalities. Charles Woodruff, an officer with General Alfred Terry and Colonel Gibbon's rescue party, said that from what he saw Reno's retreat was nothing but a "horse race." The Fourth Battalion had gone into the Valley with 116 enlisted men and 137 government horses. Of these, fifty-eight horses of the Fourth Battalion would be killed, and another eight rendered unserviceable. Some of these horses were killed later on Reno Hill, but most had been killed in the timber. This was something that was suppressed by those involved in the Reno Valley Fight. The led horses were exposed to infiltrating sniper fire by their poor placement on the dry river channel bed, surrounded by heavy timber. Company G had the greatest losses of both men and horses, all them in the Valley Fight. Lieutenant Wallace reported that when he reached Reno's Hill, he had but three men from Company G!

Only sixty percent of the Fourth Battalion's enlisted men would arrive on the bluff with their commanding officer, Major Reno. Over twenty-five percent would never show up as they were left dead in the valley. Reno and his partner in crime, Myles Moylan, would lead their "charge" all the way across a river where there was no ford, and then arrive ahead of anyone else some 300 feet up what would later be referred to as "Reno Hill." He left behind three officers and thirty-two enlisted men in his flight from the Valley Fight. Also, three civilians and two Arikara Scouts were killed in the valley. Another seven men wounded men made it to his hill top retreat position.

During the siege which followed, another twelve enlisted men would be killed on his "Hill." But, Reno's worst legacy was his abandonment of Lieutenant McIntosh along with twenty some enlisted men, attached civilians and Scouts in the timber. They were simply abandoned when he decided to leave the woods without warning. At least the Court was able to bring out that there were no bugle calls issued when Reno left. Even more tragic were the deaths of a dozen or so dismounted men who tried in vain to catch up with their mounted company men. They ran out onto the valley floor after their quickly disappearing mounted comrades. These were the same men that Benteen and Godfrey observed from Gerard's Second Knoll. Warriors were riding through their ragged line on the valley floor and decimating them. Some of the valley fleeing men wisely decided to return to the safety of the woods. One of those was Lieutenant Charles DeRudio, who with another enlisted man would later rejoin Reno and Benteen on the hilltop two days later. However, within an hour of the retreat more then a dozen of abandoned men, most from Company G, would be able to climb the buffs on foot with the civilian guide George Herendeen. A few, like Sergeant Charles White, of Company M were walking wounded.

It was Private Daniel Newell of Company M who best summed up the retreat. He told Walter Camp that it was "every man for himself, and the Sioux took the hindmost. " He had been wounded in the thigh as he was mounting his horse in the woods. This proves that no defensive action was taken to provide a covering fire for the movement from the timber. Newell's horse was then hit on the way to the second crossing and hit again in the river. Then his mount was stuck again half way up the bluffs. At this point Private Newell abandoned his poor horse and made it on foot to the top where he found the rest of his company. He told Camp that he was the last man to cross the river during the retreat. He survived his wound, but he left the Army as soon as his five year enlistment was up in 1878. Many of the others who survived the Battle of the Little Bighorn did the same thing. But, Newell lived long enough to tell Walter Camp about his experience in the early 1900s. **BYU 439 (Newell)**

Reno's Drinking: Camp recorded in his notes that Reno was known to have been a hard drinker before and after the 1876 Sioux Campaign. And eventually he would be dismissed from the Army for raising a drunken row in 1880. Reno admitted in his testimony to drinking alcohol during the Battle of the Little Bighorn. Reno stated that that he only took a "sip" to wet his lips! Camp's informants thought otherwise. **M71**

Camp noted some of Reno's "peculiar" actions on June 25. They were trying to have Doctor Porter take his carbine, only to "lose" it along with his hat and revolver during his retreat out of the valley. Some wittiness said that he had emptied and then thrown his revolver away. Camp concluded that Reno had hastily retreated in disorder from the timber without communication to the whole command. More damning were the proven allegations that no effort was made to cover the retreat neither in the valley nor at the second crossing of the river. Particularly, as Camp stated, that there was no considerable body of Indians in pursuit!

After reaching the safety of the bluffs, Reno became cool enough to start firing his loaned revolver at Indians that were now a full three quarters of a mile away! Soon after this Reno would go back down to his second crossing, with a few men, to find Second Lieutenant Hodgson's body and to "get a drink of water," as Sergeant Ferdinand Culbertson, of Company A would later testify. Here, he remained for a full thirty to forty-five minutes away from his command, and ended up leaving Mister Hodgson's body. After all, how do you easily transport a dead body? Returning to his "Hill," Reno noticed that the Pack Train had now arrived, and he ordered Captain French to take a detail and shovels to go down and bury his Lieutenant's body.

Reno then recalled him almost as soon as he had started. It is now apparent that Reno was missing from about 4:00 to 4: 45 PM. French was recalled when the "command" (Benteen and Godfrey) started to leave to advance toward Custer's position. French's Company M then went with them. This aborted move was made at least one hour and fifteen minutes after they had arrived on Reno Hill.

Walter Camp's personal objection to the actions of the Reno Court was that it would not permit Doctor Henry Porter to testify as to the physical condition of Reno as he went into the fight in the valley. Reno's attorney objected to this line of questioning and the Court upheld the objection. This was but one of many of objections made by Reno's attorney, and the three member board upheld almost all of them. After all, Reno's deceased wife's family did supply him with a high powered "Philadelphia" lawyer. Camp wrote that Frederick Gerard told him that Reno was already intoxicated before he went into the valley. But Porter and Gerard were civilians; perhaps the U.S. Amy's reluctance to have civilians testifying against commissioned officers might have influenced the Court.

Walter Camp quoted another of his informants who said that Reno appeared to be "dazed in some manner." He described Reno as walking around in the timber and holding a cocked revolver in front of his face and he appeared not to be aware of what was going on around him. His unidentified informant was in the valley fight and he had observed Reno's behavior just before the retreat from the timber! Camp's informant said that Reno seemed to have displayed neither cowardice nor excitement. "It occurred to me at the time that Reno did not know what he was doing," Camp quoted his mystery informer.

Camp thought Reno's decision to leave the timber was an "error in judgment." He also surmised that it would be hard for the Court to judge what level of censorship Reno deserved, but his retreat from the Valley had been a great mistake. The sitting Board turned a blind eye to the most likely reason for Reno's strange behavior, his being drunk.

Prosecutor Jessie Lee told Camp that when the Court acquitted Reno of the specific charges of drunkenness and cowardliness, Colonel Wesley Merritt used the phrase that they had "dammed him with faint praise. " With his statement, one might conclude that it was not the military that had initiated these serious charges. After all, it was all of those trouble making civilians, Fred Gerard, Doctor Porter and Custer's unofficial biographer, Frederick Whittaker that started all those nasty post-battle rumors. In 1879, Whittaker, during the height of the Reno Court of Inquiry published a newspaper article in the *New York Sun*. In it he questioned not just the role of Reno, but also of Benteen at the Custer Battle. Whittaker was also the first to point out that Custer's former Civil War newspaper critic, General Wesley Merritt, was now in charge of the only official U.S. Army Inquiry into Custer's last fight.

Robert Price sent Benteen a copy of the scurrilous Whittaker article to his former Civil War commander. In his reply to Price, Benteen referred to Whitaker as a "Nigger" concerning his allegations against Benteen in the *Sun* article. Apparently Benteen's post-Civil War attitude was markedly different than that of his former commander, Armstrong Custer. **M37, pg. 325.**

One of Colonel W. A. Graham's retired army informants had told him that the conception of the Reno Inquiry was instigated by a well known U.S. Army General. This unnamed General wanted to squelch those defamatory rumors about the disaster along the Little Bighorn. Graham went on to describe this unnamed officer's headquarters as being "west of Washington, but east of St. Paul." Obviously, these Victorian-age euphemistic words referred to General Phillip Sheridan. The Chicago based Sheridan was "west" of Sherman, but still "east" of Custer's immediate commander, General Terry and his St. Paul headquarters.

If Sheridan hoped to exonerate his fair haired Custer, then it backfired. And if Philip Sheridan was behind the Reno Inquiry then the dainty footsteps of Elizabeth Custer were not far behind. Sheridan's 1865 gift of the Appomattox surrender table from the McLean house to Elizabeth Custer shines like the Holy Grail of the Custer Mystery. She outlived everyone and by the time of her death in 1933 much of the historical record of Reno's erratic behavior at the Custer Fight had been irretrievably lost. All except for the research collected by the Pennsylvanian, Walter Camp; only to be become lost again, but resurrected once more by this author who is also from Pennsylvania. Walter Camp was able to collect a large number of accounts of Reno's drinking from the surviving Custer Battle participants. Both his military and civilian sources told him that Reno had been drinking copious amounts of hard liquor before, during, and after the Valley Fight. That included three of the commissioned officers that had remained silent during the Inquiry. Two of them asked Camp not to publish their statements. Camp was never to publish any of his research material, but their statements were preserved for posterity so now we know the rest of the story.

As retired Captain R. G. Carter pointed out to Graham, it was Wesley Merritt who said that the witnesses at the Inquiry untruthfully testified to uphold the "honor of the Seventh U.S. Cavalry." Merritt was a well known critic of the Great Custer during the Civil War, but in 1879 he sat as the ranking officer on the Reno Board of Inquiry. **M37, pg 337; & M73, pg. 244-246 (Ovies)**

It is apparent that Reno had consumed enough alcohol to be considered drunk. He had started to drink at least twenty minutes before his action in the valley. That is enough time to be considered impaired in his judgment. And apparently he stayed that way for the next two days. But, it was Lieutenant Mathey and Captain McDougall who were willing to tell Walter Camp the full story behind Reno's odd behavior. Mathey said that when he had arrived with the packs, he thought that Reno was inebriated. McDougall also told Camp that as soon as he arrived he reported to Reno that the pack train was now up. Reno did not pay any attention as to what he was saying. He said that his only response was, "Bennie is lying down right over there," a reference to Second Lieutenant Benjamin Hodgson, who was killed at his second crossing. It was the half empty whiskey flask in Reno's hand that attracted McDougall's attention! As he later humorously told Camp, the fact that he was Irish and that he was very thirsty it made him mad that Reno did not offer him any of his whiskey.

And it was not just the military witnesses that saw Reno drinking. Starting earlier at the mouth of the Rosebud, J. M. Sipes, a civilian barber aboard the Far West steamer told Camp that on the evening of June 21 he saw Reno very drunk. This was when the civilian Sutler, J. W. Smith, was allowed to open his floating "whiskey saloon." One of the enlisted men described Smith's riverbank "bar" as being several wood planks laid across some barrels. The officers' section was sectioned off from the lowly enlisted side by a stack of whiskey cases. But it was all the same 180 proof variety of the Wild West "Rot Gut" garden variety of whiskey. **LILLY 606 (Sipes)**

While the enlisted men were limited to the amount of whiskey they could buy, the officers could buy all they wanted. Perhaps this was when Reno stocked up on his supply of quart size bottles? After all, it was going to be a long time before he would see Mr. Smith and his floating whiskey saloon again. But first he had to sample a few "sips, just to wet his lips." Peter Thompson, a Private from Company C, said that later that same night, Reno woke them up with his drunken "bellowing," when he entered their camp site long after the men went to sleep. **R4**

And it was not just the officers and civilians who observed Reno's drunkenness. Private Henry Lange assigned to his Company E's packs, on the day after the valley fight saw Major Reno staggering "drunk" among the packs. Another of Camp's enlisted informants had looked back from the mounted advance going down the valley and he saw Reno taking a drink from a quart "flask" and then passing it on to Mister Hodgson. The proper position for officers during such a maneuver was behind the line, and not in front like the all those Hollywood movies. Reno must have gotten the flask back, because soon after Frederick Gerard saw him drinking from it again, but now it was almost empty. **M40, pg. 150 (fn 3, Taylor)**

Even Reno's own personal orderly, Sergeant Edward Davern, was quoted as saying at the Court of Inquiry that Reno was already drunk while he was still in the timber! And there were the civilian packers, B. F. Churchill and John Frett. They testified in Chicago that they had both had seen Reno drunk on the evening of June 25. According to Fret's testimony, Reno had slapped him in the face and at the same time spilled whiskey on him from an open bottle that he was holding. Reno was staggering at the time, like a drunken man. Reno said that he was going to shoot him and he leveled a carbine at him, sounds like it was some of those damn civilians making trouble again.

Doctor H. R. Porter and Frederick Gerard were the original troublemakers responsible for the drunkenness "rumor" that resulted in the 1879 Court of Inquiry. But, there was another Seventh Cavalry commissioned officer willing to speak the truth. Lieutenant Charles DeRudio added his name to the growing list. He testified that he saw Reno "finish" a bottle at the skirmish line. This supports Gerard's statement made to Walter Camp. DeRudio thought that Reno was perhaps already intoxicated when he observed this incident. Frederick Benteen tried to discredit DeRudio's European nobility by calling him "The Count, of No Account." Of course, DeRudio's valid story of his escape from the French penal colony at Devils Island made him an unreliable witness? And there were others, such as Private Patrick Corcoran, of Company K. He had been wounded on the morning of June 26, and he saw Reno take a big drink out of a quart bottle of whiskey in the "hospital" area on Reno Hill, in broad daylight that same morning. **M40, pg. 150 (Corcoran)**

Marcus. Reno's military career speaks volumes as to his emotional instability. Even during his early days at West Point, he was set back for a year in his senior year for immaturity. He served in the regular Army as a lowly Lieutenant for the next four years, primarily in the Pacific Northwest. After the beginning of the Civil War he served with the Army of the Potomac as a Captain. However, that does not mean that he had command experience as a company commander. The Civil War was overstaffed with captains; often majors served as company commanders. After May of 1863, Reno was on extended sick leave for his only war "wound;" he had herniated himself by falling off his horse. Had his drinking problem started that early? **M84**

He went on extended recruiting duty while recovering from his "war wound." In July 1863, Reno joined a Pennsylvania volunteer regiment and he was dropped from the Regular U.S. Army rolls. There he served on staff duty and was assigned to non-combat duties for the next six months. But like a bad penny, Reno once again returned to the Regular Army for the next year with the U.S. Army Inspector General Office. Here he spent most of his time on recruiting and horse procurement duties. It was when he was assigned to Philadelphia that he met his future wife. In January 1865, through his wife's family influence, Reno purchased a Colonelcy in another Pennsylvania volunteer cavalry regiment. During the closing months of the War, he was engaged in Western Virginia in minor skirmishes as a regimental commander until a week before the surrender at Appomattox. He was "brevetted" as a Brigadier General of volunteers after the War, as were many other Civil War officers. The highest brevet rank that he held in the Regular Army was Lieutenant Colonel. This quaint military system of temporary brevet rank allowed him by Army ethics to be formally addressed as a "Colonel" during his post-war service. Similarly, both Benteen and Custer in 1876 were addressed as "Colonel" and "General" for their highest Regular Army brevets. But at least Benteen had earned his brevet rank the hard way, as a commander of a Missouri volunteer cavalry regiment for the duration of the War.

After the War, as with all other Regular Army officers, Reno was reduced in rank to a Captain. This was his highest regular rank that he had held during the War. Custer was also reduced to a Captaincy. But because of Custer's spectacular War career, he was later recommended to a full regimental Colonelcy, which he turned down when he refused to accept the command of an all black cavalry regiment, the newly formed Tenth Regiment. But Reno was offered the prestigious assignment as assistant instructor of Infantry tactics at the Military Academy at West Point. Reno soon requested another assignment when his wife would not live in the "hovel" assigned to him. His Philadelphia aristocratic wife convinced him that he deserved better than what the army was offering.

So he resigned from the assignment and turned the West Point instructorship offer down. This was not a good career promoting choice. The army complied by sending him to their southern form of "Siberia," the newly formed Freeman's Bureau in New Orleans. Here he was expected to transform former salves to being property owners of their former plantations. He did not stay here for very long either, and after six months he was put on leave and reassigned once again to the Inspector General Office. The Army just did not seem to know what to do with Reno! He just did not seem to fit in any of the assignments that they gave him.

However, Reno struck pay dirt when in December 1868 when he was promoted to the permanent rank of Major and assigned to the newly founded Seventh Regiment of Cavalry. Here he would serve on various duties in Reconstruction duty throughout the Southern States. But in 1876, both he and Benteen had to live under the shadow of the "Great Custer" of the Civil War, who was now the executive officer of the Seventh Regiment. Before the Little Bighorn, Reno had been assigned to railroad survey protection in Dakota Territory, but again his wife refused to live with him in any of those "rough" conditions.

Soon there was a major incident in Reno's dysfunctional life that occurred in the early 1870s. That was when his wife died unexpectedly in Philadelphia, and the army refused to grant him an emergency leave of absence to go to her funeral. Those that knew of his drinking problem said that it then became a lot worse. The irony of the Little Bighorn was that Reno had never served with the Regimental Staff until late November of 1875. That was when Reno was assigned to replace Custer who went on extended leave of absence in New York City during the harsh winter of 1875-76. After all, being a Colonel does have its privileges!

In the spring Custer did not return to the Regiment as expected. He had become embroiled in Washington, D.C., with the pending U.S. Congressional investigation into the illegal activities of President Grant's brother Orville Grant and General William Belknap who was Grant's Secretary of War. General Belknap was a Civil War crony of the General of the Army, William Sherman. The result was Custer's bogus "house arrest" by President Grant, leaving General Alfred Terry to be put in charge of the 1876 Sioux Campaign. The direct result of this fiasco was the disaster on the Little Bighorn, where Custer's most bitterest military enemies, Marcus Reno and Frederick Benteen, were now self assured by Grant's censure of Custer and that they would now be able to circumvent the Great Custer. In the late fall of 1875, Reno had assumed the duties as acting executive officer at Fort Abraham Lincoln for the next six months until Custer's return in mid-May of 1876. This is important to remember because during this time period, little or no daily mounted drill was carried out. This meant that a large number of raw recruits now being sent to the regiment never received the prescribed horsemanship training. The direct result was that some 100 men had to walk from Dakota Territory to the Powder River in Montana. This number amounted to almost fifteen percent of the original strength of the regiment.

When Custer returned to duty at Fort Abraham Lincoln in mid-May, he went after Reno for his failure to carry out this very important responsibility. Of course it did not make much difference to Custer that the entire northern mid-west had been under many feet of snow from the Great Blizzard of 1875-76. This was the historic winter that impacted the Great Plains for many months. It would have been impossible to perform daily mounted drill on a parade ground covered with four feet of frozen snow. But the snow did melt in the early spring and daily mounted drill was possible for at least a couple of months before the expedition started to Montana.

Custer's main concern, as a horseman, was that the regiment's horses were not now in the optimum physical condition for the proposed march to Montana. This was due to the lack of the normal routine of daily mounted drill. He laid the blame squarely on Reno's shoulders, and rightfully so.

Reno had busied himself with the logistics of preparing for the Grant Administration's mandated Sioux Campaign of 1876. He assigned all available men to warehouse and routine post duties and suspended the mounted drill. Peter Thompson gives us additional insight into Reno's executive abilities. Thompson tells of a "war" that developed between Reno and the newly assigned commander of Company C, Thomas W. Custer. It seems that Reno had it in for this unruly company that was now commanded by the brother of the Great Custer, whose nepotism had placed him there. Tom Custer was well known for his laid back military demeanor, but it was not wise to pick on the younger brother of your commanding officer. **R4, BYU 215 (Lange)**

In the late spring of 1876 Reno demonstrated his military pettiness while he was still in charge of the regiment. It seems that a large number of Sioux had been sighted gathering to the west on the Little Missouri River His immediate supercilious recommendation was that he would take the now assembled six companies of the Seventh and go out and whip the whole Sioux Nation! Nobody took him seriously and, with his regiment's preparedness in disarray, Reno's inane suggestion went nowhere. This was very much like another army officer named William Fetterman, who ten years earlier thought that he could take on the whole Sioux Nation with but eighty men. However, an up and coming Ogallala-Sioux war leader named Crazy Horse put a stop to that silly notion. Crazy Horse would also be at the Custer Fight in 1876.

In mid-June Reno incurred the wrath of his overall commanding officer, General Alfred Terry. On his Powder River reconnaissance patrol, Reno had violated Terry's orders. He had over marched his orders in miles and days. He also willfully disobeyed Terry's additional verbal orders not to cross over to the Rosebud River Valley. But he did just that! On June 15 Reno decided to take Mitch Bouyer's suggestion to take the pass over from Greenleaf Creek in hopes that they could catch up with some of the villages on the Rosebud. This little side trip of well over one hundred miles of extra marching cost Terry's methodical planning some five days. Another factor was the logistical nightmare of having to re-supply his six companies. On June 25, five of these companies would ride to their death with Custer, the same companies of Reno's over-marched Powder River Scout. **M39**

But what really aggravated Terry was his proposed abandonment of the Gatling gun assigned to him on the Powder River Scout. But when it fell into a ravine Reno ordered it to be left behind. However, the young Lieutenant in charge of the Battery refused to abandon it, and without Reno's permission, he went back with volunteers and ropes. By brute force they righted the heavy gun caisson, and got it back on the trail! Reno's ill-advised decision was duly reported to General Terry. One of the newspaper reporters wrote from the field that "Custer was going to go after Reno with a sharp stick!" But it was more likely that General Terry wanted Reno's military hide tacked onto his headquarters door. There can not be much doubt that if the Great Custer had not been killed a week later that Reno would have faced disciplinary action as promised by General Terry.

He was furious over Reno's blatant disobedience of his written and verbal orders. But it was Reno's damn poor excuse for using a civilian guide's recommendation for departing from Terry's expressed orders that most angered Custer. In the U.S. Army, there is an unwritten edict that civilians are always out of the loop when it comes to military operations. But it was Reno's immature decision to leave the Gatling gun behind that really torqued off General Terry. Now we are talking about some big bucks with the loss of very expensive government property. And right in the middle of your enemy's territory!

The Inquiry Board did criticize at least one aspect of the Reno Valley Fight. However, it was directed to the line sergeants of Reno's Battalion. The Board did not think that they had done enough to control the men's firing while on the skirmish line! Was not that the responsibility of the company officers who for the most part were hiding in the woods? **M71**

What ever mistakes Reno made at the Custer Battle, he did it to the best of his abilities, even if he may have been impaired by the copious amount of alcohol that he had consumed. It is possible that the whole Reno Court of Inquiry was nothing but a "smoke and mirrors" effort to cover up perhaps other allegations that may have been surfacing from a source other than the civilians? Perhaps rumors about another subordinate officer other then Major Reno? Frederick Whittaker, the self promoting and unauthorized biographer for the dead Custer thought so and he named Frederick Benteen in his newspaper article for his refusal to go to Custer's aid in a timely manner. The possibility of other orders that did not mention anything about the Pack Train looms large. Especially, if Walter Camp's informants are correct in seeing a number of messengers other then John Martin report to Benteen. And his response by having his horses unsaddled soon after reaching Reno's hilltop retreat position was also a telling point!

Reno was responsible for his own actions and the tactical errors that he made in the in the Valley. But, Benteen was insubordinate and derelict in his duty. On either charge he would have surely been convicted. Benteen said that he did not tell the Inquiry all he knew about the Battle. Was his "missing information" about the Pack Train or the other messengers sent from Custer's Headquarters Staff?

His fellow officers supported his trickery, primarily due to his heroic role after being asked to replace Reno as commander during the two day struggle for survival on Reno's Hill. Perhaps the reader will now understand why Godfrey opposed having either Reno or Benteen's name to appear on the proposed monument that now stands their besieged hilltop. No names appear on the monument now located there. The stage has now been set for additional judgmental "mistakes" made by the other officers on June 25 on the banks of the Little Bighorn.

1874
Frederick Benteen
Courtesy of the Little Bighorn
Battlefield National Monument

1876
Armstrong Custer
Courtesy of the Little Bighorn
Battlefield National Monument

Despite Benteen's graying hair, he was less then five and one half years senior of Custer's age in June 1876. Custer was then thirty-six.

CHAPTER THREE

THE BAD BLOOD BETWEEN BENTEEN AND CUSTER

Benteen's vindictiveness was very pronounced.
Lieutenant James M. Bell

Benteen's Relationship With Custer: Before we can fully understand the consequences of the disaster of the Custer Fight, we must look deeper into the role played by Frederick Benteen, especially to his claim that it was John Martin who delivered the "bring packs" message. Benteen's animosity towards Custer has been well documented. Perhaps it started with their very first meeting in 1866. It was during the army's obligatory official call to meet his new executive officer, Lieutenant Colonel Custer; when Benteen was assigned to the newly formed U.S. Seventh Regiment of Cavalry.

In his later writings, Benteen recalled finding Custer's "order book" blatantly displayed in the orderly room! It was full of praise of the Great Custer's spectacular Civil War record and military awards. With his own meager but hard won war record in mind, perhaps Benteen resented the "Great Custer" and his stunning Army of the Potomac record? After all, the Civil War military action in the West was highly overlooked by the eastern newspapers of that time.

Later in 1869, Custer became enraged when Benteen's "anonymous" letter was reprinted in the New York Times; one that Custer thought to be critical of his role in the Washita Battle. Custer, in a boastful manner, threatened to "horse whip" the miscreant who had written that scurrilous letter. But, much to Custer's great surprise, it was Benteen who stepped forward and announced that it was he who had written the offending letter. Supposedly, in Benteen's retelling of this incident he had unsnapped his holster just in case Custer had started to use the riding crop on him. Benteen's psychology suggests that in reality he was afraid of Custer, if indeed the holster event ever occurred? In his later personal letters, Benteen accused Custer of not only being a murderer, but also an adulterer. He accursed Custer of having being very loose with U.S. Government funds while in Texas on reconstruction duty. It was hearsay evidence, as Benteen never served under Custer in Texas. **M37, pg. 208 (Benteen's holster story), pg. 213 (Benteen's "Washita" letter)**

J. M. Bell was one of Walter Camp's Seventh Regimental officer informants who had served under Benteen. He said that Custer's Headquarters Staff considered Benteen as one of the poorest company officers in the Regiment.

At the mouth of the Rosebud River on June 21, at an informal officer's call, Benteen openly challenged Custer when he asked if the pending battle was going to another Washita affair. Custer responded by publicly chiding Benteen about the misgivings that he had over the killing of a young Indian boy at the Washita Battle. Apparently, Custer was bringing up Benteen's New York Times "Washita" letter again. Lieutenant Richard E. Thompson would later tell Walter Camp that the conversation "waxed hotly" and it was easy to see that Benteen hated Custer! **BYU 261**

The next day at the evening officers' call, Custer bought up the issue of a Seventh Regiment officer who had jumped the chain of command, and had lodged an official complaint against him to his commander, General Terry. Custer apparently suggested that "Lieutenants" where doing their jobs better than the "Captains." Benteen immediately took exception to Custer's reference to "Captains," and jumped to the conclusion that Custer was referring to him. He was not, and it may be now suggested that the "Lieutenant" in this case may have been none other then Lieutenant Edward Godfrey. After all, Godfrey did hold a grudge against Custer over his role in the Washita Fight. However, this little incident but three days before the Little Bighorn shows how much Benteen's paranoia of Custer had grown. He was known in the regiment as the "Old Grumbler". **LILLY 93-94**

Two days later, on June 24, on the march up the Rosebud, Lieutenant Mathey had to report to Benteen that Custer was very displeased with his Company H's performance with their company packs. Mathey said that Benteen did not take the news very well. On the day of the Battle, at the officers' call at the Divide, Benteen pulled his crowning scam on Custer. He put Custer on the spot by demanding since his company was always the first to carry out Custer's orders that he be given the lead down Ash Creek. Benteen just "knew" that his preparatory orders had already been carried out, and that his Company H was already prepared. Benteen was then reluctantly given the lead over the Divide, at least for a short time. Within the first quarter mile he was "reined" in by Custer, who complained that he was setting too fast of a pace. It is not nice to torque off your superior. When Benteen discovered that Captain Weir's company was assigned to his battalion, he requested that Weir be replaced with another company commander from the Right Wing.

When Benteen was sent off on his "Valley Hunting" he complained about not having a surgeon being sent with him. Sure does sound like grumbling does it not? Hugh Scott said years later that Benteen was positive that Custer had intended to keep him out of the pending action by sending off on his senseless "scouting" order. Benteen would later claim that he marched over ten miles on his "Left Scout." In reality it was less then six miles. He later greatly exaggerated the poor condition of the regiment's horses and criticized Custer's "forced" marches up the Rosebud. Conversely, of all the officers that Camp interviewed, all stated just the opposite.

The horses were in good condition. Even the civilian contract surgeon, Doctor Porter said that the regiment's horses were in very good shape. All agreed except Godfrey, who in 1867 had been considered by a U.S. Army review board as not being good cavalry material. The Rosebud Valley was noted for its superior grass for grazing animals. But it was Godfrey that best summed up Benteen's quirky behavior, when he passed him off as having an "artistic" nature. Godfrey may have been referring to the Washita Battle letter, rather then his art ability.

James M. Bell, who served under Benteen, gave the best summary of his mindset. Bell said that Benteen's weakness was his vindictiveness, which he said was very pronounced. According to Bell, Benteen was very indifferent to what he considered to be unimportant disciplinary matters in his company. Consequently his Company H always had the poorest rating in the Regiment. Bell also thought that, since Benteen had once been a Colonel of a full cavalry regimental during the Civil War he never took an interest in being just a mere Captain in the Seventh. On the same hand, Godfrey said the same thing about Custer, saying that he did not seem interested in being a mere Lieutenant Colonel rather than a Brigadier General. **LILLY 5**

W. B. Jordan, a civilian trader, said that it was well known the Benteen was a "horrible drunk," and that one time he went on a four-day drunken binge while arguing in the officers club. Benteen's military attitude can be best summed up with how his U.S. Army career ended. In the 1880s, Benteen was sent to Utah to supervise the construction of a government irrigation canal project on the Ute-Ouray Indian Reservation. He had been on extended drinking binges for the duration of his assignment. For this behavior, Major Benteen was charged with Dereliction of Duty by the commander of his regiment. A charge for which he would surly would have been convicted. Under the pressure of a certain conviction, Benteen was allowed to "honorably" resign from the U.S. Army. Co-authors, Barry Johnson and Bill Boyes have covered Benteen's downhill slide in their excellent article published in the Little Bighorn Associates Research Review article. **LILLY 667, also M6**

Bob Doran 2007

Sergeant-Major William Sharrow with a set of fours delivers his first order to Benteen at approximately 2:00 PM while on his Left Scout. Sharrow was sent from the South Fork of Ash (Reno) Creek after it was discovered that there were no villages camped there. This was Benteen's "valley" he was looking for, not the more distance Little Bighorn Valley. Sharrow may have delivered a second message while Benteen was still at his "watering" halt waiting for the Pack Train. Lt. Gibson's advanced detail can be seen in the right foreground.

CHAPTER FOUR

THE LEFT SCOUT TO RENO HILL AND BEYOND

Benteen came in and met Reno and unsaddled
Private John Hammon, Company H

Benteen's Route: Godfrey told Walter Camp that he and the other officers in Benteen's Battalion did not know that Reno had been given a separate command. Benteen was positive that his "scout" was a separate detail and a ruse by Custer to keep him out of the impending action! However on his "Left Scout" his overall rate of march of three and one-quarter miles per hour was a very respectful rate considering the terrain that he covered.

Benteen always claimed the he had been sent on a senseless "valley hunting" side trip. He also tried to convince everyone that it was the Little Bighorn Valley that he was hunting. But, is it not possible that the "valley' he was hunting was the closer South Fork of Ash Creek? Bouyer and his Crow scouts could have forewarned Custer of the major trail that ran up the South Fork. In fact, when the Big Flat warriors went after Crook on the Rosebud they used this trail to reach the Otter Creek pass. The additional fact that Benteen was twice ordered by first Chief Bugler Henry Voss and later by Sergeant Major William Sharrow to regulate his march indicates that he was not expected to remain very long his "Left Scout."

The military importance of the South Fork valley was that other villages could have been camped there, and that would leave them in Custer's rear as he advanced down Ash Creek proper. Benteen's battalion had been on the Left Scout for nearly two hours. Was Benteen ordered by Major-Sergeant Sharrow to return to the main Ash Creek? He reached the main trail by 2:10 PM. Benteen was now but fifty minutes behind the Custer battalions. But after another three and three quarter miles, his battalion had reached the Hartung Morass by 2:45 PM. The Yates, Keogh and the Reno battalions had crossed over this same point but forty-five minutes earlier. Benteen's was now closing the gap. His rate of march was now six and one half miles per hour that of a slow trot. This proves that Benteen was not "dawdling" up to this point in time.

When Benteen reached the Hartung Morass, he claimed that he just happened to decide to halt here to water his horses and allow his men to fill their canteens. There is adage among all good horsemen that when horses that have been ridden for some time and they were considered to be hot, that you do not water them upon halting. An hour after reaching the evening campsite was the army's normal time before the horses could be watered. This mandated cooling down was a regulated procedure. It is very doubtful that the men or the horses were interested in drinking the bitter tasting water in Ash Creek.

This non-horseman story has gone unchallenged for too long. Perhaps some of the horses may have sipped the alkaline and coal-tar flavored water, but there was no regulated watering halt, it just was not army protocol for this time of day. In retrospect, was this "watering halt" rationale just another of Benteen's absurdities? Is there another possible reason for Benteen's sudden halt here? Perhaps it was the arrival of another missing messenger with another one of those inane orders from Custer. And, if the order had been for Benteen to halt and to wait for the Packs, he might just as well go ahead and "water" his horses. This could have been an excuse to cover up his indignation for what he thought was but another one of Custer's attempt to keep him out of the fighting. However, an even more disturbing scenario emerges.

Did Benteen just say, the hell with Custer and remain at the Morass, despite earlier orders to advance quickly to Custer's front? And later additional orders carried by Sergeant Kanipe was they wanted Benteen *up there as quickly as he could*, according to what Daniel Kanipe told Walter Camp. Perhaps Benteen's watering halt was just a ruse to tell Custer what he could do with Custer's June 21 exposure about the Washita "Indian Boy" incident that must have been a horrible mortifying experience for Benteen, especially in front of his peers. Perhaps Benteen's vindictiveness and his horns were now beginning to grow? **(See CHAPTER THREE, pg. 102)**

To have officially watered his horses by the mandated army procedure, would have required dismounting and spreading the horses out along long lines at a "good" watering area. Today the narrow neck of the southern end of the Hartung Morass is not a good watering place, especially for that many horses. Even so, Benteen could have "watered" all of the horses in his entire battalion within the next ten minutes. But he stayed here for at least thirty minutes. The known rate of march for the Pack train tells us that!

Horsemanship, "Watering Call": By their primal nature as being preyed upon herbivores (grass eaters) horses have evolved to drink water but once a day. In their natural state they would gather around a "watering hole" at the same time of day to avoid predators. Here they would consume their required daily amount of water equal in weight on a ratio of the number of pounds of digestible vegetable matter (hay or grass) eaten in the same twenty-four hour period. When stabled in an army garrison a "Water Call" was performed each day at the same time. Horses thrive on routine. The horses would be led by platoons or squads to troughs filled from a deep well near the stables. The ratio of digestible matter to water can be as high as five to one in weight. If a horse had eaten twenty pounds of grass, he will need 100 pounds of water that amounts to about twelve gallons. Since water weighs just over eight pounds per gallon, a 1000 pound horse can drink as much as eight to sixteen gallons of water a day all at one time.

The Army had a regulated procedure for watering on a campaign. At least one hour after halting for a cooling down period, a small number of mounted men would take the linked company horses to a pre-selected place suitable for watering. Usually they were arranged in a wide front along a non-marshy stream. The curb bit bridle with its restricting chin strap was removed to prevent impeding water from going down their gullet. Then the so-called "watering bridle" with its snaffle bit would be slipped over the halter after the curb bit bridle had been previously removed by its rider. This was done so the mounted guard could still have control over the horses. The snaffle or "broken-bit" watering bridle with its own set of reins replaced the curb bit bridle. By nature, since a horse drinks only once a day, a horse can drink up to a pint of water per sip, and a full "watering" could amount to ten gallons. It would have taken less than five minutes to fully water the horses; that is, if they wanted to drink that much. Assuming that all of the battalion's horses were watered at the same time, then it should have taken Benteen far less than fifteen minutes for dismounting, watering, and mounting again.

There is no way for Benteen to have stretched a simple Watering Call into nearly a half an hour. Benteen was simply waiting for the Pack Train to arrive! Within at least the next ten minutes of his arrival and halting to water his horses, the unmistakable sounds of Reno's skirmish line in the valley resounded up Ash Creek by at least 2:55 PM This sound was to have a profound effect on Captain Weir, who was not aware of Custer's latest order to Benteen and he complained bitterly about the delay in leaving the so-called watering halt. According to Godfrey's guarded statement it was an "another" officer (Weir) that now questioned why was "the Old Man is keeping us here so long?" Weir confronted Benteen and told him that they "ought to be over there," at the sounds of the fighting! **M40, pg. 75. Godfrey.**

Within fifteen minutes of the sounds of fighting from the valley, Captain Weir mounted up his company, and without orders from his battalion commander left the Hartung Morass. However, Benteen would stay at least for another five minutes. This would be the nominal amount of time required to mount up and form into a column of fours again. But, when the head of the packs did arrive, Benteen quickly abandoned them to go play "catch-up" with his loose cannon, the unruly Captain Weir! Is this one of the "secrets" that Benteen bragged that he kept from the Reno Court of Inquiry? Or, was there a mutual agreement between Reno's attorney and certain officers that were involved with the incident?

When the head of the Packs arrived at 3:15 PM it forced Benteen to leave and make room for them along the trail. He had now been at the Morass for a minimum of thirty minutes, three times longer than the normal time needed to have watered his entire battalion. Was he now on a mission to rein in the unmanageable Captain Weir? After leaving the Hartung Morass,

Benteen within the next ten minutes would meet Sergeant Kanipe. Based on a seven mile per hour rate of march Benteen would have met Kanipe by 3:25 PM. This places Kanipe's interception near the junction of the North Fork trail that connects with Mathey's Knoll. This will soon become Custer's mandated "shortcut" for Benteen and the Pack Train. It is but one mile between the Hartung Morass and the turn-off to the North Fork crossing and the Big Flat trail that now turns south across the Echleman Fords.

Here the mystery concerning McDougall's later use of the Custer "shortcut" now widens. Daniel Kanipe was not requested to testify at the Court of Inquiry. But fortunately for the sake of history and generations of "Custer Buffs" to come, Walter Camp interviewed him in 1908. Not only was this an extensive interview, but Kanipe went with Camp to the Battlefield the very next year. During their Court of Inquiry testimony both McDougall, and Mathey vehemently denied receiving any orders from Custer at this point in time.

Is it possible that someone else communicated Custer's shortcut mandate to McDougall, someone like Frederick Benteen? After all, Martin did testify that he or someone else was sent back to McDougall. Is it possible that Martin was covering for another member of Company H who may have been the mystery fourth messenger? And did not Benteen tell Kanipe that he was not responsible for the packs? **M71, pg. 390**

Benteen's "Two Horns of a Dilemma": Upon reaching the North Fork trail junction, Benteen choose to continue to follow the distinct cavalry trail that now turned to the left. At this point, Benteen was now in strict disobedience to Custer's mandated shortcut order, the one that Sergeant Kanipe had just delivered. Crossing again to the left bank of Ash Creek at the Echleman Fords, the main travois then continues to follow the present county gravel road. However, Benteen continued to follow the distinct cavalry trail that now departed from the original Ash Creek trail. Soon Benteen would come to a major separation in the cavalry trail that he was following. About one mile from Kanipe's interception he would arrive at what he would latter refer to as being his "Two Horns of a Dilemma ".

Unknown to Benteen was that the left hand trail had been created an hour earlier by Reno, and just now by Captain Weir's missing Company D. Custer had taken the right hand northward bound trail. This pronounced trail would soon lead to Martin's "Marshy Place" crossing of Lower Ash Creek. How do we know that Reno had taken this trail that intersected with the main Ash Creek trail near the Echleman Fords? In 1919 Hugh Scott and Colonel Tim McCoy, later an early cowboy movie star, traveled to the Battlefield together. Four of the original Crow scouts that were with Custer now guided them over the environs. In Scott's description of this trip, as recorded in Graham's *The Custer Myth*, one of the Crows pointed out the trail that Reno had taken to reach the river. He said that it went by the "Spear Camp" sheep sheds! **M17, pg. 17**

At the turn of the century, the Speer Ranch was a vast holding, with their headquarters located on the Rosebud. Those traveling south on Montana State Highway 314, toward the site of the June 17, 1876 Rosebud Battlefield State Park, will pass by the old Speer Victorian mansion located on the right side of Highway 314, some ten miles south of Busby, Montana. In the 1980s, Hank Weibert showed this author where the original Speer Ranch sheep sheds had been located on lower Ash Creek. These early spring birthing sheds for the ewes were common before cattle became the major livestock by the turn of the Twentieth Century. Sheep ranching was prevalent in Southeastern Montana before cattle ranching. These sheds were located along a major trail and were torn down by the Weibert family. The trail could still be seen in the 1930s before it was plowed under for a wheat field.

Benteen, reaching his "Two Horns of a Dilemma" in the trail, continues to follow the heavier right hand cavalry trail. This shows that he was heading to the bluffs where he had been ordered to advance without the Pack Train. Benteen claims he did not know whom it was that had taken the left hand trail; the one that would lead to Reno's first crossing. Benteen was now following the trail of the so-called Custer Squadrons, the First and Second Battalions. But is it possible that he did know whose trail he was following? John Burkman, Custer's former personal orderly, was with the Pack Train. From a point just west of the South Fork fords, at the first rise east of the present Fellows Ranch, he could see army units marching over what is now called Benteen and Reno Hill. This was about the same time that Benteen's battalion had just arrived at his watering halt. Burkman could see the Gray Horse Company assigned to Yate's Second Battalion. Did Benteen have the same sighting of Custer's men now silhouetted on the bluffs?

Within the next 100 yards past his "Two Horns" separation point, Benteen's battalion minus Weir's Company D, started to pass by Gerard's Second Knoll. It was then that they head the distinct sounds of a rolling gun fight coming toward them from the Valley. Forming into a single rank and drawing their revolvers, the men of Company H and K were ready for whatever action seemed to be in front of them. From Gerard's pronounced high ground, Godfrey said that they could see an army unit fleeing in disorder in the valley. He said that they could see them through a "gap in the trees. " It was from Gerard's Second Knoll that Benteen and Godfrey now halted their mounted skirmish lines and continued to observe the very end of the Reno retreat from the valley. The distance was less then two miles. **LILLY 609**

What is not well understood is that the vegetation seen today in Southeastern Montana is not what it was in the late 1800s. The trampling and selective browsing of the large herds of buffalo, elk, antelope and white-tail deer prevented the growth of unwanted brush and the proliferation of larger trees. Since the introduction of modern farming non-indigenous plant species soon changed the landscape to a large degree. As many of the historical photographs taken soon after the Custer Battle proves that there were far fewer cottonwood and other softwood trees then today along the Little Bighorn River.

The elevation and prominence of Gerard's Second Knoll allowed for a good view of the area where Reno would flee from the valley floor. Actually, some of Reno's men reported that at this time they could see a group of mounted men on high ground near the mouth of Ash Creek. It was of course Benteen's two companies now aligned in a line along Gerard's Second knoll.

While Benteen and Godfrey were observing the tail end of Reno's retreat, the sudden appearance of Wier's missing company made their presence known to them. Weir had gone to Reno's first crossing, less then one quarter mile below Gerard's Second Knoll. And now, without even a hello or a goodbye, Weir's company flew by its battalion commander. They were now headed northward. Weir had also observed the army's retreat from the valley, now headed toward the bluffs to the north. After all, Weir was doing what any good fighting officer would do; he was hurrying the sounds of the fighting of his comrades. Ticked off by Weir's arrogant action, Benteen now took off with his orderly, perusing the disappearing company, and leaving Gibson and Godfrey behind with their now reforming companies. Making a wild dash to get ahead of Weir, Benteen reined up in front of Weir, as much to say do not do that again. After all, Benteen must have felt that the Custer sycophant was thumbing his nose at him, again. And, it was not the first time that Weir had disrespected his battalion commander. Only twenty minutes earlier at the Morass, Weir had mounted and left with his company without permission. He had reached the river at least five minutes ahead of Gibson and Godfrey's companies. In a fit of bravado, Benteen now raced to get ahead of Captain Weir, as if to show him who was the boss. All of this action took place above and below Martin's Marshy Place crossing on Lower Ash Creek. The time now was 3:30 PM.

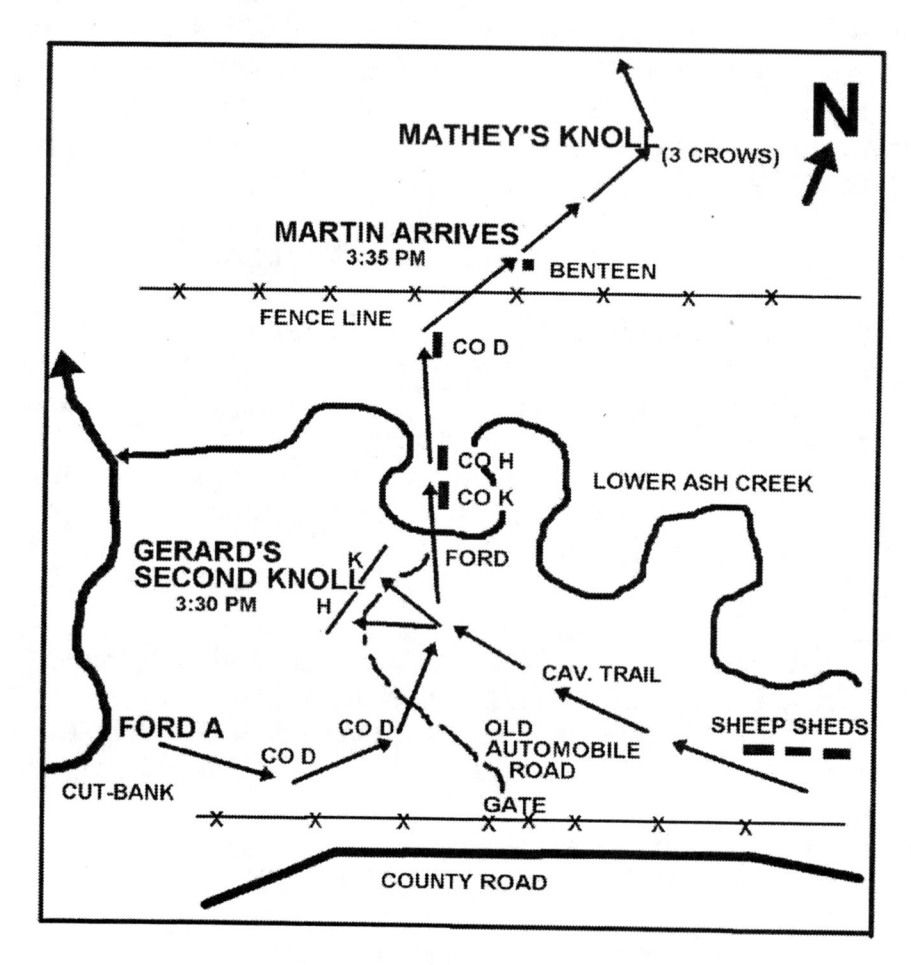

THE WEIR AND BENTEEN INCIDENT
NOT TO SCALE

Weir was insubordinate with his battalion commander at least four times on June 25. This incident was the second time that his Company D went flying by Benteen leaving him in the dust. Benteen and his orderly ran him down and within moments of John Martin arrival that defused the show down. Weir was a well known Custer sycophant and the two would have to be separated later in the campaign by General Terry. Both were sent on recruiting duty, the army's equivalent of being sent to Siberia. We know that this little incident happened, as Benteen later bragged about it at the 1879 Court of Inquiry. Red flags should have gone up at this point and it might have raised a few eyebrows; but the sitting members of the Board did not asked a single question about this braggadocio tale of Benteen's ego. Benteen even claimed that now he was some four or five hundred yards ahead of Captain Weir when his Bugler, John Martin arrived. As battalion commander, he was expected to be somewhat in the advance, but not over a quarter of a mile ahead!

The Court consisted of three members, of which two were members of the Mounted Service, and they never challenged this typical Benteen exaggeration. In fact not a single member of the sitting board ever challenged Benteen on any of his absurdities. Was this just another of Benteen's embroidery on his contrived role in the battle? Or was his message simply to say that all of his problems were being caused by that Custer-lover, Thomas Weir!

The Myth is Born: As the now reinstated battalion commander, Benteen was riding well in advance of Weir's company. Due to their deployment as mounted skirmishers, his other two companies were still in the distant rear. This "horsemanship" fact is pointed out so the reader will soon detect the deception of the pro-Benteen officer's in their contemporary letter writings and their later testimony at the Reno Inquiry of their versions of what occurred next.

At a point about one quarter mile below Mathey's Knoll, John Martin arrived with his written order. According to Martin, after Benteen had read his message, he placed it into his pocket. But later Edgerly and Gibson, in their later testimony and letter writings, would claim to have been shown Martin's written message at the time of its arrival. This somewhat implies that a halt occurred which we know did not happen. But at least Benteen would have had halted, as Edgerly said that when his Company D reached Benteen, both he and Captain Weir were shown Martin's newly arrived order. Remember, Benteen said that he was four or five hundred yards ahead of Weir's company?

Even Lieutenant Gibson, the titular Commander of Company H, which had been far in the rear of Company D, now gets into the act. He too claimed to have seen the Martin message when it arrived! It was when he caught up with Benteen's advanced position, even though his company had been well in the rear. It sounds like it was getting pretty crowded around Benteen at this time. All these little stories sound kind of rehearsed. The problem is that they may have never happened!

The question to ask is how did Lieutenant Gibson ever get to see Martin's message if his Company H had been at more than one quarter mile in the rear? What did Benteen do, ride back along the ranks until he got to his First Lieutenant just to let him see the note? Most likely Benteen's exaggerated testimony was nothing but a smokescreen. Some thirty-five years later, Edgerly was still able to quote Benteen as saying at this time, "Well, if he (Custer) wants me in a hurry, how does he expect that I can bring the packs? I think that I had better not to wait for the packs." If there was any truth in this attributed statement, then one can see Benteen's pronounced hatred for Custer. However, all of these contrived scenarios may have occurred long after Benteen reached Reno's retreat position. If so, was Benteen passing around Martin's message just to underline his doubt of Custer's managerial ability to issue logical orders?

Just as J. M. Bell said, Benteen's vindictiveness was very pronounced. But Benteen had already made the decision "not (to) wait for the packs," over twenty-five minutes earlier when he had left them behind at the morass.

Reno Hill: Benteen claims that it was the presence of the three Crow Scouts on Mathey's

Knoll that now caused him to advance to the soon to be hill top position of Reno's beleaguered battalion. That is doubtful, since the rampaging Captain Weir now had the bit between his teeth; Benteen was simply following his equally ranked, but subordinate battalion officer. A very embarrassing leadership position to be in! **M40, pg. 76 (Godfrey)**

Continuing to follow the Custer trail over the Second Ridge, Benteen's Battalion soon reached Reno's retreat position. More or less, both commands arrived at about the same time. Some of Reno's men said that Benteen's men were already there as they struggled up the steep bluffs. The time was now 3:50 PM. When Benteen arrived, an enlisted man said that he saw a fishing net (seine) hanging from Benteen's saddle. He thought that Benteen had been fishing, but we know that he was now on another kind of "fishing" expedition.

Within twenty to thirty minutes of his arrival on Reno Hill, Benteen's next horsemanship action gives us a good clue as to his real motivation concerning Custer's order to "Come on, Be Quick!" He simply had his horses unsaddled! **BYU 444 & 463**

This was as much as saying that he was not planning on going any further. Or, was he just waiting for the Packs again? According to Edgerly's testimony, as soon as Company D arrived Captain Weir had his men dismounted and formed into a skirmish line. However, we do not know if Godfrey followed suit, but most likely he also dismounted his men. But why did Benteen later order the saddles to be removed? Was it the appearance of the "Packs" now arriving on Reno Hill? Benteen's ordering the saddles to be taken off from at least his own Company H gives us greater insight into his motives. It is an established practice among all good horsemen not to remove saddles from horses that have been ridden for period of time, as they will have a hot back. Not if you are planning to ride them again within the next thirty minutes or so.

Horsemanship: The reason for leaving the saddle on is to give the horse a "cooling down" period. If the saddles are removed too quickly, the horses will develop "heat bumps." These are normal blister-like swellings that expand in the lose skin along the back. While heat bumps are not debilitating, you cannot replace the saddle and ride again, until they have dissipated. The weight of a rider can cause the saddle to quickly rub raw the heat bumps into a festering open sore. Severe galling, or "saddle sores," will then occur, placing the animal out of service. However, if the saddle is left on for at least twenty to thirty minutes, the back will cool down, and then the horse can be ridden at any time.

If a breach of this good "horse sense" occurs and severe galling is the result, the animal is then put out of service for weeks, perhaps months, until these saddle sores are healed properly. During the time that the sore is open, an internal bacterial infection can developed into a fistula, causing a slow death. This cooling down was an established U.S. Army protocol and no experienced cavalry officer would even think about saddling up again until the heat blisters had time enough to dissipate the fluid-build up after the cooling down period.

Benteen's True Motives: If Benteen had his saddles removed soon after arriving, then it proves that he was not planning to have his men mount up and begin to ride again at least within a half hour. Having his saddles removed means two things, one that he had already been on Reno Hill for thirty minutes and the other is that Benteen was not planning to travel any farther. However, it is interesting to note that the end of this decent cooling down period would be about the same the time that the Pack Train arrived on Reno Hill. Perhaps, he thought that he fulfilled his Pack Train order, an order delivered one hour and forty minutes earlier at the Morass. The same order that Benteen tried to convince the Court of Inquiry to believe that John Martin had carried. Is this why he had Martin to commit perjury? **(See Chapter Five, pg 143)**

Within minutes of Benteen's arrival on Reno Hill, two heavy volleys were heard from Custer's advanced position. Additional heavy volleying for the next twenty minutes would soon follow. About the same time that Benteen decided to unsaddle his horses the head of the Pack Train was arriving. Lieutenant Mathey reported that they had heard heavy volleying when the packs had been halted on the Big Flat. The time of arrival of the Pack train on Reno Hill was at 4:20 PM, according to Godfrey's field diary entry. **C8**

By using the known rate of march of the Pack Train, its arrival on Reno Hill at Godfery's stated time is very accurate. Years later, Colonel Graham would try to convince Godfrey that his field diary entry was wrong. Graham placed the arrival of the packs at a much later time. His time distortion is not a realistic calculation, as the entire Pack Train would have to have many more halts than is known. Four legged livestock cannot travel any slower than their normal walking pace, so Graham's time reconstruction is flawed. He never traveled to the Montana battlefield to make a on the ground evaluation of the terrain. Evidentially, Graham may have been a good desk jockey, but he sure was not an experienced horseman.

A more appropriate "Benteenism" is found in Camp's interview with Private Isaac Fowler, of Company C, who had been with his company packs. He quoted Benteen as saying, "If Custer with his companies *cannot take care of the Indians*, what we can do to help him out *with the Pack Train* on our hand?" (Italics by author) Fowler said that this remark occurred at the time that heavy volleying was being heard from the *north*. Since Fowler was with his company packs on June 25, it had to be after their arrival by 4:30 PM. If Benteen in fact did make this remark is he now using the packs as an excuse for not going to Custer's relief? Did he not tell Kanipe earlier that he was not in charge of the Pack Train?

The "Weird" Weir Point Episode: Just before the Packs arrived, Weir jumped ship again, now for the third time. It happened within fifteen minutes of his arrival on Reno Hill, when he and Company D just disappeared again. Soon after heavier volleying was heard from the north, Captain Weir asked Lieutenant Edgerly to covertly leave with the company. According to the traditional Court of Inquiry version, this occurred after an altercation between Weir and *Reno*. Weir had supposedly asked Major Reno for permission to go forward to the sounds of Custer's fighting.

Why would he be asking Reno; was not that the prerogative of his battalion commander, Frederick Benteen? Just because Reno held higher rank does not mean he had command authority over any of Benteen's company commanders. The sitting board never challenged this touchy question! The question to ask is why? Military regulations are quite clear in this matter; unless there had been a restructuring of the command authority, Captain Weir was still under Benteen's command.

The answer to this perplexing conundrum was that the so-called "argument" was not between Weir and *Reno* at all. According to some of Camp's informants, the debate was between Weir and *Benteen* and no one else! It was all about Benteen's reluctance to go forward to the obvious sounds of Custer's fighting. There is no mention for Reno of being involved. In fact, when this event occurred at approximately 4:10 PM, Reno may not have even been on the bluffs. Some time soon after Benteen's arrival Reno had gone back down to his second crossing with a small detail looking for Mister Hodgon's body. The false concept of Reno being involved in a "blow up" with Weir was nothing more then a smoke screen contrived by some of the officers that wanted to protect Benteen.

Having covertly pre-warned his Company D subordinate, Lieutenant Edgerly, Captain Weir now rode off to the *north* with just his orderly. Apparently he was following Custer's distinct cavalry trail that had gone over Sharpshooter's Ridge. Dutifully, Edgerly mounted up the company and for a short distance followed the Custer trail, but he soon turned to his right and within minutes was out of sight. This is what his annotation on Walter Camp's blueprint map shows. Sometime after Company D had left, Benteen started asking as to where they had gone. Not knowing where one third of your command is hardly a sign of an observant commanding officer. That damn Weir had done it again!

It was at least twenty minutes after Company D left that Benteen started to inquire about his missing company. That was about the same time that the Pack Train was now arriving on Reno Hill. Was Benteen planning to go forward with the packs and he needed all of his battalion company commanders? The answer is no, because of the above horsemanship factor concerning the unsaddling of horses that have been ridden and had "hot backs". Benteen now ordered the saddles to be removed from at least his Company H horses. This proves that he was not planning to go any further forward.

According to Edgerly's annotated Camp blueprint map, he had taken Company D to the southeast base of Sharpshooter's Ridge some 300 yards *north* of Reno's retreat position. However, he soon turned to the right and went down into what geographically can be described as the "South" Medicine Tail drainage.

Weir simply continued to follow the Custer Trail over the Sharpshooter's Ridge complex until he reached the additional high ground that Walter Camp would refer to as "Weir's Hill." According to Camp's field note description, this location is on the northern end of the Sharpshooter's Ridge 100 yards north of the present National Park Service north boundary fence line of the Reno-Benteen Battle Site. Camp's "Weir's Hill" is not to be confused with the present site designated today as Weir Point. However, Company D would soon travel there.
LILLY 120

This was the first high place where Weir and Edgerly halted briefly to observe fighting far off to the *north*. Edgerly, with Company D, had paralleled Sharpshooter's Ridge some 750 yards farther to the *east* for at least one half mile. From his higher ground, Weir saw warriors coming up Medicine Tail Coulee and he signaled Edgerly to seek his higher ground. Edgerly did so in a very unorthodox military manner. He simply had the company circle clock-wise and cross over their trail! Was it not only the enlisted men who were poorly horse trained, but also some their officers? Or was this another symptom of how poorly the men were trained? Perhaps it was easier for Edgerly just to have his men execute this lackadaisical method, rather the prescribed army way. Reaching Weir's higher position, together they now traveled west, crossing over the shallow head of Cedar Gorge, and by following the bluffs they arrived at newer high ground now called Weir Point. The time of their arrival here was about 4:30 PM.

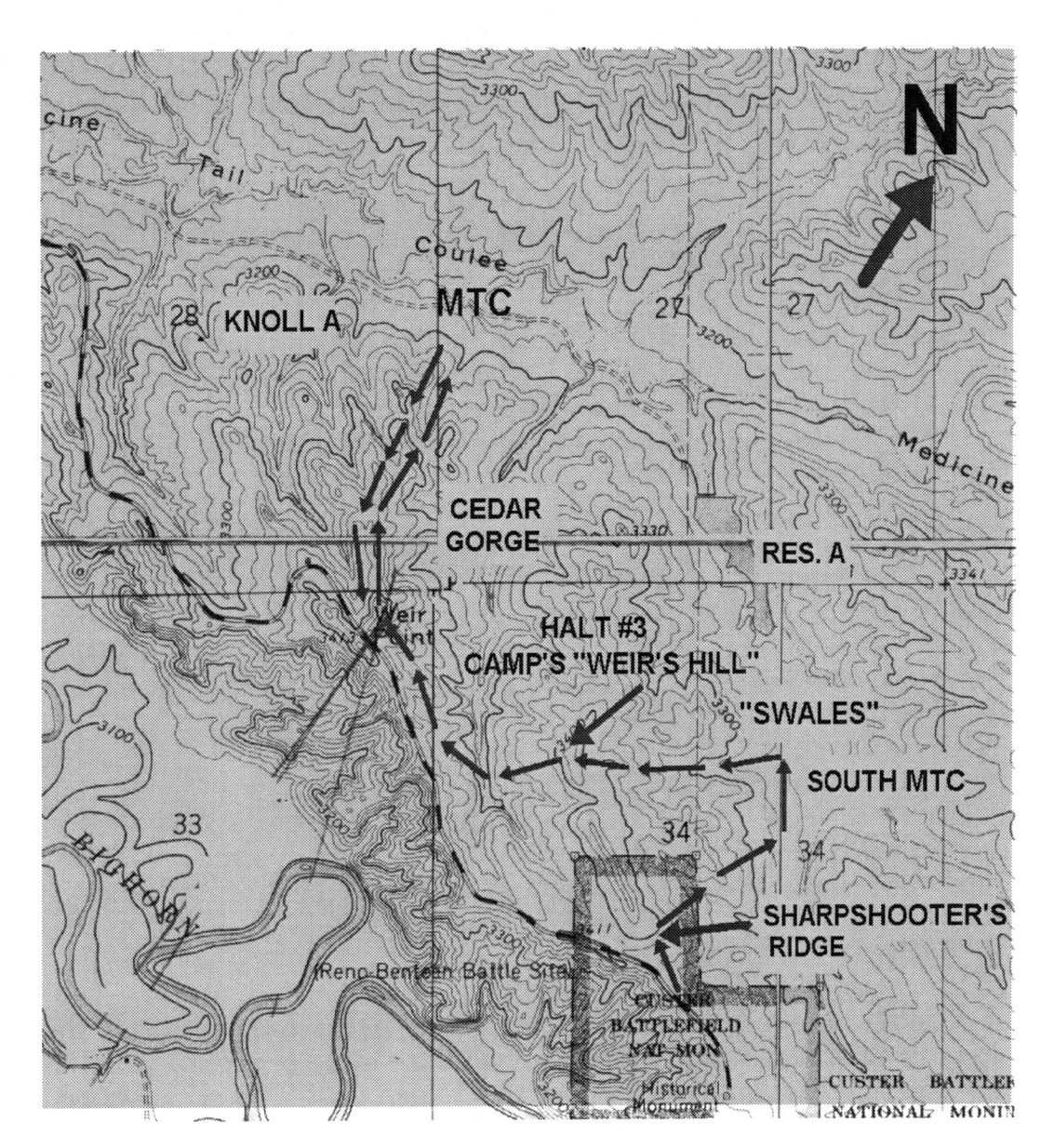

EDGERLY WITH COMPANY D

SCALE: ------------- 1/4 MILE

When Lt. Edgerly left Reno Hill with Company D he soon turned right into South Medicine Tail Coulee (MTC) drainage. He was signaled to by Captain Weir to join him on his high ground Walter Camp identified this high ground as being his "Weir's Hill."

In the Reno Court National Archives record Edgerly stated that he passed by some "swills," sic, swales. **(See EDGERLY WITH COMPANY D, pg. 115)** He and Captain Weir observed the early fighting on the Custer Field from Camp's "Weir's Hill" at 4:20 PM when the men on Calhoun Hill were being forced to flee to the Keogh area. From Camp's "Weir's Hill", Company D cut across the head of Cedar Gorge and reached the present Weir Point area by 4:30 PM. Edgerly with Company D may have then traveled as far as Medicine Tail Coulee **(MTC)** proper. Upon Company D's return to Weir Point they fled in haste along with Captain Weir to Reno's retreat position were the Pack Train was still located. Soon after, Benteen and his group would also retreat to Reno Hill arriving by 5:30 PM. Godfrey's sighting of the inrush of warriors on Custer Hill which marked the end of the fighting on the Custer Battlefield.

The Weir Point Episode: Here Company D formed a mounted skirmish line and for a period of time they just sat observing the fighting on Custer Field. This unauthorized "reconnoitering" was something that was suppressed at the Inquiry. The question is why?

From this point Edgerly may have taken Company D farther ahead and perhaps as far as Medicine Tail Coulee. Again, Captain Weir stayed on the high ground. When Walter Camp interviewed Company D's First Sergeant, Michael Martin, he strongly inferred that his company traveled far beyond the high ground where Captain Weir remained. Sergeant Martin mentioned of going past a "sugar loaf" looking knoll. This may have been Knoll A, near the First Battalion's Fourth Halt in Medicine Tail Coulee. **See pg. 115**

This distinctive conical knoll is easily accessible from Weir Point by a long ridge that leads northward from Weir Point. If so, Company D may have come very close to the First Battalion's halt in Medicine Tail. Apparently, Captain Weir continued to stay on his higher observation point. Walter Camp ambiguously refers to Weir Peak and Edgerly's Peaks (plural) as being separate entities. Perhaps the twin knolls that can be seen about a quarter mile northeast of the Weir Point ridge may be his "Edgerly Peaks."

Camp was well aware that Edgerly with Company D had gone much further than what is called Weir Point today while Captain Weir stayed behind. When Camp first visited the area in 1903, no one knew where "Weir's Point" was located. Camp already had a good deal of knowledge from reading the Reno Court of Inquiry verbatim record housed at his hometown Chicago library. The majority of the proceedings had been published daily in the Chicago newspapers on a daily basis in 1879.

Edgerly vehemently denied that either he or Weir ever saw Custer's trail during this unauthorized reconnoitering. But Weir would be soon deceased before the year was out, so how could Edgerly speak for a dead man? Perhaps Edgerly's denial was due to the fact that if he admitted having followed Custer's trail the Court might have asked why he did not continue to follow it to Custer's aid. It is the same pattern of denial that Edgerly would later use to convince William Graham that he had never met Walter Camp! **(See CHAPTER FIVE, pg. 144)**

At some point in time, Edgerly and Company D would soon return to Weir's higher position in a very big hurry. And, then together, Captain Weir with Company D would again fly past their battalion commander, Benteen now for the fourth time! Weir's First Sergeant Martin describes how they arrived in a very undignified military fashion back at Weir's high ground. Of course, by now Benteen, Godfrey and French had arrived with their companies. First Sergeant Martin said that while they were at their advanced position, the warriors in a "gully" **(MTC)** had approached them in ever increasing numbers. Sergeant Martin threw his reins over his neck in order to deploy his weapon. He said they then just "rode like "Blazes" (Hell) to get out of there." Perhaps, it was also the sergeants that were not well horse trained. Company D would now stampede along with its company commander from the present Weir Point area and back to Reno's hilltop position. Benteen and the rest would soon follow! **Camp's interview with Sergeant Thomas W. Harrison, Company D, supplied to author by Bruce Liddic.**

Logically, Edgerly's forward advance probably occurred during the same twenty minute period spent by Benteen's group traveling on its way to the present Weir Point area. Now, with Captain Weir's rapid exit from his high point, they all fled back to Major Reno's hilltop position, the one that Reno had never left. Along the way, Company D lost acting Lance Corporal Vincent Charley who was shot through the hip and blatantly abandoned along the cavalry trail on the bluffs. Edgerly promised him that he would return and rescue him. However, no one would rescue him. Out of the 140 some enlisted men and six commissioned officers that fled Weir Point, none bothered to attend to the plight of the poor Corporal. Was this heartless action just another sign of the continuing breakdown of military order, just like Reno's rout from the valley? After all, the men were just following their fearless leaders.

Mister Hare's Role: Second Lieutenant (Mister) Luther Hare was Godfrey's Company K subordinate officer. However, on the day of the Custer Fight, he was assigned to the Indian Scouts, along with Lieutenant Varnum. But after retreating with Major Reno to the bluffs he soon rejoined Company K, which was part of Benteen's battalion. Within minutes of Benteen's arrival, Mister Hare would be sent back to find the Pack Train and to expedite the arrival of reserve ammunition as soon as possible. Hare's assignment to Benteen's battalion strongly infers that it was Benteen that ordered him back

Mister Hare was able to make his two and half mile round trip in twenty minutes, having met Lieutenant Mathey on his land mark knoll by 4:10 PM. He would testify that on his return he reported to "Major *Reno*," giving the Court the false impression that it was Major Reno who had ordered him back to the Pack Train. However, we know that Major Reno was not even on his Hill at the time. He was down at his Second Crossing still looking for Bennie Hodgson's body and to drink some "water" according to Sergeant Culbertson's testimony.

However, within fifteen minutes of Hare's return, Benteen's missing Company D was now silhouetted on the horizon of the present Weir Point area. And no one could have failed to see them. Supposedly it was Major *Reno* who ordered Mister Hare to go forward to Weir's unauthorized advanced position and, according to Hare, to "open communication" with General Custer.

It is strange that Benteen would use the same wording as his excuse for going forward to Weir Point, some thirty minutes later. But as the author suspect, this statement is just another one of Benteen's many distortions of the truth. But, Mister Hare actually never said that it was *Reno* who ordered him, only that he reported to him after returning from his quick trip to the Pack Train. Was it possible that the very same officer that had ordered Hare back to the packs was the very same one that now sent him to retrieve Weir and that was his battalion commander, Frederick Benteen? This deliberate vagueness was perhaps one of the singular biggest deceptions perpetrated on the Court of "Iniquity. " The poor Mister Hare dutifully went, but after a long period of time he started back alone, most likely with a glum face. Weir's response to Benteen's obvious request of an immediate return was probably not printable in the Inquiry's record. So, if Weir would not return, than Benteen would have to go to Weir! In 1910, Hare would tell Walter Camp that he did not issue any orders when he reached Captain Weir's advance position, at least not to the angry Captain Weir, who would have eaten the green Second Lieutenant alive, who had just graduated from West Point in 1874.

All that Hare would testify to was that he was told to have Weir open "communication" with Custer. This is a bizarre statement even if one believes all of the other fairy tales told at the

Inquiry. However, it was Walter Camp's consensus following his interviews that Weir was ordered by Benteen to return to Reno Hill. If you substitute Reno's name with Benteen, every time Reno's name is evoked in the record, than you will start to understand what was going on. Everybody knew that by then *Reno* was out of the loop as far as being able to command anyone. And Benteen's obvious attitude was, the Hell with Custer! **M40, pg. 64 (Hare)**

As Captain McDougall would tell Camp, when he first arrived on Reno Hill, nothing but confusion existed. Ask yourself; was it Reno that sent Hare to retrieve Benteen's wayward officer? Most likely it was Benteen. About the same time that Hare was dutifully riding out to Weir, something happened on Reno Hill that caused Benteen to have a change of heart. He now decided to go forward and "communicate" with Custer! Was not what he was ordered to do at least an hour and half earlier?. It was now past 4:45 PM. Reaching Captain Weir's advanced position, Hare now found him alone, as Edgerly with Company D was now well to the north. After a period of time, perhaps as much as thirty minutes, Mister Hare would leave Weir to return to Benteen, who was still on Reno Hill. But, just a short distance from Reno Hill, he would meet the "command" now on its way to Weir's advanced position. Hare's use of the word "command" is but another one of those euphemisms that are so prevalent in the Inquiry testimonies.

We know today that Hare's "command" was Benteen now on his way forward. Hare does not ever seem to have reported back to Reno at this time. Especially, if one examines his evasive responses to Prosecutor Lee's searching questions. Mister Hare never says exactly where it was that he found Reno. The mystery is solved when one understands that Hare never reached Reno Hill. He simply joined the now advancing "command" (Benteen) and returned to Weir's advanced position with Benteen. And just where was Reno? Why he was still on his "Hill," as he had never left his place of refuge. Perhaps he just did not want to leave the Pack Train and his private stash of Mr. Smith's floating saloon whiskey bottles.

All of the officer's tried to make the Inquiry Board believe that it was Major Reno who was in charge of Hare's "command" now marching to Captain Weir's advanced position and to open "communication" with Custer! As Dr. Charles Kuhlman expressed it in his classic *Legend Into History*; if you believe all of the rhetoric in the Court of Inquiry one can almost hear the regimental band playing as Major Reno marches to Weir Point!

This mystery was cleared up when Camp's informants explained that Major Reno had never left his retreat position in the first place. The second clue is that all of them considered Reno incapable of commanding anyone at his point in time. He had stayed behind with the small remnant of Company G, Company A and the Pack Train. His only known military activity was to have the buglers insistently blow the "recall" command after Benteen left. Some time after the last of the pack mules arrived by 4:30 PM. Benteen suddenly ordered his horses to be saddled up again. Within the next thirty minutes, Benteen would start forward in an abortive attempt to "communicate" with Custer. Something that he was supposed to have done two hours earlier! **M49**

Lieutenant Mathey said that it was at least thirty minutes after they arrived before the packs were started again. They traveled but a quarter of a mile before returning once again to Reno's hilltop position. That places the time of Benteen's departure as 4:50 to 5:00 PM. B. F. Churchill, the civilian packer, said that the original two boxes of ammunition which he and Fred Mann had rushed forward were unpacked, but they were never opened. He said that they had to repack them again "minutes later" when the Pack Train was ordered forward again. Again, exactly who it was that ordered them forward has never been discovered. We know that it was not Major Reno! **M71, pg. 468 (Churchill) & pg. 515 (Mathey)**

It is doubtful that the Pack Train traveled very far. Obviously, the whole "Weird Point" episode was orchestrated by Benteen, and not by any of Reno's motivation. But the question must be asked: why did Benteen now go forward to Weir's advanced position? After all, it was Weir who had gone out on his own hook. Edgerly was also to tell Camp that Weir later confessed to him that he had not even asked permission from either Reno or Benteen. He just went out on his own hook, just like Major Elliot at the Washita.

Was there an incident that may have occurred that caused Benteen to make a shabby attempt to carry out his previous mandates, which was to expedite the Pack Train or to "Come on, Be quick," depending on which version one prefers. There may have been such an event if we are to believe another of Walter Camp's fragmented notes. In another of his disjointed memos was the story that another messenger from Custer had arrived on Reno Hill, after Benteen had arrived. And it was not Bugler John Martin!

Camp's suggestion of yet another messenger arriving on Reno Hill comes from Sergeant Richard ("Dick") Hanley of Company C, through Private James Wilber of Company M. Wilber had arrived on Reno Hill with the rest of the survivors of the Valley Fight. Hanley arrived with his companies packs. Hanley said that a man from Company "C" had left Custer and had arrived *after* John Martin. The Medal of Honor winner Hanley was a reliable source for Camp. It had to have been after 4:30 PM, when the Hanley/Wilber incident occurred.

As we suspect, it was most likely it was Corporal Eldon French of company C that delivered Benteen's third message at 2:45 PM, the one that ordered him and wait for the Pack Train. Corporal French is officially listed as being Killed In Action (K.I.A.). It has been assumed that he died on the Custer Battlefield, as there are no suggestions that he was killed on Reno Hill. There were fourteen survivors from Company C and they have all been accounted for in the roster studies. Is it possible that yet another messenger arrived on Reno Hill having been sent direct from the Custer Battlefield? The answer may be yes if we look at another of Camp's antidotal stories. In another one of his unpublished notes, Camp simply states that a rumor circulated on Reno Hill that "Calhoun had been wounded." If this story started before the exodus of Benteen and his colleagues, this antidotal story might be worth investigating. How could anyone on Reno Hill have known that Calhoun, an officer with the Custer Battalions, had been wounded? It is possible that this army "scuttlebutt" may have been started with the arrival of another messenger from Custer, as suggested by the Hanley/Wilber rumor? **(SEE CHAPTER FIVE, pg. 127, THE PIVOTAL THIRD ORDER)**

Something had to have motivated Benteen for him to start making the appearance that he was carrying out at least one of his three "Custer" orders that he had received within the past two hours? What other kind of incident could have motivated Benteen enough to make him move northward? The arrival of yet another messenger could have been enough motivation. Did Sergeant Hanley's mystery messenger from "Company C" arrive while Benteen was still on Reno Hill? The sudden fear of a Court Martial conviction for overt insubordination may have been the major factor for Benteen's sudden departure from Reno Hill?

And it was Captain Weir that could have initiated those charges. After all, the "fear factor" of a living Captain Weir was very valid. That is until early July when Weir was forced to leave the campaign. Tradition has it that that his leaving was due to an undisclosed "illness," However, Weir was still at Fort Abraham Lincoln in September, as the Post Returns show. He was at Fort Lincoln until October 1, and he was acting as post commander from September 19 to 26.

Where had Benteen been all this time? Why he was in St. Louis on recruiting duty. It appears the Benteen had been asked to leave General Terry's reorganized campaign by early August. According to the Fort Abraham Lincoln Post Returns, we know that Captain Thomas Weir left there on October 1, enroute to St. Louis "to relive one Captain Benteen from Recruiting Service in that city." However, less then six months after the Custer disaster Weir would die in New York City. There is a long standing tradition in the U.S. Army that when a commanding officer is dissatisfied with a subordinate, he is transferred to the army's equivalent of Siberia. In this case recruiting duty in St Louis! Perhaps General Terry was trying to keep the warring Weir and Benteen separated and out of his reorganized expedition?

When General Terry arrived on Reno Hill on June 27, and announced that the rest of the Seventh now lay dead some four miles north of Reno's Hill. Benteen challenged Terry's startling statement and was supposed to have said that he did not believe it, that he thought that Custer was just picketing his horses somewhere, and that he had probably taken off like he did at the Washita Fight. It is that "Washita" thing again!

Terry immediately and curtly ordered Benteen to personally take a detail and go identify the newly discovered dead, especially the body of Benteen's archenemy, the Great Custer! Benteen did not seem to know when to keep his mouth shut in front of his superiors. Benteen has been quoted, that upon finding Custer's body, as saying, "Well, there he is, he won't fight anymore". One can almost see him kicking dirt on the body of the Dead Lion.

The question that must be asked is why the rumor of yet another Custer messenger did not spread like wildfire? After all, Walter Camp did interview some thirty enlisted men known to have been at the Little Bighorn Battle. Four of these men were from Company H. They were Jacob Adams, John Martin, Henry Mecklin and George Glenn (a.k.a. Glease). Adams was with the Pack Train, and Martin's role is too close to the subject. Mecklin arrived on Reno Hill with Benteen and later had an extensive interview with Camp. But, Glenn was discharged in 1877 as a deserter. Was he forced to desert because of what he knew about another messenger? Only one informant, Richard Hanley, out of nearly seventy interviews is not a compelling argument for the rumor that Calhoun was wounded. However, when there is smoke there is a fire. And Benteen could have squelched that fire very quickly when he retuned to Fort Rice in October, from St. Louis, where he had been on recruiting duty. Was this when John Martin replaced Custer's other messengers?

Benteen discovered as early as July just how important his Custer "battle relic" might play in the future, perhaps in saving his military buttocks from a Court-Martial roasting. Otherwise, why on July 4, did he write his wife telling her that the "last lines Cooke ever wrote," were to be preserved as the "matter (investigation) may of interest hereafter (later), likewise of use (evidence)." At the Reno Inquiry two and a half years later, Benteen would enter as evidence his "Martin" order. The Court did not keep the original order as an exhibit, but it was entered into the official transcript, in Benteen's verbatim wording. Soon after this Benteen did not seem to have any further use of it, so he just gave it away! **See CHAPTER FIVE, pg. 137.**

His "closed mouth" testimony and the "secrets" that he withheld seemed to have protected him from military repercussions. Lieutenant Godfrey, a retired Brigadier General in 1922, protested having either Reno or Benteen's name placed on the monument that was later erected at the hilltop defensive site. Perhaps by then his enthusiasm might have waned for his former battalion commander, Frederick Benteen? The U.S. Army was and still is a tight knit group! Certainly by 1888 Godfrey knew of both Reno's and Benteen's ignoble exit from their nearly thirty year tours of military service. But the most important factor at the Inquiry was the respect that Benteen had won from his fellow officers and enlisted men alike for his leadership during the hilltop siege on June 25-27. This may have saved Benteen's reputation for the time but twelve years later his bad habit of alcohol abuse and dereliction of duty would force him forever out of the U.S. Army. After all, did Benteen not say that he did not tell all that he knew at the Court of Inquiry?

Bob Doran 2007

WHAT MARTIN SAW

Martin said that he saw Custer's entire command retreating from the river. What he was seeing was the passage of Company F and L as they continued to advance over the south slope of the Nye-Cartwright Ridge. Due to the terrain, he could not see Company E that had already been dismounted to counter the attack of the Young Warriors on the Second Battalion flanks and rear. (See pg. 168-170)

CHAPTER FIVE

MARTIN'S TRUE ORDER

They want you up there as quick as you can get there (*Be Quick*). The have struck a big Indian camp (*Big Villages*) **(See pg. 130)**
Sergeant Daniel Kanipe, his verbal message to Captain Benteen

Then Captain Benteen took the dispatch, read it, and put it into his pocket, and gave me an order to take to Captain McDougall to bring up the pack train and keep it well up.
John Martin's perjury at the Reno Court of Inquiry

The Fourth Halt: It would have been about the time of Bouyer's arrival in upper Medicine Tail that the "Custer" Squadrons were once again halted. This was now the fourth time since the Battalion Formation Halt near the divide. The major factor for this unexpected halt may have been Bouyer's news of additional villages further downstream, now partly visible to Custer from his Medicine Tail position. The so-called "Custer Battalions" had been in a double pincer (envelopment) attack on the Upper Camps, the very same encampment that Reno was now attacking. The sound of his skirmishing had been heard for the past fifteen minutes, but now it was quite, too quite! At this new halt the sounds of Reno's skirmishing had ceased, by now the men had fled into the woods position where all effective fighting stopped.

A hurried discussion now ensued between Custer and Adjutant Cooke who then wrote out a message and handed it to John Martin. It was to be taken to Captain Frederick Benteen, the reserve battalion commander. As the Camp material makes quite clear, this may have been the sixth order sent to Benteen. The content of one of these known messages would later become an icon of the Custer Fight. But, more important, what was the military strategy that prompted Martin's written communication? At this point in the chain of events the Benteen/Martin's historical version of what was to happen has no military rationale. It is contradictorily in nature. Benteen is now being told to "be quick, "but at the same time to wait for the Pack Train. History researchers in the past have never challenged this enigmatic icon. **See Facsimile A, pg. 48**

There was already a large escort assigned to the Packs. A total of over 110 company "packers" along with Captain McDougall's Company B, as an escort, now numbered some 160 men, which equaled twenty-five percent of Custer's entire military force. No matter how many men Custer ordered to hurry up the Pack Train, the heavily loaded pack mules could not travel any faster. Forty minutes earlier, from Mathey's Knoll, Custer knew where the Pack Train was located. It would take the "Packs" a minimum of another hour and forty-five minutes just to reach the Medicine Tail/Martin dispatch point. There are two major reasons to believe that Martin did not carry the Historic "Pack Train" message as it is historically written. They are:

1. What if the Packs were delayed and became exposed to an attack from the flanks and rear? The "Martin" message, as worded reveals has no strategic military planning by Custer at the time it was supposed to have been written. Custer had just become aware of additional villages downstream!

2. An order had already been previous sent that countermanded any future Pack Train expediting order, which is the expressed intent of the historic Martin order. Sergeant Daniel Kanipe had carried this over-looked order some twenty-five minutes earlier. **(See pg. 129)**

At the established marching rate of three and one half miles per hour of the Pack Train, it would take far too long for it to reach even the Medicine Tail Coulee halt. The Pack Train would not be able to arrive there until nearly 5:00 PM. When Martin was sent back at 3:10 PM, the Pack Train was still five and one half miles on Custer's back-trail. His apparent new Double Envelopment plan of attack the Onion Creek encampments in the valley were dependent on a quick attack on what he may have thought to be a series of very small villages. Even if only the "ammo" mules were sent they would not have arrived any quicker than the entire Pack Train. The sorting out the nearly two dozen ammunition mules would have been a logistical nightmare. The result would have added many minutes before they could be sent forward. Only one non-commissioned officer had been assigned to each of the company packs. Where would the supervisory personnel come from for the now separate company pack details? Common Enlisted men are just never turned loose; the army always has a supervisor over them!

When Martin arrived at Benteen's position by 3:35 PM, Custer was now attempting to cross at Ford B and attack the Onion Creek camps. Within the next few minutes, heavy firing and later long term skirmishing from Custer's position was clearly heard on Reno Hill for over an hour after Benteen's arrival by 3:50 PM. When Benteen returned to the main trail on upper Ash Creek at 2:10 PM, Reno's battalion had just been sent forward to pursue Gerard's Fleeing Village. The First and Second Battalion were soon to divert from Reno's trail and cross at Lower Ash Creek at Martin's "Marshy Place. " Custer was now committed to a pincer movement on the upstream encampment just reported by Lieutenant Varnum.

In 1879, when Lieutenant Lee questioned Benteen about his delay in carrying out Custer's mandate, Benteen, realizing the trap being set by the Prosecutor, interjected this evasive reply, "I wish to say before that order reached me that I believe that General Custer and his whole command were (already) dead." Was this typical Benteen absurdity his real mental state on June 25, or his irrational guilt confession, one that he had developed by the time of his appearance in Chicago? **M71, pg. 430.**

Benteen was now less then four miles on the back-trail. By Custer's orders, Benteen had been ordered off of his "Left Scout" and returned to the main trail. By the faster rate of march that he would start to use, he would reach the 2:00 PM Custer/Reno (Hartung Morass) crossing of Middle Ash Creek within the next thirty minutes. Had he already received an order to hurry up? But during the next thirty minutes Benteen would remain motionless at what would become his "Morass". We now need to look at Custer's original Battle Plan, the one that he first created when he first saw the Hunkpapa village from Mathey's Knoll at 2:30 PM.

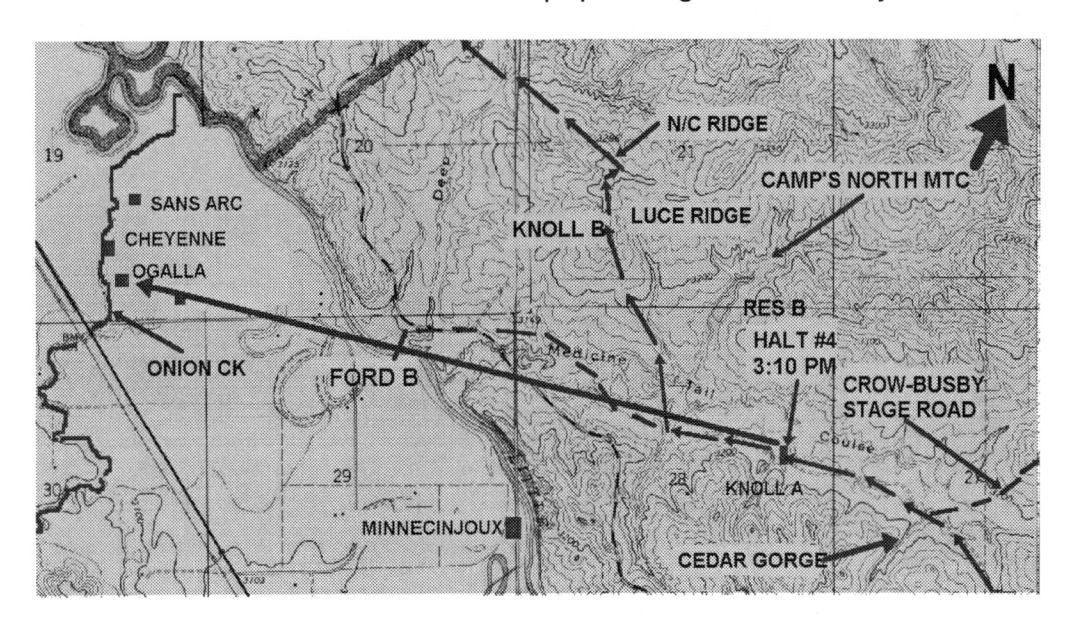

WHAT CUSTER SAW AT 3:10 PM

When Bouyer arrived with the news of additional villages downstream, Custer again halted the two battalions at 3:10 PM. The Second Battalion will now be sent northward.

SCALE: -------- 1/4 MILE

The problem with these new villages on Onion Creek was that they were well within supporting distance of their upstream neighbors. If Custer needed anything, it was not the entire Pack Train or ammo mules. What he needed now was additional reinforcements, such as Benteen's reserve battalion, and as quickly as possible.

The Three Military Options: When Custer was on Mathey's Knoll, he had three viable military options available to him. In the order of the most military importance they were:

1. Custer could order Benteen's reserve battalion to escort the entire Pack Train to a more protected position on the bluffs.

2. Custer could order Benteen's battalion alone into the Valley, as reinforcement to support Reno's attack on the upstream side of the village.

3. Custer could order Benteen forward to support his pincer movement on the exposed downstream side of Varnum's village, leavening the Pack Train to fend on its own.

What Custer did next proves that he selected the first option, to have Benteen bring the "Packs" to a more secure defensive position on the bluffs. At this point in the Battle, this was the most viable military scenario. It was from Mathey's Knoll that Custer now sent the first of several directives to Benteen defining his role in the pending battle. It would now be the third order sent to Benteen's since the halt near the Divide. This order would remain a mystery until one of the many fragmentary notes of Walter Camp gives us insight into to the enigma of Benteen's "dawdling" at his Morass. To fully understand the full military situation at the halt in Medicine Tail Coulee, we must consider an earlier incident that occurred when Custer first saw the upper villages from Mathey's Knoll.

Another Staff Messenger Is Sent to Benteen: A very important clue is found in the Camp Collection at Brigham Young University. Camp noted to himself that a high-ranking non-commissioned officer, from the Headquarters Staff, had been seen delivering an order to Benteen while he was still at his "Morass." Could this have been the regiment's Sergeant-Major, the highest ranking NCO in the regiment? Sergeant-Major William Henry Sharrow's special chevron markings would make him stand out to any enlisted man that might have seen him at or near Benteen's Morass.

If this "rumor" is true, then this "missing" messenger could have delivered another new order to Benteen, and what was the content of this order? Could this new order hold an explanation of Benteen's erratic behavior and his refusal to march to the sounds of battle only minutes after his arrival at the 2:00 PM/Hartung Morass? **(See Bibliography. BYU Uninventoried Note No. 1, pg 227)**

The first occasion that Custer had to observe Benteen battalion's and its relationship with the Pack Train was when he arrived on Mathey's Knoll by 2:30 PM. At that time, Benteen's battalion was just ten minutes from entering the Custer/Reno 2:00 PM Hartung crossing of the Lower Ash Creek. At the same time, the head of the Pack Train was now crossing the South Fork fords, but one and one half mile and thirty minutes behind Benteen. If a messenger had been sent from Mathey's Knoll by 2:30 PM, he could have reached Benteen as early as 2:45 PM. It is but two miles to the Hartung Morass, where we suspect Benteen had halted to "water" his horses. We need to look closer at the role that Frederick Benteen may have played in the "bring packs" historic message. This author suspects that Benteen's actions was being controlled by his detested commander, Armstrong Custer. Benteen left us with the perception that he decided to halt and water his horses just might not be quite true?

Was there another possible reason for his halting at this time? After all, it should have taken only ten to fifteen minutes to water his entire battalion, not the thirty minutes that he stayed at his "Morass." And we now know that his horses were never watered. Is it possible that Benteen was ordered to halt and wait for the Pack Train?

Was it possible that a crucial battle order was delivered to Benteen by the regiments' top ranking non-commissioned officer at this point in time and what was the content of this order?

If additional messengers had been sent before Kanipe and Martin, then what was the military motive for this order? Was it possible that Benteen was officially ordered to halt and wait for the Pack Train by an even earlier messenger, one that we do not know about? Another mystery messenger, so to speak? Camp's high placed NCO could have countermanded the previous messenger sent from Mathey's Knoll, the first one that ordered him to halt and wait for the Pack Train. After all, we have only Benteen's word that it was John Martin that carried the latter famous "bring packs, PS bring pacs", one that Benteen said was "Custer's Last Message".

The Pivotal Third Order: If a messenger was sent from Mathey's Knoll, as we suspect, was it Sergeant-Major Sharrow who delivered it? No, not if we look at his earlier dispatch assignments. Sharrow was sent by 1:45 PM from the junction of Upper Ash Creek and its South Fork. This was the second known order to be sent to Benteen and Sharrow had arrived by 2:00 PM. Was this just another one of those little "Custer" burrs under Benteen's saddle? The distance that Sharrow would be required to ride back to the main trail, and then play catch up with the more rapidly advancing Headquarters Staff would not have allowed him to have quite enough time to reach Mathey's Knoll just to be sent back to Benteen again. Someone else from the Headquarters Staff would have to be sent. But can we identify that messenger?

Thanks again to Peter Thompson we now know the probable name of this mystery messenger. Thompson tells of an incident that occurred before the regiment reached the Powder River. And the incident concerns an enlisted man named "French" who was the blunt of Custer's peculiar habits. We can now identify him, as there was but one enlisted man in the entire regiment that was surnamed French. He was Corporal (Henry) Eldon French and interestingly enough he was also from Company C, and Thompson knew him well as they were both from the same company. He referred to him as the "Poor French," because Custer ill-treated him. Custer's nickname in the regiment was "Iron Ass" Custer, due to his ability to ride long and hard hours in the saddle. He expected others to be able to keep up with him on his many "wild" rides!

According to Peter Thompson, on one late afternoon search for a good camp site for the regiment, Custer had sent Corporal French to find a good watering spot. When the "Poor French" reported back that he had not found a suitable watering spot, Custer called him a lair and accused him of not going to where he had sent him because he was lazy. Not only was Custer psychologically abusive to his men, but he rode his horses and orderlies to their exhaustion, or perhaps even to their deaths, depending on how one looks at the result of the soon to come disaster at the Battle of the Little Bighorn? **R4**

Corporal French's Role: The third messenger could have been Peter Thomson's "Poor French", Corporal Eldon French, of Company C. If he had been on Custer's Staff in mid-June, was still assigned on June 25, perhaps he was the same enlisted man that John Martin passed on this way back to Benteen? The man from Company C whose face Martin knew but not his name. The one who asked Martin where the Headquarters Staff was; and Martin had advised him to fall back to the Packs. Corporal Eldon French is officially listed as having been killed on June 25 with his company. **M40, pg. 104 (See text pg. 128)**

If we are correct in assuming a third messenger was now sent to Benteen from Mathey's Knoll, to order Benteen to halt and wait for the Pack Train, then is it not possible that yet another countermanding order would again be sent soon after Mathey's Knoll? The answer is yes, if we believe in the statement made by another of Camp's informant officers. And, that was the statement from Hugh Scott that Custer had the reputation for issuing an order, and to turn around with an almost immediate change of the order.

Not to become embroiled in Custer's personality, but it seems that among some of his officers he had reputation of being just a little bit quirky. He did exhibit the "normal" West Point academy trait of the belief in group punishment for the misconduct of one individual. He also had a bad habit of disrespecting some of his men. Hugh Scott said that Custer was well known for his one and only known vice and that was gambling! While stationed at Fort Lincoln, Scott was told that Custer seemed to enjoy taking gambling money from newly assigned Lieutenants, or force them to write him an IOU. Of course, there is no evidence that Custer ever called up his debts from his green Lieutenants. In one of his letters to Theodore Goldin, Benteen somewhat bitterly mentioned having to pay back one of his debts that he owed Custer. Was this one of Custer's personal traits that would come back to haunt him on the banks of the Little Bighorn? **LILLY 824, The Benteen/Goldin letters, BYU Mss 1130.**

The Fourth Order: Sergeant-Major Sharrow was also most likely not the fourth messenger now sent back to Benteen. He had just managed to catch up with Custer's Staff on or about area know today as "Benteen Hill" on the N.P.S. Reno-Benteen Defensive site. The rumor of a high placed non-commissioned officer being seen delivering an order to Benteen while he was still at his morass infers strongly that it was Sharrow. However, If Custer did send this fourth order to Benteen at this time, and then he would have to been sent from a point beyond Mathey's Knoll. From the heights of the present Benteen Hill area, Custer was now able to observe more of the Blackfoot and Minneconjou Sioux encampments located downstream from Varnum's Hunkpapa village. Perhaps from here Benteen was now counter-manned to abandoned the Pack Train and now advance forward without the burden of the slow moving packs?

On or near the area known toady as Benteen Hill, Custer may have changed his mind about the Pack Train movement. Is it possible that he now sent another Headquarters Staff member back to Benteen? Custer may have countermanded Corporal French's previous order sent just ten minutes earlier from Mathey's Knoll?

Benteen would now be directed to no longer wait for the Pack Train. Was this the reason the Benteen was to tell Sergeant Kanipe in the next fifteen minutes that he was not in charge of the Pack Train? This scenario would also account for the rumor of a non-commissioned officer at Benteen's watering halt at the time of the Pack Train's arrival. Remember that at the army then considered a Corporal to also be a non-commissioned officer. Can this mystery messenger be identified?

Corporal Alexander Bishop: John Martin said that a man named "Bishop," had also been assigned to Custer's Staff, on June 25, the day of the Battle. Unfortunately for us, there were two enlisted men surnamed "Bishop" in the Seventh Regiment and they were both assigned to Benteen's Company H. And, they were both known to have survived the Battle. If one of them had been with John Martin on Custer's Staff, how is it that both of the Bishops' survival be explained? On June 30, they were both at the camp near the mouth of the Bighorn for the quarterly Pay Muster. This was but the second payroll muster of the year. No enlisted men are ever going to miss his pay muster. And it is that Benteen thing again; both Bishops were members of his Company H. Benteen had promoted Alexander Bishop to Corporal just before they left Dakota Territory in May. Peter Thompson said that a man named "Bishop" was Custer's personal orderly by the time they reached the Powder River. **R4, pg. 10a**

However, on the evening of June 25, Alexander Bishop received a life threatening wound in the right arm during the fighting on Reno Hill. He was transported on the Steamer Far West on July 2, to the regimental hospital at Fort Lincoln. He remained there until August 12 when he was sent onto to Fort Rice for recuperation where his Company H was posted. During the time that he was at Forts Lincoln and Rice the balance of his company was still in the field as part of General Terry's reorganized campaign. However, his company commander, Frederick Benteen was not with them! By August, Benteen was given permission to leave the expedition. Only General Terry could have authorized that absence. Company H arrived back at Fort Lincoln on September 27 without its commander. By early October they reached Fort Rice some sixty miles downstream on the Missouri River.

By October 29, 1876, the now Sergeant Alexander Bishop was discharged for a medical disability. Benteen had arrived back at Fort Rice after mid-October. There was an overlap of less then a two week period during which Bishop could have been promoted to Sergeant before his discharge. Obviously, it was Benteen who elevated Bishop's rank as only a company commander can do so. And just where had Benteen been during all this time after he left Terry's field campaign and before he mysteriously shows up again at Fort Rice? Why he was in St. Louis on recruiting duty! Was this General Terry's way of separating him from Captain Weir? That answer is forthcoming when we look deeper at the mystery of the two Bishops. Is it possible that with the discharge of Alexander Bishop, soon after the return of his company comrades, that Benteen may have been able suppressed any stories of his role as an additional messenger from Custer? The four men from Company H that Camp contacted never mentioned anything about either of the Bishops in their company. History is not known for coincidents, but the two Bishops seem to have been proverbial twins!

The regiment's other Bishop was Private Charles Bishop. Both Alexander and Charles had been recruited in New Orleans on the same day, and by the same officer, Frederick Benteen. Ironically, Charles was also wounded in the right arm on the same day as Alexander. Both would be taken together down the Missouri River on the steamboat *Far West*. However, Charles Bishop would soon recover and was discharged honorably at the end of his five year enlistment. Both men were still alive at age seventy-seven in 1927. Unfortunately, Camp never contacted either of the Bishops.

The Fifth Order; The Role of Sergeant Daniel Kanipe: Within five minutes of sending messenger number four, Sergeant Daniel Kanipe was now ordered back to Captain McDougall. He was sent by Captain Thomas Custer, acting as Aid de Camp on his brother's Staff. Now we have three messengers all being sent within a fifteen minute period. Was Custer's fondness for changing his mind now showing up? Although Kanipe's verbal order was directed to McDougall, he was also told to relay the same order to Benteen, that is if he happened to intercept him.

In 1908, Kanipe told Walter Camp that the order he was to convey to Captain McDougall was if any of the packs got loose, they were to be cut off, unless they were ammunition packs. Kanipe quoting Captain Thomas Custer added this proviso, "and, if see Benteen, *tell him to come on quick...a big Indian camp*". In additional Camp notes, Kanipe was also told to tell Benteen, "They want you up there (*Come on*), and for you to get there as fast as you can get there. (*Be quick*)." (Italics by author) Benteen was also to be told, "That they had *struck a big Indian camp*". Does this not sound a lot like Martin's famous written order that would be sent twenty-five minutes later? **M40, pg. 92 pp; LILLY 35**

Essentially Kanipe's order contains all of the elements of "Martin's" written order to Benteen. However, one important factor is missing in Kanipe's verbal order. There is no mention of any "Packs." Additionally, both McDougall and Benteen were told to "come across country," in other words for the both of them to take a shortcut to the bluffs. Why would Custer "want (Benteen) up there as quick as (he) could get there," if Martin's "bring packs" order had not yet been sent?

Fortunately for us today, Walter Camp took Daniel Kanipe and Peter Thompson with him in 1908 on one of his annual trips to the Battlefield. Kanipe was able to show him where he was sent back and the route that he used to reach Benteen and the Pack Train. What is interesting is that Kanipe told Walter Camp that he had not reported to either McDougall or Mathey! The question is how did McDougall or Mathey know to take Custer's proposed "shortcut" if Kanipe never reported it them? Kanipe said that he could not find Mathey. But Kanipe's order was directed to McDougall. At the time of Kanipe's arrival, Lieutenant Mathey was at the rear of the Packs, and McDougall would have been there also, as he was with the rear guard company. Kanipe told Camp that he reported to a civilian, William Waggoner, the Chief Packer! This was a serious breech of military protocol. Civilians were always out of the loop when it comes to military orders.

We know from one of Walter Camp's annotated "Blueprint" maps that Kanipe was sent from a point one quarter of a mile *north* of Reno's hill top position. Camp had annotated Kanipe's departure with a red colored pencil on the so-called "Edgerly" map. At a point above the present parking lot, but just below the knoll now called Sharpshooter's Ridge, Kanipe was sent back to McDougall. During his first visit since the Custer Fight, Kanipe had pointed out his exact route back to Benteen and the Packs. He had not followed Custer's back trail over Martin's Marshy Place and the Echleman Fords; instead he took a ridge further to the east. He could see the dust from the Pack Train. Kanipe would meet Benteen on the Big Flat, very near the now burning Lone Tepee Number Two.

Benteen quickly sent Kanipe on his way, with a curt remark that he was not "responsible for the packs! " He was abruptly told to go see Captain McDougall. It was at this point that the Pack Train issue becomes troublesome. Was it Benteen's pronounced indifference, or a simple misunderstanding on his part of a straightforward verbal order that would soon create confusion and insubordination? Benteen was at the time following the Custer/Reno cavalry trail that crossed over the Hartung Morass. However, soon after Sergeant Kanipe's arrival, Benteen arrived at the North Fork trail diversion. Since there were no signs that shod cavalry horses had taken this unused trail and Benteen continued to follow the fresh heavy cavalry trail. It now turned to the left and soon crossed over Middle Ash Creek again at the so-called Echleman Fords. **(See pg. 64, ASH CREEK, LOWER)**

The fact that both Lieutenant Edgerly and Gibson were to claim that they were shown

Martin's message is not in question. There is no doubt that they both saw a written message, but the question is when? Seems strange that in the heat of battle, a battalion commander is pandering his commanders written orders to his subordinates! What's wrong with this picture? Does it not sound somewhat contrived?

Edgerly seems to had an excellent memory because nine days after the Custer Fight he was able to quote his viewing of Lieutenant Cooke's written message word for word in his letter to his wife. However, Benteen's fellow officers and their collective "remembrances" continue to sound contrived when some thirty-five years later, Edgerly was again able to "quote" verbatim, the entire "Martin" message to Walter Camp. On July 4, the same day that Edgerly and the others wrote to their wives, Lieutenant Gibson came close to summarizing it in a letter to his wife. Is it possible that Benteen may have been passing the message around the July 4 camp, just to make sure they got it right?

Except for the soon to be deceased Captain Weir, Lieutenants Edgerly and Gibson were the only other officers that claimed to have seen Martin's message at the time it was delivered. Edgerly was the only one to testify at the Inquiry. There he paraphrased "Martin's" message as "we have struck a *big village, hurry up* and *bring up the packs*" and as a postscript, "*bring up the packs*." (Italics by author) Sounds very much like Godfrey's Army-Navy Journal version of his "push on with packs." messenger. The one where Godfrey said he saw a messenger ride up and talk to Benteen soon after they had returned to the main trail on Upper Ash Creek. **M3**

Was Godfrey referring to Corporal French's verbal order (number three) that caused Benteen to halt at the Hartung Morass and wait for the Packs? In Edgerly's letter to his wife written on July 4, he attributes this same event as occurring about a mile past the "watering place." And, after another "one to two miles," they came to the "burning tepee." From our reconstruction of battle events, the "Burning Lodge" was but one mile, or less, past the Hartung Morass. Considering the distance distortion, it seems that Edgerly might have been referring to the Hartung Morass as where Benteen had received Godfrey's Army-Navy order to "bring up the pack."

There is no doubt that the two officers may have seen "Martin's" note, but the real question is when? Was it on June 25, the day of the Battle or later at the Yellowstone River campsite in early July? Their collective memories seem to be very good for an event that happens during the fog of war.

Some two years after the Custer Battle, Major Reno "requested" that an official U.S. Army inquiry be conducted into the "rumors" about the charges of his cowardliness and drunkenness that were now being circulated by certain civilian participants. Namely, they were Frederick Gerard and Doctor Henry Porter both whom had been with Reno in his Valley Fight. Now, in Chicago, rehearsals became the order of the day during the "Reno" Inquiry. We know that at this official "investigation" in 1879, Reno's attorney needed Benteen's full support for his client's defense. Reno, at the time was serving a two-year dismissal from the U.S. Amy, having been convicted by a Court-Martial Board on the serious charge of the rape of a fellow officer's wife. But why were there several closed door testimony sessions and daily "couching" for Reno's fellow officers?

Perhaps an earlier dress rehearsal was conducted at the camp on the Yellowstone in July.

Benteen may have passed around his altered version of "Martin" order just to make sure that they saw the eventual historic version, and not its original wording? In the unlikely event that there were two written messages, more likely the real "Martin" message was simply made to disappear by its alteration? Take your choice; Benteen's "artistic" ability was just that creative.

There is the possibility of two related written orders being sent to Benteen, but that seems unlikely since in the reality of military warfare, a commander usually does not repeat himself. The Kanipe countermanding Pack Train order sent to McDougall earlier proves that John Martin could not have carried the bogus "bring packs" memorandum. Is it possible that the original text connotation was changed by the simple inclusion of additional wording, After all, the addition of "bring pack, P.S. bring packs" now changes a simple request for reinforcements to one of expediting the entire Pack Train. Benteen's suspected "alteration" now changes the original meaning. Could this scenario have happened? The answered is yes, if we look at the role that Frederick Benteen may have played in this sordid event.

Benteen's Role: Indeed, Benteen seems to have been very concerned that there might be an investigation, perhaps into his dereliction of duty at the Battle of the Little Bighorn. His letter to his wife, written on July 4, suggests his concern. After all, it was Benteen's alcoholism and dereliction to duty that later terminated his twenty-one year army career in Utah. Benteen's track record leaves room for suspicion, especially his antics after the Custer Battle. After all, it was on the Yellowstone at the mouth of the Bighorn, on July 2, that the fraudulent "Enlisted Man's Petition" first surfaced. In this spurious effort Benteen tries to gain a field promotion for his and Reno's "heroic" role at the Battle. Since the "Great Custer" was now dead, why should not he and Reno be advanced in rank? It is very doubtful that Reno had anything to do with this blatant self promoting scheme. **M26**

Considering the fact that it was Benteen's First Sergeant, Joseph McCurry, who later became the chief suspect in this piece of fiction. It was also an improper military request, as witnessed by General W. T. Sherman's rebuttal. Field promotions had been done away after the Civil War and Benteen, as a Regular Army commissioned officer, should have been aware of that fact. Walter Camp was well aware of the Enlisted Men's Petition, he had seen it as part of the Chicago newspapers file coverage of the Inquiry as Exhibit 10. And he had asked at least fifteen of his enlisted men informants whether they remembered the Petition? Not one even knew about it, let alone having signed it, yet many of their names appear on the Petition. **M26**

This same time frame could also have been when Martin's altered "bring pack" message could have first surfaced publicly. After all, we have only Benteen's word that the message that he claimed to have been delivered by John Martin and was still in its original text.

Orders to Benteen at the Morass: But why did not any of the other officers ever mention that they knew of additional orders being delivered to Benteen while at his morass? Lieutenant Gibson, Edgerly, and Godfrey all failed to mention knowing of any such incidents at this time. Is there a reasonable explanation for this anomaly?

There is if one looks at the physical layout of the Hartung Morass. Its narrow entry neck would have prevented the three companies from watering their horses in close proximity to each other. They would have had to spread themselves out along the existing alkali dry packed trail. Benteen's battalion reached the Hartung Morass by 2:45 PM some thirty minutes after returning the main trail. Godfrey said that he saw a messenger ride up and talk to Benteen, "soon after" reaching the main trail. Was his mystery courier Corporal Eldon French of Company C? Corporals are considered to be non-commissioned officers and French was from the Regimental Headquarters Staff.

But at least one enlisted man in Benteen's battalion did notice the presence of the mystery non-commissioned officer and his subsequent delivery of an order to Benteen, again at his watering place. It may have been an enlisted man from Benteen's own Company H, such as his orderly and he spread the "rumor" of the non-com from the Staff. After all, someone had to have started the rumor that another messenger had been seen delivering a message to Benteen at or near this watering place. It is possible that Benteen as the Battalion Commander, and being in the lead, he was the only officer in the vicinity when the fourth messenger arrived.

It may have been a verbal order. Being a verbal order, and with the entire Headquarters Staff now being deceased, Benteen no longer had proof to justify his "dawdling" at the Morass. He may have been ordered earlier to expedite the Packs to the bluffs, but nothing further. Was this an order that he considered to another of Custer's attempts to keep him out of the pending battle? This may have been the major factor of Benteen having John Martin lie, under oath at the Reno Court of Inquiry by saying Benteen had sent him back to the Pack Train as soon as he arrived? Another factor in Benteen not carrying out this new directive, whether it was written or verbal was Captain Weir's sudden departure from the Benteen morass.

This impulsive move of Weir compromised Benteen's leadership. Perhaps Benteen was embarrassed that he could not control his "Loose Cannon, "the impetuous" Captain Weir, who was also a well-known Custer sycophant. But, after another five minutes of his continued "dawdling" at the Morass, the arrival of the head of the Pack Train would force Benteen's two remaining companies from his "fishing" spot! Perhaps Benteen did not want us to know about Kanipe's order that countermanded Martin's Pack Train expediting order, before it was sent, the one that Benteen made so little effort to carry out. Was this one of many of Benteen's "secrets" that he withheld from the Reno Court of Inquiry?

The intent of the third order may have been for Benteen to halt and wait for the soon expected arrival of the Pack Train? When Custer first arrived on Mathey's Knoll, he could not have failed to see the relative position of Benteen's battalion and the Pack Train, now both located west of the South Fork fords. It was at the Hartung Morass, that thirty minutes earlier, the advanced battalions with Custer crossed over to the right bank of Ash Creek. Reno's Battalion was ordered to follow. At 2:30 PM, Benteen was now ten minutes from reaching this same crossing that the advanced battalions had reached at 2:00 PM. It is ten and one half miles by the trail down Ash Creek to the Hartung Morass. This trail can be seen on the 1890s Blake/Marshall survey published for the first time in **Chapter One, pg. 51. Also MAP. pg. 56 (The Hartung Morass)**

The Pack Train was still some forty-five minutes from arriving at this same point. Upon seeing the relative positions of these units, Custer could have ordered Benteen to wait for the packs to close the gap and then have Benteen reserve battalion escort them to a safer position on the bluffs. At the time, Benteen was not more than three miles behind Custer's advanced Squadrons. Custer may have thought that it was worth the time to have Benteen expedite the Pack Train to the bluffs. Is it possible that Custer wanted the Pack Train to reach a safety of the bluffs, as opposed to being caught in the open valley of Ash Creek?

A little over seven years earlier, at the Washita Battle, the Seventh Regiment had lost part of its wagon train. Then roving warriors had captured their winter overcoats. But Captain James Bell's quick thinking saved the day when he rushed the balance of the wagon train and its reserve ammunition into Black Kettle's captured village.

On June 25, in Montana, the regimental Pack Train contained some 30,000 rounds of reserve carbine ammunition. Its loss would be a major concern. If we accept the scenario that Custer did indeed send such an expediting order to Benteen, then we need to look closer at the major players, Benteen, Mathey and McDougall. Their subsequent actions speak many words concerning their role with the Pack Train in the Battle of the Little Bighorn. This deconstruction of the Pack Train has never been done before.

If Sergeant-Major Sharrow, or any other messenger, had been sent from Mathey's Knoll at 2:30 PM, it would have taken fifteen minutes to reach Benteen. The messenger would have intercepted Benteen just before he entered the Hartung Morass. This places the messenger's interception by 2:45 PM, the probable time that Benteen arrived at the Hartung Morass.

It is less then ten miles from where Benteen was ordered to start Left Scout to the Hartung Morass. This gives him a four mile per hour average gait, that of a regulated walk. We know today that Benteen retuned to the main trail on Upper Ash Creek at approximately 2:10 PM. If we use six miles as the total distance traveled on his Left Scout, his battalion by then averaged three miles per hour for just less than two hours. This is less than a walking pace and not the exaggerated horse killing impression gait that Benteen and Godfrey tried to leave. Perhaps they were motivated by a factor other than proper horsemanship.

Lieutenant Godfrey, in his Army-Navy Journal article, written in early August of 1876, described their horses on the Left Scout as already jaded and becoming exhausted. His description does not explain Benteen's walking gait. It was while Benteen was still at the morass that the rumor stated about the high ranking *sergeant from Custer's staff* being seen delivering an order to Benteen. The rumor soon spread though the ranks. Is it possible that Benteen did what he was ordered and that was to halt and wait for the Packs?

Other Seventh Regiment officers told Camp that Benteen believed that Custer was trying to keep him out of the Battle. Perhaps it was the feud over the Washita Battle letter incident that enraged Custer years ago? Benteen again bought the subject up again at the June 21 campsite on the Yellowstone. The result was that Custer humiliated Benteen by telling the other officers about Benteen's unsettling experience of having to kill a young Cheyenne boy during the Washita Fight. Benteen's ill-manners bought the Custer scab to a bleeding sore again. Perhaps, to save face, Benteen decided that this was now a good time to stop and "water" his horses!

The process of an official army "Watering Call" is a "cut and dry" daily routine and it was a highly regulated army procedure. It should not have taken much more then ten minutes to water his entire battalion. A "good watering place" was described in the Army Regulations as being at a non-boggy place along a stream, where a few mounted men would take as many as two ranks of linked horses to drink their fill. Army horses normally were watered daily at the same time of day, and only after a prescribed amount of time after being fed grain. This time honored "horse sense" was to prevent advanced colic which is always a fatal condition.

Sergeant Daniel Kanipe was sent back with a verbal order to McDougall to "hurry up" the Packs. But far more important the Pack Train was to take a "shortcut" to the bluffs. This mandated shortcut was a more direct route from the Big Flat to Mathey's Knoll over a crossing on the North Fork of Ash Creek. After all, Custer could hardly have failed to notice this shorter route when he was on Mathey's Knoll at 2:30 PM. It intersected with the Big Flat trail and the now burning "Lone Tepee." But Benteen told Kanipe that he was not in charge of the Packs, and without delay Kanipe was sent on his way to McDougall. At the Reno Court of Inquiry, both McDougall and Mathey vehemently denied of ever receiving any orders from Custer since near the Divide!

Daniel Kanipe was not invited to testify at the Inquiry, so the Court did not know of Custer's shortcut order issued to McDougall and Benteen. But why did McDougall and Mathey deny receiving such an order from Custer? Kanipe cleared up that mystery when he told Walter Camp in 1908 that he had never delivered this important order to either McDougall or Mathey. Instead, he delivered it to the Chief Packer, William Waggoner, who was a civilian under military contract. Kanipe never explained this serious breach of army protocol. Civilians were always out of the loop, when involved with military orders.

More revealing are the personal letters written by Godfrey and Benteen soon after the Battle! In his letter to the editor of the Army-Navy Journal, Godfrey explained that "*soon after*" Benteen had returned to the "trail of the main column," he had received another order from Adjutant Cooke. It was an order to "*push on with the packs.*" (Italics by author) There was no mention whether it was an oral or a written order, or who delivered it. Godfrey's estimate was that this event occurred when they were still six miles from Reno Hill. If Godfrey was referring to the written order delivered by John Martin, his "six miles" can hardly refer to the same messenger. Martin's arrival came when Benteen was within one and a half miles of Reno Hill and not Godfrey's estimated six miles. We know today that Benteen's return entry point on the Upper Ash Creek trail, was one and one quarter mile east of the present county road bridge located near the South Fork junction. Did Godfrey's "soon after" imply that his "push on with the pack" order arrived somewhere near the South Fork? In his Army-Navy Journal letter first published on September 2, 1876, Godfrey never mentions the "bring packs" message, or if it was John Martin who carried it.

From the Divide to Benteen's reentry point on Upper Ash Creek trail it is six and three quarter miles. That leaves just over seven miles to Reno Hill, by the trail that we know that Benteen would use. Does this place Godfrey's "push on with the packs" order near Benteen's reentry point? Not if we look closer to the rate of march of the Pack Train. Godfrey noted in his field diary 4:20 PM as when the head of the Pack Train arrived on Reno Hill. His time entry can now be used as a good time and distance indicator for the travel of the Pack Train. McDougall said that the Pack train crossed the Divide at 12:20 PM. The thirteen and three quarter mile distance from the Divide to Reno Hill was covered in three hours and forty-five minutes, a respectable 3.66 mile per hour rate of march. We also know that the packs were running thirty minutes behind Benteen. If the Pack Train had to travel another six miles that Godfrey estimated to reach Reno Hill, and they reached Benteen's reentry point by 2:20 PM, then Godfrey's field diary entry of 4:20 PM is very correct!

It is seven miles from Benteen's reentry point to Reno Hill. At the nominal rate of march of seven miles per hour (the "magic" Pont Express rate) from Benteen's reentry point it would have taken his battalion another hour to reach Reno Hill. Benteen should have then reached Reno Hill by 3:10 PM, but we know that he did not arrive there until at least 3:40 PM, a thirty minute difference which would be the time he spent watering his horses!

Benteen's known rate of march after his returning to the main trail down Ash Creek now makes his watering halt much closer to the Hartung Morass, rather then the South Fork area which is a favorite choice today by many Custer Buffs. This makes the Hartung crossing the most likely candidate as being the true Benteen morass. At this point on the property formerly owned by Robert Hartung, there is a pronounced five-acre "sinkhole" that holds water even in dry years. The travois trail used by the Cheyenne and Sioux villages on June 16 traversed across the south end of the Hartung Morass. From the Hartung Morass to Mathey's Knoll, by the North Fork trial, is less then two miles distance in an almost straight line. This is Custer's proposed "shortcut" trail. How do we know that the Hartung Morass is exactly the same "boggy" place where Benteen watered his horses? We know from using the timing of the Reno's Fight in the Little Bighorn Valley.

If the beginning of Reno's retreat was at 3:25 PM, and Benteen and Godfrey arrived at Gerard's Second Knoll by 3:30 PM, then we have a very good time indicator of how long Benteen was at the morass. If Benteen and Godfrey arrived at Gerard's Second Knoll one hour and twenty minutes after they returned to the main trail at 2:10 PM then we have a good idea of where his morass was located. The distance from the reentry point to Gerard's Second Knoll, by the known trail that they used is five and one three quarter miles.

The distance between the Hartung Morass and Gerard's Second Knoll is but two miles. Benteen could have traveled this distance in fifteen minutes. Even at the at the rate of seven miles per hour their total travel time would be fifty-five minutes, leaving thirty minutes at his "watering halt." This places his departure from his "watering place" by 3:15 PM, the estimated time of arrival of the head of the Pack Train at the Hartung Morass. The sounds of Reno's skirmishing started within ten minutes after Benteen's arrival at his morass. Camp's mystery messenger could have delivered his order as early as 2:45 PM, ten minutes before Reno's valley firing began. Captain Weir would leave at least fifteen minutes after hearing the advanced fighting. This places his early departure by 3:10 PM, a full five minutes before Benteen.

There are now several scenarios that can be created with Camp's revelation of a messenger having arrived at Benteen's morass. If this order was a verbal order, then we have but one scenario. Martin's historical written order had to have been altered. If the missing messenger carried another written order, than there had to been two different written orders, one that that John Martin carried, and the earlier messenger as reported to Camp. In the first scenario, Benteen was verbally ordered to halt and wait for the Packs. After their arrival, he was to expedite the entire Pack Train to the bluffs via the North Fork Trail which was Custer's mandated "shortcut." This he never did, except only to wait long enough for the head of the Packs to arrive.

The second scenario assumes that were two written messages and means that the earlier messenger delivered the famous "bring packs" order long attributed to John Martin. As written, this enigmatic order fits perfectly for an earlier delivery. However, as historically written, the Martin "bring packs" message is not in accordance with an accepted military scenario of having being sent from Medicine Tail Coulee, some thirty-five minutes after the Mathey Knoll order. However, if John Martin was the carrier of a singular written message to Benteen, then it had to have been altered!

The inclusion of the words "bring pack," and the additional "PS bring packs" could have been added later by Benteen to suit a post morass delivery? Delete these phrases, and Martin's written message now becomes more of a reasonable scenario for a Medicine Tail Coulee order. This unchallenged piece of history may have been the creation of the guilt-ridden mind of Frederick Benteen? If true, then when was it altered?

Benteen's letter to his wife, written on July 4, 1876, contains "guarded" wording! A man writing to his wife does not expect his private thoughts to be shared with history years later. Written at the camp on the Yellowstone, near the mouth of the Bighorn River, this letter may hold a clue to Benteen's frame of mind regarding his Custer memento. In this letter Benteen quoted his "Martin" message verbatim. He thought that since it was badly torn that the content should be preserved. He advised his wife to keep his letter, "as the matter *may be of importance* hereafter, *likewise of use*". (Italics by author) Either Benteen was being prophetic, that one day this memento would be of great historical interest, or was he more likely reflecting on an expected government investigation into the causes of the Battle of the Little Bighorn disaster?

Apparently Benteen was not a Romantic, nor did he want Custer's "Last Message" to become an icon to the memory of his late and detested military commander. Perhaps the answer to this perplexing question may be found in another of Benteen's letters concerning his Custer Battle relic. In a letter written March 6, 1879, Benteen now sends his altered "bring packs" message to Captain Robert Newton Price, of Philadelphia.

Captain Price, a former subordinate officer under Benteen in Missouri, had sent him a copy of Frederick Whittaker's newspaper article in which Benteen's role in the Custer Battle was challenged. Price requested that Benteen send him his "Martin" message, since he had read about it in the newspaper coverage of the Court of Inquiry. Benteen quickly acquiesces to this request and sends it on to Price. However, Benteen makes no mention that it was the very same one carried to him by John Martin. His excuse for giving his Custer souvenir away is very revealing. It seems that Benteen no longer had any use for it! **M37, pg. 325**

He had entered his verbatim version of Custer's "last order" into the Inquiry record as evidence on his own behalf. Was this the same "important matter" that he wrote to his wife about two and half years earlier? But what is important to note is that Benteen sent his useless Custer memorabilia twenty-three days after the closure of the Reno Court Inquiry in Chicago! We know that Benteen's Battle relic sent to Price had the same wording as quoted in his wife's letter, and the same wording that was entered as evidence at the Court of Inquiry. However, is it possible that it was not written on the day of the Custer Battle, but perhaps soon afterwards?

That would have been when Benteen realized that he did not have any proof of what originally may have been just a verbal order? But in 1879 it was now just a useless piece of scrap paper. In the same letter to Captain Price, Benteen stated that Lyman Gilbert, Reno's attorney, had informed him that "his testimony at the Inquiry had been very *satisfactory to the Army people*!" (Italics by author) Was Gilbert's plural usage "Army people" perhaps referring to Sherman, Terry, and other Generals whose careers were on the line? Benteen continued by writing that while he had been "closed mouthed" at the Inquiry, he was regretful that he had not been allowed to "turn loose on Custer." It seems now that Benteen could have had Martin's original written order altered to one that more suited his needs? **M37, pg. 325**

The Subterfuge at the Court of Inquiry: Since two and half years had passed since Benteen's Pack Train orders (plural) were issued, it was possible for collusion and obstruction of justice to occur at the Reno Court Of Inquiry. And it helped to create the myth that John Martin carried "the last lines that Cooke ever wrote." We now know there was an earlier verbal order, the one carried by Daniel Kanipe, which perhaps McDougall nor Mathey never received, but was delivered to Benteen. Perhaps John Martin carried a second written order, but it was either altered or simply made to disappear.

If the famous "bring pack, P.S. bring pacs" has not been altered and is in its original wording, then someone else had to have delivered it. The military situation in Medicine Tail Coulee does not allow for a Pack Train expediting order, which is the intended wording of Benteen's "Martin" memo. Custer had now set into motion a Double Envelopment (pincer) maneuver on the Lower Camps on Onion Creek. His two battalions would be operating now as separate units. Exactly to which battalion was the Pack Train (or ammo mules) supposed to report to by 5:00 PM, which was the earliest time that the Packs could have arrived in Medicine Tail Coulee?

That means there had to have been a second written message, one that Benteen says never existed when he wrote his wife but nine days later. He used the words the "*the last lines that Cooke ever wrote, which was an order to me.*" (Italics by author) And that possibility is not likely due to the above scenario reconstructed by the author based on his Western ranch and military horseman experience and the Camp and Stands In Timber research. Someone has to lying, and the most likely candidate was Frederick Benteen.

After all, it was Frederick Benteen that had the most to gain by altering Martin's true and only written message! Not Walter Camp, John Stands In Timber and certainly not this author. The authors' startling and logical conclusion that John Martin could not have carried the Icon of the Custer Battle came about secondary after the discovery of Custer dividing his force in Medicine Tail Coulee. We know from Walter Camp's interview with John Martin's and his honesty about his forced perjury at the Reno Inquiry that his Medicine Tail order was a written one. Or is there a far more sinister implication that the Benteen's version may have never existed? Is it possible that the additional words "bring pack, PS Bring pacs" were added to Custer's original simple reinforcement order, the one that he sent from Medicine Tail Coulee at 3:10 PM? If there has been no alteration or additional wording, or no complete forgery; then the famous. "Martin" message had to have been delivered much earlier!

If delivered as historically written by an earlier messenger, then there had to have been a second written message, the one carried by Martin. Did Custer in Medicine Tail Coulee send Benteen a second written order to advance with his reserve battalion without any mention of the "Packs", and what would the wording of such a message be and what happen to it? **See Author's Facsimile B, pg. 141**

Having a second written order to Benteen is unlikely. Is it possible that John Martin was used to create the subterfuge needed to protect Benteen from the inquiring minds of a future

Inquiry Board, one that came about in 1879? If so, we need to look at the role that John Martin played in this possible deception.

The True Role of John Martin: It was Adajunt Cooke, and not Custer, that personally selected Bugler John Martin to deliver his hand written note to Benteen. Many Custer researchers have made an issue about this selection of a foreign born native, who may have not spoken good English. The myth that Martin was given a written message because of his nationality was created in the mind of Colonel William A. Graham! His major contribution to this study was his verbatim copy of the Reno Court of Inquiry in 1923.

Walter Camp had already read the *Chicago Tribune* newspaper account of the Court of Inquiry's verbatim record at least twenty years before Graham's publication of the original copy that he found stored in the military archives. But, it was in his 1923 "reconstructed" story of John Martin's role that Graham falls short. In his scenario of Martins' role in the Custer Battle, Graham tries to make us believe that Custer and Martin had gone to the top of a "Big Hill," while the command had halted at its base. From his observation from this "Big Hill" Custer thought that the squaws and children were playing, and that the "Indians (warriors) must be in their tents asleep".

Graham also created the misleading concept that Cooke's "hurriedly" written message was done on the "jump" while the "Custer" companies were galloping headlong into the valley! The same contrived scenario was later presented in his book, *The Custer Myth*, first published in 1953. He has Custer barking out an order to Martin, and then Cooke, fearful that the poor English speaking Martin probably did not understand the verbal order, writes out the message! All the time the "command" was in motion. This muddied scenario concludes that Custer gave the order personally and verbally to Martin, who then checked (reined in) his horse when Cooke said, "Wait, orderly, I'll give you a message!" The phrase "checked his horse," leads us to believe that the entire command was still galloping "Hell Bent for Leather" and onward to disaster. Graham also has Martin being "told" by Custer to tell Benteen not only to be quick, but too bring the "ammunition packs." There is no written evidence that the word ammunition was ever used in any of the orders issued on June 25.

In his sworn testimony at the Inquiry, Martin never mentions the words ammunition packs. What is more important is that in his several interviews with Walter Camp, Martin never mentions being told about the Pack Train or the ammo packs. In fact, Martin never mentioned ammunition packs in any of his letter writings. Graham's textual picture reads like a John Wayne movie. The problem with his pulp-fiction style of writing is like a "Hollywood Scenario." It simply never happened!

Graham's usage of ammunition packs was first contrived in his 1923 version. Sounds good, but it just does not serve history. Graham may have been able to ride a pretty good judicial desk, but obliviously he was not a horseman. His "checked his horse" is an example of his subjective style of writing "history." As far as it is known, Graham never visited the battlefield about which he helped to create so many myths.

The proper place for an Adjutant was on his commanding officer's right. Martin's position was behind and to Custer's left. Graham's assumption is that Cooke was able to hear every word of Custer's verbal order with his head turned to the left, and that Cooke would be able to rephrase it word for word. Not exactly how a well-organized Adjutant in the field works.

Graham's conjectured story was first published in 1923, a year after his interview with Martin who died in 1922. Even Martin's own Inquiry testimony forty-three years earlier runs contrary to Graham's fictional story.

Walter Camp had interviewed John Martin in 1908 and 1910, some thirteen to fifteen years before Graham created his contrived story. In the much earlier Camp interviews, Martin said that it was only after they had come into full view of the (downstream) village(s) that Custer again halted the entire command. Custer and Cooke hurriedly discussed the matter at the halt. Only than did Cooke write the order and hand it to Martin. It was only after Martin had started to leave that Custer spoke to him as if an afterthought. Custer, not Cooke then verbally ordered Martin to go back and see if he could find Benteen. Then if it was safe, Martin was to return to the Staff. If not, he was to come back with Benteen. **M40, pg. 100-101**

This proves that Custer only wanted Benteen's reserve battalion since there is never any mention of ammunition packs. This post verbal order also shows that Custer was not worried about Martin's supposed lack of English. Any one of the other orderlies assigned to the Headquarters Staff who all spoke English, could have been selected. These include Sergeant Henry Dose, Regimental Sergeant-Major William Sharrow, Sergeant Robert Hughes, and John Vickory, and Corporal Alexander Bishop. Also on the Staff was the elusive Corporal Eldon French.

It now appears that Custer wanted Martin to go find Benteen. What Custer did not know was that ever since Sergeant Kanipe had been sent twenty-five minutes earlier, Benteen had been on an extended "fishing expedition" at his morass.

What Was Martin's Real Order? The text of the historic Benteen/Martin order, as written, would have been valid if sent forty minutes earlier, when Custer was on Mathey's Knoll. However, what if the "historic" message is not in its original text? What if the words, "bring pack, P.S. bring packs" were added at a later time? The important question was whether Corporal Bishop's order was an oral or a written one? The addition of these words drastically change the original intent of this order from an explicit demand for Benteen's reserve reinforcements, to a more benign "Pack Train" expediting order. We know from the military situation that existed and the logistics of a Pack Train expediting order being sent from Medicine Tail Coulee at 3:10 PM, that John Martin could not have carried Benteen's version of the historic "bring packs" order. We also know that another messenger was sent earlier to Benteen with what amounts to a Pack Train countermanding order. And that messenger, Sergeant Daniel Kanipe, was sent at least twenty-five minutes before John Martin. **M40. pg. 92-93, 130 (Kanipe)**

WAS THIS MARTIN'S ORIGINAL ORDER?

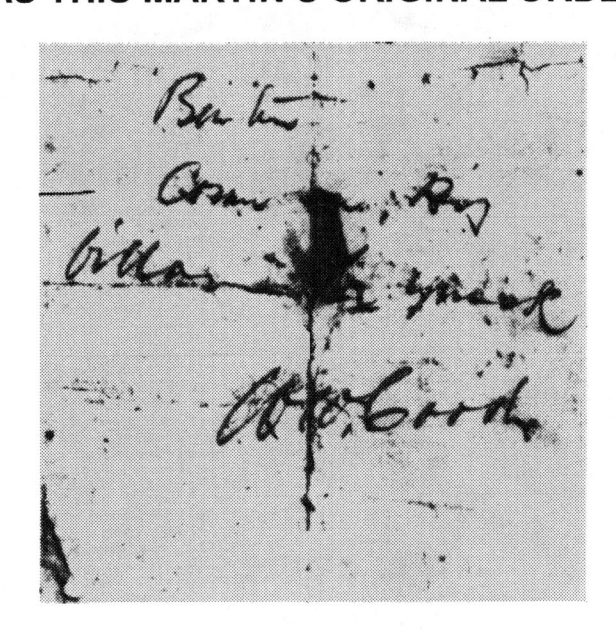

FACSIMILE B

*Benteen may have altered **FACSIMILE A (See pg. 48)** by the addition of the two lines, "bring pack" and "PS bring pacs." This inclusion would change a reinforcement order to a more benign Pack Train expediting order. It would give Benteen an excuse for his failure to go to Custer's advance front in a timely manner. John Martin's original text **(FACSIMILE B, above)** may have been altered nine days after the disaster on the Little Bighorn River, while in camp on the Yellowstone River near the mouth of the Bighorn River, on or about July 4, 1876. This was the same time frame that the fraudulent Enlisted Men's Petition was first circulated. It is to be noted that Benteen's First Sergeant Joseph McCurry was the FBI's prime suspect in adding names to the petition requesting the field promotion of Benteen and Reno. Walter Camp interviewed a number of enlisted men who had no remembrance of its existence, but yet their names appeared on this illegitimate document which was entered as Exhibit 10 at the Reno Court of Inquiry. When Godfrey described Benteen of having "artistic ability" was he referring to his ability to create bogus documents?*

Martin's Short Cut: When Martin left, he was told to follow their back trail. Instead, he took a "shortcut!" After traveling about three-quarter mile up Medicine Tail Coulee, he crossed over the original trail that came down from the same ridge from his "Big Hill. " This was the same trail that Custer was forced to abandon due the narrowness of the crest of the ridge. Apparently Martin understood that this was the same Indian trail that they had been following, and in spite of his maligned intelligence, he realized that he could save time by taking this shortcut. Martin's thinking saved him at least five minutes of travel time, the saving resulting from his by not taking Custer's longer South Medicine Tail trail, the same one as suggested by Godfrey's more "eastern" route. **M40, pg. 101**

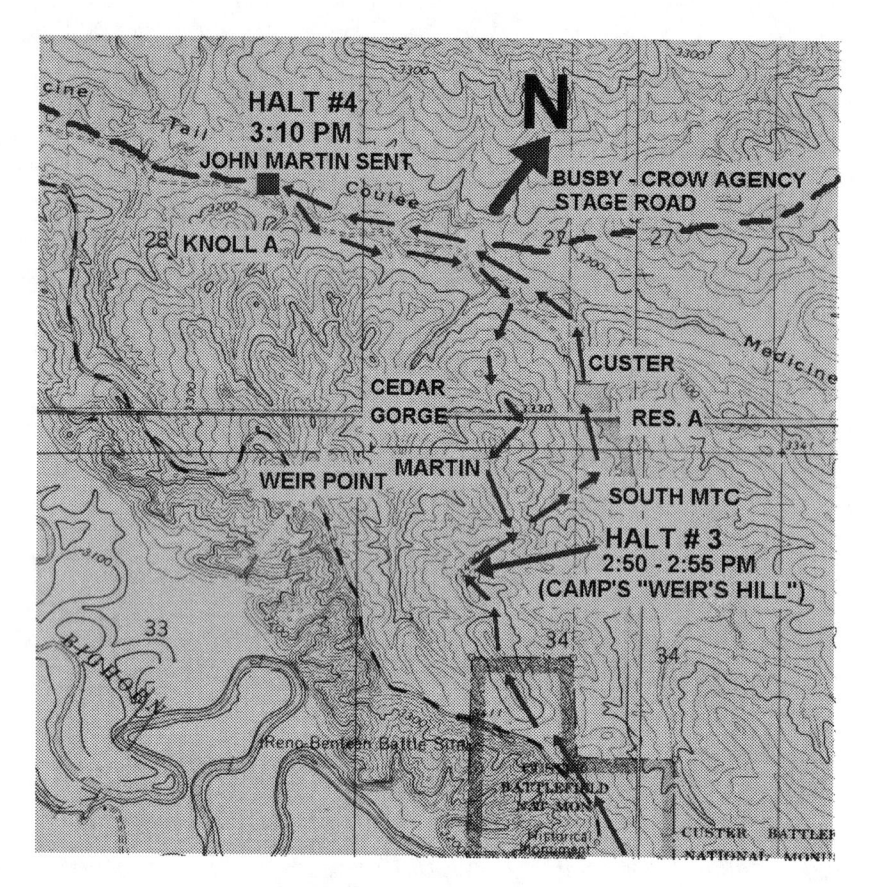

MARTIN'S SHORTCUT

SCALE: ----------- 1/4 MILE

John Martin was ordered to take the cavalry back trail, but he used a shortcut to reach his "Big Hill" where Halt Three occurred. He used the original trail that was too narrow for the sixty foot column of Custer's advancing battalions. It saved him at least five minutes of travel time. As much as Benteen tried to malign Martin's intelligence, he was a good soldier. In the area south of the Camp's "Weir's Hill" Martin had to have passed Corporal Henry Eldon French on his way forward to rejoin the Headquarters Staff. Corporal French was earlier assigned at the Powder River to Staff duty and he may have issued the pivotal order to Benteen that caused him to halt and wait for the Pack Train. The Pack Train was but thirty minutes behind Benteen's reserve battalion which was the length of time he spent "watering" his horses.

Martin's Retreating Command: After about one mile of travel, Martin reached the highest elevation on the northern end of what may be now called "Martin's Ridge." He heard the sounds of gunfire to his right rear and as he told Walter Camp, he saw "Custer's command...falling back from the river". Martin misinterpreted the sounds of fighting of the now dismounted Company E as Custer's entire battalions now retreating from the river. **See Art Work, pg. 123**

At the Court of Inquiry, Martin did not mention the incident of seeing what he thought was a retreat from the river or passing Boston Custer or the man from Company C. Martin told Camp in 1908, that in Chicago it was not desired that he should tell everything that he knew.

Sounds like that someone got to Martin in his pre-testimony session. Was it Reno's attorney or his commanding officer, Frederick Benteen? **M40, pg. 101**

But we also know today, from John Stands In Timber's published account of his interviews with his fellow Northern Cheyenne battle participants, that Captain George Yate's battalion was now under attack by what appeared to be a threatening group young warriors. They were attacking the rear flanks of the Second Battalion which was on its way northward to the lower fords. This pre-emptive strike occurred on the south slope of the Nye-Cartwright/Luce Ridge area. The time was now 3:20 PM.

Soon after Martin's misinterpreted sighting, Boston Custer passed by him on his way to catch up with his brother's headquarters. He had gone back from the South Fork area earlier to the Pack Train to exchange horses. When asked where the command was, Martin may have hesitated in telling him because of what he just saw. Soon after, Martin would pass an enlisted man from Company C. This errant enlisted man wanted to know where the "command" was by now. Was this Peter Thompson's "Poor French" who was assigned to staff duty, and is why Martin recognized him? The timing is correct if Corporal French was returning from the Hartung Morass.

The Halt in Medicine Tail Coulee: Walter Camp used this incident of Boston Custer appearance as proof that there was a lengthy halt in Medicine Tail Coulee. After all, Boston was able to catch up with his brothers, as he body was later found on the present Custer Battlefield, over two miles north of Medicine Tail. A little farther on, Martin would pass by the enlisted man from Company C trying to catch up with Custer's command. This does not sound like a straggler but someone more like Thompson's "Poor French".

Martin's Court of Inquiry Perjury: Martin stated during his Court of Inquiry testimony that as soon as he delivered his message to Benteen he was sent on back to McDougall. It is obvious that Martin's declaration was a voluntary one, as there was no previous line of questioning by Lieutenant Lee. Prosecutor Lee was astounded by this claim and he persistently dug for the truth. Martin's saying he was now sent to McDougall becomes very apparent as a fabrication in the ensuing questions and answers. But, being a good soldier, Martin stuck to his story. Martin testified the day before Benteen was recalled back to the stand. In 1910, when Walter Camp asked Martin about Benteen sending him back to McDougall, he freely admitted that he had been forced to make that statement. He said, "They made me say that! " Since Camp had already read Martin's testimony, he was taken back by his frankness. Martin had committed perjury at the Inquiry. Martin explained that "they" made him say that, referring to his sworn statement of having been sent to the Pack Train commander. The question is who were the "they" and why was Martin forced to commit perjury? **M71, pg 390 (Martin)**

Edgerly's Blueprint Map: (See pg. 146) In the Brigham Young University (BYU) portion of the Camp Collection, there are three "blueprint" copies of Camp's map. All are made from the same "master" drawing of his second revised map. Apparently there was an earlier version, but the only known circulated blueprint copies are those currently in the BYU Collection and these are copies of the later revision. One blueprint copy had been mailed to Private James M. Rooney, of Company F, as the attached accompanying letter identifies Rooney as being the recipient.

Of major interest to this Custer study is that one of the blueprint copies was labeled in Camp's handwriting in red pencil as being the "W. S. Edgerly" copy. The obvious reference is to Lieutenant Winfield S. Edgerly, who was the subordinate officer of Captain Weir's Company D. Edgerly would later deny that he had ever met Water Camp, but the existence of the "Edgerly" blueprint map strongly suggests that he had been in contact with Walter Camp, and as early as 1909 when the master map was made.

Benteen's version of "Martin" order **(Facsimile A, pg. 48)** may have been shown to Edgerly and Gibson on July 4, which was when all three wrote letters to their wives. Was it on June 25 or July 4, that their ability to paraphrase, and in Edgerly's case, to be able to quote the actual text verbatim from Benteen's "Martin" version. Edgerly's memory of nine days after the Custer Battle is very remarkable, even if there was but one version. Benteen must have trotted out his "Dog and Pony" show on July 4 after he had thought about his insubordinate role that may surface in the expected investigation into the debacle at the Little Bighorn. This was also about the same time that Benteen's fraudulent "Enlisted Men's Petition" first surfaced. **See Chapter Five, pg. 123**

At BYU there are three letters written by Edgerly to Camp and they are listed in the correspondence index. His last letter was written in 1911. Edgerly was a master of plausible denial. While he may have never met Camp face to face, what about the U.S. Mail? All of the BYU Camp Blueprint maps have fold lines as if they had been mailed. When Colonel Graham asked Edgerly in 1925 about his extensive interview with Walter Camp, he denied having ever met him. Graham, in his July 9, 1925 letter to Edgerly, quoted an unidentified officer recently retired from the U.S. Army. He wanted Edgerly to be aware of "certain statements" attributed to a Mr. W. M. Camp, of Chicago. The statements were about Graham's unidentified officer's personal knowledge of daily rehearsals of certain Seventh Regiment officers while appearing at the Reno Court of Inquiry in 1879. According to Graham, these allegations were of such a fallacious nature that Edgerly should comment on them. **M37, pg. 323 (Edgerly to Graham, July 15, 1925)**

Was Graham's mysterious source none other General Edward S. Godfrey, who had retired from the U.S. Army in 1907? The following year, Godfrey started corresponding with Walter Camp. The allegations from Graham's unidentified source were that Camp had "positive evidence" that Reno had been drunk on June 25-26, 1876 and that nearly all of the officers at the 1879 Reno Court had "gathered in Reno's (hotel) room and rehearsed (their testimony) for the next day". They were able to do that because their daily testimony was being published in the Chicago newspapers. Graham goes on to dismiss Camp's silly notions that when Reno fled the valley Custer was not yet engaged. And Graham, again quoting Camp, reported that Reno had fled in a "disorderly, disorganized mob, with no leadership whatever." Furthermore, Graham thought that Camp was wrong about his theory that Custer had made a lengthy halt after Martin was sent back. However, today all of these Camp "allegations" are known to be valid, as this study will prove.**M37, pg. 322 (Graham to Edgerly, July 9, 1925)**

Edgerly would vehemently deny to Graham that he had ever "*been in Reno's room.* " He said he personally had not discussed his testimony with another officer, except his "most intimate friend, Lieutenant George D. Wallace." (Italics by author) But he does not say anything about not being in Reno's attorney's or perhaps Benteen's room! Again, Edgerly was perhaps a master in plausible denial. Was his denial designed to distance himself from his earlier letters and lengthy interviews with Walter Camp? After all, Colonel Graham was a retired U.S. Army

Judge Advocate. Perhaps Edgerly did not want his and other officers' perjury to be made known to Graham. In 1921, Graham would discover the original verbatim copy of the Reno Court of Inquiry record in the military archives. It became permanently deposited in the U.S. National Archives by 1941. Later, in 1951, Graham would publish his condensed version of the Reno Court of Inquiry. But Edgerly's annotated Camp "blueprint" map tells a much different story from what he testified to under oath at the Reno Court of Inquiry in 1879. Edgerly suggested to Graham that perhaps Camp had extracted his so-called seven hours of interviews from his correspondence with Edgerly. **M37, pg. 323 (Edgerly to Graham, July 15, 1915)**

But today we have Edgerly's interview with Camp as published by Dr. Hammer in his book, *Custer In ' 76*. And again, there is the annotated blueprint map housed at BYU which discredits Edgerly's denial that he had contacted Walter Camp. Edgerly's protests to the Camp's informant (Godfrey) to the claims there was a cover-up now sound hollow. Graham was blindsided when it came to the possibility that an "Officer and a Gentleman" of the U.S. Army would lie under oath. He just did not ask Edgerly about Benteen's role!

Camp's "Edgerly" blueprint map is annotated showing where Edgerly and Company D traveled when they went forward to the sounds of Custer's fighting. Faintly seen in a different colored yellow pencil marking, there is a wide looping "trail" that was apparently added by Edgerly. It is of a different color and a heavier line weight that Camp used when he marked his other blueprint copies. Camp could not have conjectured exactly where Edgerly had traveled. This Edgerly annotation shows that he and Weir did not travel direct to what will become known today as Weir Point. The meaning of this little known side trip was discussed in Chapter Four.

Perhaps Camp's blue print copy was mailed to Edgerly and he annotated it and mailed it back to Camp. The "Edgerly" map at BYU does have severe fold lines, but so do the other two. The original size of the blue print copies measures about one and half by three feet so Camp may have folded them for mailing and his convenience when traveling. But, no mater what, one cannot dismiss Edgerly's obvious annotation of his copy or his published personal interview with Camp. Was it Reno's attorney and his little collection of Seventh Regiment officers who on a daily basis would rehearse their testimony in someone's hotel room before each day of testimony? Or was it an independent effort on Benteen's part alone to make sure that his Company Bugler had it right? Congress may have made them Officers and Gentlemen, but some were a long way from being either.

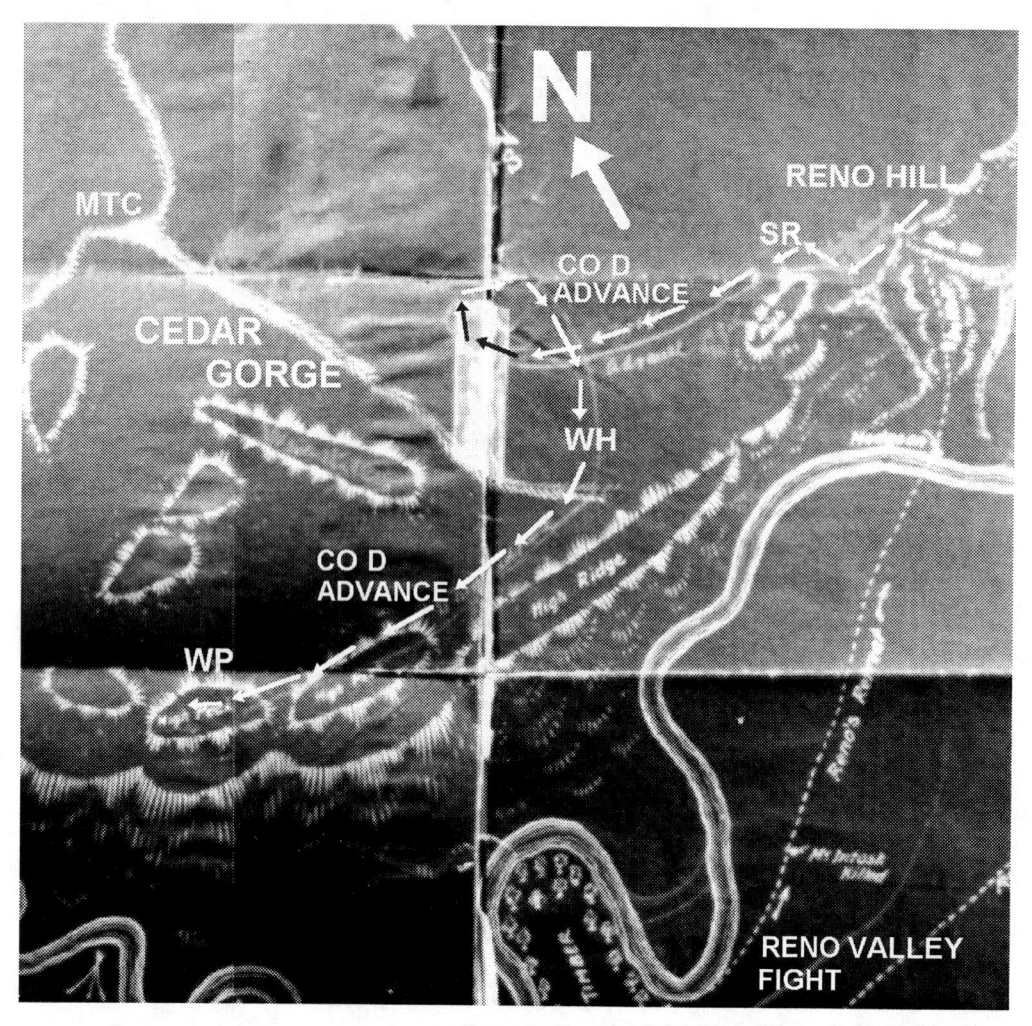

SEGMENT OF THE EDGERLY BLUEPRINT MAP

(ANNOTATIONS IN WHITE BY AUTHOR)

SCALE: -------------------------- 1/4 MILE

*Lt. Winfield Edgerly annotated Walter Camp's blueprint map showing where he and Company D traveled after leaving Reno Hill by 4:10 PM. His yellow colored pencil marking can be seen making a looping trail down into what the author calls the South Medicine Tail Coulee drainage or Godfrey's "Eastwardly Route" Camp used a red pencil to annotate his maps that he mailed or hand carried to his informants. Camp's "Weir's Hill" can be seen where Company D's trail crosses over itself when Edgerly went to join Captain Weir on his high ground **(WH)**. This high point is located two tenths west of the NPS fence line on the Reno-Benteen defensive area. Sharpshooter's Ridge can be seen at **(SR)**. Edgerly and Weir would than go to the present NPS site now designated as Weir Point **(WP)**. Company D may have traveled a considerable distance past this point, and possibly as far as Medicine Tail Coulee.* **(See Edgerly with Company D, pg. 115)**

Or was it Benteen alone, on a damage control mission of his own that forced a lowly enlisted man from his own company to commit perjury by having Martin to say he had been sent back to the Pack Train? It is far more important to learn why Martin was forced to say that? Martin's plural usage of word "they" implies that there was more then one person involved. Perhaps, it was Benteen along with Reno's attorney. Apparently, the answer to this perplexing conundrum is found in the politician's favorite phrase: quid pro quo, you scratch my back and I will scratch yours. Who had the most to gain by Martin's perjury? The question that must be asked is why did "they" make Martin lie about his being sent back to the Pack Train? If we have correctly identified Frederick Benteen as the culprit, the answer is forthcoming.

Benteen may have anticipated that the Court would ask the obvious question: why was his name on a Pack Train expediting order? Why did not Cooke address it to McDougall or Mathey? After all, if it was a true Pack Train expediting order, then why was it addressed to Benteen? Did not Benteen tell Sergeant Kanipe that he was not responsible for the Pack Train? There is no doubt that Martin did deliver a written order to Benteen, but was it the famous "bring packs" message? Could there have been other written orders sent on the day of the Battle? We know of other written message that was sent on June 25. **M40, pg. 134 (Dose), pg. 147 (Foley), Robert E. Doran, *The Man Who Got to the Rosebud*, Little Big Horn Associates Research Review, Winter 2003**

Only minutes after Martin was sent back, Private Nathan Short, of Company C, was given a written dispatch to be delivered to General Terry, which was the promised "Herendeen" dispatch! The body of Bugler Henry Dose, of Custer's Staff was found in Medicine Tail Coulee with a remnant of a written message grasped in his fingers! Adjutant Cooke was found on Monument Hill with a note addressed to Captain Henry Nolan, his "last will and testament," directing disposal of his personal effects. And there was those "memorandums" of the battalion assignments. Who is to say that the Custer/Cooke/Martin order was the only memo ever to be written on June 25?

At the Reno Court of Inquiry, Prosecutor Jessie Lee unexpectedly asked John Martin if he had seen anyone on his trip back to Benteen. Martin quickly denied that he saw anyone. But we know that he passed Boston Custer and at least two stray Company C men. Why did he say that? And, more important, why did Lieutenant Lee asked that particular question in the first place? If a non-commissioned officer did indeed travel to the Hartung/Benteen morass, for whatever reason, he would have had to pass Martin on his return trip to the Headquarters Staff. In our time and distance reconstruction they would have had to pass each other at least by 3:20 PM, near the area of his "Big Hill". Martin could not have failed to have seen the messenger. But if he accidentally blurted out that he had, the next question would be where had the other Staff's messenger been, and why? **M71, pg. 390 (Martin)**

Was Benteen substituting his Martin for the other messenger? Was that why he had Martin "volunteer" the statement that he was sent back to McDougall? After all, Benteen did have Martin's written order in his pocket, but the other messenger's order was verbal and was now blowing in the wind. Benteen's behavior at the Morass now starts to make sense. Had he been ordered to wait for the "packs" to arrive at the morass?

But, as soon as the head of the Pack Train arrived, Benteen took off, and he began to follow the heavy cavalry trail down Ash Creek. Then why did not Benteen stay with the packs and expedite them to the buffs, as apparently he was ordered. After all, is not that what Martin's supposed order told him to do? At the Court of Inquiry, this issue could have become a sore point with those officers that were involved, McDougall, Mathey and Benteen. Is this why Martin's true order was covered up? And the cover up apparently started very early on in the aftermath of the disaster on the Little Bighorn.

The Decision in Medicine Tail and Martin's True Order: According to what Martin told Camp, it was in Medicine Tail Coulee, while at the Fourth Halt that Adjutant Cooke wrote out the message that he was to carry to Benteen. Historically, we have been led to believe that this order was the better known "bring pack, PS bring pacs" message. Since Martin did not look at his order, he never knew the exact wording of his message. When Martin received it, Benteen was just leaving the Hartung Morass after a long unexplained thirty-minute halt. Is there another possible scenario that would offer more logical military sense? Is there perhaps another messenger who is missing from the chronological order of events, one that we were never told about? The author's conclusion that is that his **Facsimile B** is what Martin's message would have logically looked like. **See Facsimile B, pg. 141**

If we are correct that Martin did not carry Benteen's famous "bring pack" message, if it ever existed at all, than who did? And, what was the intent of the one that Martin did carry. Based on military logic, the missing order would have been a countermanding order. Benteen had earlier been ordered to expedite the packs but now he was being told to rush his reserve companies forward to Custer's advanced front! There was no reasonable military rational for the entire Pack Train or for any of the individual companies' ammo mules. What Custer needed now was Benteen's reserve battalion, Neither he nor any of his other officers were expecting a protracted fight so the reserve ammunition from the packs for a defensive stand was far from their minds.

In the unlikely event that there were two back-to-back written messages sent to Benteen, did he wrongly substitute the earlier written message with Martin's message? He could have placed them both in his pocket and later possibly confused the two. After all Benteen may have shown the other order to the other officers by accident, or was it by design?

This author doubts that this happened. What the author suspects is that Benteen simply had Martin's reinforcement order made to vanish, or seemingly to "disappear" by its alteration? After all, if the fourth order delivered earlier by Corporal Bishop to Benteen was a verbal one than Benteen would not want it to come out that a non-commissioned officer of Custer's Staff had delivered such an order. Especially, if later the army launched a high level investigation. No matter how Martin's written order was worded, Benteen failed to carry out either scenario. He did not quite "expedite" the Pack, nor did he "come on" by being "quick" and rush to Custer's aid. And the U.S. Army considers that an overt act of insubordination!

By July 4, everyone knew that they were to be repercussions for what happen on the Little Bighorn. From General Terry, who was a former lawyer, Staff officer Captain Robert P. Hughes, another attorney and down to the lowest buck private, it was in their bones that "someone" was going to have to pay for this fiasco. However, a dead commander does make a better "scapegoat" rather than the living "Hero of Reno Hill," Frederick Benteen. He may have tried to outwit the Court by having John Martin "voluntarily" testify that he had indeed been sent back to the Pack Train commander.

Was this Benteen's way of correcting Custer's mistake of sending two back to back verbal orders by Bishop and Kanipe that now counter-manned his earlier wait for the Pack Train order. But, to Benteen's credit, the very next day when he testified, he blurted out in the middle of a reply to a benign question that no matter what Martin had just said the day before, if he went back to McDougall than he went on his own. Benteen denied having ordered Martin back to McDougall. This un-requested "confession" may have been Benteen's method of distancing himself from Martin's perjury or was it guilt? His spontaneous outburst also proves that Benteen was keeping up with the testimony that was being published daily in the local Chicago newspapers. **M71, pg. 434**

Or was Benteen trying to suppress that he knew who the other messenger was? After all, if it was Alexander Bishop and he that he stayed with his company commander from the Morass all the way to Reno Hill, than John Martin's being sent back to McDougall would answer how the Pack Train knew to take Custer's short-cut. But, it was a moot point, the now Sergeant Bishop was long gone from the army, but Martin was still there, lying his heart out on the witness stand for his company commander.

McDougall's Complicity: What is not clear was just how did McDougall know to take the "shortcut" to the bluffs? After all, Sergeant Kanipe never reported Custer's order to him. Then exactly how and when did McDougall become a clairvoyant? At approximately 3:45 PM, McDougall stopped following the distinct Custer/Reno/ and Benteen cavalry trail, the same one that he had been following for the last three hours. And now he began to take the unused North Fork trail, the one that led directly to Mathey's Knoll. The same "shortcut" that Custer had mandated two hours earlier. The mystery is why did McDougall take this shortcut in the first place? Is it possible that Benteen may have passed Kanipe's verbal order on to McDougall, and initiated the "missing" order"?

Did Benteen try to legitimize his earlier verbal order from Corporal French, the one he could no longer prove, because the entire Headquarters Staff were now dead? However an altered version of Martin's written order would now make him responsible for expediting the Packs. And provide also a good excuse for his "dawdling" at the Morass and then, another excuse for not going to Custer's aid in a timely manner!

Another interesting event, as revealed in the Walter Camp Collection, was the fact that when the Pack Train came into view on Reno Hill, Benteen ordered his horses to be unsaddled. Apparently, he was not planning to go any farther. Had his order to bring the packs to the bluffs been carried out? Was this the real secret that he bragged about when he boasted of withholding information from the Court of Inquiry? After all, Reno's attorney needed Benteen's full cooperation to save his client from the charges of drunkenness and cowardice. Was this the reason for all the "closed door" testimony, and an almost daily "rehearsal" of certain officers' testimony? It seems to center around the role that Benteen, McDougall and Mathey played with the Pack Train during the Battle of the Little Bighorn. **(See Summary of Orders to Benteen, June 25, 1876, pg. 211)**

Bob Doran 2007

The First Battalion being pursued to the Finley/Calhoun Hill area now dismounted after their fifth halt on Greasy Grass Hill (foreground). Curly accurately described the "Flankers as Skirmishers" formation (see page 201) on one of his many field trips with Walter Camp.

CHAPTER SIX

MEDICINE TAIL TO FINLEY HILL AND BEYOND

The Sioux gave voice to a heap big yell, like a dog (and then) heap shoot, bang, bang, bang!
Walter Camp quoting Curly

Forget what you know about the Battle of the Little Bighorn! This study is based on the known tactical deployment and horsemanship aspects of the Custer era cavalry; and it will reveal a very untraditional reconstruction. It will not be based on the Hollywood non-military thinking and the many false theories called "Custer Myths." It will be based on the horse clues that Walter Camp recorded during his twenty-three years of research with participants who were there. And, as a horseman, this author's thirty years of unraveling their memories.

For the most part the fighting on the Custer Battlefield was a dismounted infantry action. The warriors also fought dismounted except when moving from action scene to another. They just followed what the army did, when they dismounted to fight on foot in one place, so did the warriors.

When Curly took Walter Camp over the Battlefield environs in 1908, Camp soon became convinced that some, if not all of Custer's companies, had tried to cross at the Minneconjou Ford, (Ford B) at the mouth of Medicine Tail Coulee. On the same hand, Camp's contemporary, John Stands In Timber, was convinced that at least some of "Custer's" soldiers had gone to another set of fords farther to the *north*. His conviction was formed when his fellow Cheyenne informants guided him over a trail that went *northward* from Medicine Tail Coulee to a set of fords a considerable distance downstream. If the battalions with Custer were operating as separate military units, than both sources of information could be correct. Did Custer divide his forces and if he did, why?

We know from Walter Camp's research that it was the First Battalion that went to the Ford B area. And, eventually being forced to retreat after an aborted crossing, they would be deployed on what is now known as the Finley and Calhoun Hill areas. That leaves the Second Battalion to have been Strands In Timber's northbound soldiers that attempted to cross at the lower fords. This startling conclusion is based on knowing the correct battalion assignments made on June 25. **See Chapter One, pg. 53 (Battalion Assignments)**

For far too long, writers have placed Company L in the wrong battalion! Along with the now identifiable terrain that the two "Custer" Battalions traveled over, and with the army's regulated rate of march of their horses, we can now create a "blueprint" of the time, distance and events as they unfolded. Thanks to modern day cavalry reenactors, who with great diligence have reconstructed the protocol for the deployment of the "Custer" era Cavalry, we can now fill in the blanks. This new knowledge gives us far more logical military scenarios.

The Strategic Role of the Second Battalion: Within minutes of the departure of John Martin from the Fourth Halt in Medicine Tail Coulee, Custer ordered Yates's Second Battalion, consisting of Companies E, F and L, into motion. Their mission was to circle around to the *north*, and attack the rear of these new encampments on Onion Creek. To do this they would have to cross the river farther downstream. Once across the river, they were to attack the Onion Creek villages from the downstream (north) side. This flanking movement was like the multi-front deployment at the Washita Fight against Black Kettle's winter village. **See Villages, pg. 69 (See also WHAT CUSTER SAW At 3:10 PM, pg. 123)**

The startling conclusion that the Great Custer divided his forces in the face of a superior number of enemy flies in the face of most Custer researchers. But the simple fact that two separate army units were now in operation cannot be denied, not if both Walter Camp's and John Stands In Timber's sources are correct. By having two military units moving in two different directions is the military strategy of a double envelopment, a "pincer" movement with two separate attack fronts.

This was the original intent of Custer, who at first thought the villages that Varnum had seen were just in the upper valley. Custer's earlier departure from the Lower Ash Creek Valley proves that he intended to execute the same style of pincer movement on the downstream side of the Upper Camps, those that Reno had been ordered to attack from the upstream side. But now, in Medicine Tail Coulee he discovered that there were additional villages much farther downstream. If he continued the attack the northern side of the Upper Camps, he would leave warriors from these new villages in his rear. This was not an acceptable military scenario.

If he attacked the *southern* end of the new Onion Creek camps, then their *north* side would be left open for the possible escape of the lodges. By sending one of the two battalions on an end run northward was standard protocol for any experienced combat officer. What is not apparent was that Custer did not seem to be aware of the size and strength of these downstream villages. Nor, did he expect the total failure of his subordinates, Reno and Benteen, either to hold their positions or to coming to his aid with reinforcements. Custer now needed Benteen's reserve Fourth Battalion to replace the Second Battalion, now on its way *north* to attack these new encampments. Two previous orders had already been sent to Benteen to come to Custer's advanced front now in Medicine Tail Coulee, without the Packs. **See Facsimile B pg. 141.**

The First Battalion, Halt Number Four: The result was an extended halt for the First Battalion. They would now have wait for Yates's Second Battalion to come around to the rear of the Onion Creek encampments. Walter Camp was the very first Custer researcher to ever suggest that such a halt did occur in Medicine Tail Coulee. Camp also thought correctly that a halt would also give Benteen time to close up the distance between the separated units. He measured the distance from the Minneconjou Crossing (Ford B) to where he was shown where the soldiers had halted in Medicine Tail Coulee. His primary source was Curly. His wheel odometer measurement was just over one and one quarter mile. **LILLY 131**

After being ordered *north* the Second Battalion traveled down Medicine Tail Coulee for about a quarter of a mile when the advanced foragers from Company F located a well-defined trail that went *north*. It would take the Yates's Battalion over what was to become known as the "Nye-Cartwright" Ridge area and across what is now the present Custer Battlefield. And then down into the Little Bighorn Valley and the expected lower ford crossings.

Bouyer Sent Back To Crow Hill: Soon after the departure of the Second Battalion, Custer may have noticed that he could no longer hear the sounds from Reno's engagement in the upper valley. The sounds of Reno's skirmish line had been heard for the last ten minutes, ever since leaving Martin's "Big Hill." Bouyer was now sent back to the bluffs again. Custer not only wanted to know what happened to Reno's advance in the valley, but also what the villagers were doing, especially those in the Lower Camps where Yates's Battalion was now headed. **(See pg. 160, FIRST BATTALION RETREAT TO FINLEY HILL)**

Bouyer took Curly, who by now had caught up with the Headquarters Staff. A five-man detail was sent with them. It would have taken them less than five minutes to reach the high ground now called "Bouyer Hill", due to its short distance from the Fourth Halt in Medicine Tail Coulee. It was while Bouyer and Curly were here they observed Reno's sudden departure from the valley at 3:25 PM. Three men, Bouyer, Curly and perhaps the supervising N.C.O. of the escort detail then waved their hats to get Custer's attention. **See Map pg. 160**

Lieutenant Charles DeRudio observed this event while he was still in the timber in the valley on the left bank of Little Bighorn River. His sighting of what he thought was Custer, Adjutant Cooke and a third man was *just before* Reno's retreat from his "Woods Fight." They were silhouetted against the sky on a high point due *north* of his position in the valley. However, he must have had remarkable eye sight since it is almost one mile distance to Bouyer Hill. Custer still had DeRudio's expensive European field glasses and DeRudio's sighting was made with the naked eye. At the time of Reno's retreat the Second Battalion was still in motion on the *south* slope of the Nye-Cartwright/Luce Ridge area. But, at that this very moment, an incident occurred that would prematurely send the First Battalion into the valley.

The First Battalion Is Sent Forward To Ford B: When the Second Battalion reached a point on the lower south slope of the Nye-Cartwright Ridge, a little known event occurred.

They were attacked by a band of "Young Warriors" on the right rear of the column as it was advancing up the south slope. Suddenly, this large band of pre-warrior society teenage "boys" appeared out of the mouth of the North Medicine Tail Coulee drainage.

Horsemanship Note: This sudden attack on the flanks and rear of his battalion caused Captain Yates to have Company E dismount and to fight on foot to meet this new threat. The obvious reason that Company E was selected is an established protocol of the U.S. Army. Because the default dress alignment is to the right, and the Gray Horse Company was on the left flank of the battalion, Company E was the logical one to be dismounted without affecting the alignment of the battalion. **O3 & O4 See pg. 169, YOUNG WARRIORS ROUTE**

Yates's Tactical Error: Yates's premature decision would keep Company E out of support for the next hour! When this attack occurred, the Second Battalion was still 600 yards from the First Battalion's halt in Medicine Tail Coulee. As soon as the Young Warriors assault on the Second Battalion was verified, Custer was forced to send Myles Keogh's First Battalion into motion towards the valley. This premature offensive move came by 3:25 PM, approximately ten minutes after the Second Battalion had started its northward movement from Medicine Tail Coulee.

More Horsemanship: How do we know that it was the First Battalion that was now sent down Medicine Tail Coulee? After the Custer Fight, both Lieutenants Charles DeRudio and Edward McClernand saw organized shod tracks in lower Medicine Tail Coulee. These tracks were in a double column of fours, eight files wide. This trail was created by the Keogh's First Battalion as this was the only battalion that had two companies. They were still marching in a Civil War "Squadron" formation. These tracks went all the way to Ford B. In at least one instance they momentarily changed into a column of twos, so reported Lieutenant DeRudio. This change probably occurred at the crossing of the lower Medicine Trail Coulee drainage about one quarter mile east of the present National Park Service Bridge on the tourist road to Reno Hill. **LILLY 546 (McClernand), DPL 97 (DeRudio)**

This premature deployment of the First Battalion was in response to the Young Warriors attack on the Second Battalion. While John Martin was taking his "shortcut" he heard the opening volleys of Company E at 3:20 PM. He told Walter Camp he thought that he was observing Custer's entire Command "retreating" up the south slope of the Luce Ridge area! What he was seeing at a fleeting glance was the Second Battalion, now minus. Company E, continuing its mounted advance northward and over the Nye-Cartwright Ridge. **M40, pg. 101 (Martin)**

The Seventh Messenger Is Sent: When Bouyer and Curley rejoined the advancing Head Quarters Staff in Medicine Tail Coulee, Custer would send yet another messenger. This order may have been directed to Captain McDougall, who now needed to know of Reno's retreat now headed for Ash Creek and the Pack Train. Army regulations require a retreating column to withdraw on their back trail and that appeared were Reno was headed. McDougall needed to beware of the danger of the warriors falling onto the Pack Train as they chased Reno up Ash Creek. Martin had been sent only twenty minutes earlier to Benteen. Martin's order would have been a logical countermanding directive for Benteen to come forward quickly, the same orders sent earlier by Corporal Bishop and Kanipe. Right now, Custer did not know where the Pack Train was located. He last saw them from Martin's "Big Hill" over thirty minutes earlier yet twenty minutes from the 2:00 PM crossing of Middle Ash Creek. Military commanders assume that their orders will be carried out. But the person that wrote that military axiom obviously did not know Frederick Benteen. Custer still did not know where Benteen was located. Benteen was approaching Mathey's Knoll and still fifty minutes behind Custer. The messenger now sent to McDougall may have been Bugler Henry Dose of Company G. He had been assigned to the Headquarters Staff and his body was later discovered in Medicine Tail Coulee. **LILLY 578 (Dose)**

Custer, having just been told of Reno's retreat from the Valley, realized this was a cause for great concern. The Pack Train would be exposed if Reno followed his back trial up Ash Creek. The First Battalion and the Staff were now approaching the Ford B area. Probably in response to Bouyer's dire news about Reno's flight from the Valley, Custer now ordered all of the Buglers to be massed in front of the Staff and then to incessantly blow cavalry calls! Apparently Custer wanted the Onion Creek camps to know of his immediate presence in the lower Medicine Tail Coulee area? Or was this a ploy to take the pressure off of Reno's retreating men? If it was, it worked too well, for within the next thirty minutes ninety percent of the entire warrior force would converge on the Custer Battalions.

The main reason for the massing of the warrior force against Custer at this time was due to the arrival of additional troops (Benteen's battalion) at Reno's chosen hilltop position. As Walter Camp pointed out in his notes that the Indians knew the first soldiers (Reno) were no longer a threat. By having these new soldiers (Benteen) join those on the bluffs prevented them from an immediate attack on the villages. If the new soldiers continued to advance northward they could easily be cut-off by flanking attacks in the rough ground of the bluffs, fighting that favored the Indians! **LILLY 29**

However, the knowledge of other soldiers attacking the lower villages sent at least ninety percent of the warrior's northward to combat this new threat. But as the First Battalion was approaching the Onion Creek camps, an event occurred on behalf of the warriors. It nearly spelled a disaster for the villagers, but as events unfolded it would assure defeat for the First Battalion at Ford B. It involved the young pony herd boys whose job was to watch over the massive and free grazing horse herds of the villagers.

The Pony Herd Boys: A providential incident occurred within the last hour that would change the fortunes of war in favor of the villagers. The Onion Creek camps were located over two and one half miles downstream from where Reno's skirmish line was formed. When the soldiers opened fire, the population of the lower camps went into immediate action. The women and children started to strike their lodges and pack their household belongings preparing to escape. There is evidence that the Northern Cheyenne village already had begun to break camp, even before the Reno attack.

The Northern Plains Indians had an established tradition to travel a short distance in the late afternoon to their new camp sites. The Northern Cheyenne camp would be the first to break camp, as they were on the downstream side of the villages. The Old Men councils had already decided to move the villages to the mouth of the Little Bighorn, where a large herd of antelope had been spotted in the vicinity of present day Hardin, Montana. But, the following little known event would soon swing the balance of the battle to favor the villagers. The young pony boys, assigned to watch over and guard the pony herds, had failed in their critical roles to assure tribal survival. The lower camp's pony herds had been put out to graze on the bench-lands west of Onion and Squaw Creeks. These essential guards were to insure that the herds would stay close to the lodges so, if needed, they could be herded quickly into the camps. But, typical of young boys, and it being a hot day, many had gone swimming in the Little Horn River. The others were just goofing off in general. **M40, pg. 157 (Curly)**

When Reno opened fire, sheer pandemonium broke out. This incident proves that Custer's mid-afternoon attack was indeed a surprise. When the herds were not immediately driven in, the adult men where forced to ride out and round up their family horses and herd them into the villages. However, as they approached the scattered herds, many of the ponies became frightened and begun to run away from the rapidly approaching riders from the villages. This breech of security by the pony boys cost the Cheyenne and Ogallala warrior's critical time in setting up their defense posture. The women were unable to acquire their drag ponies needed to haul their household goods and their highly valuable lodge covers. The possibility exists that Custer may have witnessed this this weakness as early as 3:10 PM, when he first halted in Medicine Tail Coulee. It could have given the appearance of a camp already on the move?

The Ford B Snipers: This delaying incident was a blessing in disguise for the warriors. Some forty minutes after the opening shots by Reno's battalion, the First Battalion made its appearance in lower Medicine Tail Coulee. Due to the pony boy's negligence, a small number of Cheyenne warriors (not yet mounted) saw what was happening when the soldiers made their sudden appearance at the mouth of Medicine Tail Coulee.

The brief and light skirmishing between John Stands In Timber's Young Warriors and the dismounted Company E on the slope of the Nye-Cartwright area some fifteen minutes earlier had already alerted them. But now seeing that these new soldiers were headed directly towards their camps, they ran on foot to the left bank of the Minneconjou crossing (Ford B). Here they quickly sought positions in the heavy brush on the upper bench across from the wide crossing. This act by the dismounted warriors would become the beginning of end of the offensive attack by the army. The distance beyond Ford B to the Onion Creek camps was but three-quarter of a mile and the mounted soldiers could have covered this distance in a matter of minutes. **NA4, pg. 124-125 (Miller names five of these warriors)**

The Real Ford B: In the multitude of Custer writings there are much confusion on where the Court of Inquiry's "Ford B" was located. Credit must be given to Owen B. Williams, a premier "Custer Battle" researcher of the 1960 and 1970s, for determining where it was located. Williams was a retired civil surveyor from the U.S. Corps of Engineers, and like Walter Camp, he was able to correctly identify the correct Ford B. There are two apparent ford crossings in this area today. The lower downstream one (where the Real Bird family holds their annual reenactment) is not the Minneconjou Ford, usually referred to as Ford B. This minor crossing was mentioned by some of the Battle participants as being a good watering place for horses. And that is its primary purpose today as many of the local Crow horses are taken here to be watered. It has a very narrow exit trough on the left hand bank, one far too narrow for the passage of a column of fours. The major crossing, which has been there for time immemorial, is located about four tenths mile upstream from the lesser Real Bird crossing. This very old and traditional ford had been a prominent crossing long before the Custer Battle.

The Lack of Fighting at Ford B: Mister (Second Lieutenant) Harrington, of Company C, was junior in grade to First Lieutenant James Porter of Company I. It would be Porter who was given the honor to advance across Ford B. It was a time honored military ethical edict that gave him the honor of leading the first company over the river for an attack on the Onion Creek encampments. Curly told Camp that the fighting in this area was very unimpressive to him. He did not see where much action had taken place. However, Curly did see a mounted sergeant ride across the river and disappear among the warriors on the other side. The Headquarters Staff and Company C would have remained on the upper bench on the east bank. Mister Harrington's Company C was most likely formed into a single mounted rank ready to cross by files behind Company I.

Captain Keogh, as the battalion commander, would have waited with the Staff as army protocol dictated. When Company I tried to cross in a column of fours, Lieutenant Porter and his buglers would be in the lead. The dismounted warriors, hidden in the brush along on the upper west bench, opened up with a blistering fire of several volleys. At least two of the soldiers were immediately were shot out of their saddles in midstream! This may have been Lieutenant Porter and one of his buglers. Porter was later officially listed as missing in action, but his blouse coat was later found in the village. Bullet holes in his coat showed that he had been shot in the back, and on through the chest with a large bore weapon and at a relatively close range. Assuming that their revolvers may have been deployed this early there is a strong possibility that Lieutenant Porter was shot by one of his own men.

The training of the enlisted men with the deployment of side arms, while mounted was almost non-existent. This author on more then one occasion has unintentionally discharged the same single-action revolver as carried by the army. The deployment of the revolver was done by the numbers. If the hammer had been mistakenly pulled back to full cock, an accidental discharge is very plausible. The fact remains that Porter may have been shot in the back by one of his own men due to the lack of proper weapons training then so prevalent in the army.

Warriors said that they saw one of the bugler's body float downstream. However, due to the higher respect paid for commissioned officers, Lieutenant Porter's lifeless body may have been retrieved and taken along with the troops as they retreated to higher ground. If so, his body was never identified on the field. After the Battle, the body of a sergeant from Company I, along with his horse, was found some distance west of "Custer's Ford." Camp surmised identified this body was that of Sergeant James Bustard, who was one the of two platoon sergeants known to have gone down Medicine Tail Coulee. If so, Company I was now left with but one platoon sergeant, three corporals and their First Sergeant to maintain military order. Keep this mind, as these anomalies will appear later. As battalion commander, it would have been Captain Keogh who now ordered a withdrawal by the "March to the Rear," bugle command. Company I, now without any of its officers now managed to reverse itself in midstream and marched back to the right bank, where Company C and Custer's Staff was still waiting.

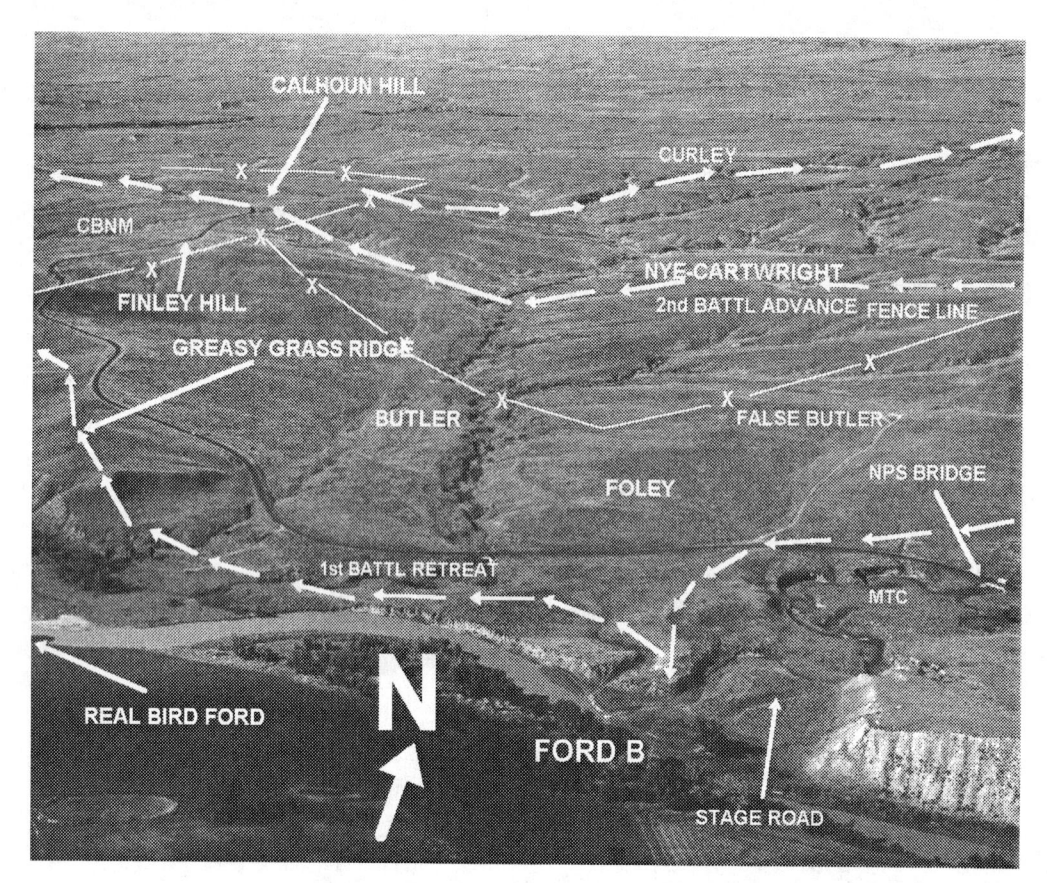

AERIAL VIEW OF FORD B AND NYE-CARTWRIGHT AREA

(3:35 to 4:00 PM)

SCALE: -------------------- 1/4 MILE

This aerial photograph shows the Ford B area. Here a small number of dismounted warriors held off the attempt of the First battalion to cross at 3:35 PM. The First Battalion withdrew and began a northern retreat to Greasy Grass Ridge. By then, overwhelming numbers of mounted warriors were arriving from the defunct Reno Valley Fight.

*The earlier advance of the Second Battalion is shown over the Nye-Cartwright area, as part of a double envelopment (pincer) movement against the Onion Creek encampments. Only part of the upstream Ogallala village could be seen **(See Villages, pg. 69)**. The Second Battalion was sent twenty-five minutes earlier and was attacked by the Young Warriors **(See pg. 164)** causing a premature advance of the First Battalion down Medicine Tail Coulee to the Ford B area. **(See Map pg. 125)***

The Minneconjou Ford: The Crow still call it the Minneconjou Ford named after the Sioux encampment that was located just upstream at the time of the Battle. Walter Camp mentioned that this crossing was the most prominent ford in this area. It is located the northeast 1/4 section of Township Section 29. This well established ford would later be used by the Indian Reservation systems as a stage road crossing. The Blake/Marshall Survey **(Seen on page 55-56)** shows the Crow Agency to Busby stage route crossing at the

Minneconjou Ford. This is the traditional Native American name for this very wide and hard bottom crossing. It lies just above the natural terminal end of Medicine Tail Coulee drainage.

The First Battalion Retreats: At this point, Custer ordered an immediate general retreat by a right flank movement to higher ground. U.S. Army regulations did not leave him much choice. They state that when a unit attempts to cross an "obstacle," such as a river crossing, and faces an unknown enemy strength "entrenched" on the other side, then that unit is required to retreat on its own back trail! Curly said that it was at this point in time that the warriors now begun to cross to the right bank of the river in many places. The First Battalion retreated, but not on its back trail. They did not go back up the Medicine Tail Coulee trail. Striking out to the *north*, Custer was perhaps now looking for another unguarded crossing farther downstream. **O3 &O4**

Or the possibility exists that he may have been trying to reunite with his best military friend, George Yates and his Second Battalion. Too many "Custer" buffs have insisted that the "Charge the Camp" Custer would have never retreated from any situation! This is a false assumption due a procedure called a Court of Inquiry. Army officers were subject to disciplinary review when there was a large lost of government property, especially if it was the horses. God help them if they lost any of the Government horses; their career was soon over!

The First Battalion's Retreat To Finley Hill: This action now took the First Battalion to higher ground now called Greasy Grass Ridge. They still maintained the same "squadron" formation, with both companies files parallel to each other. Traveling mounted for the one mile distance; they now halted and dismounted just outside of the original "South" fence line of the future Custer Battlefield.

In the early 1900s, Camp often referred to the existence of a "**South**" boundary fence line at the Custer Battlefield. Here he was referring to part of the original fence line constructed by James Campbell around the Custer Battlefield during the 1890s. About one hundred yards west of the present automobile gate, Camp's "south" fence line then diverted northwest toward the mouth of the Gray Horse ravine. In the mid-1900s, a governmental boundary adjustment caused this original fence line to be abandoned. The First Battalion would now halt and be deployed as dismounted skirmishers just south of the original fence line on the highest portion of Greasy Grass Hill. **M40, pg. 167 (Also pg. 160, FIRST BATTALION RETREAT TO FINLEY HILL)**

From this halt the men began intermittent and long range light skirmishing with the mounted warriors. The soldiers now moved in a magnetic north direction on foot. The warriors simply stayed outside of the army's effective carbine range of about a quarter mile. They would soon arrive at what Walter Camp would designate as "Finley Hill," named after Company C's second platoon leader, Jeremiah Finley. Daniel Kanipe showed him where Company Cs' Sergeants Finley and Finckle were found and buried. The movement to Finley Hill was strenuous for the dismounted skirmishers. By standard army procedure all dismounted action was done at the "Double" or "Quick" time of marching!

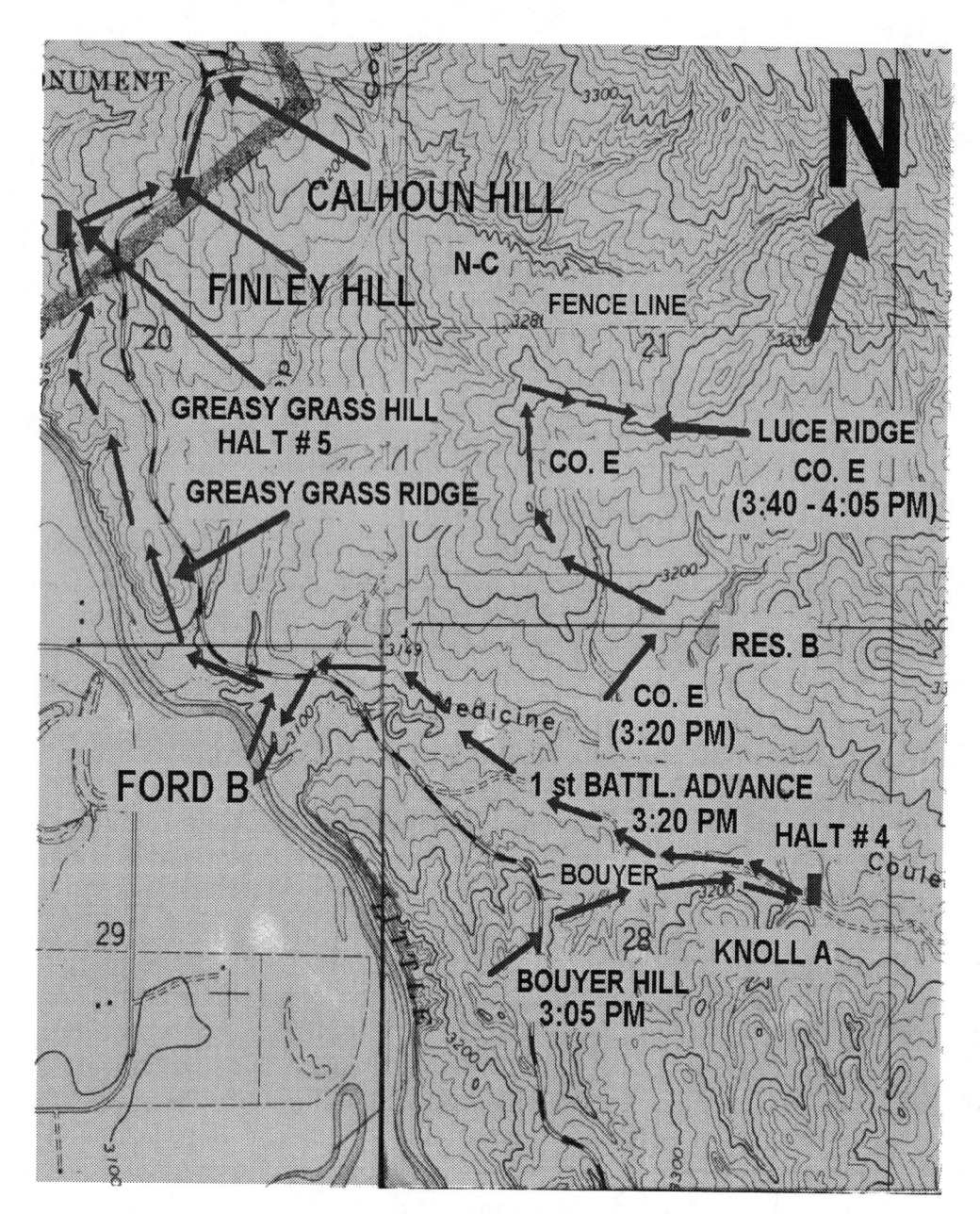

FIRST BATTALION ADVANCE AND RETREAT TO FINLEY HILL

3:25 to 4;:00 PM

SCALE: --------------- 1/4 MILE

*Custer prematurely sends the First Battalion into the valley, after the unexpected attack of the Young Warriors on the Second Battalion now on its way north. The result was the aborted passage at Ford B when a small number of dismounted warriors prevented the battalion from crossing. After Lt. Porter's death in mid-stream, the battalion was ordered northward to Greasy Grass Ridge and perhaps another crossing. The retreating battalion was dismounted and formed into Flankers as Skirmishers **(See Appendix: pg. 201)** on Greasy Grass Hill **(Halt #5)**. Company C was posted on Finley Hill after firing two volleys that were heard on Reno Hill at 3:55 PM. Meanwhile, Custer's Staff and Company I continue to the future Calhoun Hill, in search of a defensive "Good Ground" to fight on.*

According to Curly it was during this early phase of fighting that Custer told Mitch Bouyer that he was now looking for good ground on which to fight. This is the "Bouyer" remark from the Camp material that Charles Kuhlman wrote about in his book, *Legend Into History.* He was referring to research material sent to him in the late 1930s by Robert Ellison. According to Curly, Bouyer said that Custer was now seeking a high place to wait for the arrival of the other troops. However, Bouyer did not think that they would come, having been "scared out" of the territory. Were these other troops Benteen's reserve battalion? Curly would also tell Camp that the warriors were now driving the men like buffalo. They were on all three sides, only their front was left open. **LILLY 29, BYU 434, M40, pg. 158 (Curly), M 44, (Kuhlman) pg. 160**

The Fifth Halt of the First Battalion: This was the very first time since leaving the Divide, that the First Battalion was dismounted. Here they formed into two parallel ranks of skirmishers on the flanks. The double sets of fours of the led horses were kept between the two lines of flanking skirmishers. This is a standard army tactical formation referred in the cavalry manuals as "Skirmishers as Flankers." **See APPENDIX: Skirmishers as Flankers, pg. 201**

When the word got out that there were other soldiers now approaching the lower camps, the warriors galloped to this new scene of action. The majority of them arrived soon after the non-fighting at Ford B and the resulting retreat of the First Battalion to higher ground. Curly said that he did not actual see any of the soldiers killed or wounded along this retreat to Finley Hill, but he could not understand how there would not have been some causalities. However, his mentor, Mitch Bouyer did lose his horse along this retreat. There is a remote possibility that Custer, from the height of Greasy Grass Hill, may have been able to see the Second Battalion also now retreating from their abortive Lower Ford crossing. The two battalions were now separated by one and half mile distance. Both battalion commanders were adhering to the old military adage, that when you have lost the offensive, "seize the high ground!"

The First Battalion was still dismounted when they reached Finley Hill, a good quarter mile from where they had dismounted. Here Company C halted and deployed into a poorly formed skirmish line. Whether is was Keogh or Custer who ordered this desperate attempt to fend off the ever increasing and aggressive number of warriors that now threatened their flanks, the attempt would soon come back to haunt them. This meager effort now becomes the first skirmish line to be established within the present boundaries of the Custer Battlefield. This now becomes the author's "East Skirmish Line."

Curly said that two volleys were now fired from new halt near Finley Hill. He thought that they were some kind of a signal to the other soldiers. These volleys were heard on Reno Hill and they were described as being sort of a crash-crash sound. Even the hard of hearing Godfrey heard them and did others like Frederick Benteen, who had normal hearing. This brings us to the very beginning of the fighting on the Custer Field. Up to now, only light skirmishing and maneuvering for a better defensive position had occurred which was a prelude to the more serious fighting to come. The time was now 4:00 PM.

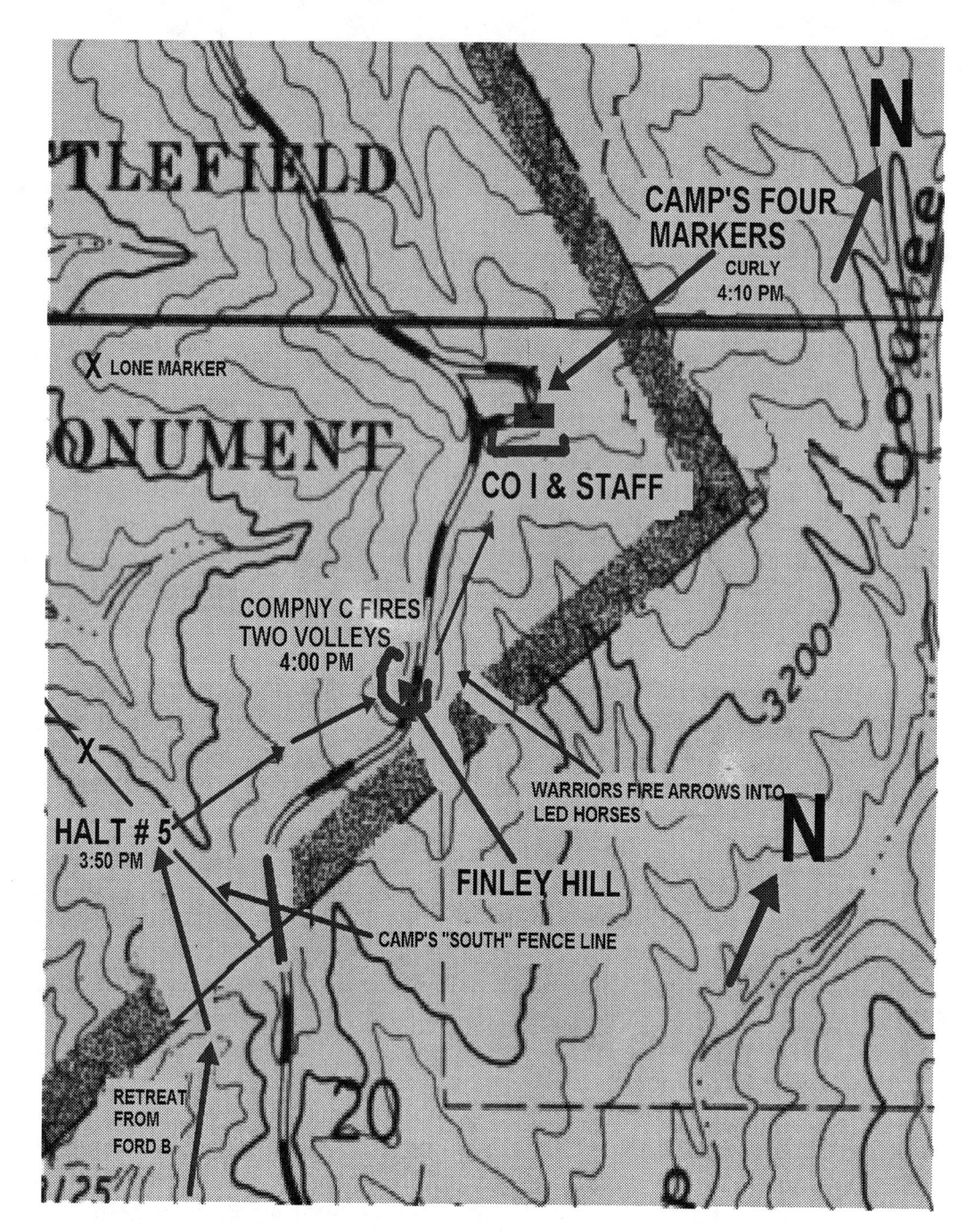

EAST SKIRMISH LINE

(4:00 to 4:10 PM)

SCALE: -- 1/4 MILE

Walter Camp was the first Custer researcher to identify Finley Hill as where Company C had been posted. His source was Daniel Kanipe, who along with Peter Thompson had traveled with Camp to the Custer Battlefield in 1908. Obviously, it was Company I that fought on Calhoun Hill along with Company L when it arrived later from the West Skirmish Line by 4:20 PM. **See CUSTER FIGHT - PHASE 1, pg. 202**

Bob Doran 2007

ARCHERS ON FINLEY HILL
(See "Disaster on Finley Hill," page 165)

CHAPTER SEVEN

THE CUSTER FIGHT

Our people were all around the hill on every side by this time. I heard some of our men shouting: "They are gone!" And I saw many of the soldier's horses had broken loose and were running away. Everywhere our warriors began to yelling Hoka Hey, Hurry!"
Standing Bear, from Black Elk Speaks, by John G. Neihardt

Note on directional headings: Up to now, mostly the United States Geological Survey (U.S.G.S.) references have been used. They are based on longitudinal True North, and do not reflect the sixteen degrees of magnetic variation in this region. In this chapter all geographical directions in or near the Custer Battlefield will be given as general magnetic compass directions. For example Calhoun Hill is on the east end of the Battle Ridge, while Monument Hill is on the west. This is done in deference to the already established usage to the South Skirmish Line, which correctly should be expressed as the West Skirmish Line, if using U.S.G.S. orientation.

The East Skirmish Line, Finley Hill: After firing the two volleys, Company C was formed into an extended skirmish line. Assuming that they had no causalities along the retreat from Ford B, Mister Harrington would have but twenty-one men to place on the line. Company C had at least eight un-ridden reserve horses. Extra led horse holders would be needed. This cut into the number of skirmishes that could be placed on the line. The normal prescribed interval between skirmishers was set at six yards. At this interval Company C's normally extended line would be some 125 yards long if deployed as a single rank. But due to the understaffed company it was most likely deployed as a double rank. This is where a double rank of knelling and standing men from each platoon would be deployed. They may have been placed in a semi-circle around the highest part of Finley Hill. Peter Thompson reported in his 1900 narrative as seeing his Company C formed in a semi-circle from his advanced position as a straggler and dropout in the river bottom.

Normally, when men were posted on high ground they were deployed along what the military called a "military crest. " This was where they were deployed some distance down the slope so that they would not be silhouetted on the horizon. For some reason this practice was not carried out on Finley Hill! Perhaps, the non-standard deployment was due to Mister Harrington's inexperience. He had left West Point just under two years earlier and this was his first combat experience!

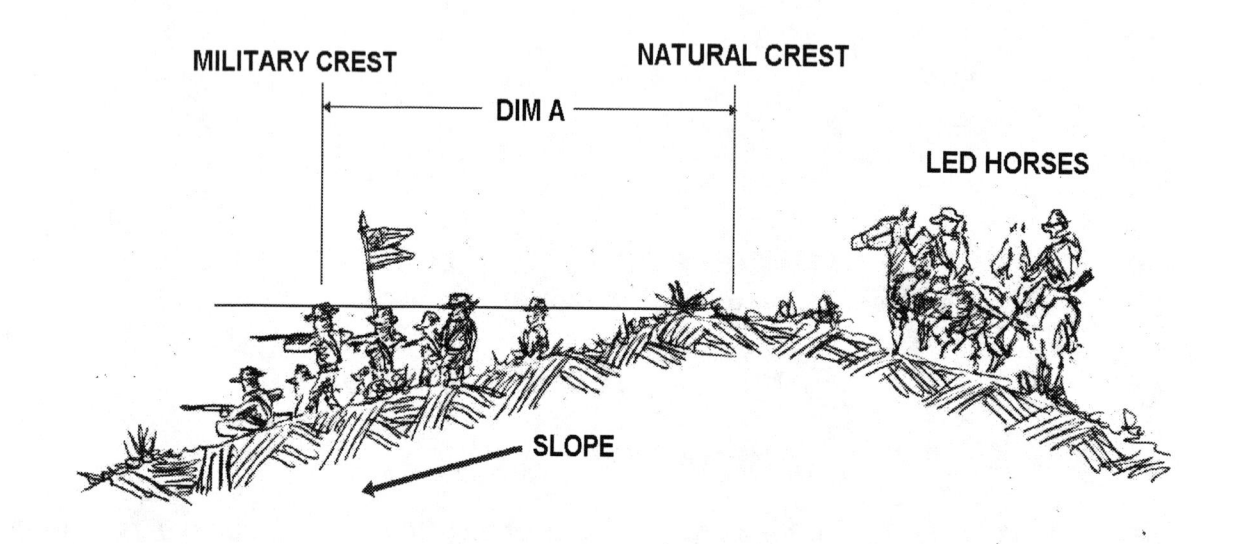

Bob Doran 2007

MILITARY CREST DEPLOYMENT

NOT TO SCALE

However, the major military problem with Finley Hill was that the area was just too large for such of a small defensive force. The "fighting" here was not very effective for the soldiers. They did not have any real targets to shoot as the majority of the warriors by now were dismounted and crawling up along the slopes. The terrain allowed this lone company to be soon encircled on at least three sides. However, the rear of the line was left open due to lack of cover for the warriors in this direction. **See Appendix: The Custer Fight, Phase 1, pg. 202**

Custer Goes to Calhoun Hill: At this early point in the Battle, the Headquarters Staff along with Company I continued north to what is now called Calhoun Hill. Company I may have been able to remount when Company C fired its two volleys. It was another quarter mile to this higher ground and the men were now becoming tired from the double time marching effort after being dismounted. Upon reaching the higher elevation of Calhoun Hill, the Headquarters Staff and Company I now halted and was deployed along a new line near present N.P.S. battlefield road entrance to the Calhoun Hill area. The most probable cause for this movement may have been two fold? Custer may have wanted to observe what the Second Battalion was now doing? . **M40, pg. 158 (Curly)**

There is a high blocking terrain known as the "Lone Marker" ridge west of Finley Hill that prevented seeing Yates's battalion, also now retreating away from the abortive "Willy Bends" crossing in the valley. The other factor may have been the sudden appearance of the orphaned Company E, which was now skirmishing dismounted down the North Slope of the Nye-Cartwright Ridge. They had heard the skirmishing from Greasy Grass Hill to Finley Hill and were now responding to the action from what will become the Custer Battlefield. Did Custer confuse Company E's appearance as an advance unit from Benteen's expected arrival with the needed reinforcements?

It would have been at this time that a courier with a five man detail was sent to Captain Yates from Custer's new high ground defensive position (Calhoun Hill). By the time that the Headquarters staff had reached Calhoun Hill, the Second Battalion was now forming a defensive skirmish line at the west end of the present day National Cemetery complex. Custer needed the two battalions to be reunited as soon as possible. It is this author's contention that the Calhoun Hill area was Custer's proposed "Good Ground" to wait for the arrival of Benteen's expected reinforcements. It was at this point that Bouyer came to Curly and told him that the Scouts had been ordered to get out as soon as they could. Custer, through Thomas Custer had told Bouyer that "they were going to be taken (killed)." It appears that even during this early segment of the fighting Custer realized that his small command was going to be overrun and annihilated! **M40, pg. 167 (Bouyer), LILLY 29, BYU 434, M40, pg. 159 (Curly) M 49, (Kuhlman) pg. 160**

Disaster on Finley Hill: After less then ten minutes of long range sniping on Finley Hill, the left flank of Company C was rolled up. The shattered company then fled in wild disorder. A little known tactical deployment by the dismounted warriors gained the advantage over the "modern" U.S. Army. The weapon that created this advantage is surprising; it was the archaic bow and arrow! **See APPENDIX: The Custer Fight, Phase 2 pg. 203**

A shallow depression in the terrain to the east of the left rear of Company C's line allowed for the infiltration of dismounted warriors who were able to lob arrows in a high parabolic flight into the flanks of the led horses and their mounted holders. Within minutes, the horses were being hit by very painful arrow strikes. Very soon sheer pandemonium would break out among the horses and the men of Company C's Second Platoon skirmish line. **NA4, pg. 232, NA6, pg. 230 (Bow & arrow usage)**

Screaming and kicking the led horses of the Second Platoon bolted through the line. When frightened, horses emit pheromones (chemical odor) that cause other calm horses to suddenly become unmanageable. When horses become frightened, their "flight or fight" instincts kick in. They will always flee away from the source of what is spooking them. The led horses started to stampede and they fled southward through the Finley Hill skirmish line. Curly, from his position on Calhoun Hill, described how "the men that had been left behind" were now running for their horses. He said that "they just would not stand." This observation proves that men on Calhoun Hill were posted where they could still see Company C's position on Finley Hill. **M40, pg. 158-159 (Curly)**

Curly was seeing Sergeant Finley's Second Platoon fleeing in panic to get to their horses. In time the companies line supervisors, Sergeants Finley and Finckle, would be killed behind their respected platoon positions. It was at this point that all control over the men ceased. Soon the First Platoon along with Mister Harrington was in full retreat, a repeat of Reno's rout almost an hour earlier. The panicked men fled for their lives. They left behind a total of eighteen men dead on Finley Hill, the majority behind the skirmish line. How do we know that it was Company C that had fought here? When Walter Camp took Daniel Kanipe and Peter Thompson to the Battlefield in 1909, it was former Company C Sergeant Kanipe who pointed out the exact burial locations of Company C's platoon leaders, Sergeants Jeremiah Finley and August Finckle. Camp then coined the term "Finley Hill" to designate where Company C had fought.

In 1877, Trumpeter A. F. Mulford reported that during his reburial trip to the Custer Battlefield he saw the "uncovered remains of eighteen men, in six piles, with a piece of a tepee pole sticking in the ground at each pile." Is it possible that these eighteen men represented Company C's Second Platoon? On one of these poles, Trooper Mulford saw a "white sombrero" with obvious battle related damage. In 1876, Company C was one of three companies issued the new gray felt campaign hat. **M37, pg. 379**

It is obvious that during the original burials the bodies were dragged around and placed into piles, similar to the Civil War methods of cleaning up a battlefield. This is to be kept in mind that when the army would place stone grave markers on the battlefield in 1890. They were deceived by this unorthodox manner. The "barrow" dirt dug out from around the "six piles" of three men each, confused the grave marker soldiers.

When Company C had its left flank rolled up, they left behind eighteen men dead on Finley Hill. At least three additional men were killed running on foot trying to catch up with their mounted comrades. But the remnant of Company C continued to flee mounted past the Headquarters Staff's position with no apparent notice of their presence. The one dozen or so mounted survivors now turned west into "Ravine A," the one that leads down to what will soon become known as the Keogh area.

As the fleeing men approached this area, about one quarter of a mile west of Calhoun Hill, some turned to the left and fled mounted southward over the Battle Ridge. The sudden appearance of mounted warriors in their front, in the deeper reaches of Ravine A, caused an abrupt change in direction. However, a few Company C men, possibly a set of fours, continued on to the plateau where later the remnants of Company I will also retreat and reform in the soon to be designated "Keogh" area. One of these men was the First Sergeant Edwin Bobo, who had lost his horse near the Calhoun Hill area. In 1909, Daniel Kanipe showed Walter Camp the exact location of Sergeant Bobo's body in the Keogh area. He also pointed out the where Bobo's horse, "Carlo," had been shot down and had fallen down the left embankment of Ravine A. Most likely it was one of Company C's mounted man that picked up the dismounted Sergeant Bobo and they were able to reach the Keogh area. Walter Camp carefully marked his "Markers" field survey were First Sergeant Bobo and horse had fallen. The normal position for the First Sergeant in a skirmish line is behind the right platoon. When the company fled, Bobo may have been left behind and a set of stragglers rescued him when his horse went down with him. **M40, pg. 95 (fn 15) Kanipe, 199**

The balance of about a dozen men now fled south along an established trail that ran parallel to what is now called the "Gray Horse Ravine." (Ravine B) It led to a good ford crossing across from the mouth of Onion Creek. At least five other men, along with Harrington, were able to cross at this ford and continue to travel towards the *west* bluffs. Here they would lose another two men. After the battle, Frederick Gerard would discover two dead enlisted men out the valley across from the crossing at the mouth of the Gray Horse Gully. Later in the 1950s, Hank Weibert would discover an authentic Custer era cavalry spur in a hay field in the northeast 1/4 section of Township Section 29. Perhaps it might be related to the dead men discovered by Gerard. **LILLY 671 (Gerard)**

Mister Harrington and his remaining three men now continued to flee south along the bluffs towards the mouth of Bear In The Middle Creek. Apparently, they were now headed back to the mouth of Ash Creek. However, they were out guessed by pursuing warriors, who took the faster valley route and then headed them off. In 1877, Crow families returning to the Little Bighorn valley discovered the skeletal remains of an officer along with three enlisted men near the mouth of Bear-In-Middle Creek, some six miles away from Finley Hill. Pretty Shields, the wife of the Crow Scout Goes Ahead, told Frank Linderman about this discovery in his biography *Red Mother*.

The remaining Company C men that did not cross the river now turned upstream along the right bank of the Little Bighorn and soon they would reach the top of Greasy Grass Hill. A number of army artifacts found by the National Park Service in Ravine D may be further evidence of these men trying to reach the remainder of their battalion now on Calhoun Hill? However, being closely pursued, they were soon killed near the top of Greasy Grass Hill, just outside of the Walter Camp's original "South" boundary fence line. Only thirty minutes earlier they had dismounted here on their way to Finley Hill. Walter Camp wrote about finding human phalange (finger and toe) bones on Greasy Grass Hill. By simply scraping away the loose soil around what were shallow grave depressions, he discovered the tell-tale signs of the original 1876 burials. Other Camp informants, such as Major Fred Grant verified these burials. The President's son had been in charge of the recovery of many of the officers' remains in 1877. **LILLY 55-56 (Camp on Grant)**

The Corporal Foley Incident: As Harrington and his men passed by the mouth of Ravine C, one man turned and entered the deepest part of this branch of the Gray Horse Gully. He was Corporal John Foley of Company C. Later, the final location of Corporal Foley's burial will become confused with Sergeant James Butler's burial site. But, to the 1876 participants the question of John Foley's body was not in doubt. Nor was it to Walter Camp when he did his research some thirty years later. Foley became the very first of the Custer dead to be discovered when Benteen and the other burial parties traveled down Medicine Tail Coulee. Camp carefully recorded the location of both of the Foley and Butler sites. He also recorded statement that Sergeant James Flanagan, of Company D had seen Corporal Foley riding out and being killed when his company was on Weir Point. The small remaining balance of Company C, now consisting of only three to four men, along with their dismounted First Sergeant Bobo, were now struggling to survive alone in the Keogh area. However, they were soon to be joined by the men now fighting on Calhoun Hill. **See BUTLER-FOLEY MAP, pg. 180, LILLY 672 (Flanagan)**

The Second Battalion Advance and the Young Warriors: After leaving the First Battalion in Medicine Tail Coulee by 3:15 PM, Captain Yates took his three companies over the *north* bound trail that passes over the future Nye-Cartwright/Luce Ridge and the soon to be Custer

Battlefield. After traveling approximately seventh tenths mile along the trail, they were attacked from the rear by a rag-tagged group of teenage "boys," who for all appearances seemed to be full-fledged warriors. This band of at least fifty of these "Young Warriors" emerged from the mouth of Camp's North Medicine Tail Coulee. Poorly armed and not yet recognized as having full warrior society status. These "wannabe" apprenticed pre-society teenagers were out to make a mark on their own. The night before a number of these young Cheyenne boys, in a public ceremony in the village, pledged that in the next fight with the bluecoat soldiers they would "throw their lives away." The ceremony has been described as the "Dying Dance".Some anthropologist researchers have incorrectly described them as being the "Suicide Boys." **M25, M53, pg. 194, 197-201, M54, M76, & M78.**

In the Native American culture, taking one's life was an unthinkable "sin," just as it is in the Judean/Christian culture. These young pre-warrior "boys" represented the symbol of the new raising "Red Power" movement centered on the mysticism of Sitting Bull. After the Indians' clear cut victory over General Crook's command, on the Rosebud eight days before, this pledging to defend their families and their homeland was the promise of things to come. They were willing to throw their lives away, as John Stands In Timber expressed their motivation. These young warriors would prove to do just that, as nearly all (if not all) would soon die during the June 25 battle. In the early afternoon of the Custer Fight, an unknown number of these Young Warriors, estimated as least fifty, gathered near the mouth of Custer Creek, some two and one half miles downstream from the Onion Creek camps. They had avoided the village's military police that had full authority to punish any tribesman severely, even to kill them, by who blatantly challenge the established tribal rules.

Sometime near 3:00 PM, they had traveled about five miles up Custer Creek. They had hoped to intercept the soldiers who were known to have been in the vicinity of the "Big Bend' of the Rosebud, near the present town of Busby. But they did not know of Custer's night march and his preemptive afternoon movement down Ash Creek. At a point one mile west of present Squaw Teat Butte a Sioux military society "policeman" summoned them to the top of a ridge located near present Highway 212. **M53, pg. 197-201**

From here they could see Custer's two battalions now moving down into the South Medicine Tail drainage from John Martin's Big Hill. They hurriedly advanced down a branch of Camp's North Medicine Tail Coulee drainage. At about 3:20 PM, they struck the rear of the Yates's advancing Second Battalion, now moving up the south slope to the Nye-Cartwright Ridge area. It was here that the legend of the "Gray Horse" Company started when they were dismounted and deployed against this sudden attack on the rear flanks of their moving column.

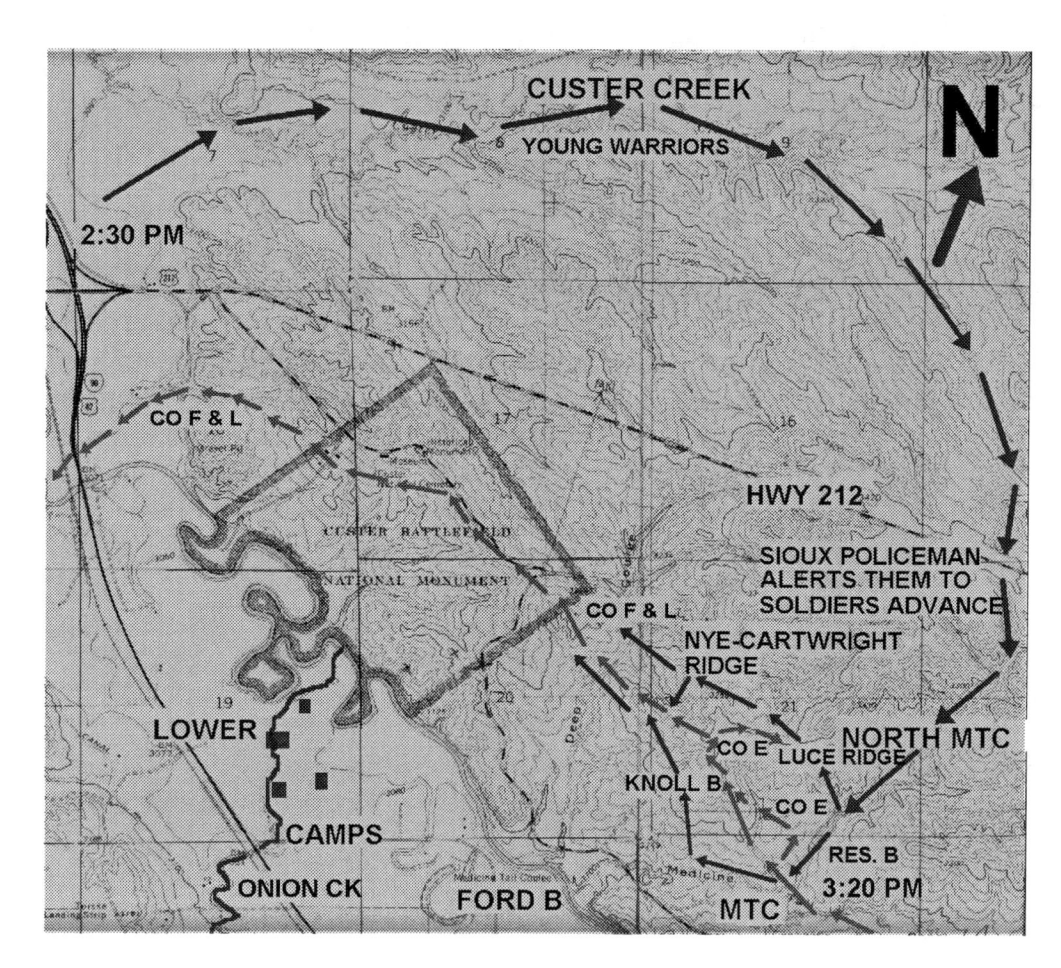

YOUNG WARRIORS ROUTE

SCALE: -------- 1/4 MILE

*In the early afternoon of the Battle, some fifty pre-society "Young Warriors" slipped through the village police lines and gathered near the mouth of Custer Creek (upper left corner). The evening before the Young Warriors had pledged themselves in a public ceremony to fight the army even to their deaths. Their intent was to find the soldiers and on the main Hwy 212 trail and attack them. John Stands Timber referred to them as "Suicide Warriors," those willing to throw their lives away in combat. They were unaware of Custer's night advance up Davis Creek. About 3:00 PM they were alerted to Custer's advance over Martin's Big Hill to Medicine Tail Coulee by a Sioux policeman on Hwy 212. They intercepted the Second Battalion's advance near Reservoir B at the mouth of North Medicine Tail Coulee drainage **(RES. B)**. Company E was dismounted to counter this unexpected flanking attack. Companies F and L continued mounted to the Lower Fords. The Young Warriors split up with some following Companies F and L over the future Custer Battlefield. Unable to prevent them from entering the valley, they halted near Monument Hill and watched company F and L attempt to cross at the "Willy Bends" crossing. The others stayed to harass Company E that by now had halted on the Luce Ridge. Here they would be soon joined with full-fledged warriors from the defunct Reno Valley Fight. **(See Company F & L Advance to the Lower Fords, pg. 171)***

The Gray Horse Company: The phantom like appearance of Company E in the antidotal Indian accounts may now be altogether resolved! When this seemingly threatening attack occurred, Captain Yates committed a tactical error. He had Company E, which was located on the left flank of his command, to be halted and dismounted. This act would keep Company E out of the mainstream military action for the next one hour. Company E would form a "By the Right Flank" skirmish line that now faced to the northeast, the direction from which the Young Warrior's were attacking. But, with the fluidity of the Plains Indian's way of fighting, they simply divided and quickly created separated lines of rapidly moving and harassing attacks on both sides of the advancing Second Battalion.

Soon the Young Warriors separated, with some staying to continue their harassment of the dismounted Company E men, while the others chased after Companies F and L, who were still mounted and continuing to advance on the *northbound* Nye-Cartwright trail. By the time that the Young Warriors had reached the present Monument Hill area their smaller ponies were played out. They halted here as they realized that they would not be able to prevent the soldiers from getting into the valley. John Stands In Timber's uncle was one these Young Warriors. Meantime, Company E had moved on foot for about a quarter of a mile than turning almost ninety degrees to the left, they headed back to the trail Companies F and L had just taken. This direction would lead them over Knoll B and onto the present Nye-Cartwright Ridge. **(See pg. 169, YOUNG WARRIORS ROUTE)**

The Luce Ridge Skirmish Line: Lieutenant Algeron Smith finding the summit of the Nye-Cartwright Ridge area too large to defend with just one small company moved some 350 yards to the east to an adjacent pronounced ridge now called the "Luce" Ridge. Here, for the next thirty minutes, Company E would skirmish ineffectively with the residual Young Warriors and the ever-increasing full-fledged warriors now arriving from the defunct Reno Fight. The myth of the ghost-like early battle presence of the men with the Gray Horses was now born!

The Willy Bends Crossing: In the meantime the balance of the Second Battalion (Companies F and L) attempted to ford the Little Bighorn at a crossing later identified by John Stands In Timber as being at the old "Willy Bend's" homestead. This early 1900s house, with its green pyramid roof, now lies in shambles on the ground. There still is a pronounced trough north of the old building ruins on the (south) left hand bank of the river. But the companion trough on the opposite side has been eroded away by flooding and there is now a small island downstream This strategically located natural hard bottom crossing is located 280 yards west of the 1880's railroad bridge that parallels the present Interstate highway. It is located in northwest corner of the southeast quarter section of Section 19. **(See pg. 171, COMPANY F & L ADVANCE TO LOWER FORDS)**

The valley warriors had out guessed the motives of the soldiers. When they saw them trotting along the Custer Battle Ridge, they rode quickly to block all of the fords downstream of the lower camps. At these crossings they dismounted and waited in the heavy brush for the soldiers to arrive. When Company F and L arrived at the Willy Bends ford they were forced to withdraw for the very same reason that the First Battalion had discovered fifteen minutes earlier at Ford B. An unknown number of entrenched enemies at this natural obstacle (ford) caused Captain Yates to order a general retreat. Indian accounts tell of at least one soldier being taken along when they retreated. He had been bucked off his horse during the brief fighting at the crossing. Perhaps this was Lieutenant Calhoun?

On the most western (magnetic) end of the National Cemetery complex, Companies F and L formed a dismounted skirmish line along the south military crest of the extended ridge west of the present N.P.S. ranger's housing units. It lies outside of the Little Bighorn National Monument boundary. This skirmish line becomes the author's "West Skirmish" Line. After nor being able to cross at the Willy Bend's Ford they lost the offensive and were now operating in a defensive mode. It was now approximately 4:00 PM, about same time when the East Skirmish Line was being established on Finley Hill. The two battalions were now separated by just over one mile distance.

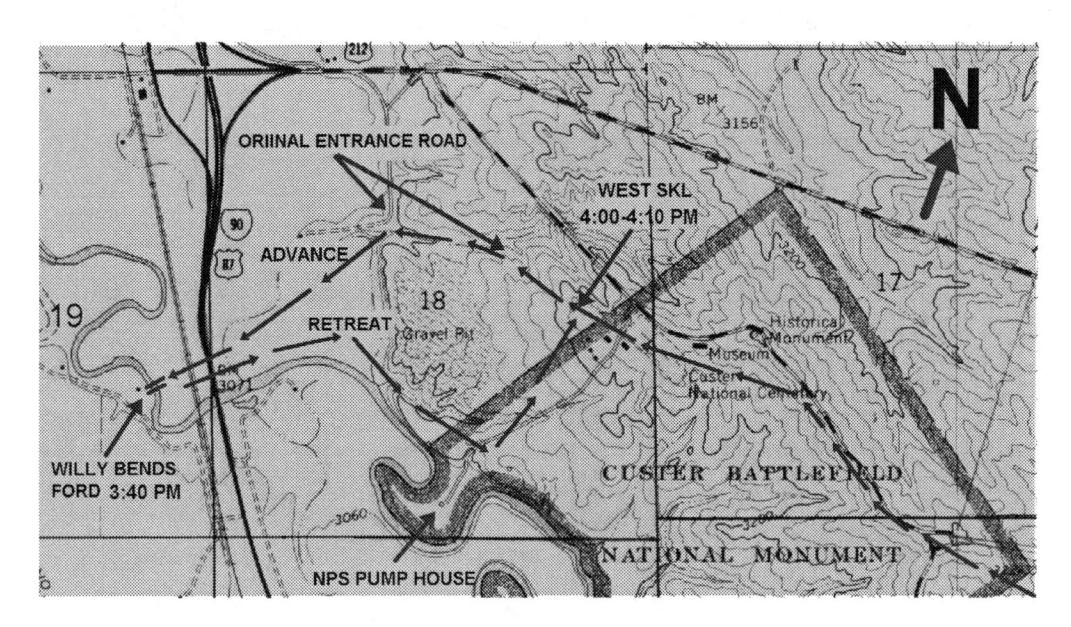

COMPANY F & L ADVANCE TO LOWER FORDS

SCALE: --------------- 1/4 MILE

The Second Battalion without Company E traveled to a major crossing located in Section 19 ***(Willy Bends Ford)*** *seen in the lower left. Unable to affect a crossing they retreated to high ground on the northern end of the National Cemetery hill area. Here they formed the West Skirmish Line* ***(West SKL)*** *until summoned by Custer to move to his chosen defensive position now called Calhoun Hill.*

The West Skirmish Line: Just like the First Battalion, Yates did not retreat on his exact back trail. His two companies now circled back to the southeast and traveled between the present gravel pit and the river channel. They ended up inside the horseshoe loop where the present N.P.S. pump house is now located. Just like the First Battalion, they were looking for another unguarded crossing. But, they were headed east toward the First Battalion's position, which was now advancing west along Greasy Grass Ridge. Perhaps reuniting the two battalions was their primary factor? Finding large numbers of warriors blocking any farther movement in that direction, Yates was forced to turn to the left (north) and seek higher ground for safety. The abbreviated Second Battalion would end up on the west end of the present National Cemetery area. Some 200 yards outside the present N.P.S. boundary fence, they dismounted for the first time since leaving the Divide Halt.

After less than ten minutes of ineffective dismounted skirmishing with the warriors that had crossed the river and were chasing after the beleaguered battalion. It was becoming another Finley Hill disaster. The five man detail sent by Custer from Calhoun Hill by 4:00 PM had now arrived by 4:10 PM. Yates would immediate mount up and withdraw his men. The order carried by the five man detail was for Yates to come to Custer's high ground defensive position. The two companies now started to advance eastward along the Battle Ridge. Approximately six tenths mile east of Monument Hill, they were confronted with the sudden appearance of Mister Harrington and his handful of Company C men, who were now in full flight from the Battlefield. As they crested the ridge, Yates responded by having Company F deployed on foot along the north side of the Battle Ridge. This action was to give assistance to the few remaining men from Company C now arriving in the Keogh area. **(See pg. 202)**

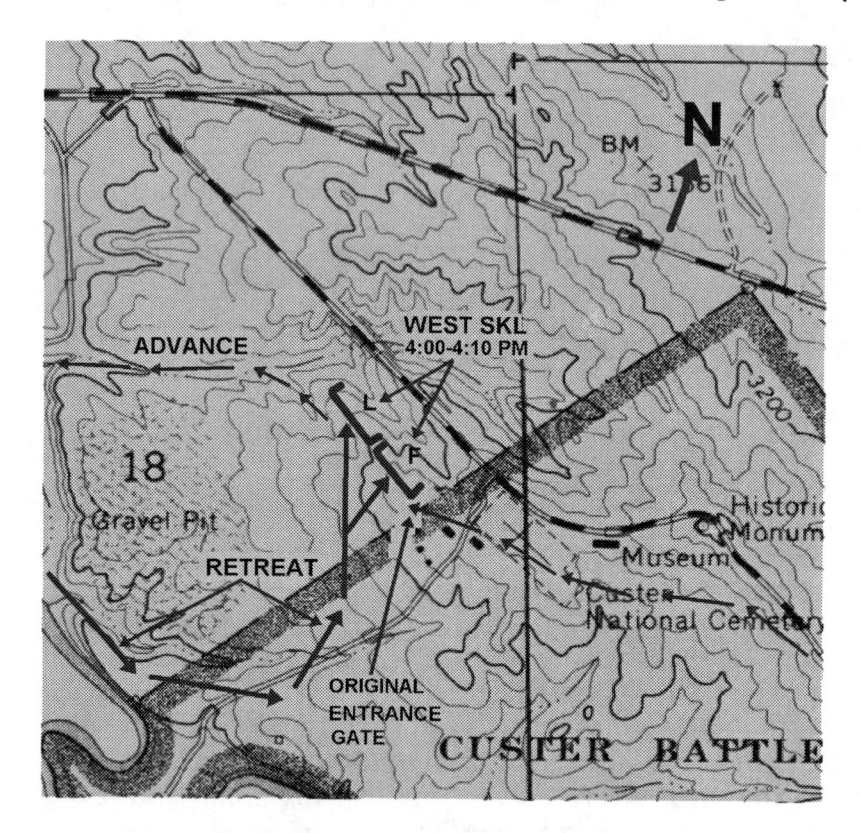

WEST SKIRMISH LINE

(4:00 TO 4:10 PM)

SCALE: ---------------------- **1/4 MILE**

In the 1960s, John Stands In Timber was the very first researcher to suggest this skirmish line location just where his fellow Northern Cheyenne battle informants had shown him. Margot Liberty, who authored his biography, **Cheyenne Memories** *in 1967, along with Bill Gary (NPS) and J. W. Vaughn all have discovered expended army rounds on this site. Unfortunately, in the 1970s, subsequent local treasure hunters with metal detectors scoured this skirmish line that most researchers were not even aware of its existence of this historical site. These illegally taken shell finds were sold to collectors at a minimum of $100 per shell. Again, history was lost to the White Man's greed!* **M19, M20**

The Battle Ridge Deployment: Captain Yates would post Company F on the Battle Ridge and send Lt. Calhoun with Company L forward to the place that now bares his name. This little known action is based on the correct company assignments, for far too long other researchers have placed Company L in the First Battalion to account for the presence of their officers being found on Calhoun Hill. This is working history backwards to make their theories work; one cannot just create a false premise without creating more Custer Myths! **See APPENDIX: Custer Fight-Phase 1, pg. 202**

There was another important military need for this action. The dismounted warriors that had earlier encircled Yate's temporary West Skirmish Line, were now mounted and chasing the "fleeing" battalion eastward along the Battle Ridge on the North slope. These were the warriors that confronted Harrington's fleeing men in Ravine A. Second Lieutenant William Reily deployed his Company F along the north facing military crest just below the nominal crest of the Battle Ridge. But, the company's led horses were now forced to be posted over the ridge on the south slope. This move would leave their horses exposed to the now mounted warriors who were in hot pursuit of the Second Battalion. Apparently Captain Yates elected to stay with Company F, although as overall battalion commander he was not officially in charge of his own company.

Company L Goes to Calhoun Hill: First Lieutenant James Calhoun with Company L continued toward the high ground that now bares his name, but already occupied by the Headquarters Staff, Company I and the just arrived orphaned Company E. Immediately upon arriving Company L was dismounted and placed along a southward facing line ninety degrees to the existing skirmish line of Company I. They would stay here for but a very brief time, while the Staff decided what to do. With sixty percent of the two battalions' originally already undermanned strength now missing, Custer had a hard decision to make. But any decision he would make would be tempered by the aggressiveness of the great number of warriors that were now forcing them off of Calhoun Hill. This is what Curly was now observing from high ground during his brief halt one mile east of Calhoun Hill. The time was now 4:20 PM.

Company E Again! By 4:20 PM, the orphaned "Gray Horse" Company E arrived at Custer's Headquarters position about the same time of Company L's arrival. At least fifteen minutes earlier, Lieutenant Algernon Smith had decided to abandon his useless skirmish line on Luce Ridge. Hearing Company C's two volleys fired from Finley Hill at 4:00 PM, Company E began to move dismounted *northward* toward Calhoun Hill. Here Company I and the Headquarters Staff were now visibly located on the future Calhoun Hill area.

By 4:05 PM, just east of the present cross section fence line in Township Section 21 on the crest of the now designated Nye-Cartwright Ridge, Company E would fire three additional resounding volleys. It was these simultaneous volleys fired at 4:05 PM caused Captain Weir, who was with Benteen's battalion, to start his advance towards the sounds of this stage of the fighting. In this area, just east (magnetic) of the fence line and along the north slope of the Nye-Cartwright Ridge, a number of expended casings have been located in piles of three. They are all located in the proper skirmish intervals of eighteen feet along this line. Also, they are about thirty feet below the horizon for a proper "military crest" location. **(See Art Work pg. 164)**

All expended casings that have been found along this line were fired by the First Platoon of Company E. The company was still dismounted and marching in platoons, at the double time. This is where each platoon was parallel on both sides of the Nye-Cartwright Ridge. Their led horses were being held between skirmishers now deployed as flankers.

At the same time, the Second Platoon most likely also fired volleys from the south slope of the Nye-Cartwright Ridge. When ordered to volley the men would halt and half-face to the right or left, and then fire. They continued this platoon skirmishing for the next four tenths of a mile, leaving hundreds of expended casings now along the west downward slope of the Nye-Cartwright Ridge. It was Company E alone that fired all of these expended casings in this area. At some point on the down slope, Company E was able to become mounted again. From a point east (magnetic) of Deep Coulee they continued onward mounted to Calhoun Hill, arriving there at least by 4:20 PM. **See APPENDIX: Skirmishers as Flankers, pg. 201**

As soon as they arrived, Lieutenant Smith was ordered to continue advancing westward to Company F's dismounted position along the Battle Ridge, some 800 yards west of Calhoun Hill. Since we suspect that Captain Yates had stayed with Lieutenant Reily, then the decision to have Company E not to stay on Calhoun Hill must have been made by Colonel Custer. Was this a clue to what he may have been planning at this moment? Originally, Custer may have planned to have all of his battalions to rally around the high ground now known as Calhoun Hill. This would have been for a defensive measure to wait for Benteen's expected reinforcement. But now, Custer may have decided to take his last military option and seek the relative safety in the valley's timber bottom. His men were now firing away their meager supply of ammunition. They had not planned on a protracted defensive stand.

This theory has compelling support from Curly, the Crow Scout; He told Walter Camp that from his new observation point, east of the battlefield, he made a most intriguing sighting. He had seen soldiers fighting for their lives in a ravine. Dr. Charles Kuhlman theorized that this was the famous Gray Horse ravine. But it cannot be seen over the Battle Ridge from Curly's eastern observation point. Curly described that many warriors now surrounded these men on all sides. He was positive that they would all soon be killed in that ravine. He could not see how any of them could have survived and the horror of this stuck with him for the rest of his life! The ravine in question was Ravine A, again being used as an avenue of escape.

Curly had made his observation some ten minutes after he left Calhoun Hill. But the most intriguing observation was that at the same time he was seeing the doomed men in Ravine A those with the Gray Horses were now moving along the Battle Ridge in a normal manner. **M40, pg. 159 (Curly)**

Curly Revisited: Bouyer and Curly had traveled with the Staff to Calhoun Hill. Located four tenths mile of a north of Finley Hill, this open high ground may have been what Custer was searching for, his "Good Ground" on which to make a defensive stand. Another informative Custer remark again relayed by his acting aid-de-camp his brother, Captain Thomas Custer, to Bouyer was that *"they were going to go down there!"* **BYU 434-435**

It is one of the most enigmatic clues for current researchers to interpret. Is it possible that Custer this early may have intended "they" (the command) would have to "go down there," meaning the relative safety of the timber in the valley? The men were now expending their meager ammunition supply at too fast and the startling reality of Bouyer's prediction that Benteen would not show up may have struck home with Custer. It was at the time of this hurried conversation with Bouyer that Curly was ordered to get out while he could. Bouyer promised him that he would also leave as soon as he could find another horse. He never did, as his body has now been identified by forensic science as one of those being buried along the South Skirmish Line. Curly left Calhoun Hill by 4:10 PM.

Camp recorded Curly's departure point as being at the "four markers," located on the northern end of the loop road on Calhoun Hill. The National Park Service has erected an interpretive marker located at this point. Camp's compass heading of Curly's escape route was recorded as being 087 Degrees. This direction of travel was nearly due east. This compass heading points to the most northern branch of "Deep Coulee" that runs parallel to the Nye-Cartwright Ridge.

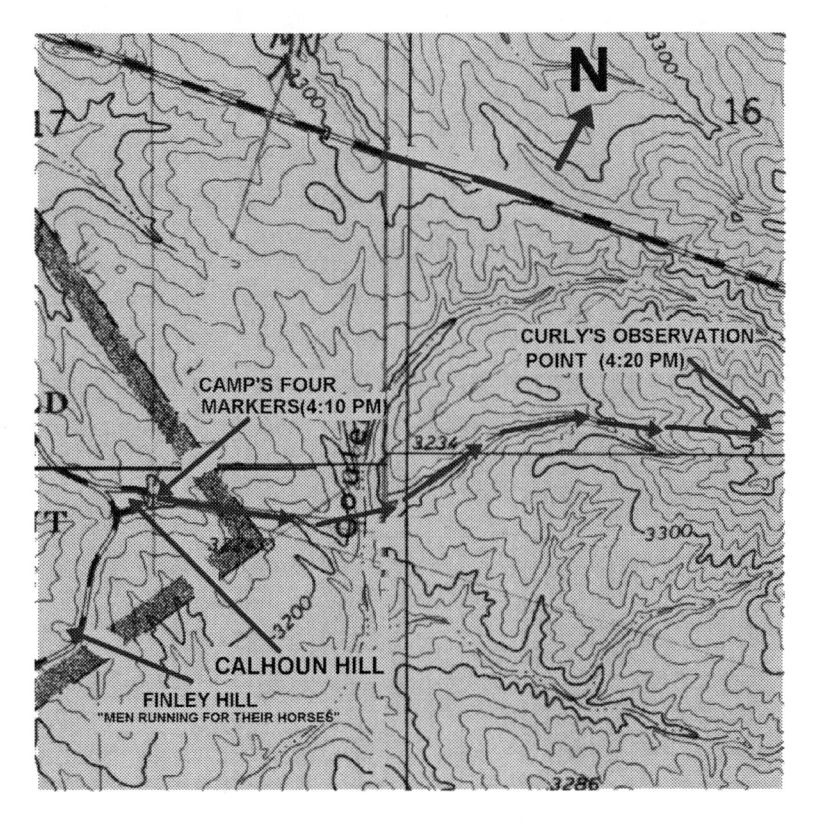

CURLEY'S ESCAPE

4:10 PM

SCALE: -------------------- 1/4 MILE

Curley and Mitch Bouyer were ordered to get out by Custer (through his Aide Camp, Tom Custer) by 4:10 PM. This was at the same time that the men on Finley Hill (Company C) were running for their horses. Curley travel for one and one quarter mile east of Calhoun Hill. From here he observed men with bay horses fighting for their lives in a ravine. However, at the same time he also saw men who had Gray Horses (Company E) traveling along the Battle Ridge in a normal manner. After leaving his observation point by 4:20 PM, Curly went to the Crow's "Custer Last lookout," a traditional war observation high peak located six and five tenth miles east of the battlefield entrance roads on Highway 212.

Curly's Escape: The straight line distance from Camp's four markers on Calhoun Hill to Curly's easterly high ground observation point is one and a quarter mile. Curly stopped twice on his way to this high observation point, located to the south of present Highway 212. The first time was to retrieve a dead Sioux warrior's blanket, Spencer rifle and ammunition, as he had fired all of his own ammunition for his Winchester rifle on Calhoun Hill. His next brief halt was to take possession of an abandoned Sioux pony. All of these "spoils of war" were still with Curly when he arrived at the steamer Far West on June 28. But it was from his high ground place that he witnessed the events occurring on Calhoun Hill. He described how the men with bay horses were all jumbled up in a ravine, but at the same time those with the Gray Horses were moving mounted along the Battle Ridge. Where were they going and why?

We know that from Walter Camp's exacting interviews with Curly that he now traveled north to what is known in the Crow Nation as a war observation known as the "Lookout". It is a high point on that Little Bighorn and Tullock's Fork divide that looks pyramid in shape. It is located six and one half mile east on U.S. Highway 212 , one half mile north. From here Curly observed the fighting on Reno Hill until dark. That night he camped on the West Fork of Tullock's Creek. The next day he traveled down Sarpy Creek to the Yellowstone River. By late evening on June 27, he was observed by Lieutenant Edwin Booth at the army base camp near the mouth of the Big Horn River. At mid-day he arrived at the steamer Far West on June 28. He had traveled some 150 miles in sixty hours.

Another Retreat Down Ravine A: Soon after the arrival of Company L, Custer may have ordered a planned withdrawal from Calhoun Hill. With the collapse of the skirmish line on Finley Hill, he must have known that now, with just Company I and L they would not be able to hold Calhoun Hill for very long. So why did he now order Company E to continue westward along the Battle Ridge if he was planning to leave there?

The only avenue open for an exit from Calhoun Hill was by going down Ravine A to the Keogh area, with covering fire of Company F from the adjacent crest of the Battle Ridge. But the presence of the bodies of officers of Company L found on Calhoun Hill, each in their respective platoon position, indicates something other than a planned and orderly withdrawal. Also, at this time, Custer may have attempted to communicate again with Benteen. A five man detail from Company L, possibly including Sergeant Hanley's mystery messenger that started the "Calhoun was wounded" rumor, may have been sent at this time?. **NA6, pg. 232 (Five man detail) M40, Camp/Hammer pg. 149 (Wilber)**

Is there any evidence of this attempted communication? Frank Bethune, a local Crow rancher in the late 1890s, discovered four sets of soldier skeletons along the *south* slope of the Nye-Cartwright Ridge area. These remains included two horse skeletons, along with their horse tack. Two of the human skeletons were found between the protective legs of one of the downed horses. These artifacts may have been what remained of the five-man detail that may have included the "Calhoun was wounded" messenger. **(CBNM Files, Bethune)**

We know that Bethune's discoveries were located in the same area where Company E had earlier skirmished with John Stands In Timber's Young Warriors. However, Bethune's artifacts may not have been casualties from this early stage of fighting. The chance of the of this many men being left behind was remote, considering how poorly armed the teenage warriors were, and the Young Warriors could not have inflicted that much damage to the well ordered skirmishing that Lieutenant Smith would have conducted. He was a well-experienced Civil War officer and he would not have abandoned any of his men, dead or alive! **M7 (The "Blummer" manuscript)**

Anyone hit on the retreat to what has become known as the Luce Ridge would have been taken along. This explanation of a five man detail with yet another messenger is offered to answer the antidotal story that (Lieutenant) "Calhoun had been wounded." A rumor that circulated on Reno Hill after the Pack Train had arrived. Combined with the other rumor attributed to Sergeant Hanley that another messenger from Company C had arrived from Custer on Reno Hill, and it was not John Martin. Walter Camp carefully recorded both of these antidotal stories as having occurred on Reno Hill, soon after the packs had arrived. They were army "scuttlebutt" that circulated in the events between the time of the arrival of the Pack Train and the advance of Benteen to the present Weir Point area. It had to have been someone who had been on Calhoun Hill that knew of the wounding of Lieutenant Calhoun and he had just come in from Custer!

Both rumors could be associated with the artifact finds credited to Frank Bethune (the four bodies and horses) of a possible five men detail located on the south slope of the Nye-Cartwright Ridge area. But no matter, how do we explain Corporal Alexander Bishop's survival if he was with Custer's Staff on June 25, just as John Martin told Camp that "Bishop" was there!

As pointed out by Peter Thompson and John Martin, Corporal Bishop's presence on the Headquarters Staff makes it possible for him to have been sent back at some point. Bishop's arrival on Reno Hill would help to explain either rumor, that of an additional messenger or the wounding of Lieutenant Calhoun. Benteen sure had a lot of "scuttlebutt" to cover up, and both Alexander Bishop and John Martin were under his direct control as members of his company! But the identity of the "Calhoun was wounded" mystery messenger still remains just that, a mystery!

It is possible that one of the enlisted men that was officially killed on Reno Hill may have been the mystery messenger? The messenger would have been from Company I or L, as they were the only two companies posted on Calhoun Hill when we theorize that the five man detail was sent by 4:20 PM. By subtracting the known number of the men assigned to the Pack train, we have four "extra" men from Companies I and L. The most likely candidate for the "Calhoun" rumor could have been Private David Cooney of Company I. He was seriously wounded by being shot through the hip on June 26. He was transported to Fort Abraham Lincoln on the *Far West* with the other wounded men. He died there at the post hospital on July 20. It is possible that in the aftermath of the struggle on Reno Hill that his role as a messenger went unnoticed and forgotten with his death?

The Enigma of Private Cooney: Two days after his wounding on Reno Hill, Private Cooney was promoted two grades to Sergeant! If we rule out Reno or Benteen as having done this field promotion that leaves General Alfred Terry as the only military commander to have the authority to do so. His company commander, Captain Miles Keogh, was now dead. The real question to ask is what Private Cooney did to deserve such an unusual field promotion, for he was the singular enlisted man to have this extraordinary privilege. No other enlisted man was treated in this manner! Is it possible that his role as Custer's true last messenger was recognized by General Terry? This inscrutable event may explain Sergeant Hanley's rumor of another messenger that came in from Custer (his "Company C" man) long after John Martin. This was scuttlebutt that started on Reno Hill identified by Walter Camp along with the associated "Calhoun was wounded" anecdotal story.

If so, Private Cooney would have left Calhoun Hill by 4:20 PM. The four men and their dead horses as discovered by Frank Bethune may also be associated with Cooney's flight to Reno Hill. His arrival on Reno Hill (4:50 PM) after a thirty minute trip (four miles at eight miles per hour) could account for Benteen's sudden departure from Reno Hill, one hour of his "dawdling" after he had his horses unsaddled.

The Collapse of Calhoun Hill: By now a total of almost ninety men had gathered on Calhoun Hill, Custer's proposed defensive position. Now they were forced to retreat down Ravine A. If the present markers found here are correct then twelve just men were killed in the retreat down Ravine A. The markers today are all located in the bottom of the ravine. This amounts to less than fifteen percent loss of the men who fled Calhoun Hill. Unless the present markers on Calhoun Hill do not represent the actual number of burials there, the number of dead left behind is relatively insignificant. Only nine markers exist on Calhoun Hill and two represent officers.

Except for the anomaly of the deaths of both officers of Company L, only seven other dead men were left behind. Under the usual circumstance, when their officers were killed, a wild stampede of the enlisted men follows. It might have been the presence of Captain Keogh and Custer's Staff that created a seemingly ordered retreat down Ravine A. Walter Camp made a mistake in not questioning Curly more closely about his observation of the men with the bay horses fighting for their lives in this ravine. Curly could have solved this mystery by telling us if the men were mounted or not?

Company I and L, along with the Staff and the civilians were now forced off from Calhoun Hill, and they retreated down Ravine A. This was the same ravine where Curly saw men with bay horses being surrounded by many Sioux. It seems that it would have been very difficult to become mounted with the pressure from the large number of mounted warriors that Curly observed at 4:20 PM. **See APPENDIX: The Custer Fight, Phase 3, pg. 204**

By the method that Daniel Kanipe suggested (only one burial where three or more grave markers were seen) the fourteen grave markers found today in Ravine A today suggests the men that fled down this ravine *were not mounted*. Mounted men would have covered the distance to the Keogh area very quickly with far less causalities. However, by following the pattern of the First Battalion's retreat, Curly's men may have been deployed as flankers as skirmishers. If so, there may have been a well formed resistance as they retreated downward to the "Keogh" area.

The conclusion is that they were dismounted and they were able to withdraw in an orderly manner. Curly's assessment of their danger can now be minimized. Apparently, the some fifty dismounted skirmishers of Company I and L were able to defend themselves quite effectively. The warriors would be exposed as they rode along the higher ground (now called "Henryville" after the 1984-85 archaeological excavations) and come within the soldier's close range of fire. At that close range the striking power of the issued .45 caliber Springfield carbine would knock a horse off its feet if it struck hard bone. Other "soft" targets such as human arms or legs would be simply torn away from the body!

Artifact finds of spent .45 caliber soft lead slugs have been found on the Custer Battlefield mushroomed into flattened fifty cent size shape from such wounds. And the mounted warriors would be firing at random rapidly into the orderly dismounted retreat. Unlike the parody portrayed by the Hollywood movie makers, the Dakota warriors were not unintelligent; they would have backed off and waited for a better opportunity to strike. Two emerging theories now come to light about this retreat down Ravine A. The first is that all military order had broken down and that the men were not traveling in any known regulated movement. Remember that on Reno's retreat it was everybody for himself.

So was the first retreat down Ravine A, when Harrington's Company C men fled mounted in wild disorder down this same ravine but some ten minutes earlier. It would seem that there would be many more grave markers in Ravine today.

The second theory is if the "Flankers as Skirmishers" deployment was used, than their causalities could have been light along the upper sides of the ravine. It is possible that their bodies were latter washed or moved down to the bottom of the ravine when the 1876 burial parties knew that they would not stay covered on the sloping sides of the ravine?

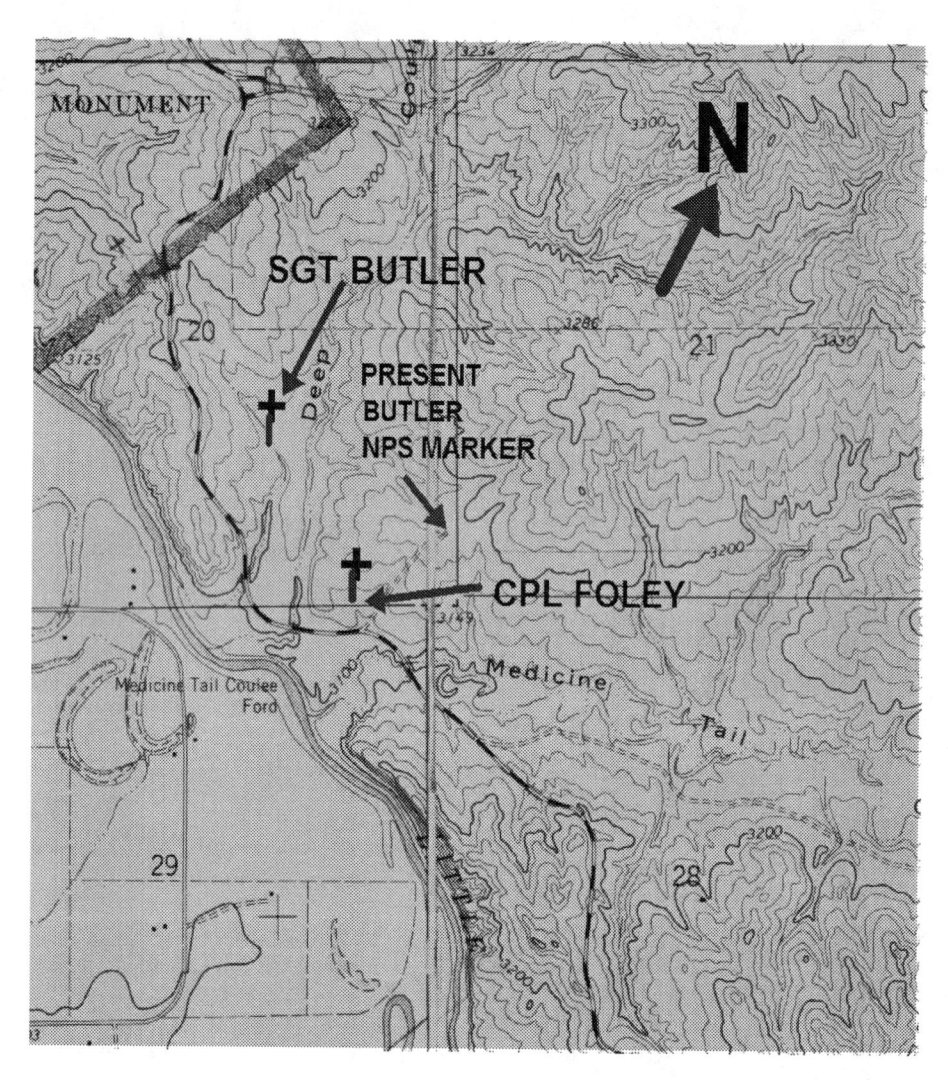

BUTLER AND FOLEY

SCALE: ---------------- 1/4 MILE

According to one of Camp's Blueprint maps, Corporal Foley was discovered and buried in the southeast 1/4 section of Section 20. In 1908, the remains of what may have been Sergeant Butler was recovered from where Camp was shown where Butler was found (See above) and was reburied in the National Cemetery. The location of the original burial was identified by a Cheyenne battle participant from Lamedeer. He described the soldier of being one of the last to be killed and that he had three markings on his sleeve. **Source: LILLY 687 (Roy), CBNM Files (Luce).**

The Keogh Restaging Area: However, it will become obvious that men on the slopes of the Keogh area would fight dismounted in a series of stands in two lines of skirmishers. It does not seem that they would have been mounted, just to be dismounted again in such a short distance. If Custer's plan was to reach the timber for a better defensive position, they could have continued to ride mounted all the way to the river bottom. Or did he realize that a Reno style of retreat would occur? After all, Company E had just been deployed westward for some reason. Out of the ninety some men that fled Calhoun Hill, about seventy-eight would reached the Keogh area. This temporary restaging area now held the remnants of

Companies I, C, L, and Custer's Staff, along with the civilians. Eventually, about thirty-five of those that arrived would be left dead in the Keogh area. They fought in a series of stands, with both residual battalions parallel with each other, and diagonally up the North Slope of the Battle Ridge. Here they would be joined with survivors from the soon to be formed South Skirmish Line.

Where Was Company E Going? We left Company E heading to Company F's position on the Battle Ridge, now giving covering fire for the retreating men in the Keogh area. Curly described seeing the Gray Horsemen riding in a normal manner westward along the Battle Ridge. But before Lieutenant Smith could reach Company F's position, something happened to divert Company E down to what will become known as the South Skirmish Line.

On June 28, Lieutenant Edward McClernand had examined the Custer Battlefield when he noticed a very important clue. He had just left Calhoun Hill and was headed along the Battle Ridge to go to "Custer's Knoll." He described seeing a distinct cavalry trail of "fours" going off on a left oblique soon after leaving Calhoun Hill. That trail diverted at about a thirty degree angle heading (northwest) direct to what is now called the South Skirmish Line. The point where this change of direction occurred is adjacent to the Keogh area. This new direction would lead Company E down to where later the bodies of both Company E and F would be found. Is there any possible relationship that would coincide with the retreat of the men from Calhoun Hill and possible new orders that concerned the Gray Horse Company? **LILLY 546**

There still remains the mystery of why the South Skirmish Line was placed so far removed from the serious fighting going on in the Keogh area. Why did Lieutenant Smith take his company some 300 yards away from the relative safety of the high ground on the Battle Ridge? This distance is close to the maximum effective range of the carbine. The high plateau were Lieutenant Smith would soon establish his new line overlooks an established trail that leads to a ford crossing at the mouth of the Gray Horse Gully (Ravine B).

Mister Harrington and his Company C survivors had taken this same trail only twenty minutes earlier. However, Company F would soon join Company E on this new established line. The fact that men from Company F were also found in this area lends credence to the theory of an orderly withdrawal to the timber. Indian battle accounts tell of soldiers running on foot, as if they were tired, down the south slope of the Battle Ridge.

Other soldiers behind them were mounted on horses. The method by which the dismounted Company F men traveled down to Company E's new line was by the prescribed army method of the "double-time" infantry marching step. This highly animated British Army action makes men look like they are "tired" by their regulated high stepping leg movement. The "mounted men" would have been Company F's led horses' holders. Army regulations and good horse sense requires that they stay mounted. **O3 &O4**

From the above scenario it is now apparent that the men of Company F were withdrawn in an orderly manner from the north side of the Battle Ridge. After an "About Face," they then "ran" at the double-time down the south slope to join Company E. Their led horses would have followed them and placed in the rear of the new line. Company F was now positioned on the right flank of Company E, and closer to the east (south) end of the National Cemetery Ridge. This action would soon have serious consequences for the soldiers now assembled here and for the rest of men in general! John Stands In Timber's Young Warriors would soon again visit them, and they will crush any hope for survival in the valley timber bottom!

The Destruction of the South Skirmish Line: The combined Companies of E and F could post only seventy men and officers on this new line. Only a total of about fifty skirmishers could be placed on this "South" Skirmish Line. According to Indian accounts, the warriors for the most part had been dismounted in this area. But they soon recovered from their surprise when the mounted Gray Horse soldiers came "charging" down from the east end of the Battle Ridge. As the warriors fled back down into deeper cross ravines to retrieve their horses they were challenged by Lame White Man to go back and attack this new soldier line. It was at this time that the rumor circulated that the Young Warriors were about to charge, mounted from the adjacent Cemetery Hill. And that is just what happened. **M53 (Liberty) pg. 200-201**

This rag-tied band of fifty or more of teenage boy warriors aggressively charged right into the right flank of Company F's horse holders. Here with the Civil War era cap-and-ball revolver, along with their archaic bow and arrow, they were became very effective and soon created panic among the soldiers. Soon a general stampede of men and horses started eastward across Ravine B, and over the "Lone Marker" ridge located north of Finley Hill. They left behind five dead horse holders in the swale behind the line. At least eight other mounted horse holders made into Ravine C leading up to Finley Hill. Company F's Private Richard Saunders, was most likely the N.P.S. archaeological excavation's "Big Mike," one of the last to be run down mounted and killed along this line of fleeing men. Charles Kuhlman was the first to suggest that these "fleeing men" had fled from the South Skirmish Line. **M49, pg. 188**

The impact of Lame White Man's dismounted attack on the center of the line caused the First Platoon of Company E to retreat up the south slope of the Battle Ridge. Along the way, they would be joined with other survivors from the South Skirmish Line. They were from both of the platoons of Company F and soon a total of about twenty-five men and three officers would reach the crest of the Battle Ridge. Lieutenant McClernand said that he saw a total of about ten dead men between Custer Hill and the Gray Horse Gully. **M53, pg. 204-205**

Second Lieutenant James Sturgis' Second Platoon was forced to flee into the upper reaches of Gray Horse Gully (Ravine B). A number of Company E's horses were later found, shot down to form a barricade, along the crest of the west side of the ravine. At least three of Company F's men were also found among the dead of Company E in the ubiquitous shallow head of the Gray Horse Ravine. Only eighteen men were found here which represented the approximate number of men in Company E's Second Platoon. A small number of other fleeing men, apparently not mounted, were discovered in the lower reaches of Ravine C. One of them was Private John Briody, of Company F, whose leg had been cut-off at the hip and thrown over his face. This butchering was the mark of the women who were the animal butchers for the tribe. John Stands In Timber said that it was Southern Cheyenne women who were survivors of the infamous Sand Creek massacre in Eastern Colorado that did most of the butchering of Custer's soldiers. However, at least one man from Company F, Private William Brown, was later found west of the Little Bighorn, across from the mouth of the Gray Horse Ravine! Obviously he "escaped" mounted as his horse was with him. If Custer had hoped to gain the safety of the timber, then Private Brown was the only man known to make it.

The Great Custer Killed: When some two dozen survivors of the South Skirmish Line reached the summit of the Battle Ridge, they were joined with another thirty-nine men from the Keogh restaging area. This now gives us a total of sixty-three men now headed for higher ground of what will become known as Monument Hill. Along the north slope of the Battle Ridge, now designated by a N.P.S. interpretive marker as where Company F and E had fought, "Custer's Luck" ran out! A lateral gun shot through the upper left chest fatally wounded him. The exit wound clipped the rear of his upper arm. Most likely he was mounted at the time. His lifeless body was taken along with the rest of the retreating men to Monument Hill, some 300 yards further to the west end of the Battle Ridge. **M37, pg. 56 (Red Horse)**

The momentum of the retreating men from the South Skirmish Line spilled over onto the north side of the Battle Ridge. The men from the Keogh area flowed over to the south side, and they now started to run on foot towards the same high place, what is to become known as "Custer's Knoll."

Along south side of the ridge, markers show that an additional eight men were lost, representing enlisted men from Companies I and L from the Keogh area. However, the remaining members of the Staff may have joined in with the South Skirmish Line survivors, Companies E and F, now reforming on the North Slope. Here they would lose another six men.

The Last Stand The Northern Cheyenne accounts of John Stands In Timber indicate that the men were now running as if they were tired and not just from the army's regulated double time marching effect. And rightfully so, as by now most have been fighting for over an hour and they were by now very frightened. The early skirmishing of Company E on the south slope of the Nye-Cartwright area started one hour and forty minutes before. And with all of the maneuvering on foot around the greater part of the one square mile battlefield, it must have proven to be very exhausting. There can be no doubt that the men were now physically worn out and in a panicked state.

A Sioux warrior describes what he saw at this time. The soldiers were now leading their horses on foot, running and trying to shoot at the same time. Most were now using their "little guns". This is not a description of an orderly movement of troops! Approximately fifty men would reach the summit of Monument Hill.

There is a continuing Custer Myth that the men on the Last Stand Hill had shot down their horses to provide protection. What really happened should dispel this erroneous assumption. A protective wall of horse flesh was created by having all of their horses formed into a semi-circle on the sloping south side of Monument Hill. Here forty-two officers and enlisted men would seek shelter by standing on the inside of their living wall of horse flesh. They tried to fire over their saddles at an almost invisible circle of dismounted warriors along the National Cemetery complex and the other surrounding high terrain. This long range sniping action would last for perhaps the next twenty minutes. The myth was born of Custer's Last Stand!

Only the freed spirit of the Great Custer would be aware of the struggle of his men for survival, for his dead mortal body was carried here from the north slope of the Battle Ridge were he received his chest wound which may not have been immediate fatal. There is the scenario offered by the Doctor Porter that he removed a small caliber revolver bullet from the back of Custer's neck. Perhaps it was Tom Custer that supplied the small caliber non-bleeding head wound as the coup de grace to prevent further mutilation to his wounded brother, whom he thought to be still alive?

The remaining four or five sorrel horses from Company C were shot down to form a small horse barricade located on the very summit where the Battle Monument now stands. It was for the ranking enlisted men from the Headquarters Staff and the attached civilians. A total of seven men would now be placed behind these dead horses. They were: Chief Bugler Henry Voss, Flag Bearer Robert Hughes, John Vickory and the four civilians. The balance of the survivors, representing the remnant of the former two battalions, circled downward on the south slope of the "Last Stand" hillside. The angle of the slope was too great for a barricade of dead horses, so the men attempted at first to use their standing horses as shelter from the incoming rein of fire from the encircling dismounted warriors. The remaining members of the Second Battalion formed the right flank of the west side of the circle. The remainder of the First Battalion now gathered along the left flank, or the east side. **DPL 97 (DeRudio) Also Photo, pg. 187**

As suggested by many of other researchers, the men did not shoot down their horses, least not at the beginning of the "Last Stand. " Several of the burial officers made this observation. Horsemen are reluctant to shoot their horses, when in their minds there might exist some hope of getting away mounted. Beside, the steepness of the terrain offered little hope of protection from downed horses. The men's prone bodies would still be exposed to incoming fire, particularly those on the upper side of the horseshoe loop. By now the warrior force at a safe distance had completely encircled the Last Stand Hill.

From a long range the warriors fired at the larger living horses. The linked-up horses were up to three abreast along the outside perimeter of the beleaguered group of men. At first the men tried to remain standing on the inside of the circle of their horses. But quickly attrition took place, and by groups of threes and fours the wounded linked horses started to flee or they danced around in a frenzy of fear and pain. In the early part of this fighting some of the soldiers had to have been seriously injured or killed by their own horses. Eventually, nearly all of the horses would soon be on the ground, either motionless or in the throes of dying. Perhaps by now some were by being shot down in desperation by the men.

As the men became more exposed to the warriors sniping fire, attrition took over and within twenty minutes or less, all firing had ceased from the soldiers. Then the great circle of front line warriors and many hundreds of mounted spectators now started to converge on the dead men on the hillside. However it came to them as a great surprise when a small group of men got up from behind the horse barricade on the summit and begun to run downhill toward the river.

The Last Seven: Most likely the first to run was Chief Bugler Henry Voss. According to Camp's information his body was found a considerable distance past the present west boundary of the battlefield and that it was far to the west of Monument Hill. Camp's contemporary accounts place his body toward the river. For some time a lone marker stood outside of the present entrance gate and to the south of the paved entrance road. Sometime in the 1940s it disappeared. Mark Donahue in his Custer Battlefield Historical & Museum Association's *Greasy Grass (*May 2002, Vol. 19) article about Mark Kellogg, shows a 1930s photo of what might be the final resting place for Henry Voss. The Donahue photo shows this 1930s marker to be the northwest corner of the southeast 1/16 section of the northeast 1/4 section of Section 18. The shallow ravine where this stray marker was located leads onto the original entrance gravel road that led to the original ornamental cast-iron gate then located near the present N.P.S. rangers' quarters. This was the same original trail that earlier Companies F and L used to reach the valley and the Willy Bends crossing. Chief-Bugler Voss may have been following Mark Kellogg's flight to the timber in the valley. The distance from Monument Hill to this now missing marker is about 700 yards.

Boston Custer and Autie Reed were able to reach a point about 150 yards southeast of the Last Stand group. The two lone markers represent their original burial sites. Lieutenant Godfrey supervised their burial. Mitch Bouyer and at least one other unidentified enlisted man from the Staff reached the right flank of the defunct South Skirmish Line. Here among the bodies of Company F's skirmishers, they were bought down in one final act of war.

Bob Doran 2007

THE LAST STAND

At first, the only dead horse barricade of four to five Company C horses was formed for the Staff NCOs and the civilians on the highest point of "Custer Knoll". See page 182-183 (View Looking West)

The Last Man to Fall: This left Mark Kellogg, who apparently had started to run in the same direction as Henry Voss. He was able to travel a considerable distance past the present automobile entrance gate. He continued along the route of the future gravel road. entrance. Someone said that his body was but a "stone's throw" away from the river. Some of the observers of his body suggested that the newspaper reporter might have been roped and dragged for some distance. On June 28, Colonel Gibbon's inspection party discovered the body of Mark Kellogg. His body was identified by his civilian boots that had straps over the insteps. Mark Kellogg had written that he was going with Custer to be "at the death" in his last known dispatch dated June 21, 1876, written at the mouth of the Rosebud River. He got his wish but not the news story of the Century!

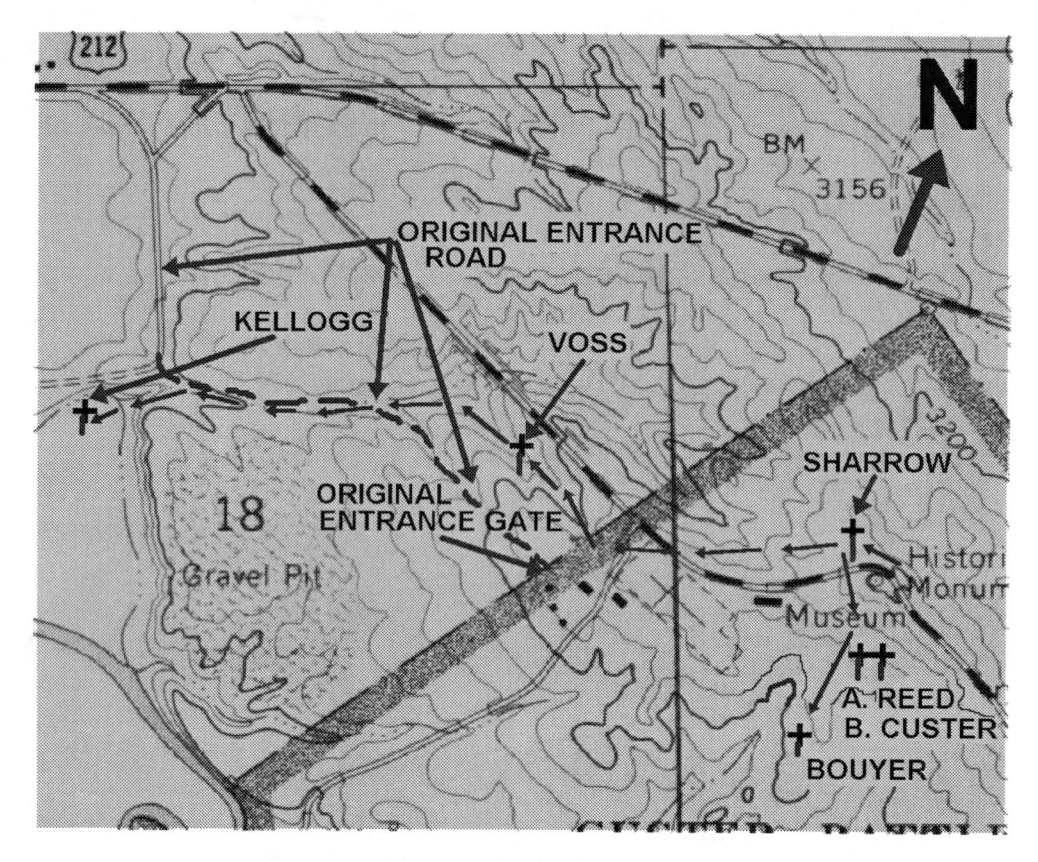

THE LAST SEVEN

SCALE: -------------------- 1/4 MILE

The last seven men from behind the Company C horse barricade on Monument Hill made an effort to reach the safety of the timber in the valley bottom. They were Sergeant-Major William Sharrow, Chief-Bugler Henry Voss, and the four civilians, Mark Kellogg, Boston Custer, Autie Reed and Mitch Bouyer. One other staff N.C.O., Robert Hughes of Company K may have also been with them. They had been placed inside the remaining sorrel horses from company C that were shot down for their protection. This smaller circle of four to five dead horses represented Custer's headquarters staff last command post.

Mark Kellogg, the civilian reporter sent on the expedition by General Terry was found on the valley floor near a ravine that was used earlier by the Second Battalion. His body was the last to be discovered by the Terry/Gibbon inspection party. Although many expended army cartridge casings were found here, no bodies were discovered behind this small horse barricade that was on the highest summit of the "Custer Knoll" were the Battle Monument now strands. **(See pg. 187)**

Courtesy of the Little Bighorn Battlefield National Monument

THE COMPANY C HORSE BARRICADE

Believed to have been taken by S. J. Morrow in 1879. View looking west.

The Custer Hill Finality: It was then that the large circle of mounted Indian non-combatants, acting as spectators, and the front rank of dismounted sniper warriors began a great inward rush towards the dead soldier circle. Meantime, on Weir Point, over 150 officers and men of the Seventh Regiment had watched the final destruction of their comrades. Lieutenant Godfrey, who was the last man to leave Weir Point, observed a huge black circle of humanity and horses shrinking on it self. With a great dust cloud and tremendous victory shout that was heard on Weir Point, Custer's Last Stand was over! The time was at least 5:30 PM. **M40**

Other Horses and Animals at the Custer Fight: U.S. Government horses and mules were not the only animals to be taken to Montana in 1876. Many of the officers and men had bought along their dogs. Lieutenant Godfrey relates a story of how one of Custer's personal hounds had come back to Fort Abraham Lincoln in 1876. He was starved; the hound was kept around the guard house. Later, when Godfrey was transferred to Fort Yates the same dog would recognize and befriended Godfrey and his children. **BYU 184 (Godfrey)**

One of Walter Camp's sources told him about the "mascot" of Company I who was recovered from the Indians years after the Battle. He was described as a black and white bull dog named "Joe Bush." He trusted a soldier or an Indian, but not a white civilian. Private John Creighton, of Company K, tells of another bulldog named "Red," who was considered by the soldiers to have been a veteran of the Battle. Charging Hawk, a Brule-Sioux told Camp that as an eight year boy in the villages at the Little Horn battle, he often heard the story of a soldier dog seen during the battle running along the back trail with a hand written note tied to his collar. The Indians shot at the dog but he escaped the fighting. The Arikara Scouts tell of how Bobtail Bull's horse traveled all the way back to their Missouri River reservation, after his rider killed in the Valley fighting. **BYU 184, Lilly 66, Lilly 87, 667**

Napoleon, the Other Survivor: The well publicized Company I horse, "Comanche," was not the sole surviving government horse from the Custer Fight. Private Francis O'Toole, of Company E, told of the recovery of another government horse that has gone unnoticed. His name was "Napoleon", a gray horse from Company E. "Nap," just like Comanche, was found on the battlefield with serious wounds. Both horses, along with others, were ordered to be destroyed by a callous officer, but these two horse survivors just "happen to follow" the enlisted men back to the mouth of the Bighorn River crossing. Along with the men they were then transported over the Yellowstone aboard the steamboat *Far West*. Later, in early August, they would be both transported by the *Durfee* back to Lincoln. Apparently "Nap" died well before Comanche, who lived until 1891. **See page 189**

Both horses were official U.S. Government company horses, contrary to the Hollywood version that Captain Keogh "owned" Comanche. He had been assigned to Private John McGinness, of Company I who had been left behind at the Fort Lincoln hospital. Apparently Keogh had usurped one of his own enlisted men's company horses for his own use, something that the army frowned upon. Keogh was known for getting drunk and striking enlisted men with his "shillelagh" (Irish walking cane), something that the army did not frown on. **LILLY 78, 89, BYU 394 (O'Toole)**

Godfrey tells of an Indian horse that he found in the Deep Coulee area, very near the same point that Curly discovered his Sioux pony. As spoils of war, Godfrey retrieved and rode this gray Indian pony until the horse was shot from under him in the Nez Perce War of 1877. **BYU 184 (Godfrey)**

The Horse Memorial: In 1881, a fifteen ton memorial stone shaft was erected on Custer Hill, to honor all of the U.S. Army soldiers killed on both battlefields. Earlier in 1879, as part of a battlefield cleanup conducted from nearby Fort Custer, all of the horse bones that could be found were gathered up and enclosed in a cordwood "monument." It was located on the exact site where the horse barricade had been created for the Staff's non-commissioned officers and the civilians on the very top of the Custer Knoll.

Some time before the Custer Hill memorial monument was erected in 1881, the earlier horse cordwood memorial was dismantled to make room for the present granite shaft. Soldiers from Fort Custer dug a twenty foot by fifty foot trench and reburied the bones of approximately ninety horses that were killed on the Custer Field in 1876. In 1941, this "horse cemetery" was accidentally rediscovered during an N.P.S. construction project. The small numbers of disturbed horse bones were reburied, but the site of the horse "cemetery" was lost to history once more.

When the present Indian Memorial was under construction in 2002, the 1881/1941 horse burial site was once again rediscovered. This resulted from a mandated impact study being conducted by the N.P.S., and a partial archaeological excavation on a small segment of the shallow horse cemetery followed. By 2004 the National Park Service erected a marble memorial marker denoting the original 1881 below ground burial site of the Seventh Regiment's horses. It is located about twenty-five yards northeast of the present Battle Monument. It is an appropriate and fitting tribute to that magnificent creature, the horse, whose pure honesty tells the real story behind all of those "Custer Myths."

Permission by Little Bighorn Battlefield National Monument

THE HORSE MEMORIAL

Courtesy of the Little Big Horn Battlefield National Monument

NAPOLEON AND COMANCHE

On the left is Napoleon, a gray horse assigned to Company E. Along with Comanche of Company I they were ferried across the Yellowstone River on the Far West on June 30. Later both were transported down to Fort Abraham Lincoln in August. Comanche outlived "Nap" but both were true survivors of the Custer Fight and both were U.S. Government company horses. It is but another "Custer Myth" that Comanche was Captain Keogh's personal horse.

SUMMARY

The clash between the U.S. Army and the Sioux and Northern Cheyenne on the Little Bighorn was fought with many errors. The Native Americans were able to take full advantage of the mistakes made by the army. As Custer's Second Battalion commander, and his best military friend, Captain George Walter Yates made a series of serious tactical errors. The first of these were the deployment of Company E as dismounted skirmishers on the southern slope of the Nye-Cartwright Ridge. This "knee-jerk" reaction would put Company E out of the mainstream of over an hour. His response to the sudden appearance of the Young Warriors was unwarranted. At this point, these poorly armed teenagers did not pose a real threat. But their large numbers and aggressiveness appeared to be a threat to the rear flanks of the advancing battalion.

Yates's second mistake was in dismounting on the Northern Cemetery Hill complex and establishing the short term West Skirmish Line. This deployment came after the abortive attempt to cross at the Willy Bends ford. The very real threat of a large warrior force now crossing at the Gray Horse Ford caused Yates to be cut-off from the First Battalion's retreat from Ford B. However, Yates needed to gain higher ground, but he would have been better served by taking the high ground along the Battle Ridge.

The third tactical error created by Yates was his deployment of Company F along the North Slope of the Battle Ridge to assist Harrington's fleeing Company C. This very small number of men did not demand this wasteful number of personnel. He had been ordered to advance to Custer's chosen rallying point on Calhoun Hill.

The destruction of Company C on Finley Hill may have caused Custer to reevaluate waiting for Benteen's expected reinforcements. This decision may have resulted in sending the newly arrived Companies E along with Company F to be deployed near the Gray Horse Gully that led to the timber in the valley. The salient "floating" line of the South Skirmish Line now had its flanks exposed to higher ground. The Young Warriors were glad to oblige them with a devastating attack on their led horses, causing a rout of the men forcing them back again to the Battle Ridge. It would be a Finley Hill rout all over again. It was the doom for the struggling dismounted men at the 'Keogh' restaging area. Any hopes that Custer entertained in seeking refuge in the timber bottom were now gone. The rest of the story was the rolling up of the flanks and the anxious hope of a "Last Stand" on Monument Hill! It was Frederick Benteen's reading of the fighting on the Custer Field, was that it was a rout and the men were "scattered like corn!"

The real cause of the defeat lay in the Grant Administration's folly of the civilian run-amok policies of the corrupt Indian Department. Under the reconstruction policies of the Post-Civil War, new western lands were wanted to boost the economy and for farm land for the newly freed slaves. And the huge areas of what were once considered as Indian land and were now up for the grabbing. The government financiers' dream of another California Gold Rush in the Black Hills sealed the Sioux and Northern Cheyenne's fate. The U.S. Supreme Court's ruling that all previous. U.S. Government treaties were now abrogated was another major factor. The War Department administration over Native Americans was then taken over by the far right quasi-religious Indian Department, created by the money-hungry Grant Administration.

There is ample evidence that when the U.S. Army was in control of the "Indian Problem," that the Indians fared better than when after the Custer disaster, when they were forced onto reservation systems. The religious "right" of its day was given a free run in Christianizing the People, while the corrupt Indian Department would make farmers out of them.

Another major factor was the lean economics of maintaining a viable military establishment. Before 1876, all cavalry companies were to have a minimum of eighty enlisted men in the ranks. When the Seventh Regiment left their post near Bismarck, Dakota Territory, the average strength of the companies was but fifty-nine enlisted men. Only seventy-three enlisted men were left behind at Fort Lincoln and the regiment started the 1876 Sioux Campaign with but 698 enlisted men in the twelve companies, a deficit of thirty percent!

This left a deficit of 189 men below their congressional mandated strength of 960 enlisted men. But it was in the ranks of commissioned officers that the Army was most understaffed! Of the thirty-six company officers that should have been at the Custer Fight, only twenty-four were available. When the "Custer" Battalions went down Medicine Tail Coulee, the five companies had just nine company officers, instead of the fifteen allowed by congressional law. The First Battalion suffered the most, with only three officers rather then the six that were mandated, a full fifty percent reduction!

The lack of non-commissioned officers caused the breakdown in discipline within the companies. At the full strength that the five companies should have had, there was a sixty percent deficit. The First Battalion's discipline breakdown in the Battle was due to the lack of supervisory personnel. The Third and Fourth Battalion had just eight company officers, a forty-five percent deficit in company officers. Only twenty-nine company and battalion commissioned officers and battalion officers and 578 enlisted men went up the Rosebud. There were an additional four officers and two enlisted men assigned to Custer's Headquarters Staff. The total of 607 of men and officers was far short of over 1000 that could have been there, amounting to a forty percent reduction. Now we know why General Terry had expressed his fears that he had sent too small a force up the Rosebud River.

Five days latter, General Terry's worst fears came to fulfillment. It was not just the human toll; there was a shortage of horses and their tack. Saddles were in short supply, as wittiness the large number of "reserve" horse taken into combat on June 25. The "Custer" Battalions had a total of fifty-five "extra" rider-less horses in their ranks. When forced to dismount and fight on foot, an additional fifteen horse holders were required to take care of these reserve mounts. This further reduced the number of men that could be put on the skirmish line.

The author's inevitable conclusion was that there was but one written message and that John Martin carried it. **(See Facsimile B, pg. 141)**The other three known orders to Benteen had all been verbal. But, there may have been as many as two additional orders sent to Benteen. It now becomes apparent that Benteen reworded the written reinforcement order delivered by John Martin to suit his need to offset any future military repercussions. His letter to his wife on July 4 says as much as this.

Whether if it was Reno or Benteen who were the primary cause of the failure at Little Bighorn is a moot point, one failed to supply positive leadership while the other supplied fearless leadership for their survival on June 26 and 27. And that was how the enlisted men looked at it, and so did many of their officers!

Not to be discounted was the growing "Red Power" movement attributed to Sitting Bull's perceived charisma. Many of the younger "summer roamers" (reservation) warriors were attracted to the growing awareness that this was to be the last great buffalo hunt in Southeastern Montana. The "winter roamers," those who resisted going onto any reservation, also knew that their days were numbered. A quiescent religious movement soon permeated Sitting Bull's people, and the reservations emptied out for one final rite of passage.

If there was indeed an eight messenger **(see pg. 211)** sent from Calhoun Hill, he could have come from Company I or L, and if he was with his company and not the packs on June 25. There were at least two "extra" unaccounted members from both Companies I and L that may have not been with the Pack Train. One was Corporal David Cooney, of Company I, a twenty-eight year old veteran of four years from Ireland. Private Cooney received a life threatening wound on Reno Hill on June 26, being shot through the hip. He was transported to the hospital at Fort Lincoln with the rest of the Seventh's more critically wounded men. He died there on July 20, just twenty-five days after the Custer Fight

Could Private Clooney have been the mystery messenger that carried the Sergeant Hanley/Wilber "Calhoun was wounded" rumor to Reno Hill? For some reason he was field promoted to Sergeant two days after his wounding. The most interesting question is who had the authority to have granted this field promotion of two grades when all of the commissioned officers of Company I were dead or not at the Battle? General Terry was the only one with that authority and why? What heroic role did Private Clooney play in the Custer Battle? It is possible that in the confusion of the aftermath of the Battle and with his serious wound that Private Clooney's role as Custer's last messenger was overlooked and forgotten soon after his death?

Corporal Eldon French delivered the first of three crucial orders concerning the movement of the Pack Train. The next two, one verbal and one written, demanded that Benteen come forward without the packs and to be quick about it! But Benteen did not pay any more attention to them as he did to Sergeant Kanipe's verbal "shortcut" order some fifteen minutes after Corporal French was sent from Mathey's Knoll. Benteen did somewhat expedite the packs to Reno Hill an hour overdue, despite all of his "dawdling" and excuse making, but that role had already been counter-mannered by Bishop, Kanipe and Martin. Even if Benteen had taken Custer's mandated shortcut and he had gone forward in a timely manner without the packs, he still would not have been able to reach Calhoun Hill much before 5:00 PM. By then it would have been too late. Benteen's post-battle assessment that Custer had out run his support was very correct!

What must not be ruled out was Custer's fondness for gambling and his bad habit of issuing orders and then he would turn around and countermand them. Benteen was told to wait for the Pack Train and then he was ordered not to wait. This rash of "Custer-Burrs" had worn Benteen's patience thin, but his spitefulness and his track record of dereliction to duty won out in the end. The fourth pivotal Staff messenger was Corporal Alexander Bishop, of Company H, a twenty-two Brooklyn born native who survived the Battle by remaining with his company commander, Fredrick Benteen. Is this why Custer told John Martin to come back, if it was safe, otherwise to come back with Benteen? He was sending back messengers but none were returning!

Overall, the major contributing factor was that there were just too many warriors consolidated in an unprecedented gathering of the tribes along the Little Bighorn. Colonel Joseph Reynolds can be given credit for this. His premature attack on March 17, 1876 on the Northern Cheyenne village on the upper Powder River caused much of this consolidation. After losing their lodges, winter food stores, household equipment, and most of their horses, the decimated Cheyenne traveled north to Montana and were taken in by the winter roaming Sioux. This unprecedented consolidation of the tribes on the Little Bighorn had never been seen before or ever again. The officers would not have expected such a massive gathering along any of the streams in the region. There were a minimum of 1000 lodges contributing to as many as 2000 "warriors" as the un-pledged "Young Warriors" would prove. These teenagers would inflect more damage to Custer men than the full-fledged "adult" warriors

The largest contingent that Custer had ever faced before was Black Kettle's village on the Washita River in 1867. Then there were about fifty lodges with a maximum of three hundred fifty villagers. On the Little Big Horn there were some 7000 people. This was twenty times the number of Black Kettle's village. The unexpected pitched battle on the Little Bighorn was doomed from the very onset, just as General Terry had feared due to the under strength status of the Seventh Regiment. Did Custer underestimate the fighting strength of the villages along the Little Bighorn River? Most likely he did due to a lack of advanced reconnoitering and the fact that his troops were still marching in an outdated Civil War squadron formation as a Reconnaissance In Force.

The civilian, Frederick Gerard, said it best. He told Walter Camp that even if Custer had kept his force together, the Seventh Cavalry would have known that they had whipped. Gerard concluded that there were just far too many Indians.

Just like in Vietnam, the ill-conceived strategy of the 1960s has a great similarity with the Indian Wars of the 1870s. In the end, unintelligent politicians send out the military that was ill-prepared to carry out their rash decisions. It was the Native Americans' physical and spiritual resistance to the intrusion of the American Government into the Dakota and Montana areas that defeated the "Elan" of the U.S. Army. It started with the Grant Administration's illegal intrusion into the Black Hills in 1874 in search for gold. This highly orchestrated "Gold Rush" was the direct result of Sherman's failed Indian Policy carried out during the corrupt Grant Administration. Author and historian, Donald Jackson in his excellent treatise *Custer's Gold* explains this sordid episode that makes some of the present war policy of recent and current national administrations pale beyond belief. President Grant as a "'war" president shares with President Eisenhower the same shameful legacy of the Vietnam War, one that is very reminiscent of the post Civil War Indian Wars. And the U.S. Army and the Native Americans become the "whipping-boys" of the morally bankrupt policy makers. .

Vine Deloria, the Ogallala-Sioux author and early civil rights leader of the 1950's "Red Power" movement said it best with the title of his book, *Custer Died for Your Sins.*

END

APPENDIX:

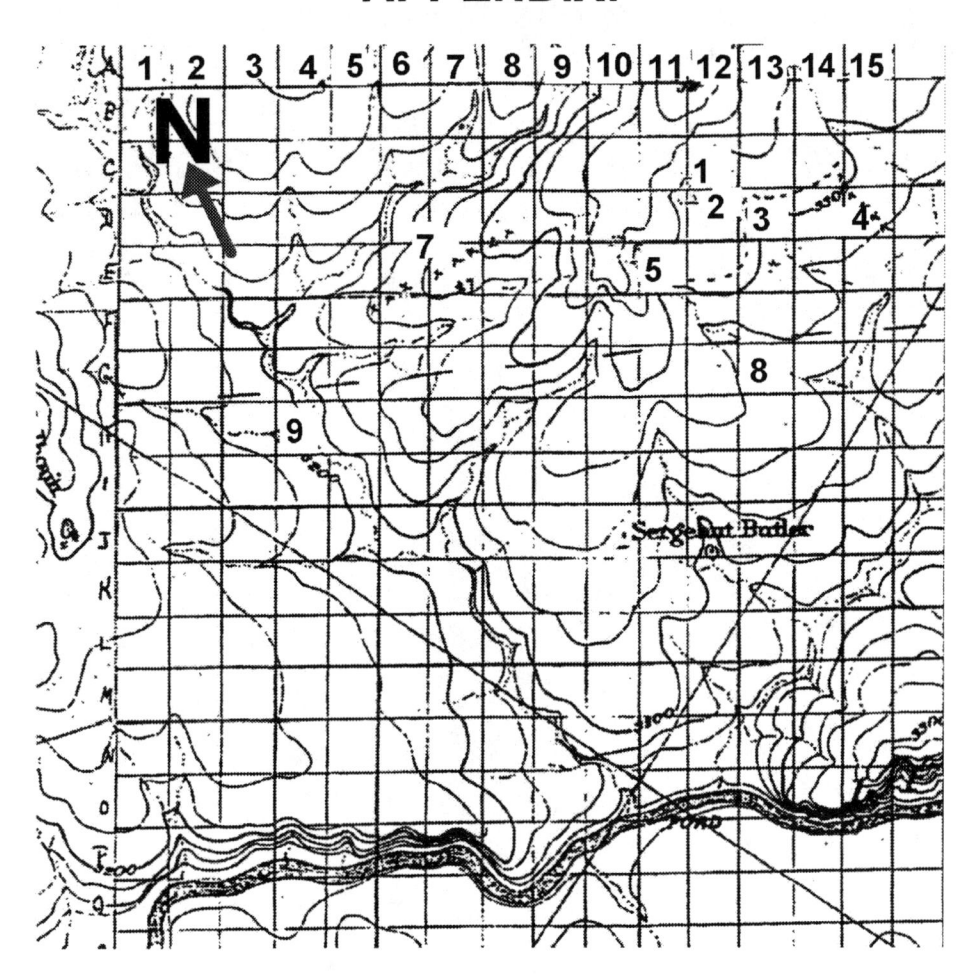

THE LUCE ARTIFACT FIND GRID MAP

SCALE: -------------------- 1/4 MILE

KEY:

ITEM	GRID	DESCRIPTION	GREENE
#1	C-12	Expended casings at 3yardt intervals.	11A
#2	D-12	(150) Expended casings (True Luce ridge)	10A
#3	D-13	Cavalry Spur with buckle.	10C
#4	D-15	Expended casings scattered at 9 yards.	18A
#5	E-11	(1) McKeever cartridge box.	11C
#7	E-7	(17) Expended casings (Blummer)	18A
#8	G-13	Horse skeleton with saddle parts.	11D
#9	H-4	(1) Winchester rifle found in 1936 (Nelson).	13C

Custer Battlefield Superintendent Major Edward Luce had a civil survey done in 1943 to locate the then known artifact finds. Luce used the east boundary fence line of the Custer Battlefield (left) as his datum point and 375 foot square grid lines. The expended casings in Luce item #4 (D-15) shows where Company E was first dismounted. It was here that Company E fired the opening shots of the Custer portion of the battle at 3:20 PM. They were posted at nine yard intervals as the expended casing finds show. The Luce Item #2 (D-12) *represents the true location of the "Luce Ridge where over 150 expended army casings had been found. This is where Company E was posted from 3:40 to 4:00 PM. But, later when Company E left the Luce Ridge at 4:00 PM they marched dismounted and fired three volleys at six yard intervals as in a **Flankers as Skirmishers** formation **(See pg. 201)**.*

Company E's dismounted movement to Calhoun Hill started on the south slide of half-section fence line in Section 21, and continued down the north slope of the Nye-Cartwright Ridge to near Deep Coulee. Here they were mounted and arrived on Calhoun Hill by 4:20 PM. At that time Curley saw the men with the Gray Horses moving in a normal manner. Source: CBNM file: Luce Bulletin #1, February 1, 1944. **Author's personal communication with Doug Scott, NPS Chief Archaeologist Mid-West Region.**

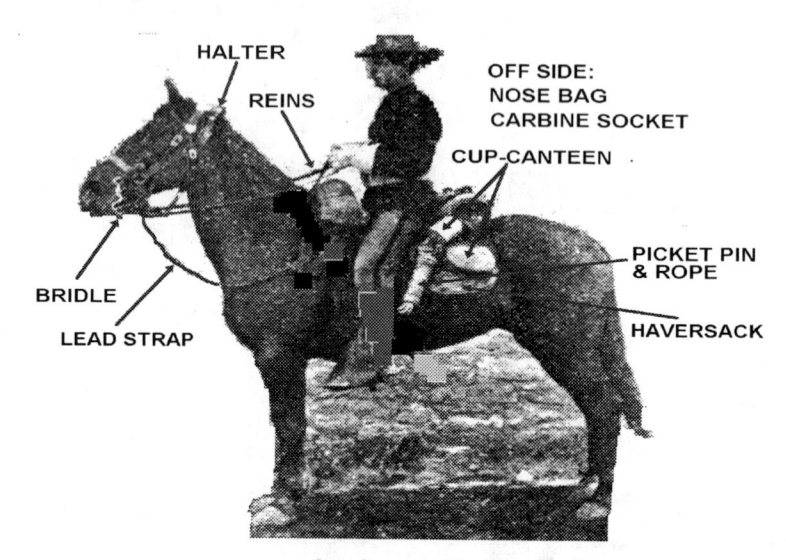

Lt. Jno. J. Boniface, *The Cavalry Horse and his Pack,* 1903

CUSTER ERA HORSEMAN
Annotations by author.

*The **Halter** was always worn under the bridle. The **Bridle** used a Shoemaker curb bit, with three degrees of severity (port height). The reins were not split like the western style, but riveted together on the riders end. The leather **Lead Strap** was snapped to the halter "D" ring and tied to the near (left) side of the pommel. The man's tin **cup**, **canteen**, and **haversack**, which contained four days of ration, eating utensils was tied to the near rear saddle ring. The "meat can" (mess kit) contained the salt pork ration. The haversack was line with a rubber coating. The bed blanket(s) was used under the saddle when the horse 'fleshed out" after a long field campaign. The heavy overcoat was tied with the "coat straps" on the pommel. The **Picket Pin** and **Rope** was fastened to the near rear saddle staple. The near (left) **saddle bag** contained the remaining cartons of reserve carbine ammunition. The off (right) saddle bag was for spare horseshoes and personal gear and perhaps reserve ammunition. The carbine leather socket was fastened to the off side rear saddle rigging strap. On the off front saddle ring hung the canvas nose "feed bag" containing the horses' curry comb, brush, hobbles and "watering" bridle. Total weight in light marching order was under sixty pounds including the seventeen pound McClellan saddle.*

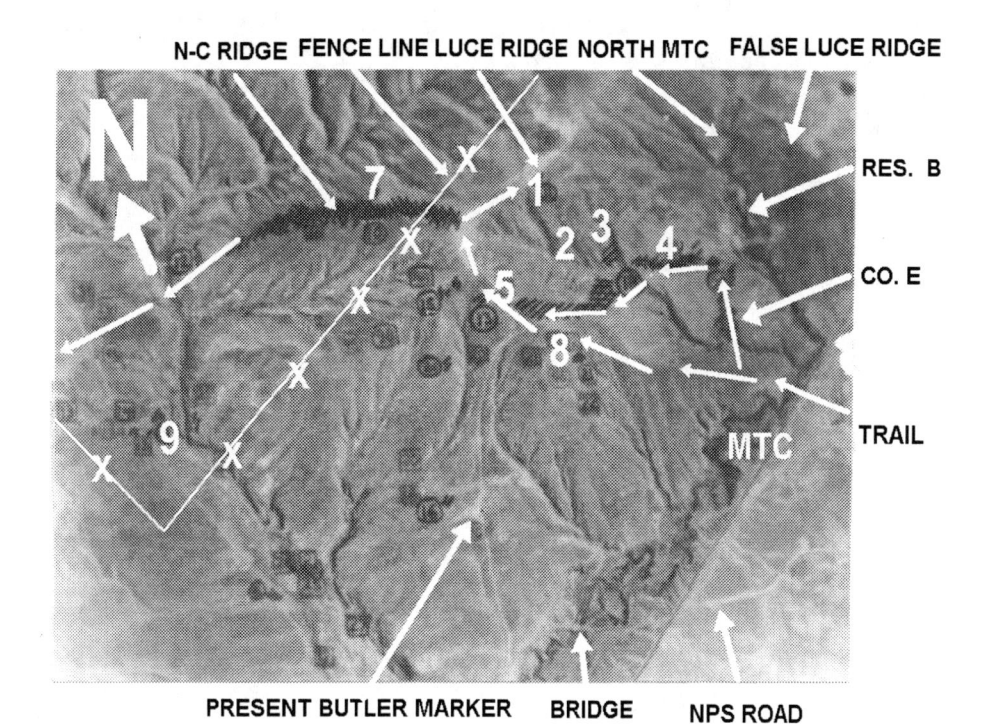

NPS MASTER ARTIFACT FINDS AERIAL PHOTO SURVEY I
(U.S.D.A. COMPOSITE AERIAL PHOTO)

Numerical annotations in white represent the 1943 Luce Grid Map 1943 artifact finds **(See pg. 195)**

SCALE: ----------------- 1/4 MILE

Based on the United States Department of Agriculture (USDA) aerial photographic surveys, this composite NPS Master Artifact Finds Survey was created by Custer Battlefield personnel in the late 1960s. They used an alphanumerical coded system to record all known artifacts finds to that date (seen in black).

KEY:

C10 = (1) Cavalry spur with buckle.
C11 = (1) McClellan saddle.
C12 = (1) Horse bones with horse tack.(Luce #8)
C20 = (2) Human skeletons.
C21 = (1) Human skeleton.
C22 = (1) Human skeleton.

D2 = Human bones.
D11 = Horse tack (see C12)

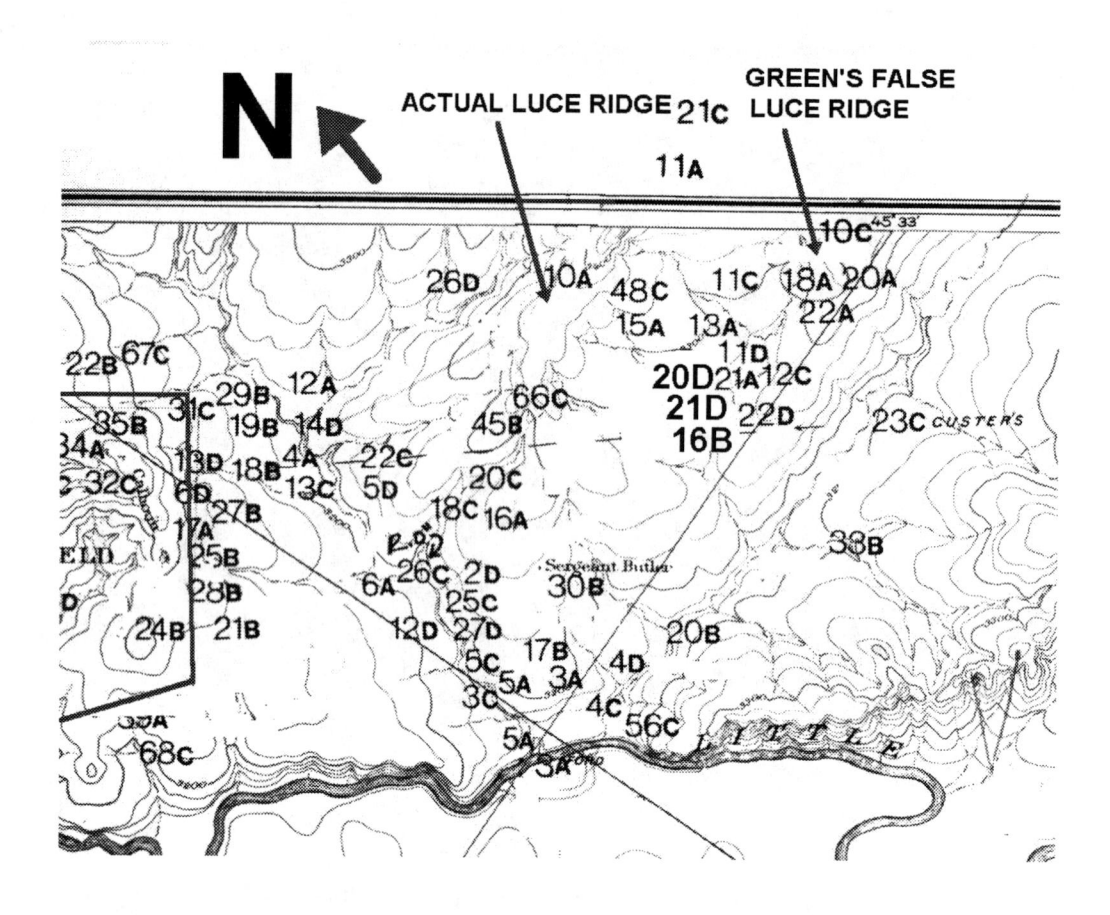

GREENE'S FOLD-OUT MAP FROM Evidence and the Custer Enigma
1889-1905 U.S.G.S. SURVEY IS SHOWN
NOTE: Walter Camp's "South" boundary fence line is shown in the lower left corner.

SCALE: -------------- 1/4 MILE

Expended Casings	Army Artifacts
10A = (105) in groups of three (Luce Item #2)	10C = Cavalry Spur.
12A = (2)	11C = (1) McKeever Cartridge Box
13A = (1)	12C + horse Bones (Luce Item #8)
18A = (152) Luce Item #4	20C = (2) Human Skeletons.
20A = Unknown Numbers.	21C = (1) human Skeleton.
22A = Many at three yard intervals (Luce Item #4)	22C = (1) Human Skeleton.

*Jerome Green transposed the 1960s NPS Master Artifact Finds alphanumerical callouts from the above NPS Master Aerial Photo Survey (**pg. 197**) for his book, Evidence and the Custer Enigma, first published in 1973. Unfortunely, the much earlier 1889-1905 United States Geological Survey (USGS) topographical survey version was used for his fold-out map. This obsolete USGS survey was done as an "Eye Ball" survey only where no actual on the ground survey was done. The area outside the Custer Battlefield is subjective and has great scale distortions as to the actual terrain contour features, especially east of the Nye-Cartwright area.*

The current USGS 1967 version as used in this book were done by aerial photogrammetric process and shows the correct terrain contours. By usage of the inaccurate older non-aerial produce survey, Greene's NPS U.S.D.A. Master Aerial Photo Survey alphanumerical callouts are grossly misplaced. The artifacts found on the actual Luce Ridge are shown up to half mile to the east, creating a second but false "Luce Ridge." The results have been that subsequent researchers continue to place artifact finds where they have never been found. This just creates another distorted view of the Custer Battle.

Only the Second Battalion traversed the Nye-Cartwright area on their way north to the lower fords. Company E was dismounted to counter the surprised attack of the Young Warriors. Consequently all of the expended army casing found in this entire area were fired alone by Company E.

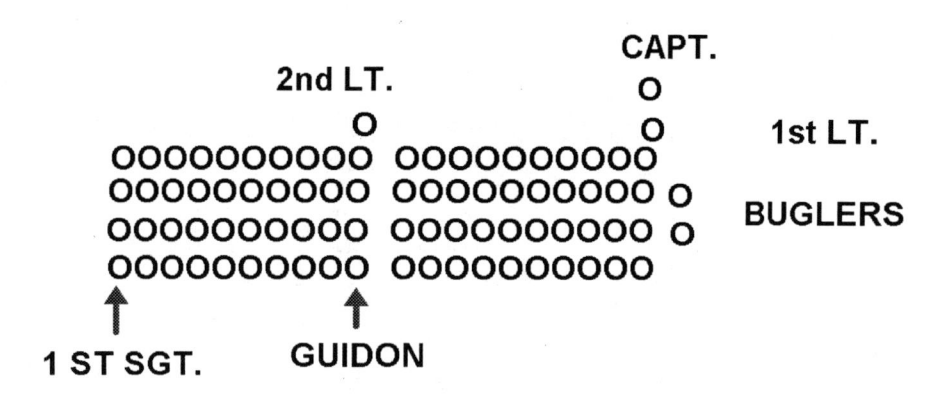

```
                                           CAPT.
               2nd LT.                       O
                  O                          O    1st LT.
          OOOOOOOOOO  OOOOOOOOOO
          OOOOOOOOOO  OOOOOOOOOO  O
          OOOOOOOOOO  OOOOOOOOOO  O    BUGLERS
          OOOOOOOOOO  OOOOOOOOOO
                ↑           ↑
           1 ST SGT.    GUIDON
```

COMPANY FORMATION IN PLATOONS
Source: Fourth Regiment 1883-4 Drill Manual, Fort Huachuca, Arizona Territory

The Custer Era standard formation was that of a column of fours marching in platoons. There are references in the Camp material using the term" Marching in Platoons". This is the correct deployment for fours in platoon formation according to the 1883-84 Drill Manual of the Fourth Regiment of cavalry while stationed at Fort Huachuca, Arizona Territory. It is not what you see in all of those Hollywood movie portrayals.

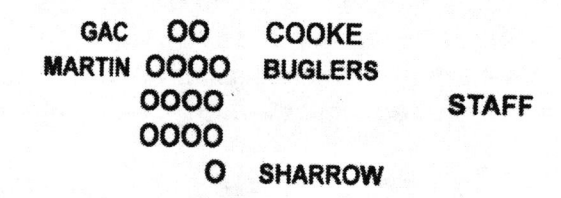

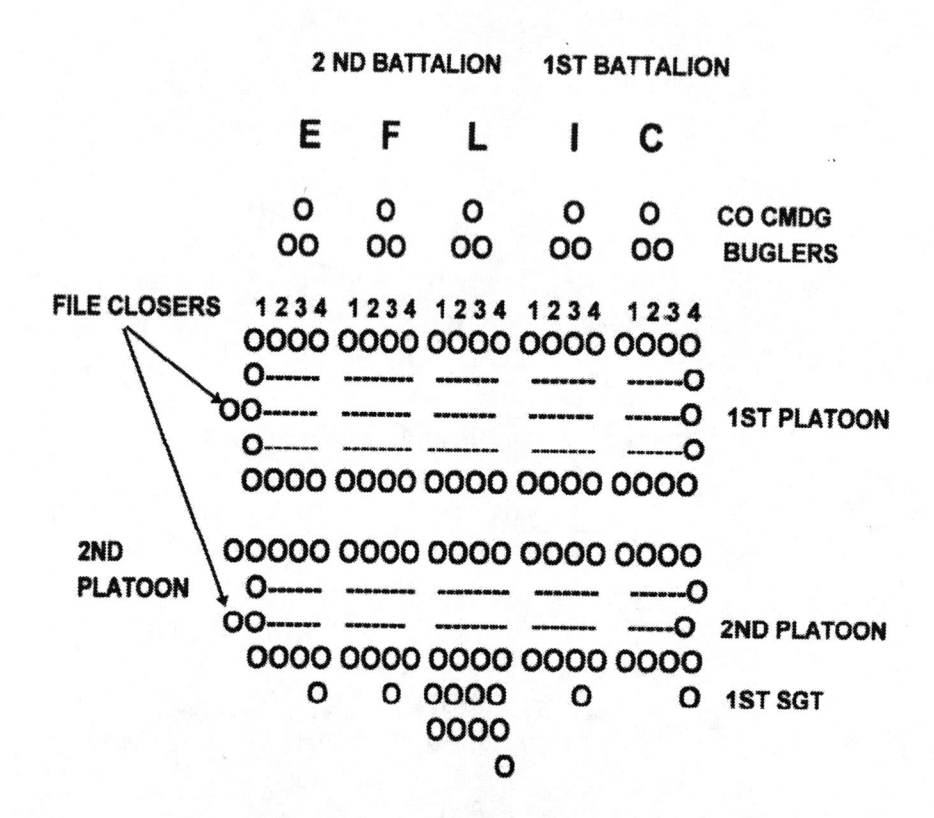

```
              GAC   OO    COOKE
           MARTIN  OOOO   BUGLERS
                   OOOO            STAFF
                   OOOO
                     O   SHARROW



            2ND BATTALION    1ST BATTALION

              E      F      L      I      C

              O      O      O      O      O     CO CMDG
             OO     OO     OO     OO     OO     BUGLERS

  FILE CLOSERS  1234  1234  1234  1234  1234
               OOOO  OOOO  OOOO  OOOO  OOOO
               O----  ----  ----  ----  ----O
              OO----  ----  ----  ----  ----O   1ST PLATOON
               O----  ----  ----  ----  ----O
               OOOO  OOOO  OOOO  OOOO  OOOO

   2ND       OOOOO OOOO  OOOO  OOOO  OOOO
  PLATOON     O----  ----  ----  ----  ----O
              OO---- ----  ----  ----  ----O    2ND PLATOON
               OOOO  OOOO  OOOO  OOOO  OOOO
                O     O   OOOO    O     O       1ST SGT
                          OOOO
                            O
```

SQUADRON FORMATION
USED BY THE FIRST & SECOND BATTALION

Custer used this Recognizance In Force formation to travel from the battalion assignment halt near the divide to the halt in Medicine Tail Coulee. Also referred as marching in platoons (or companies) this method was popular during the Civil war were the ground allowed a wide front. The major advantage was a much shorter column length as opposed to the companies being in tandem.

Lt. McGuire in his preliminary version of his Reno Court of Inquiry battlefield map shows the Custer "Squadrons." Kanipe told Walter Camp that they had marched in a column of twos with all five companies abreast of each other. This is a Civil War "Squadron" formation.

When marching in a "Squadron" style formation, the company commander and the First Lieutenant (First Platoon leader) moved to the front of the company with the buglers. The Second Lieutenant (Second Platoon leader) moved inside the ranks between the platoons. The file closers would than be on the left flank of the Squadron with the default dress alignment to the right.

```
                    O KEOGH  BATTLN CMDG

                    PORTER  HARRINGTON
                      O        O      CO CMDG
                      OO       OO     BUGLERS

    CO I                                    CO C
  SKIRMISHERS                            SKIRMISHERS
     X                                        X
                        I    C
     X
                     1 2 3 4  1 2 3 4
                     OOOO   OOOO
     X               O-----  -----O            X
                     O-----  -----O
                     O-----  -----O         1ST PLATOON
                     O-----  -----O
     X                                         X

                     O-----  -----O
     X               O-----  -----O            X
                     O-----  -----O         2ND PLATOON
                     O-----  -----O
     X               OOOO   OOOO                X
                       O       O
                     LED HORSES
     X                                         X


     X                                         X
```

SKIRMISHERS AS FLANKERS
USED BY FIRST BATTALION ON ITS RETREAT TO FINLEY HILL

*When the First Battalion halted on Greasy Grass Hill **(Halt #5)** Companies I & C formed into this protective formation. The led horse was placed in between the parallel lines of skirmishers deployed on the flanks of the dismounted column. To prove the importance of the information given by Curly to Walter Camp, he described this exact formation in detail. Curly's description is exactly as shown in the Fourth Regiment Drill Manual of 1883-4. It proves the veracity of Curly's interviews with Camp whom he described as the most exacting man who ever interviewed him.*

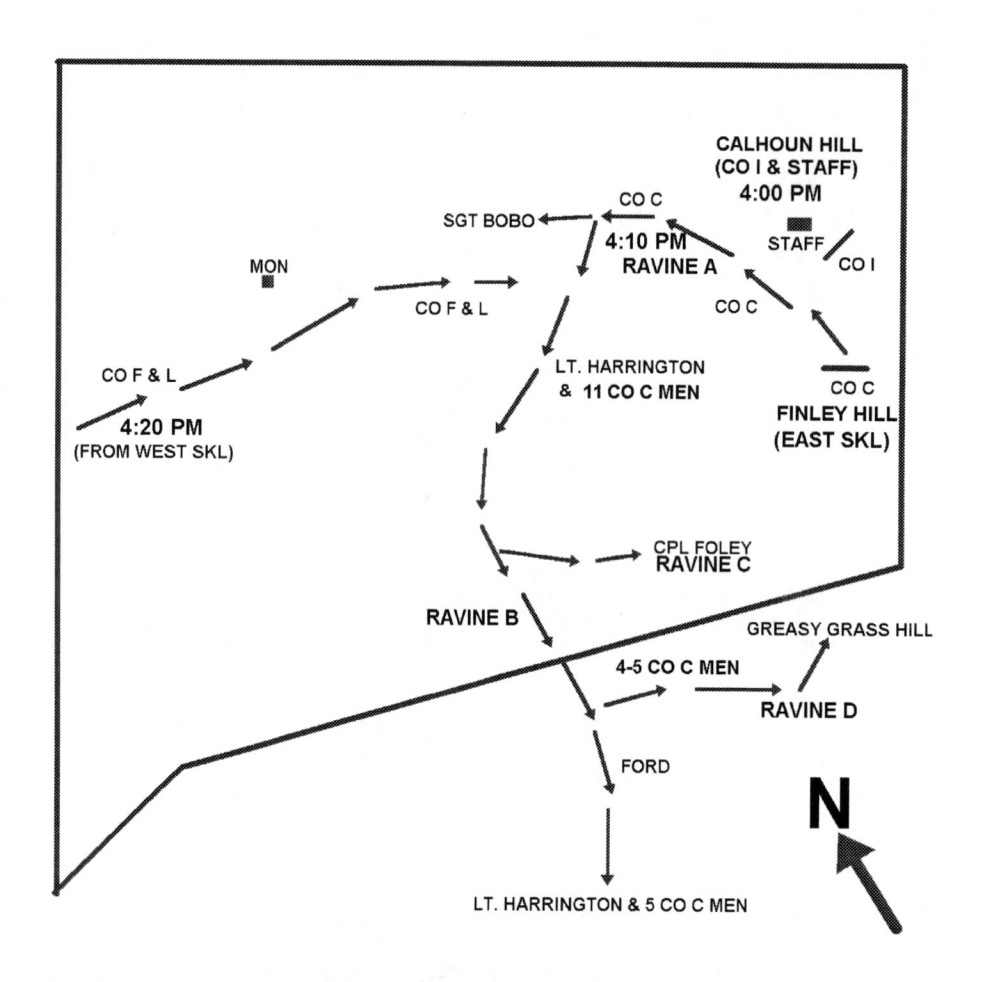

CUSTER FIGHT - PHASE 1
(4:00 - 4:10 PM)

SCALE: ------------------- 1/4 MILE

The First Phase of the Custer Fight began when Company C formed the East Skirmish Line **(EAST SKL)** on Finley Hill at 4:00 PM. Company C would be soon routed from **Finley Hill**. Their left flank was rolled up by dismounted warriors firing parabolic arrows into the led horses. Company C incurred a fifty percent loss of men on this skirmish line. Survivors of Company C fled mounted in disorder down **Ravine A**. First Sergeant Bobo lost his horse in **Ravine A** but he and a small number of Company C men made it to the future Keogh area. Lt. Harrington and about one dozen Company C men fled southward over the **Battle Ridge** and down **Ravine B** (The Gray Horse Gully). One man from Company C (Corporal John Foley) remained hidden in the lower reaches of **Ravine C**. A small number of Company C men reached **Greasy Grass Hill** by **Ravine D**. There except for Lt. Harrington and five other men was the last of company C to be killed. Their total time on the field was but ten minutes.

Company F and L were ordered to leave the West Skirmish Line **(WEST SKL)** and to advance to Custer's chosen defensive position on **Calhoun Hill**.

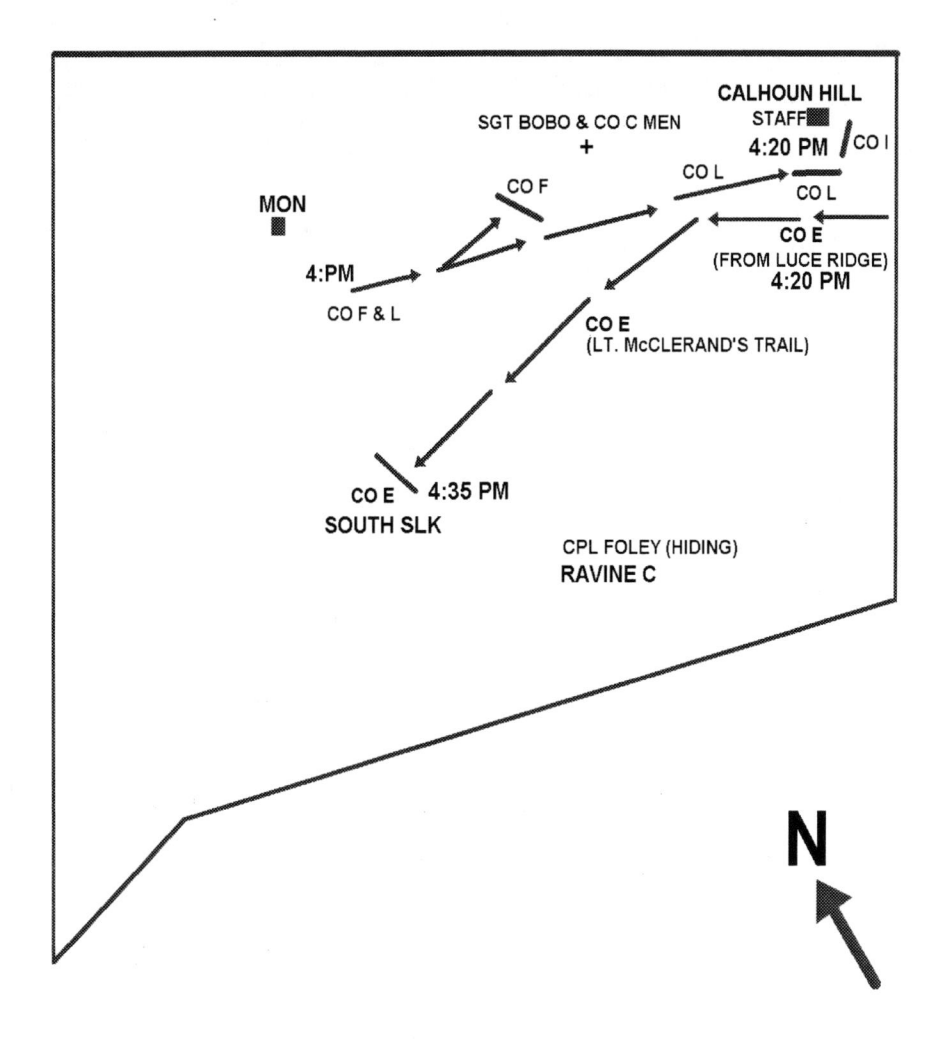

CUSTER FIGHT - PHASE 2
(4:10 - 4:15 PM)

SCALE: ------------------- 1/4 MILE

*Company F and L would intercept Company C's wild flight from the field. Captain Yates ordered Company F to be deployed dismounted on the north slope of the Battle Ridge. Lt. Calhoun continued with Company L to Custer's chosen defensive position soon to be named after him. By 4:20 PM, Company E had arrived from the Luce Ridge skirmish line only to be sent down to form the South Skirmish Line **(SOUTH SKL)**. The movement of Company E and its trail were seen by Curly and later by Lt. McClernard. This deployment of Company E may have signaled Custer's incentive to reach the relative safety of the timber in the valley bottom.*

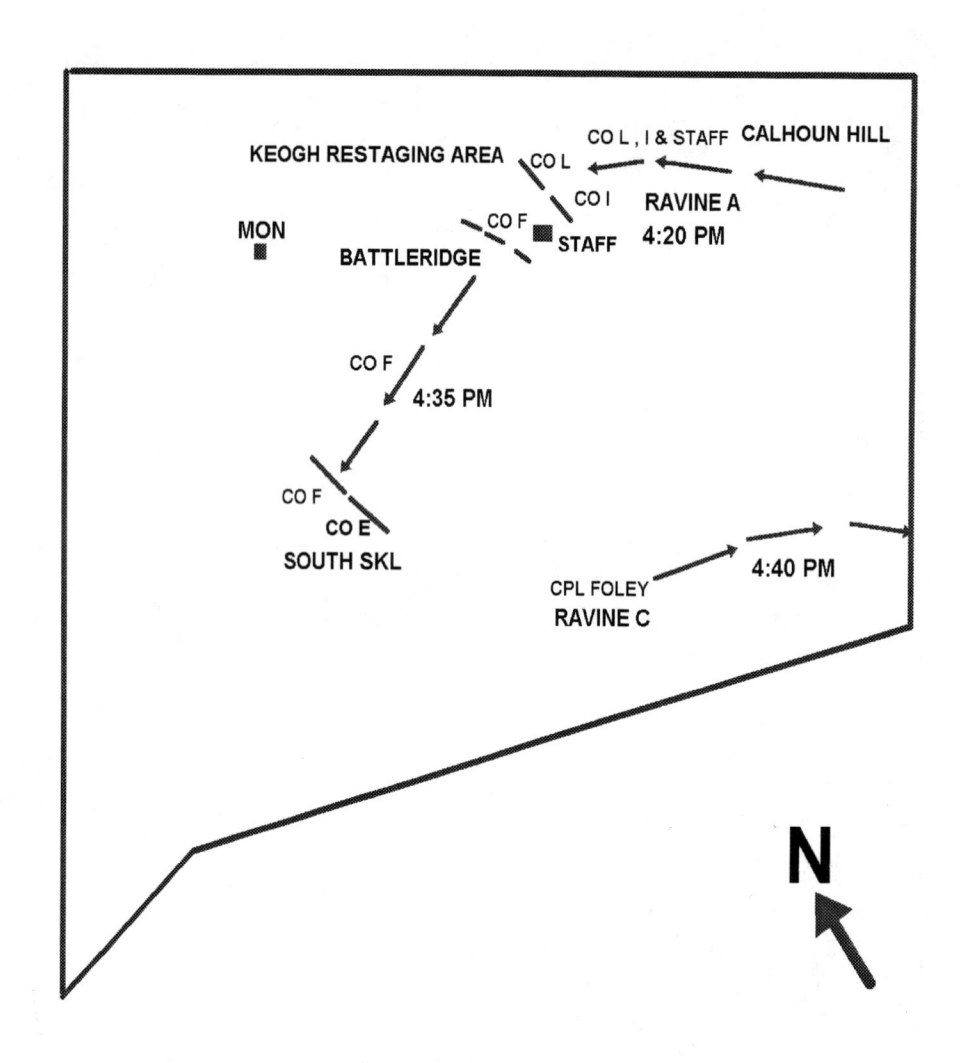

CUSTER FIGHT - PHASE 3
(4:14 - 4:30 PM)

SCALE: -------------------- 1/4 MILE

*Calhoun Hill was abandoned when a superior number of warriors forced Company I, L and the Staff to retreat dismounted in an orderly manner down **Ravine A** to the Keogh restaging area. Here they reformed in successive stands to reach the high ground of the Battle Ridge. Meantime, Company F is taken down on foot to join Company E on the new South Skirmish Line **(SOUTH SKL)**.*

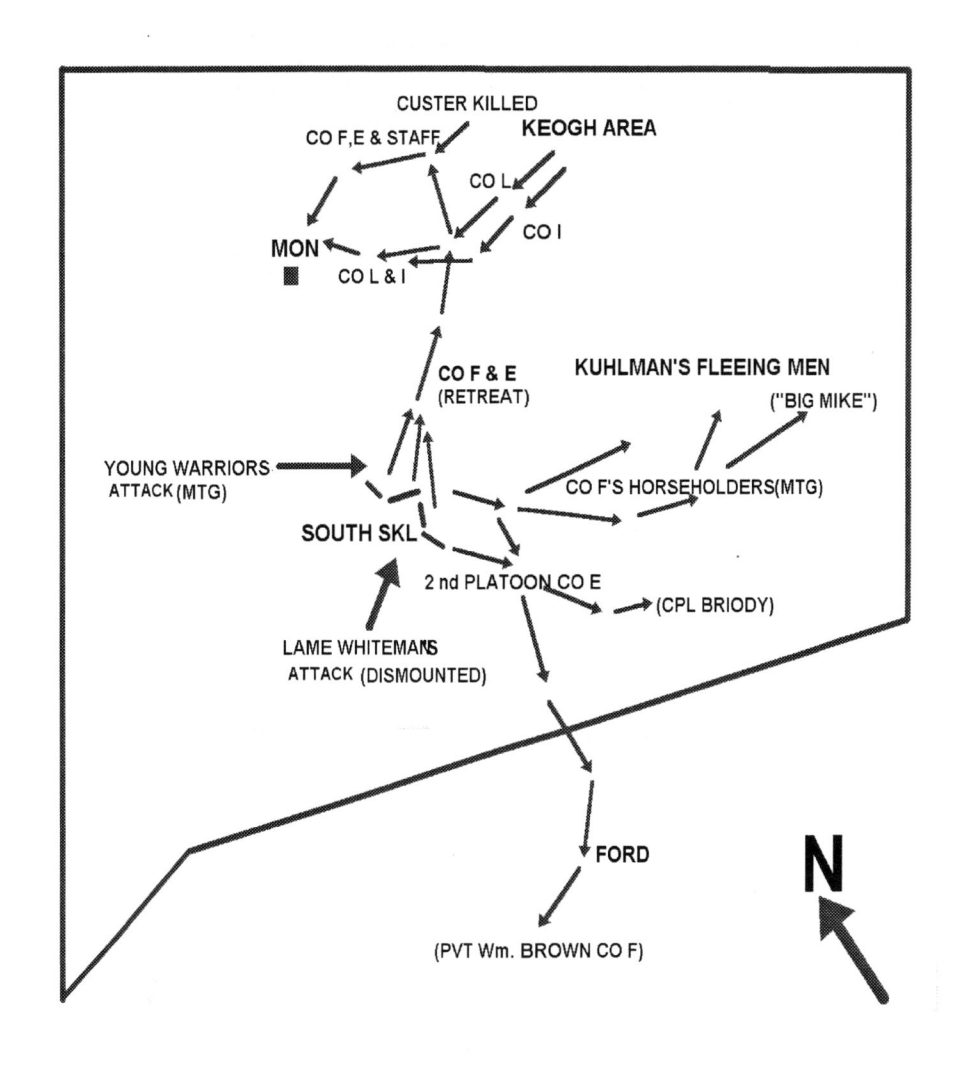

CUSTER FIGHT - PHASE 4
(4:30 - 4:45 PM)

SCALE: ------------------ 1/4 MILE

The Young Warriors decimate the **South Skirmish Line** with an unprecedented mounted attack on the right flank of Company F's led horses using the archaic bow and arrow and Civil War cap and ball revolvers. They rode into the led horse line causing the horses to stampede eastward. At the same time a frontal attack on foot by Lame White Man's warriors sealed the fate of the soldiers. Dr. Kuhlman's "fleeing men" represent the horse holders from Company F. Men from both F and E fled into **Ravine B** and **Ravine C**. Among those was the Second Platoon from company E (Mister Sturgis) whose bodies were found along with members of Company F in the upper shallow reaches of Ravine B **(Gray Horse Gully)**. Only one man, Private William Brown of Company F made it across the river.

The remnant of Company F and E retreated back to the Battle Ridge were they are joined with the survivors from the Keogh restaging area. Custer is killed on the north slope of the Battle ridge as men begin to flee to the Monument Hill area.

LAST STAND
(5:00 TO 5:20 PM)

5:20 PM MON

LAST SEVEN
RUN ON FOOT

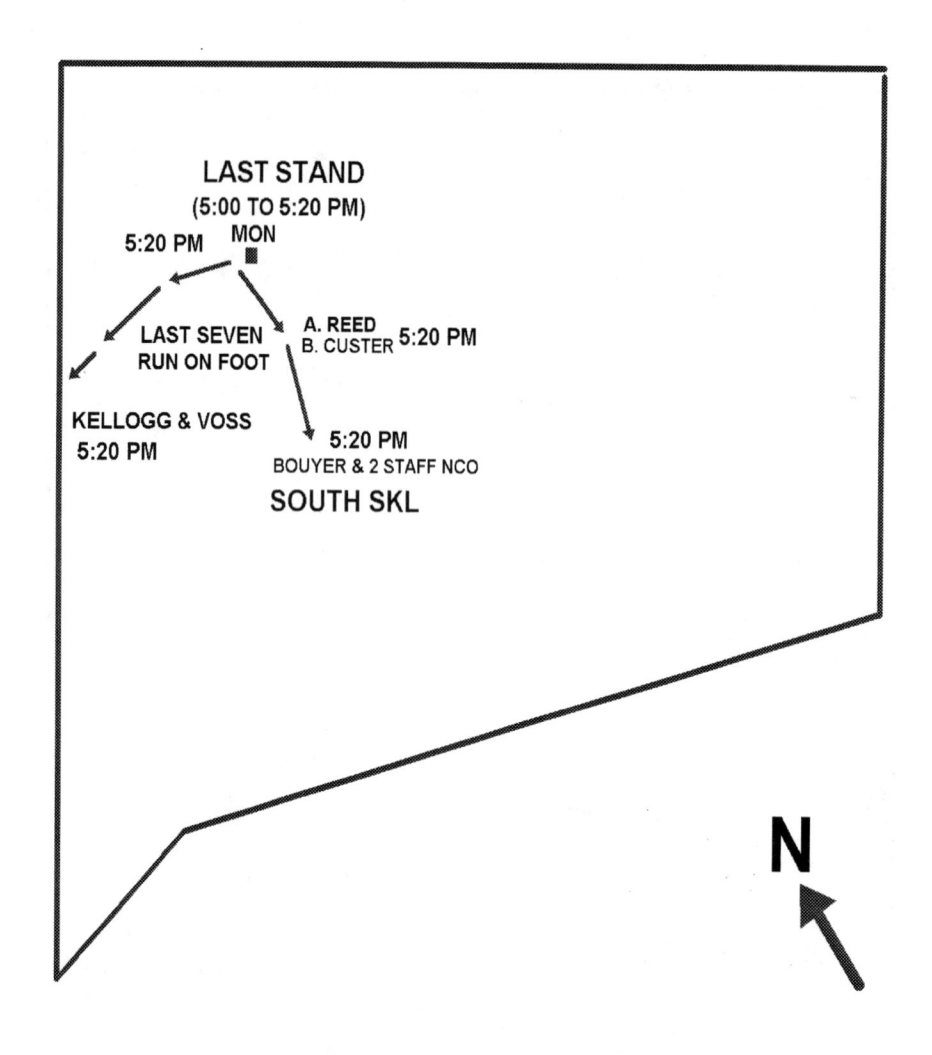

A. REED
B. CUSTER 5:20 PM

KELLOGG & VOSS
5:20 PM

5:20 PM
BOUYER & 2 STAFF NCO
SOUTH SKL

N

CUSTER FIGHT - PHASE 5
(5:00 - 5:20 PM)

SCALE: -------------------- 1/4 MILE

The **Last Stand** is formed when the survivors from the **South Skirmish Line** and the Keogh area reach Monument Hill. A barricade of Company C's horses is created on the highest point for the staff three enlisted men and the four civilians. The remainder of the men and officers stand inside a semi-circle of horses on the south slope of Monument Hill. Eventually the horses are shot down or stampede, but they were not at first deliberately shot down by the men. The men are than killed by attrition of their exposed position from distant sniping fire of the dismounted warriors on the National Cemetery complex and other surrounding high terrain. There was no romantic mounted charge until the very end when almost all of the soldiers were dead and the return firing had ceased.

The surprise ending was when the last seven men from behind the dead horse barricade on the summit of Monument Hill made a run for the valley timber. Mark Kellogg and Henry Voss made it beyond the present west boundary of the Battlefield. **(See THE LAST SEVEN pg. 184)**

SEVENTH REGIMENT ROSTER - ENLISTED MEN											
UNIT	MAY STRENGTH	LEFT AT LINCOLN	BEGAN CAMPAIGN	LEFT AT POWDER RIVER	DETACHED SERVICE & OTHER	SICK	ROSEBUD STRENGTH	SURVIVED BATTLE	KILLED	TOTAL SURVIVORS	DIED OF WOUNDS
A	55	4	51	4			47	39	8	47	1
B	71	5	66	18	2		46	44	2	69	
C	66	6	60	10			50	14	36 [4,10]	30	2
D	65	4	61	11			50	47	3	62	
E	61	7	54	7		1 [1]	46	9	37 [5]	24	
F	68	7	61	6	5		50	14	36 [11]	32	
G	65 [3]	6	59	16 [2]			43	30	13 [9]	52	
H	56	9	47	2	3		45	42 [7]	3 [13]	53	1
I	65	22	54	4			47	11	36 [6]	29	1
K	68	7	61	21	1 [13]		40	35	5 [8,12]	63	
L	67	4	63	6			57	13	44	23	
M	64	3	61	6			55	43	12	52	1
STAFF	7	2	5	3			2	0	2	5	
TOTAL	778	75	703	114	10	1	578	341	237	541	6

*Walter Camp composed these statistics from the official U.S. Army rosters. He obtained copies of them from the **GSA** (General Services Administration) in the early 1900s. These records are now deposited in the National Archives. Camp was the very first Custer researcher to compile a roster study based on his interview as to which men had actually been at the Little Bighorn.*

Notes:

1. Pvt. Ackison, Co. E, sick aboard *Far West*, June 22.
2. Lt. McIntosh's diary records 16 men left at Powder River.
3. Lt. McIntosh's diary records 66 men in Company G.
4. Company C lost one man on Reno Hill.
5. Company E lost one man on Reno Hill.
6. Company I lost one man on Reno Hill.
7. Martin, Co. H, assigned to Staff, June 25
8. Sgt. Hughes, Co. K, KIA with Staff.
9. Sgt. Dose, Co. G, KIA with Staff.
10. Cpl. French, Co. C, KIA with Staff.
11. Sgt. Vickory, Co. F, KIA with Staff.
12. Cpl. Callahan, Co K, KIA with Staff.
13. Cpl. Bishop, Co. H, Staff, June 25.
14. Pvt. Coakley, Co. K, assigned to Terry, June 22.

First Battalion	Second Battalion	Third Battalion	Fourth Battalion
B 46	F 50	D 50	A 47
C 50	E 46	H 44	G 42
I 50	L 57	K 37	M 55
146	153	131	134

Total survivors of the first and Second Battalions: 61
Pack Train:

First Battalion	Second Battalion	Third Battalion	Fourth Battalion
28	30	26	29

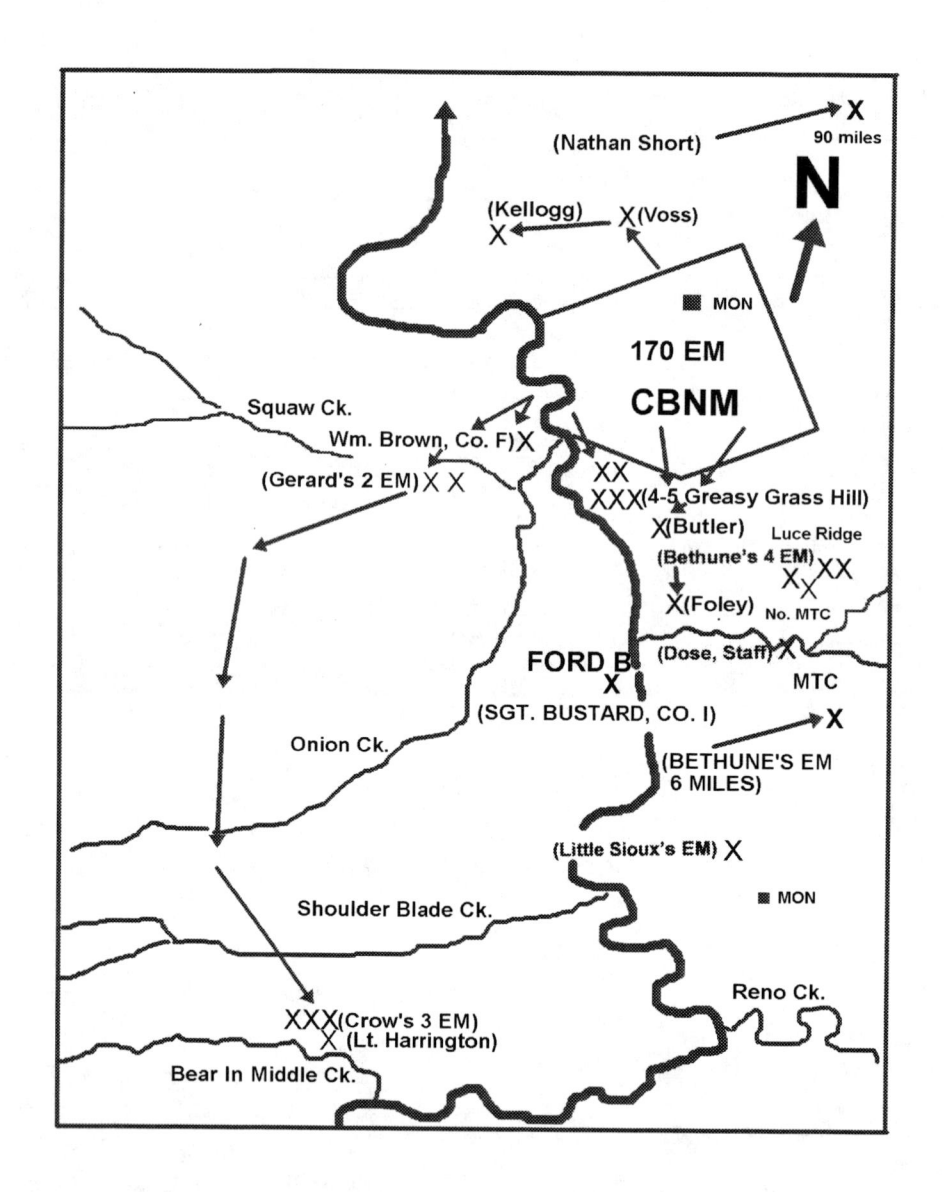

ENLISTED MEN AND OFFICERS KILLED OFF FIELD
(FROM THE FIRST AND SECOND BATTALIONS AND THE STAFF)

NOT TO SCALE

Seven enlisted men and one officer (Lt. Harrington) were known to have been found west of the Little Bighorn River. Seventeen enlisted men were known to have been found east of the river making for a total of twenty-four. This count does not include the known dead from the Reno Valley fight. They represent men from the First and Second Battalions and the regimental Headquarters Staff that traveled down Medicine Tail Coulee.

The probable twenty-four men killed off of the Custer Battlefield must be subtracted from the total number of men in the First and Second Battalions. This leaves an approximated 183 men that could have been found inside of the original boundaries of the Custer Battlefield. Camp's four to five" Greasy Grass Hill" men were originally were outside the Custer Field until the present boundary was established in the early 1900s.

COMPANY	MEN ASSIGNED TO COMPANY	HORSES ASSIGNED TO COMPANY	HORSES LOST	UNSERVICABLE HORSES	SERVICABLE HORSES
A	47	52	14	0	38
B	46	52	9	3	40
C	50	58	46	2	10
D	50	55	6	2	47
E	46	55	44	0	11
F	50	57	42	3	12
G	43	50	25	0	25
H	45	50	6	0	44
I	47	59	44	0	15
K	39	44	11	7	26
L	57	62	49	0	13
M	55	64	19	8	37
IN FORMATION	575	658	315	25	318
ASSIGNED TO STAFF	2	24	4	2	18
TOTAL	577	682	319	27	336

U.S. GOVERNMENT HORSES

The Seventh Regiment had 682 company horses, but only 577 enlisted men that went up the Rosebud River. This left a surplus of 105 reserve horses that were led in the ranks into battle. This overlooked factor made a deficit in skirmishers that could be deployed as extra horse holders were required. The average number of reserve horses in a company was seven with Company I being the exception with twelve. On Finley Hill, Company C could place but twenty-one men on the line.

A total 346 government horses were lost and made unserviceable making a fifty-one percent loss of the 682 government horses assigned to the regiment. This was a serve loss to any mounted regiment. A large number were killed on Reno hill, as seventy-five percent of the horses on the Custer Battlefield were stampeded from the field. Government horse are defined as those purchased for enlisted men as commissioned officers were required to acquire their own horses. **M41**

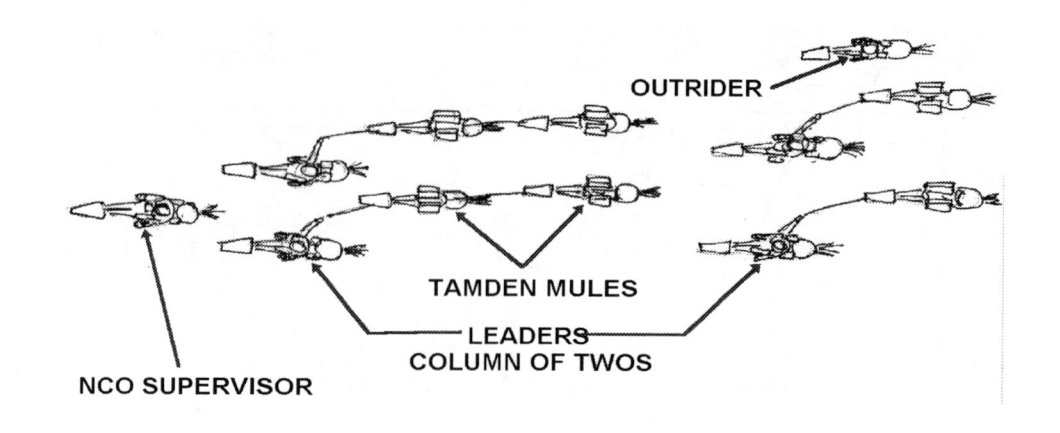

PACKS

This formation was used for the movement of the pack train. Lt. Mathey described it at the Reno Court of Inquiry. The total length of the packs would be approximately one quarter mile long (440 yards) with a normal interval of ten feet between the ranks. All those concerned with the packs said that at no time was the length over 500 yards when traveling down Ash (Reno) Creek. After the Custer Battle, Benteen and Godfrey strived to leave the impression that the packs were strung out for a much greater distance. This may have been to leave an excuse for Benteen's failure to expedite the Pack Train as ordered.

COMPANY	MEN ASSIGNED TO COMPANY	MULES ASSIGNED TO COMPANY	MEN ASSIGNED TO PACK TRAIN
A	47	13	9
B	46	13	9
C	50	14	10
D	50	14	10
E	46	13	9
F	50	14	10
G	43	12	9
H	45	12	9
I	47	13	9
K	40	11	7
L	57	16	11
M	55	15	11
TOTALS	576	160	113

PACK TRAIN

Lt. Mathey officially received 160 mules from the Quartermaster officer at the Powder River for the company packs. Additional mules were needed for the company officers, Headquarters Staff and the scouts. There could have been as many as 200 mules in the June 25 Pack Train.

SUMMARY OF ORDERS TO BENTEEN ON JUNE 25, 1876

MESSENGER	SENT	ARRIVED	CONTENT
1. Chief Bugler Voss	1:00 PM	1:30 PM	Regulated Benteen's "Left Scout"
2. Sgt. Maj. Sharrow	1:45 PM	2:00 PM	Ordered Benteen back to the Main Trail.
3. Cpl. French	2:30 PM	2:45 PM	Benteen was ordered to halt and wait for the Pack Train and then escort it to safer ground on the bluffs.
4. Cpl. Bishop	2:40 PM	3:10 PM	Benteen was now countermanded to come at once without the packs.
5. Sgt. Kanipe	2:45 PM	3:25 PM	Benteen was ordered take the short-cut to the bluffs without the packs. *"They want you up there as quick as you can get there, they have struck a big Indian Camp"*.
6. Bugler John Martin	3:10 PM	3:35 PM	The only written order. See Facsimile B, pg. 141.
7. Bugler Dose	3:30 PM	Killed	Warning that Reno was retreating on his back trail, and possibly up Ash (Reno) Creek. This order may have been intended for Capt. McDougall.
8. Unidentified	4:20 PM	4:50 PM	This messenger may have carried the "Calhoun had been wounded" rumor to Reno Hill. Was this Custer's last attempt to communicate with Benteen? The result was that Benteen saddled up his horses and went forward to Cpt. Weir's position on present Weir Point

SOURCES:
1. & 2. Common Custer sources.
2. Author's conclusion. Benteen claimed that he alone decided to return.
3. Bibliography, pg 227. BYU Uninventoried Note #1. Also R4 (Thompson, pg. 10a)
4. M40, Camp/Hammer, pg 99. M41, Bishop, pg. 157. Also R4 (Thompson, pg. 10a)
5. M40, Camp/Hammer, pg. 91, 93. Kanipe Interviews (fn 11)
6. M40, Camp/ Hammer, 99 thru 105 (The Martin Interviews)
7. M40, Camp/Hammer, pg. 99, fn #2. Also pg. 134, Henry Petring, Co. G.
8. Bibliography, pg. 227, BYU Uninventoried Note #2. (M40, Camp/Hammer, pg. 149)

TROOPER BOB DORAN
(STANDING ON THE EAST BANK OF FORD B)

If the author had served as an enlisted man in the Seventh Regiment in 1876, he would have probably hated Armstrong Custer and would have aligned with the "Hero of Reno Hill", Frederick Benteen.

BORN ONE HUNDRED YEARS TOO LATE!

NOTES ON DOCUMENTATION

This section of documentation is patterned after John S. Gray's *Centennial Campaign,* and for the very same reasons that he stated in his introduction to his documentation. In his preceding note on documentation, Doctor Gray points out that the more familiar "scholarly" form of citation has become time consuming for the author, repetitious and obtrusive for the general reader. This author might add that in the case of the Walter M. Camp Collection, it is also unworkable and not practical.

Doctor Gray admits that his new system does not permit the reader to go to a particular page or a specific item in documentary collections. The general reader is not interested in tracking down infinite page references that the serious student should have already read. The serious Custer student should be already familiar with these common sources. The egotistic need of academic authors to list how many books they have in their collection has created the prevailing citation system. Besides, quoting from someone else interpretation is neither original nor good research.

With this groundbreaking system we hope that the general reader will welcome the lack of numerical endnote references that demands you read at the end of the book. At the same time this author hopes that the serious student will accept the author's integrity and that this new bibliography format to be more useful then the archaic "scholarly" format.

Throughout the text the reader will find alphanumerical reference in bold print. The prefix **C** represents *Contemporary* accounts and is cited in Category One. They are participants' accounts written in the 1876 time frame of the Battle Little Big Horn. They represent sources such as dairies, journals, newspapers and personal interviews.

The prefix **R** represents *Reminiscent* accounts and is cited in Category Two. Walter Camp's post-battle research falls into this category, but they will be listed separately.

The prefix **NA** represents *Native American* accounts and is cited in Category Three. They include material on John Stands In Timber and Black Elk which were collected in the Twentieth Century.

The prefix **O** represents *Official* accounts and is cited in Category Four. They are those from the National Archives and U.S. Army documents.

The prefix **M** represents *Miscellaneous* research material and is cited in Category Five. They are other published books on the subject.

The prefix **H** represents *Horsemanship* research and is cited in Category Six. Since the U.S. Army horse training protocol has become a lost art, modern horsemanship techniques are listed along side the scant historical literature of the "Old Army." But, the Custer Era army was up to date if you compare it to today's accepted good horse training methods. Their horsemanship program was a hundred years ahead of contemporary horse books, videos, magazines and television clinicians such as Clinton Anderson, Chris Cox, and Pat Parelli.

Kenneth Hammer's typescripts of the Walter M. Camp collection housed at Indiana University are represented by the prefix **LILLY** in Category Seven. The widow of Robert S. Ellison deposited his portion of the Camp papers at the Indiana University **(LILLY)** after his death in the 1940s. The following number in bold allows a student to go to the exact page. Photo copies of these typescripts are available from Brigham Young University **(BYU)**..

Kenneth Hammer's typescripts of the Walter M. Camp collection housed at Brigham Young University are represented by the prefix **BYU** in Category Seven. Photo copies are available from BYU as **Mss 57.**

In the 1960s, Brigham Young University **(BYU)** purchased the bulk of the Camp Collection from the estate of Fred Rosenstock, a Denver book dealer from 1968 to 1981. Rosenstock had purchased the balance of the Ellison portion from his widow.

The BYU portion of the Camp Collection **(Mss 57)** is available in microfilm. This author has discovered not all of the BYU material has been microfilmed. In their on, off and on again microfilming process, over several years in the 1980s, it is apparent that they missed some of the collection. The massive three rolls are index by subject with five and six digit computer numbers for each item. Unfortunely, there is no separate listing as whether they are correspondence, interviews or field notes. For obvious reasons, the author had declined to attempt to overwhelm the general reader with the microfilm digital reference numbers. The other major problem would be to achieve a positive match with the author's pre-microfilm research.

The Rosenstock portion at BYU **(Mss 57)** represent the largest singular segment of the known Camp papers. In the early 1930s, Camp's research material was dispersed by his widow after his death in 1925. There are other known collections such as the Denver Public Library **(DPL)**, University of Colorado **(UC)** and the National Park Service **(NPS)**. However, in this book only one citation from the Denver Public Library **(DPL)** is referenced while none of the National Park Service **(NPS)** portion is cited. The smaller NPS collection has not yet been made available to researchers since they were discovered in the late 1980s in a barn in Northeastern Colorado. They contained the Libby Custer letters to Walter Camp.

The bulk of the "Camp Collection" at the Little Big Horn Battlefield National Monument are but copies from the BYU collection obtained in the 1980s by former NPS Historian Neil Magnum at the insistence of this author.

The numerical number in **bold** following the **LILLY**, **BYU**, and **DPL** prefix is the numerical order in which the material were typescripted by Dr. Hammer. They represent all three categories, interviews, correspondence and Camp's personal field notes.

Note: The highly fragmented nature of the Camp Collection does not allow documentation in a normal manner. Since the first "Camp" publication by Kenneth Hammer in his *Custer In ' 76*, his typescript references by the early 1980s were changed at BYU when his typescripts were removed from the archive box and folder system. It was done to save shelf space, but no master cross-reference list was made, making all of the *Custer In ' 76* citations no longer valid. Dr. Hammer's Lilly Library (Indiana University) typescripts are now inventoried in a separate BYU manuscript index titled the *Kenneth M. Hammer Collection, Mss 1473*.

Brigham Young University did prepare a pre-microfilm index register titled *The Walter Mason*

Camp Papers on the American Indian Wars and Custer, Mss 57. It was done in 1981 by Dennis Rowley and Neil Broadhurst. It contains a complete provenance of their Camp material. Its index includes separate correspondence, interview notes and Camp's research field notes, but many of the names are omitted. Again, they still have the old archive box and folder numbers. Dr. Hammer was not able to inventory all of the "Custer" material, as my research on the Nathan Short story (*The Man Who Got to the Rosebud)* was to prove. This helpful but outdated BYU index will not be cited in this work, but is available to other researchers.

However, the **LILLY** and **BYU** Hammer typescript page numbers will be cited. They are available as photocopies from Brigham Young University. The reader will have to trust this author that he did uncover and interpret the more "controversial" and unpublished Camp material that are featured in this work. For the convenience of the reader, some Camp citations from Dr. Hammer's *Custer In ' 76* are used as a cross reference. Those interested in the Walter Camp material are recommended by the author to examine Kenneth Hammer's *Custer In ' 76.* **(M40)**

BIBLIOGRAPHY:

Category One: Contemporary Accounts from Participants (Alphabetical)

C1 Benteen, Frederick W. (Captain, Co. H, Seventh Cavalry) Letters: July 2, 4 & 30, 1987 (See also M12 , Graham, W. A. *The Custer Myth*)

C2 Bradley, James H (First Lieutenant, Seventh Infantry) *Journal of.*, March 17 to June 26)

C3 Brisbane, James S. (Major, Second Cavalry) Unsigned dispatch: June 28, 1876. *N. Y. Herald,* July 8, 1876.

C4 Custer, George A. (Lieutenant Colonel, Seventh Cavalry) Dispatches: Little Missouri May 30, 1876, *N. Y. Herald,* June 19, 1876; Mouth of Powder River, June 12, 1876.

C5 DeRudio, Charles C. (First Lieutenant, Seventh Cavalry) Dispatch: Mouth of Big Horn, July 5,, 1876, *N. Y. Herald,* July 30, 1876.

C6 Edgerly, Winfield S. (First Lieutenant, Seventh Cavalry) Letter: July 4, 1876.

C7 Gibson, Francis M. (First Lieutenant, Seventh Cavalry) Letter: July 4, 1876, (See also Fougera, Katherine Gibson, *With Custer's Cavalry.*

C8 Godfrey, Edward S. (First Lieutenant, Seventh Cavalry) *The Field Diary of...,* May 17-Sept. 24, 1876

C9 Hare, Luther R. (Second Lieutenant, Seventh Cavalry) Letter: July 3, 1876.

C10 Kellogg, Mark H, *Diary of...*May 17-June 19, 1876.

C11 Pickard, Edwin H. (Private, Co. F, Seventh Cavalry) Letter: Aug. 1, 1876, Bangor, Maine, *Whig & Courier*, Aug. 16, 1876. Little Big Horn Associates *Newsletter,* April 1968.

C12 Terry, Alfred H. (Maj. General, Department of Dakota Territory Commander) *Diary of the Expedition of 1876,* May 17-Aug. 22, 1876, Mss. Library of Congress.

C13 Varnum, Charles A. (Second Lieutenant, Seventh Cavalry) Letter: July 4, 1876

Category Two: Reminiscent Accounts from Participants

R1 Adams, Jacob (Private, Co. H, Seventh Cavalry) *A Story of the Custer Massacre,* pamphlet., Vincennes, Indiana -1929

R2 Benteen Fredrick W. *Narrative,* 1890. The Benteen-Golden Letters, BYU, Mss 1130 Brigham Young University, Provo, Utah (See Also Graham, *The Custer Myth*)

R3 Burkman, John (Private, Co. L, Seventh Cavalry) Wagner, Gwendolyn, *Old Nutriment.*

R4 Thompson, Peter (Private, Co. C, Seventh Cavalry) *The Experience of a Private Soldier In the Custer Massacre.* State Historical Society of North Dakota. Originally printed in the Belle Fourche, South Dakota *Bee,* 1922-1923.

Category Three: Native American Accounts

NA1 Deloria, Vine Jr. *Custer Died For Your Sins.* Avon Books, New York- 1969.

NA2 Libby, O. G. *The Arikara Narrative of the Campaign Against the Hostile Dakotas, June 1876.* North Dakota Historical Collections, Vol. 6. - 1920.

NA3 Mails, Thomas E. *Fools Crow.* Doubleday & Company, Inc. Garden City, New York- 1976.

NA4 Miller, David Humphreys. *Custer's Fall.* Duell, Sloan and Pearce, New York-1957.

NA5 Marquis, Thomas B. *Memoirs of a White Crow Indian.* University of Nebraska Press, Lincoln, Nebraska - 1974.
NA6 Marquis, Thomas B. *Wooden Leg.* Bison Book, University of Nebraska Press-n.d.
NA7 Marquis, Thomas H. *Memories of a Crow Indian.* Bison Book, University of Nebraska Press- 1974
NA8 Neihardt, John G. *Black Elk Speaks.* Bison Book, University of Nebraska Press-1961.
NA9 Powers, William K. *Ogallala Religion.* University of Nebraska Press, Lincoln, Nebraska-1975.
NA10 Sandoz, Mari. *Crazy Horse.* Bison Book, University of Nebraska Press-1967.

Category Four: Official Accounts.

O1 Adjutant General's Office. *Chronological List of Actions &c., With Indians from January 15, 1837 to January 1891.* Old Army Press, - 1979.
O2 Casey, Col. *Cavalry to Infantry Tactics* (See also *The Custer Story*, by Marguerite Merrington, pg 179, GAC's recommendation to TWC to study)
O3 Cooke, Phillip St. George. *Cavalry Tactics or Regulations for the Instruction, Formations and Movements of the Cavalry.* J. B. Lippincott & Co., Philadelphia, Pennsylvania-1862.
O4 Forth Regiment Drill Manual, Fort Huachuca, Arizona territory-1883. (Facsimile copy supplied by the First Cavalry Division Ceremonial "Horse Platoon" at Fort Hood, Texas)
O5 Post Returns, Fort Abraham Lincoln, Dakota Territory, Nov. 1875 to Dec. 1876 (The National Archives & Records Service, General Service Administration, Washington, DC, US Government. Archives) Microfilm M617-628.
O6 Proceedings of a Court of inquiry Concerning the Conduct of Major Marcus A. Reno at the Battle of the Little Big Horn. November 25, 1878-January 21, 1879. The National Archives & Records Service, General Service Administration, US Government. Washington, DC-1964. Archives Microfilm # 592, Roll 1 7 2. Vol. 1 & 2
O7 Upton, Emery Lt. Col. *Cavalry Tactics US Army Assimilated to the Tactics of Infantry.* D. Appleton 7 Co., NY - 1874.

Category Five: Miscellaneous

M1 Adams, Jacob. *A Story of the Custer Massacre.* privately printed-1929
M2 Dick Harmon & Douglas D. Scott, "A Sharps Rifle From the Battlefield of the Little Bighorn," *A Man at Arms Special Publication,* 1988, pg. 12-15.
M3 Army - Navy Journal, September 2, 1876. letter: E. S. Godfrey, Mouth of Rosebud, M.T. August 7, 1876.
M4 Barnard, Sandy. *Digging Into Custer's Last Stand.* AST Press, Terre Haut, Indiana-1986.
M5 Barnard, Sandy. *Shovels & Speculation.* AST Press. Terre Haut, Indiana-1990.
M6 Boyes, William, *The Benteen Court Martial.* Little Big Horn Associates *Research Review,* Vol. IX, Summer, Number II, 1975.
M7 Blummer, J. D. and Doane Robinson. Custer Battlefield National Monument (The "Blummer" manuscript)
M8 Carroll, J. M. *The Court Martial of Frederick W. Benteen. 1981*
M9 Camptown Civic Club. *History of Camptown Pennsylvania, 1792-1975.* privately printed- n.d.

M10 Crow Agency, Montana. C. A. Ashbury, Superintendent. Letters: C. A. Ashbury to R. G. Cartwright. The finding of the remains of the "Unknown". Date; November 26, 1926.

M11 Custer Battlefield National Monument. CBNM Files. Letters: R. G. Cartwright to E. S. Luce, October 10, 1943.

M12 Custer Battlefield National Monument. CBNM Files. Letters: R. G. Cartwright to E. S. Luce, April 30, 1944

M13 Custer Battlefield National Monument. CBNM File Letters: R. G. Cartwright to E. S. Luce, August 29, 1946.

M14 Custer Battlefield National Monument. CBNM Files. Letters: R. G. Cartwright to E. S. Luce. July 25, 1946

M15 Custer Battlefield National Monument. CBNM Files. Letters: .E. S. Luce to R. G. Cartwright, August 3, 1946.

M16 Custer Battlefield National Monument. CBNM Files. Bulletin No. 1. The original "Luce" U.S. Geological Survey Map, 1908. Date February 1, 1944.

M17 Custer Battlefield National Monument. 0-28. Human bones on Custer Battlefield area. Date: April 2, 1941.

M18 Custer Battlefield National Monument. CBNM Files. J. S. Polland, Captain 6th Infantry. Report, Standing Rock Reservation, D. T. July 24, 1876.

M19 Custer Battlefield National Monument. CBNM Flies 4-1, J. W. Vaughn, July 2, 1963. Report on metal detection finds, Item #16 shows unidentified number of Government .45 caliber expended shell casings were found 400 - 500 yards north of the National Cemetery.

M20 Custer Battlefield National Monument. CBNM Files. 4-1, August 25, 1961. Margot Liberty & Bill Gary (NPS) picked up six Government .45 caliber expended shell casings on ridge near the ranger housing quarters, but north of the CBNM boundary fence.

M21 Custer Battlefield National Monument. CBNM Files, Mss 4-1. August 25, 1961 (Shooting of a Solitary soldier - Reported by John Stands In Timber)

M22 Custer Battlefield National Monument. CBNM Files Mss 4-1. Margot Liberty. August 20, 1961 (Mentions the Willy Bends crossing)

M23 Custer Battlefield National Monument. CBNM Files Mss 4-1. Margot Liberty, August 20, 1961 (Sites of Indian Action on Custer Battlefield)

M24 Custer Battlefield National Monument. CBNM Files Mss 4-1-29. Don Rickey, August 18, 1956 (John Stands In Timber and his uncle Wolf Tooth)

M25 Custer Battlefield National Monument. CBNM Files Mss 4-1-29. Don Rickey, August 18, 1956 (John Stands In Timber and his uncle Wolf Tooth)

M26 DuBois, Charles G.. *Kick the Dead Lion.* The Reporter Printer & Supply Co., Billings, Montana-1961

M27 DuMont, John S.. *Custer Battle Guns.* Old Army Press, Fort Collins, Colorado-1974.

M28 Edge, Robert J. *Settling the Dust.* Quick Printing Co., Sheridan, Wyoming-1968.

M29 Fougera, Katherine Gibson. *With Custer's Cavalry.* University of Nebraska Press, Lincoln 1986.

M30 Gibbon, John. *Gibbon on the Sioux Campaign of 1876.* Old Army Press, Fort Collins, Colorado-1969.

M31 Gobel, Paul. *Red Hawks Account of Custer's Last Battle.* University of Nebraska Press, Norman, Oklahoma-1969

M32 Godfrey, E. S. *Diary of the Little Big Horn* The Godfrey Papers, Library of Congress, Washington, D. C.

M33 Godfrey, Edward s. *Custer's Last Campaign.* Lewis Osborne, Palo Alto, California-1968

M34 Graham, W. A. *The Story of the Little Big Horn.* The Stackpole Company, Harrisburg, Pennsylvania-1959

M35 Graham, W. A. *The Reno Court of Inquiry* (Abstract of the Official Record of Proceedings) The Stackpole Company, Harrisburg, Pennsylvania-1954

M36 Greene, Jerome A. *Evidence and the Custer Enigma.* The Lowell Press, Kansas City, Missouri-1973

M37 Graham, William A., *The Custer Myth,* Harrisburg, PA. 1953.

M38 Grinnell, George B. *The Fighting Cheyennes.* Scribner & Sons, 1915.

M39 Gray, John S. *Centennial Campaign.* The Old Press. Fort Collins, Colorado-1979

M40 Hammer, Kenneth, *Custer In '76,* BYU Press, Provo, UT, 1976. **Hereafter called Camp/Hammer.**

M41 Hammer, Kenneth. *Biographies of the 7th Cavalry.* Old Army Press, Fort Collins, Colorado-1972

M42 Hardorff, Richard G. *Camp, Custer, and The Little Bighorn.* Upton and Sons, Publishers, El Segundo, California-1997.

M43 Hardorff. *Markers, Artifacts and Indian Testimony.* Don Horn Publications, Short Hills, Pennsylvania-1985

M44 Hutchins, James S. *Boots & Saddles at the Little Bighorn.* Old Army Press, Fort Collins, Colorado-1976.

M45 Johnson, Roy P. *Jacob Horner of the 7th Cavalry.* State Historical Society of North Dakota, Bismarck, North Dakota- Vol. 16, No. 2, April, 1949.

M46 Knight, Oliver. *Life and Manners in the Frontier Army.* University of Oklahoma Press, Norman, Oklahoma-1978.

M47 Kollbaum, Marc E. *Gateway to the West* (The History of Jefferson Barracks from 1826-1894, Vol. 1) Friends of Jefferson Barracks, St. Louis, Missouri-n.d.

M48 Koury, Michael J. *Diaries of the Little Big Horn.* The Old Army Press, Fort Collins, Colorado-1968

M49 Kuhlman, Charles. *Legend Into History.* The Stackpole Company, Harrisburg, Pennsylvania-1952.

M50 Kuhlman, Charles. *Did Custer Disobey Orders.* The Stackpole Company, Harrisburg, Pennsylvania-1957.

M51 Kuhlman, Charles. *Custer and the Gall Saga.* The Old Army Press, Fort Collins, Colorado-1969.

M52 Libby, O. G. *The Arikara Narrative of the Campaign Against the Hostile Dakota, June 1876.* State Historical Society of North Dakota. Bismarck, North Dakota-1920.

M53 Liberty, Margot. *Cheyenne Memories.* Yale University Press, New Haven, Connecticut-1967.

M54 Liberty, Margot. *Grisly Horrors at the Custer* American Heritage -1966. *(Article about John Stand In Timber's Suicide Warriors)*

M55 Luce, Edward S. *The Diary of Dr. James DeWolf.* State Historical Society of North Dakota, Vol. 25, Nos. 1 & 2. April-July 1958.

M56 Marquis, Thomas B. *Keep the Last Bullet For Yourself .* Reference Publications, Inc. Algonac, Michigan-1976.

M57 Marquis, Thomas B. *Custer on the Little Bighorn.* End-Kian Publisher Company, Lodi, California-1967.

M58 Marquis, Thomas B. *Keep the Last Bullet For Yourself.* Reference Publications, Inc. Algonac, Michigan - 1976.

M59 McChristian Doug. *Hurrah, Boys! We've Got Them!* (An Analysis of Custer's Observation Point) Custer Battlefield Historical & Museum Association, Hardin, Montana - 1989.

M60 McChristian, Douglas C. *An Army of Marksman.* The Old Army Press, Fort Collins, Colorado - 1981.

M61 McClernand, E. J. *The Fight on Custer Hill. US Cavalry Journal*

M62 McClernand, E. J. *March of the Montana Column) See M52,* Koury, Michael J., *Diaries of the Little Big Horn* 1968.

M63 McChristian, Douglas C., *The U.S. Army in the West, 1870-1880.* University of Oklahoma Press, Norman, Oklahoma-n.d.

M64 McCoy, Tim Roland. *Tim McCoy Remembers the West.* Doubleday & Company, Garden City, New York-1977.

M65 Meketa, Ray and Thomas E. Bookwalter. *The Search for the Lone Tepee.* Little Horn Press-1983

M66 Meketa, Ray. *Hidden Treasures of the Little Bighorn.* Cheechako Press, Douglas, Alaska-1984

M67 Merrington, Marguerite. *The Custer Story.* The Devin-Adair Company, New York-1950.

M68 Mills, Charles K. *Harvest of Barren Regrets.* University of Oklahoma Press, 1985.

M69 Mitchell, Thos. J. Agent Fort Peck Reservation, M. T. September 25, 1876. Reference to Lt. Harrington and Crittenden.

M70 Morris, William E. Letter to Robert Bruce, May 23, 1928

M71 Nichols, Ron H. Editor. *Reno Court of Inquiry.* Custer Battlefield Historical & Museum Association, Inc. Hardin, Montana-1996

M72 Overfield, Loyd J. II. *The Official Communcations, Documents and Reports, The Little Big Horn.* University of Nebraska Press, 1997.

M73 Ovies, Adolfo. *Crossed Sabers.* Author House, Bloomington, Indiana-2003

M74 Pickard, Edward H. "The Oregon Journal" July 31, 1923

M75 Plainfeather, Mardell Hogan. "A Personal Look at Curly's Life After the Battle of the Little Big Horn", *Greasy Grass,* Custer Battlefield Historic & Museum Association, Vol. 4, May 1988. pg 17-24.

M76 Powell, Peter J. *Sweet Medicine.* University of Oklahoma Press, Norman, 1959 (Two Volumes)

M77 Rickey, Don Jr. *Forty Miles a Day on Beans and Hay.* University of Oklahoma Press, Norman, 1963.

M78 Stands In Timber, John and Margot Liberty. *Last Ghastly Moments at the Little Bighorn.* American Heritage. pg 15 nd

M79 Scott, Douglas D. *Archaeological Perspectives on the Battle of the Little Bighorn.* University of Oklahoma Press, Norman, Oklahoma-1989.

M80 Scott, Douglas D. *Archaeological Insights into The Custer Battle.* University of Oklahoma Press, Norman, Oklahoma-1987.

M81 Scudder, Ralph E. *Custer Country.* Brinfords & Mort Publishers. Portland, Oregon-1963.

M82 Stephen, Randy, *The Horse Soldier, Vol. II, The Frontier, the Mexican War, the Civil War, the Indian wars-1851-1880.*

M83 Taunton, Francis B. *Custer's Field: A Scene of Sickening Ghastly Horror.* The J Johnson-Taunton Military Press. London-1987.

M84 Terrell, John Upton. *Faint the Trumpet Sounds.* D. McKay Co., 1966.

M85 U.S. Army Military Institute, Carlisle Barracks, PA. The E. S. Godfrey Papers. Letters: E. S. Godfrey to W. M. Camp, July 20, 1905, W. M. Camp to E. S. Godfrey, July 17, 1908, July 25, 1908, March 31, 1909

M86 Utley, Robert. *Good Guys and Bad, Changing Images of Soldier and Indian.* Custer (reprint) Battlefield Historical & Museum Association, Inc., Harding, Montana-1978.

M87 Utley, Robert. *Frontier Regulars.* Indiana University Press. Bloomington, Indiana-1973.

M88 Vaughn, J. W. Custer Battlefield National Monument. CBNM Files, July 3, 1965. Letter to Andrew Loveless (NPS Historian). Metal Detection at CBNM

M89 Vaughn, J. W. *Indian Fights and Skirmishes.* University of Oklahoma Press - 1966

M90 Werner, Fred H. *Before the Little Big Horn.* privately printed-1980.

Category Six: Horsemanship

H1 Belschner, H. G. DVSc. *Horse Diseases.* Wilshire Book Co., North Hollywood, California-1969. Former Assistant Director of Veterinary Services, First Cavalry Division, Australian Military Forces.

H2 Boniface, Jno. J. 1 st. Lieut. 4th Cavalry. *The Cavalry Horse and His Pack.* C&K Publisher Company Inc. Minneapolis, Minnesota-1977 (This is a facsimile reprint of the 1903 original)

H3 Davis, Francis W. *Horse Packing In Pictures.* Charles Scribner Sons, New York-1975.

H4 Elser, Smoke &Brown. Bill. *Packin' In on Mules and Horses.* Mountain Press Publisher Co., Missoula, Montana-1980

H5 *Equus Magazine*

H6 Devereux, Fredrick L, editor. *The Cavalry Manual of Horse Management,* United States Cavalry Scholl, Fort Riley, Kansas, 1941-42.

H7 Miller, Robert M., DVM. *Health Problems of the Horse.* Western Horseman, Colorado Springs, Colorado-1967.

H8 Simmons, Hoyt. *Horseman's Veterinary Guide.* Western Horseman, Colorado Springs, Colorado-1963.

H9 Westbrook, Ann & Perry. *Trail Horses & Trail Riding.* Wilshire Book Company, North Hollywood, California-1963.

H10 Wright, Gordon, Editor. *Horsemanship and Horse Mastership.* Wilshire Book Company, North Hollywood, California-1962. (The Official Manual of the United States Cavalry School at Fort Riley-1962

H11 U.S. War Department, *The Horseshoer,*-1941. reprinted as *A Practical Guide to Horseshoeing.* Wilshire Book Company, North Hollywood, California-1979.

CITATIONS:

Category Seven: The Walter Mason Camp Collection

Denver Public Library, Mss SC 568 Brigham Young University, Special Collections, Archives & Manuscripts. Howard B. Lee Library.

DPL 97	DeRudio, Charles	Saw Custer's trail (double set of fours) down Medicine Tail Coulee and also he saw the dead horse barricade on Custer Knoll

University of Colorado, Mss 1474. Brigham Young University, Special Collections, Archives & Manuscripts. Howard B. Lee Library. (This is the University of Colorado portion of the Camp papers of General William Brown) None cited.

Kenneth M. Hammer Collection, Mss 1473. Brigham Young University, Special Collections, Archives & Manuscripts, Howard B. Lee Library (These are Doctor Hammer's Lilly Library typescripts of the Robert S. Ellison Camp material housed at the Indiana University) The prefix represents the numerical sequence of Dr. Hammer's typescripts. Items not inventoried are cited separately. The author will supply photocopies of most of the Camp material as requested.

LILLY 5	Bell, J. M.	His opinion on Frederick Benteen
LILLY 18	Clark, Ben	Benteen wanted to know if Custer had ordered Major Elliott off at the Washita Battle and than abandoned him.
LILLY 24	Camp. W. M.	Camp's opinion on the Custer Fight that the Indians were not mounted for most of the battle.
LILLY 24	Flying By	His estimate of the length of the Custer Battle was forty-five minutes
LILLY 25	Kanipe, Daniel	Custer struck bluffs a few hundred feet above the Reno Monument. He could see the dust as he went back to the Pack Train
LILLY 25	Gerard, Frederick.	He thought that Reno's valley fight lasted only twenty minutes.
LILLY 27	Roy, Stanislas	He saw dead horses between Custer Hill and ravine where Company E's men were found.
LILLY 27	Camp. W. M.	The Company E ravine was a "wash-out" ravine.
LILLY 28	O'Toole, Francis.	He identified the body of William H. Rees of Company E in the deep gully.
LILLY 28	Martin, John	Benteen followed Custer's trail.
LILLY 29	Curly.	The "Bouyer" remark that the "others (Benteen) were sacred out of the country."
LILLY 32	Kanipe, Daniel.	Camp's sketch of Custer's Squadron formation.
LILLY 35	Kanipe, Daniel.	Company C was in Keogh's Battalion.
LILLY 55	Camp, W. M.	Describes graves on Greasy Grass Hill.

LILLY 56	Grant, Fred D.	Verifies there were graves on Greasy Grass Hill in 1877.
LILLY 61-62	Camp, W. M.	Camp's odometer mileages.
LILLY 66	Charging Hawk.	Heard about an army dog with a note tied to his collar leaving the Custer Fight.
LILLY 68	Camp, W. M.	Custer was discovered at the Divide.
LILLY 68	Wallace, George	Reno crossed at ford A at 2;20 PM (RCI) See also LILLY 89
LILLY 76	Benteen, Frederick.	General Terry's Report, Secretary of War, 1876. Benteen gives distance from Morass to Burning Lodge as two miles.
LILLY 87	"Kennally"	The company mascot of Company I was a bull dig named "Joe Bush."
LILLY 90	Woodruff, Charles.	Reno's retreat was a horse race.
LILLY 93-94	Godfrey, Edward	Custer's remark that upset Benteen about the Lieutenants doing their jobs better then the Captains was a reference attributed to General Crook.
LILLY 96	Mathey, Edward	He rode "Comanche" before Keogh.
LILLY 108	Mathey, Edward	The men were inexperienced in handling their horses.
LILLY 108	Rutten, Roman	He had to circle his horse around Reno's battalion as they neared Ford A.
LILLY 120	Camp. W. M.	Camp places Otter Creek ravine 300-400 yards west of Reno's skirmish line.
LILLY 120	Camp, W. M.	Camp's compass heading his "Weir's Hill" to present Weir Point was 317 degrees. Custer could not have seen the lower villages on Onion Creek.
LILLY 131	Camp, W. M.	Camp's odometer reading of 6184 feet from Ford B to Custer's halt in MTC.
LILLY 546	McClernand, Edward	He saw a regular set of "Double Fours" going down MTC to Ford B.
LILLY 547	McClernand, Edward	One of Custer's men was found in the river below Ford B.
LILLY 548	Camp, W. M.	Odometer reading of Rosebud trail (p.p following)
LILLY 559	Camp, W. M.	Corporal Foley's body location.
LILLY 578	Lee, Jessie M.	His quote on the Reno Court "damming Reno with faint praise." Tmp. Dose found in MTC (See pg 134, Petring (Hammer)
LILLY 579	Flower, Isaac	Benteen's remark about Custer & Pack Train.
LILLY 601	Ryan, John	Foragers got ahead of Reno's advance
LILLY 602	Ryan, John	Lt. Hodgon's on SKL
LILLY 602	Martin, John	Met Boston Custer plus 2 Co C EM (French)
LILLY 604	Camp, W. M.	Camp's opinion on Custer Fight "Long range shower of lead." Only 8-9 Indian ponies and 90 army horses
LILLY 606	Snipes, J. M.	Reno drunk on 6/21 at mouth of Rosebud
LILLY 607	Curly	Camp's opinion on Curly.
LILLY 609	Godfrey, E. S.	Weir took (left) hand trail typographical error in this typescript. Benteen and Godfrey took the right hand trail while had taken the left hand trail.

LILLY 609	Godfrey, E. S.	Sgt Hughes carried Custer's personal flag
LILLY 610	Thompson. Peter	Saw Compamny F's foragers on the Nye-Cartwright Ridge area. (See Hammer's *Custer In '76,* Camp's map, pg. 36)
LILLY 612	Camp, W. M.	Camp's Map, Shows Company F's foragers on the Nye-Cartwright Ridge.
LILLY 616	Camp, W. M.	Camp's preface.
LILLY 616	Camp, W. M.	Regimental time, May '76 Northern Pacific railroad time table.
LILLY 620	Jackson, Billy	Heard firing from Custer Field for two hours
LILLY 632	Little Wolf	Custer Field deployment (Camp's Blue-Print Map reference.)
LILLY 650	Wilson James, Sgt.	Report on Powder River Scout
LILLY 667	Creighton, John C.	Bull Dog named "Red" mascot See also Lilly 87.
LILLY 667	Jordan, W. B.	Benteen a terrible drunk
LILLY 667	Jordan, W. B.	Custer took IOU's from green Lieutenants (See also BYU 824) Scott
LILLY 671	Gerard, Frederick	Gerard saw two enlisted men's bodies in valley.
LILLY 672	Flannigan, Thomas	Bustard's body, He also saw Corporal Foley ride out from Battlefield.
LILLY 677	Camp, W. M.	Reference Custer's congressional testimony on Post Traders.
LILLY 687	Roy, Stanislaus	Foley & Butler's bodies.
LILLY 715	Camp, W. M.	Reference to newspaper account of General Terry's official report
LILLY 775	Camp, W. M.	Benteen's court martial-1888.
LILLY 775	DeRudio, Charles	Saw Reno drinking at Ford A and twenty minutes later on skirmish line.
LILLY 806-7	Camp, W. M.	Capt. Polland's report on Little Wolf on Ash Ck.
LILLY 824	Scott, Hugh	Custer's gambling habit (See also Jordan Lilly 667)
LILLY 825	Scott. Hugh	Pack Train

The Walter Mason Camp Papers on the American Indian Wars and Custer, Mss 57. Brigham Young University. Special Collections, Archives & Manuscripts. Howard B. Lee Library. (These are Doctor Hammers typescripts of the "Rosenstock" portion of the Camp Collection as purchased by BYU in 1968.)

BYU 45	Herendeen, George	Number of warriors opposing Reno were not over 200. Men and horses not tired.
BYU 51	Curley	Four Markers on Calhoun Hill & the "Bouyer" remark
BYU 112	Sweet, Owen	Set up 249 grave markers in 1889.
BYU 116	Custer, E. B.	Letter to Camp on General Terry's drinking.
BYU 139	Camp, W. M.	Reno Creek called Ash Creek.
BYU 139	Curley	Camp's interview. Hammer, *Custer In '76,* pg. 155
BYU 166	Waggoner. J. C.	Chief packer fro Pack Train
BYU 167	Kellogg, Mark	Kellogg's Notes.
BYU 168-72	Kellogg, Mark	Kellogg's Notes.
BYU 173	Boyle, James	MgGinnis's head was found in village on a pole.

BYU 182-4	Godfrey, E. S.	Found Indian pony near the Nye-Cartwright area.
BYU 195	Godfrey, E. S.	Custer's dog at Fort Yates.
BYU 215	Lange, Henry	On Tom Custer and that they had no boots for four years.
BYU 217	Roe, Charles	Custer sent Benteen on Left scout to keep him out the battle.
BYU 217	Roe, Charles	Terry's remarks to Benteen about the dead on Custer Field.
BYU 219	Adams, Jacob	Corporal Broidey's leg was cut-off.
BYU 226	Camp. W. M.	Saw many horse bones between Finley Hill and Sgt. Butler's body.
BYU 226	Logan, William	Bugler Dose's (Bouyer) body with note.
BYU 230-31	Pigford, Edward	Saw circle of Indians on Custer Field from Weir Point.
BYU 239-242	Wilson, James E.	Reno's Powder River Scout report.
BYU 252	Varnum, Charles	The White Rocks tepee on Reno Creek.
BYU 254	Bischoff, Charles	Camp's Interview.
BYU 259	Camp, W.. M.	Co's C. L & E all had the new issued "white" campaign hat
BYU 259	Thompson, R. E.	Saw nine to ten dead men between Custer Hill and the Gray Horse Gully
BYU 259	Thompson, R. E.	Kellogg's body
BYU 261	Thompson, R. E.	The Custer/Benteen feud at mouth of the Rosebud River on June 21.
BYU 291	He Dog	Little Big Horn camp's size
BYU 292-293	He Dog	Custer Fight & Ford B
BYU 297	Camp, W. M.	His "Weir's Hill" description
BYU 298-299	Camp, W. M.	His 300 degree heading from "Weir's Hill."
BYU 299	Camp, W. M.	His 202 degree heading from Weir Point to the Reno Skirmish Line.
BYU 323	Mathey, Edward	Benteen was angry about Custer's criticism of his company's packs on June 24.
BYU 323	Mathey, Edward	Kellogg's body in ravine
BYU 323	Mathey., Edward	The Libby Custer & Weir incident in Kansas.(Newspaper article perhaps by Benteen)
BYU 368	Camp, W. M.	Camp's odometer readings up Rosebud
BYU 387	Lynch, Dennis	Saw "Kanipe" ride up to Benteen at Morass
BYU 393	Heyn, William	No officers on Reno Skirmish Line.
BYU 410	Camp, W. M.	List of packers at Little Big Horn.
BYU 434	Curley	The Thomas La Forge interview. (The Bouyer remark that the "Command was going to be taken")
BYU 437	Camp, W. M.	The hardship of the enlisted man.
BYU 440-41	Camp, W. M.	Camp's criticism of Reno's actions was an "error in judgment"
BYU 441-42	Camp, W. M.	Camp's summary on Reno's drinking.
BYU 444-46	Camp, W. M.	Benteen unsaddled his horses on Reno Hill
BYU 446	Camp, W. M.	Benteen's march as a check on the length of Reno's Valley Fight.
BYU 458	Barry, D F	Benteen's criticism of Custer's Battle plan.

BYU 460	Welch, H L.	Hunkpapa village was 1000 feet in diameter.
BYU 463	Hammon, John	Benteen unsaddled his horses on Reno Hill.
BYU 468	Corcoran, Pat	Saw "Kanipe" ride up and speak to Benteen (French of Sharrow?) Also he saw Reno drunk in "hospital" on Reno Hill on June 26 AM hours.
BYU 705	Camp. W. M.	Camp's tabulation of his the sixty-one interviews of those at Little Bighorn Battle.

BYU Uninventoried Note: No. 1   A high placed non-commissioned officer from Custer's Staff was seen delivering an order to Benteen at the Morass. The author's conclusion is that it was most likely Custer's personal orderly, Alexander Bishop of Company H. **(R4, pg. 10a)**

Author's Note: This note identifies Private Dennis Lynch of Company F as being the source of the rumor. All roster studies agree that Dennis Lynch was with his company packs on June 25. Camp was able to identify Private Patrick Lynch of Company I as being the enlisted man that gave up his horse at the mouth of the Rosebud for the civilian George Herendeen who was loaned to Custer to deliver dispatches. See Hammer's *Biographies of the 7th Cavalry*. **(M41, pg. 179)**

BYU Uninventoried Note No. 2   The rumor that "Lt. Calhoun was wounded" circulated on Reno Hill. This report was attributed to Sergeant Richard Hanley as passed on to Camp by Private James Wilbur of Company M.
(M40, Camp/Hammer, James Wilber, pg. 149)

CORRESPONDENCE:

Walter M. Camp Collection (Partial listing of the hundreds of letters available at BYU)

John Martin to Walter Camp:
Jan. 5, 1909
Jan. 11, 1914

Daniel Kanipe to Walter Camp:
July 7, 1908
July 20, 1908
May 1, 1909
June 19, 1909
July 29, 1908
August 4, 1908
August 15, 1908
January 4, 1909
January 24, 1909
May 1, 1909
June 19, 1909
November 22, 1909

May 31, 1910
January 12, 1912

Walter Camp to Daniel Kanipe:
Aug. 28, 1908
Nov. 14, 1909
In all Camp and Kanipe wrote twenty-seven letters between 1908 and 1912.

Walter Camp to Peter Thompson:
April, 24, 1910

Peter Thompson to Walter Camp:
Feb. 12, 1909
June 6, 1909
April 10, 1910
June 16, 1910
Jan. 17, 1913
November 19, 1921

Dennis Lynch to Walter Camp:
Jan. 17, 1908
November 14, 1908
November 28, 1908
December 27, 1908
Feb. 27, 1909

Frederick Gerard to Walter Camp:
July 28, 1911
September 28, 1911

NOTE: Also available from Brigham Young University are the following Custer related papers:
- The Charles Kuhlman Collection, Mss 1401
- The Benteen & Goldin Letters, Mss 1130.